Communicating Embedded Systems

Communicating Embedded Systems

Software and Design

Formal Methods

Edited by
Claude Jard
Olivier H. Roux

First published 2008 in France by Hermes Science/Lavoisier entitled: *Approches formelles des systèmes embarqués communicants* © LAVOISIER 2008
First published 2010 in Great Britain and the United States by ISTE Ltd and John Wiley & Sons, Inc.

ISTE Ltd
27-37 St George's Road
London SW19 4EU
UK

www.iste.co.uk

John Wiley & Sons, Inc.
111 River Street
Hoboken, NJ 07030
USA

www.wiley.com

© ISTE Ltd 2010

Library of Congress Cataloging-in-Publication Data

Approches formelles des systèmes embarqués communicants. English
  Communicating embedded systems : software and design : formal methods / edited by Claude Jard, Olivier H. Roux.
      p. cm.
  Includes bibliographical references and index.
  ISBN 978-1-84821-143-8
  1. Embedded computer systems--Programming. 2. Embedded computer systems--Design and construction. 3. Computer software--Development. 4. Formal methods (Computer science) I. Jard, Claude. II. Roux, Olivier H. III. Title.
  TK7895.E42A387 2009
  621.39'2--dc22
                                                                                                  2009026282

British Library Cataloguing-in-Publication Data
A CIP record for this book is available from the British Library
ISBN 978-1-84821-143-8

Edited and formatted by Aptara Corporation, New Delhi, India
Printed and bound in Great Britain by CPI Antony Rowe, Chippenham and Eastbourne

FSC
Mixed Sources
Product group from well-managed
forests and other controlled sources
Cert no. SGS-COC-2953
www.fsc.org
© 1996 Forest Stewardship Council

Contents

Preface   xi
Claude JARD and Olivier H. ROUX

Chapter 1. Models for Real-Time Embedded Systems   1
Didier LIME, Olivier H. ROUX and Jiří SRBA

1.1. Introduction   1
   1.1.1. Model-checking and control problems   2
   1.1.2. Timed models   3
1.2. Notations, languages and timed transition systems   5
1.3. Timed models   8
   1.3.1. Timed Automata   8
   1.3.2. Time Petri nets   10
      1.3.2.1. T-time Petri nets   12
      1.3.2.2. Timed-arc petri nets   15
   1.3.3. Compared expressiveness of several classes of timed models . . .   19
      1.3.3.1. Bisimulation and expressiveness of timed models   19
      1.3.3.2. Compared expressiveness of different classes of TPN   20
      1.3.3.3. Compared expressiveness of TA, TPN, and TAPN   21
1.4. Models with stopwatches   23
   1.4.1. Formal models for scheduling aspects   23
      1.4.1.1. Automata and scheduling   23
      1.4.1.2. Time Petri nets and scheduling   24
   1.4.2. Stopwatch automata   25
   1.4.3. Scheduling time Petri nets   26
   1.4.4. Decidability results for stopwatch models   31
1.5. Conclusion   31
1.6. Bibliography   31

Chapter 2. Timed Model-Checking 39
Béatrice BÉRARD

   2.1. Introduction 39
   2.2. Timed models 40
      2.2.1. Timed transition system 40
      2.2.2. Timed automata 41
      2.2.3. Other models 44
   2.3. Timed logics 46
      2.3.1. Temporal logics CTL and LTL 46
      2.3.2. Timed extensions 48
         2.3.2.1. Timed CTL 48
         2.3.2.2. Timed LTL 50
   2.4. Timed model-checking 51
      2.4.1. Model-checking LTL and CTL (untimed case) 51
      2.4.2. Region automaton 53
      2.4.3. Model-checking TCTL 56
      2.4.4. Model-checking MTL 58
      2.4.5. Efficient model-checking 59
      2.4.6. Model-checking in practice 60
   2.5. Conclusion 61
   2.6. Bibliography 61

Chapter 3. Control of Timed Systems 67
Franck CASSEZ and Nicolas MARKEY

   3.1. Introduction 67
      3.1.1. Verification of timed systems 67
      3.1.2. The controller synthesis problem 68
      3.1.3. From control to game 69
      3.1.4. Game objectives 70
      3.1.5. Varieties of untimed games 71
   3.2. Timed games 72
      3.2.1. Timed game automata 72
      3.2.2. Strategies and course of the game 73
         3.2.2.1. The course of a timed game 73
         3.2.2.2. Strategies 74
   3.3. Computation of winning states and strategies 76
      3.3.1. Controllable predecessors 77
      3.3.2. Symbolic operators 79
      3.3.3. Symbolic computation of winning states 79
      3.3.4. Synthesis of winning strategies 80

3.4. Zeno strategies 82
3.5. Implementability 82
   3.5.1. Hybrid automata 83
   3.5.2. On the existence of non-implementable continuous controllers . . 84
   3.5.3. Recent results and open problems 85
3.6. Specification of control objectives 85
3.7. Optimal control 87
   3.7.1. TA with costs 87
   3.7.2. Optimal cost in timed games 89
   3.7.3. Computation of the optimal cost 90
   3.7.4. Recent results and open problems 92
3.8. Efficient algorithms for controller synthesis 92
   3.8.1. On-the-fly algorithms 93
   3.8.2. Recent results and open problems 95
3.9. Partial observation 96
3.10. Changing game rules 97
3.11. Bibliography 98

Chapter 4. Fault Diagnosis of Timed Systems 107
Franck CASSEZ and Stavros TRIPAKIS

4.1. Introduction 107
4.2. Notations 109
   4.2.1. Timed words and timed languages 109
   4.2.2. Timed automata 110
   4.2.3. Region graph of a TA 111
   4.2.4. Product of TA 111
   4.2.5. Timed automata with faults 112
4.3. Fault diagnosis problems 113
   4.3.1. Diagnoser 113
   4.3.2. The problems 114
   4.3.3. Necessary and sufficient condition for diagnosability 115
4.4. Fault diagnosis for discrete event systems 115
   4.4.1. Discrete event systems for fault diagnosis 115
   4.4.2. Checking Δ-diagnosability and diagnosability 116
      4.4.2.1. Checking Δ-diagnosability 116
      4.4.2.2. Checking diagnosability 117
   4.4.3. Computation of the maximum delay 120
   4.4.4. Synthesis of a diagnoser 121
4.5. Fault diagnosis for timed systems 122
   4.5.1. Checking Δ-diagnosability 122
   4.5.2. Checking diagnosability 123

4.5.3. Computation of the maximal delay 125
4.5.4. Synthesis of a diagnoser 126
4.5.5. Fault diagnosis with deterministic timed automata 127
4.6. Other results and open problems 136
4.7. Bibliography 136

Chapter 5. Quantitative Verification of Markov Chains 139
Susanna DONATELLI and Serge HADDAD

5.1. Introduction 139
5.2. Performance evaluation of Markov models 140
   5.2.1. A stochastic model for discrete events systems 140
   5.2.2. Discrete time Markov chains 143
   5.2.3. Continuous time Markov chain 146
5.3. Verification of discrete time Markov chain 148
   5.3.1. Temporal logics for Markov chains 148
   5.3.2. Verification of PCTL formulae 149
   5.3.3. Aggregation of Markov chains 151
   5.3.4. Verification of PLTL formulae 154
   5.3.5. Verification of $PCTL^*$ 157
5.4. Verification of continuous time Markov chain 157
   5.4.1. Limitations of standard performance indices 157
   5.4.2. A temporal logics for continuous time Markov chains 158
   5.4.3. Verification algorithm 159
5.5. State of the art in the quantitative evaluation of Markov chains 160
5.6. Bibliography 162

Chapter 6. Tools for Model-Checking Timed Systems 165
Alexandre DAVID, Gerd BEHRMANN, Peter BULYCHEV, Joakim BYG, Thomas
CHATAIN, Kim G. LARSEN, Paul PETTERSSON, Jacob Illum RASMUSSEN,
Jiří SRBA, Wang YI, Kenneth Y. JOERGENSEN, Didier LIME, Morgan MAGNIN,
Olivier H. ROUX and Louis-Marie TRAONOUEZ

6.1. Introduction 165
6.2. UPPAAL 166
   6.2.1. Timed automata and symbolic exploration 166
      6.2.1.1. Example 169
   6.2.2. Queries 170
   6.2.3. Architecture of the tool 172
   6.2.4. Reachability pipeline 173
   6.2.5. Liveness pipeline 175
   6.2.6. Leadsto pipeline 176
   6.2.7. Active clock reduction 176

6.2.8. Space reduction techniques 177
    6.2.8.1. Avoid storing all states 177
    6.2.8.2. Sharing data 178
    6.2.8.3. Minimal graph 178
    6.2.8.4. Symmetry reduction 179
6.2.9. Approximation techniques 180
    6.2.9.1. Over-approximation: convex-hull 180
    6.2.9.2. Under-approximation: bit-state hashing 180
6.2.10. Extensions 181
    6.2.10.1. Robust reachability 181
    6.2.10.2. Merging DBMs 181
    6.2.10.3. Stopwatches 181
    6.2.10.4. Supremum values 181
    6.2.10.5. Other extensions 181
6.3. UPPAAL-CORA 182
  6.3.1. Priced timed automata 182
  6.3.2. Example 184
6.4. UPPAAL-TIGA 185
  6.4.1. Timed game automata 185
  6.4.2. Reachability pipeline 187
  6.4.3. Time optimality 188
  6.4.4. Cooperative strategies 189
  6.4.5. Timed games with Büchi objectives 190
  6.4.6. Timed games with partial observability 192
    6.4.6.1. Algorithm 194
    6.4.6.2. Implementation 194
  6.4.7. Simulation checking 196
    6.4.7.1. Algorithm 197
6.5. TAPAAL 199
  6.5.1. Introduction 199
  6.5.2. Definition of timed-arc Petri nets used in TAPAAL 200
  6.5.3. TAPAAL logic 203
  6.5.4. Tool details 204
6.6. ROMÉO: a tool for the analysis of timed extensions of Petri nets 205
  6.6.1. Models 206
    6.6.1.1. Time Petri nets 206
    6.6.1.2. Petri Nets with stopwatches 208
    6.6.1.3. Parametric Petri nets with stopwatches 210
  6.6.2. Global architecture 210
  6.6.3. Systems modeling 211
  6.6.4. Verification of properties 211

6.6.4.1. On-line *model checking* 211
6.6.4.2. Off-line *model checking* 213
6.6.5. Using ROMÉO in an example 214
6.7. Bibliography 217

Chapter 7. Tools for the Analysis of Hybrid Models 227
Thao DANG, Goran FREHSE, Antoine GIRARD and Colas LE GUERNIC

7.1. Introduction 227
7.2. Hybrid automata and reachability 228
7.3. Linear hybrid automata 232
7.4. Piecewise affine hybrid systems 234
  7.4.1. Time discretization 234
    7.4.1.1. Autonomous dynamics 234
    7.4.1.2. Dynamics with inputs 236
  7.4.2. Scaling up reachability computations 237
    7.4.2.1. Reachability using zonotopes 237
    7.4.2.2. Efficient implementation for LTI systems 239
    7.4.2.3. Dealing with the discrete transitions 239
7.5. Hybridization techniques for reachability computations 241
  7.5.1. Approximation with linear hybrid automata 241
  7.5.2. Hybridization of nonlinear continuous system 243
    7.5.2.1. Properties of the approximate reachable set 244
    7.5.2.2. Approximation by hybrid systems with piecewise affine
        dynamics 245
  7.5.3. Hybridization and refinement 246
7.6. Bibliography 249

List of Authors 253

Index 259

Preface

This book stems from the global scientific priority put on the development of the research on communicating embedded systems. A worldwide scientific community is motivated by this theme and taking care of the development and promotion of formal approaches based on mathematical models and implemented by computer-automated tools. The main objective is to rise to the ever-growing challenge of mastering the quality of upcoming computer systems.

The computer systems concerned are:

– critical: a strong demand for quality comes from their handling of critical functions or a large-scale deployment;

– complex: their correct functioning depends on the careful use of resources that are mutually dependent over time. So their analysis on the basis of a formal model appears to be the most solid scientific approach.

This motivation is not new as the formal methods community has already produced a great number of results, mainly dedicated to the tasks of formal specification, verification and proof, and test synthesis. Several studies have been conducted with industrial partners, and a few of them have finally initiated some industrial software development processes. However, it remains mostly insufficient with respect to the increasing computer-related risks. Some progress is expected on the development and promotion of formal methods used in concrete computer-related problems and objects, as well as in the systematic research of new application fields and methods. Beyond the "traditional" application of formal methods to the conception of safe software, a significant impact can already be observed on areas of compiling and synthesis of controllers, diagnosis and supervision, system engineering, or security and safety engineering.

Chapter written by Claude JARD and Olivier H. ROUX.

Considering the widely acknowledged importance of the human and economic interests at stake with the future embedded systems (encompassing many economic sectors that have yet to be discovered), it is necessary to take particular interest in widely diffusing the technical advances of the domain. This is precisely the aim of this book arranged in an unified manner, such as the elements related to the current problems of embedded systems, the presentation of the achievements of new research directions on models and their use, and the presentation of available software tools. The contributing authors are renowned specialists in their respective fields. We have taken care of the coordination of the whole book, as leaders of the French national action AFSEC ("Formal Approaches for Communicating Embedded Systems"), supported by the CNRS.

Chapter 1

Models for Real-Time Embedded Systems

1.1. Introduction

The class of *real-time embedded* systems contains software components that control an application by reacting to stimuli received from a changing environment. Therefore, they are often referred to as *reactive* systems. The reaction time of these systems must be small enough to cope with the internal dynamics of the controlled or monitored application. They must thus obey the strong timing requirements, and it is crucial to ensure their correctness from both the functional and temporal points of view.

Real-time applications are often regarded as safety critical because their failures may either involve substantial financial losses or endanger human lives. It is also important to detect any error at an early stage to minimize the costs involved in its correction. This issue can be addressed by several approaches. Let us consider the following two approaches: in the first approach, from the application requirements, a model for the application and its expected properties are derived. Then a controller is proposed, using expert knowledge, to restrict the application behavior in order to satisfy the given properties. The next step is to validate the proposed controller using different techniques such as testing, theorem proving, formal verification, etc. If the controller is not acceptable, then it has to be reworked on the basis of the knowledge gained from the reported failures or counter-examples. In the second approach, the controller will be synthesized automatically from the formal model of the application. If such a

---

Chapter written by Didier LIME, Olivier H. ROUX and Jiří SRBA.

controller exists, which may not be the case, for example, if the requirements are incoherent, then a method to implement should be derived. Alternatively, if the controller model cannot be implemented, the problem has to be reworked from the beginning.

In this chapter, we will address the formal methods relating to these two approaches and those based on state-transition models. The models presented here deal with instantaneous actions and real-valued variables. The former approach usually models relevant events in the systems such as those relative to the command of the actuators or to the measures of sensors and the latter approach models durations of processes. These models thus describe subclasses of real-time embedded systems.

1.1.1. *Model-checking and control problems*

The requirements of a computer application are usually given as a natural language document. Therefore, they are subject to the interpretation of the persons who will derive the specification from them, which may result in many errors. Moreover, it is impossible for a conceptor to understand all possible interactions of the components of any reasonably sized application.

Formal methods aim at providing a mathematical framework for a clear, non-ambiguous and precise description of the systems and programs we want to develop. In this framework, the system is described by a labeled transition system or any model abstracting such a systems, e.g. automata, Petri nets, process algebra, etc. The specification may be either described in the same manner or as a property expressed in a suitable logic, such as linear temporal logics (LTL) or tree-based temporal logics (CTL), or even their timed extensions. A classical example of a real-time property is the *bounded response* property which requires that for the execution of the system, whenever some predicate P_0 on the states of the system becomes true, then some other predicate P_1 will become true, within n time units.

Among formal methods, *model-checking* is an automatic procedure that verifies whether a system satisfies a given temporal logic property. It usually works by exploring parts of the set of possible states of the system.

Controller synthesis consists of automatically synthesizing a program (the controller) that leads the interaction mechanisms with the environment (the application) and guarantees a safe and correct behavior of the coupled system. The set of actions of the system is partitioned into two disjoint subsets: a set of controllable actions and a set of uncontrollable actions. They usually correspond to the commands to actuators and the measures of sensors, respectively. The controller of the application may act on the controllable actions (and only on them) and the resulting system is said to be *closed* (as opposed to the system without the controller, which is said to be *open*).

Let us now compare the model-checking and control problems more precisely. In the model-checking problem, an already *closed* system is considered; let us call it S_{closed}. This system may be best viewed as an application S to which a controller C has been added. The expected correctness property is given by a formula φ in a suitable logic. The model-checking problem consists of deciding the question "does S_{closed} satisfy φ?" or equivalently "does S controlled by C satisfy φ?" which we will explain by:

$$\text{Does } S \parallel C \models \varphi? \tag{1.1}$$

The control problem is more general: it asks us to decide whether there exists a controller C of S such that the expected property φ is verified by S_{closed}:

$$\text{Does there exist } C \text{ such that } S \parallel C \models \varphi? \tag{1.2}$$

This problem is generally more complicated than the classical model-checking problem. To find an answer to problem [1.2], the search-space of admissible controllers has to be defined first: for example, we might want a controller with a bounded memory (modeled, e.g. as a *finite automaton* or a *Petri net*). Moreover, the controller must be restrictive enough to enforce the expected safety properties and also allow enough to avoid an excessive limitation of the behaviors of the system. Finally, there is another problem related to the control problem: the *controller synthesis* problem asks us to effectively compute the controller C.

1.1.2. *Timed models*

Considering an expected property of the system, a suitable model can be defined as an abstraction of the system such that the answer to the considered problem (verification, control, etc.) is same for both the system and its model. This implies that a model is relevant only for a given set of properties and need not perfectly match the real behaviors of the system. However, there is usually an opposition between the *expressivity* of a class of models, i.e. its ability to faithfully account for a number of characteristics of the system, and the *simplicity* in its analysis, i.e. decidability and algorithmic complexity of the verification or control problems.

The choice of an expressive-enough model avoids the pessimism inherent to the over-approximation of the real behavior of the system. Thus, a coarse model may show behaviors that are actually prevented in the real system by some device not taken into account by the model. This pessimism may lead to the conclusion that some safety property is false on the model, whereas it is actually true. It may also lead to the generation of a state-space with no finite abstraction, whereas it would have been finite with a finer model. In particular, the state-space of an untimed model may have no finite abstraction, whereas adding timing information to the model may restrict the behaviors to make a sufficient number of discrete states bounded and thus provide a finite abstraction.

Furthermore, in a number of applications, the requirements contain some properties that explicitly refer to durations between the two events. To account for such properties, a suitable model must embed some timing information rather than just the logical succession of events (logical time) expressed by models like finite automata or Petri nets. It must then model the dynamics of the application and/or the reactivity of the control system and provide *quantitative* timing information, thus enabling the verification of properties such as response times and making more precise failure causes to appear.

The models

Very general (and low-level) models such as transition systems (timed or untimed) are not directly usable for verification or control because they can represent any system without any restriction, which will usually imply the non-existence of finite representations. Therefore, we focus on higher level models, which can be analyzed using finite abstractions, but their semantics are given as transition systems.

In the untimed case, the simplest model is certainly a non-deterministic finite automaton, i.e. a labeled transition system with a finite number of states. Two other mainstream models are Petri nets and process algebras like *calculus of communicating systems* (CCS) [MIL 89]. All these models can be described in a finite way, even if their unfloodings in transition systems are usually infinite.

In the timed case, these models have been extended with timing information. Among these models, let us cite timed automata (TA) [ALU 94], extending finite automata, timed Petri nets [RAM 74], time Petri nets (TPNs) [MER 74], timed-arc Petri nets (TAPNs) [BOL 90, HAN 93], and timed process algebra such as TCCS [YI 91], one of the extensions of CCS. In this chapter, we focus on these "timed" models for which time is handled explicitly and, more precisely, on TA, TPNs and TAPNs.

Finally, the timed models can be further extended by using *stopwatches* to account for time elapsing, instead of *clocks*. These models are suspension/resumption of actions. The derivatives of the continuous variables relative to stopwatches can take only two values expressing either progression (1) or suspension (0). These models belong to the class of hybrid systems and they can model useful patterns such as pre-emptive scheduling in real-time systems.

Dense time vs. discrete time

Timed formal models account for the evolution of a system by both discrete instantaneous actions and time elapsing. The latter may be modeled either as a variable valued over a dense domain (e.g. $\mathbb{R}$) or over a discrete domain (e.g. $\mathbb{N}$). This leads to the models being called "dense time" and "discrete time,' respectively'. The choice between the two may be motivated by the following pros and cons:

– real-life applications evolve along the physical time, which is best thought of as continuous and dense. Therefore, considering a discrete time leads to an under-approximation of the real behaviors of the application. However, in view of building a controller, the application is only monitored at specific moments in time (sampling or sporadic observations);

– the controller is made of a set of tasks running on one or several processors, whose physical time is discrete. Using a dense-time model for the controller might thus add behaviors not possible in the real system (depending on the time granularity of the processors). However, it is perfectly possible to model a discrete behavior using a dense-time model.

More pragmatic considerations on computational complexity or decidability of the verification and control problems may also favor the choice of models:

– state-space computation of dense-time models can be done using symbolic methods which gather finite or infinite number of states into equivalence classes, thus mitigating the combinatorial explosion commonly found with discrete-time models, when explicitly enumerating the states. However, efficient data structures exist on the basis of extensions of *binary decision diagrams* (BDD) that can partly handle the combinatorial explosion of the number of states;

– for some models, such as those featuring stopwatches for instance, the reachability of a given state is an undecidable problem when a dense time is considered; then there exists no algorithm solving the verification problem or simply computing the state-space, but only semi-algorithms. However, using a discrete time and bounded time constraints, the reachability problem (and many others) is decidable for those models.

1.2. Notations, languages and timed transition systems

General notations

– the set $\mathbb{B}$ contains the Boolean values tt and ff;

– $\mathbb{N}, \mathbb{Q}, \mathbb{R}$ denote the sets of natural numbers, of rational numbers, and of real numbers, respectively;

– $\mathbb{R}_{\geq 0}$ is a set of non-negative real numbers and $\mathbb{R}_{>0} = \mathbb{R}_{\geq 0} \setminus \{0\}$ is a set of positive real numbers; we will also use these subscripts for $\mathbb{N}$ and $\mathbb{Q}$;

– for $n \in \mathbb{N}$, $\mathbb{R}^n$ is the space of real vectors of dimension n;

– for any finite set E, we denote the cardinality of E by $|E|$;

– B^A denotes the set of applications from A to B. If A is finite and $|A| = n$, an element in B^A is also a vector in B^n. The usual operations $+, -, <, \leq, >, \geq$, and $=$ are extended component-wise to vectors in A^n, with $A \in \{\mathbb{N}, \mathbb{Q}, \mathbb{R}\}$;

– a *valuation* ν on a set of variables X is an element of $\mathbb{R}_{\geq 0}^X$. For $\nu \in \mathbb{R}_{\geq 0}^X$ and $d \in \mathbb{R}_{\geq 0}$, $\nu + d$ denotes the valuation $(\nu + d)(x) = \nu(x) + d$, and for $X' \subseteq X$, $\nu[X' \mapsto 0]$ denotes the valuation ν' with $\nu'(x) = 0$ if $x \in X'$ and $\nu'(x) = \nu(x)$ otherwise. The symbol $\mathbf{0}$ denotes the null valuation such that $\forall x \in X, \nu(x) = 0$;

– let X be a set of variables. An *atomic constraint* on X is a formula of the form $x \sim c$ with $x \in X$, $c \in \mathbb{Q}_{\geq 0}$ and $\sim \in \{<, \leq, \geq, >\}$. $\mathcal{C}(X)$ denotes the set of *constraints* on X made from the conjunction of atomic constraints on X. Moreover, we denote by $\mathcal{C}_{dbm}(X)$ the set of conjunctions of terms of the form $x - x' \sim c$ or $x \sim c$, with $x, x' \in X$, $\sim \in \{<, \leq, =, \geq, >\}$ and $c \in \mathbb{Q}$;

– for a constraint $\varphi \in \mathcal{C}(X)$ and a valuation $\nu \in \mathbb{R}_{\geq 0}^X$, we denote by $\varphi(\nu) \in \mathbb{B}$ the truth value of φ obtained by substituting each occurrence of x in φ by $\nu(x)$. We thus define $[\![\varphi]\!] = \{\nu \in \mathbb{R}_{\geq 0}^X \mid \varphi(\nu) = \mathbf{tt}\}$.

Timed words and languages

Let Σ be a finite set called *alphabet*. Σ^* (resp. Σ^ω) is the set of finite (resp. infinite) sequences of elements of Σ and $\Sigma^\infty = \Sigma^* \cup \Sigma^\omega$. We will call *finite words* on the alphabet Σ the elements of Σ^* and *infinite words* on the alphabet Σ the elements of Σ^ω.

We define $\Sigma_\varepsilon = \Sigma \cup \{\varepsilon\}$ with $\varepsilon \notin \Sigma$, where ε represents a particular action (or letter), said to be *silent* or *non-observable*.

DEFINITION 1.1(TIMED WORD).– A *timed word* w on an alphabet Σ is a finite or infinite sequence $w = (a_0, d_0)(a_1, d_1) \cdots (a_n, d_n) \cdots$ such that for all $i \geq 0$, $a_i \in \Sigma$, $d_i \in \mathbb{R}_{\geq 0}$ and $d_{i+1} \geq d_i$.

A timed word $w = (a_0, d_0)(a_1, d_1) \cdots (a_n, d_n) \cdots$ on Σ can be considered as a pair $(a, d) \in \Sigma^\infty \times \mathbb{R}_{\geq 0}^\infty$ with $|a| = |d|$. The value d_i gives the absolute date (considering the system starts at date 0) of action a_i.

We denote $Untimed(w) = a_0 a_1 \cdots a_n \cdots$ the untimed part of w, and $Duration(w) = \sup_{d_i \in d} d_i$ the duration w.

We denote $\mathcal{TW}^*(\Sigma)$ (resp. $\mathcal{TW}^\omega(\Sigma)$) the set of finite (resp. infinite) timed words on Σ and we define $\mathcal{TW}^\infty(\Sigma) = \mathcal{TW}^*(\Sigma) \cup \mathcal{TW}^\omega(\Sigma)$.

DEFINITION 1.2(TIMED LANGUAGE).– A *timed language* L on Σ is a subset of $\mathcal{TW}^\infty(\Sigma)$.

Timed transition systems

We discuss systems that can be described by a labeled transition system, i.e. a set of states and a set of transitions between states, labeled by actions. In a given state, it is possible to change the state by executing the action by labeling one of the outgoing edges. A run in the transition system is then a sequence of transitions.

Timed transition systems (TTSs) are special transition systems for which two types of transitions are possible: action transitions and time transitions, modeling, discrete and continuous evolutions of the system, respectively.

DEFINITION 1.3(TIMED TRANSITION SYSTEM).– A (labeled) *timed transition system* is a 4-tuple $S = (Q, Q_0, \Sigma, \longrightarrow)$ where Q is a set of states, $Q_0 \subseteq Q$ is the subset of initial states, Σ is a finite set of actions (disjoint from $\mathbb{R}_{\geq 0}$), $\longrightarrow \subseteq Q \times (\Sigma \cup \mathbb{R}_{\geq 0}) \times Q$ is a set of edges called transition relation. When $(q, e, q') \in \longrightarrow$, we also write $q \xrightarrow{e} q'$. The transition relation consists of a *continuous* transition relation $\xrightarrow{d \in \mathbb{R}_{\geq 0}}$ and a *discrete* relation transition $\xrightarrow{a \in A}$.

We make the following standard assumptions on TTS:

– 0-DELAY : $q \xrightarrow{0} q'$ iff $q = q'$;

– ADDITIVITY: if $q \xrightarrow{d} q'$ and $q' \xrightarrow{d'} q''$ with $d, d' \in \mathbb{R}_{\geq 0}$, then $q \xrightarrow{d+d'} q''$;

– CONTINUITY: if $q \xrightarrow{d} q'$, then for all $d', d'' \in \mathbb{R}_{\geq 0}$ such that $d = d' + d''$, there exists q'' such that $q \xrightarrow{d'} q'' \xrightarrow{d''} q'$;

– TIME DETERMINISM: if $q \xrightarrow{d} q'$ and $q \xrightarrow{d} q''$ with $d \in \mathbb{R}_{\geq 0}$, then $q' = q''$.

DEFINITION 1.4(RUN IN A TTS).– A *run* ρ in a TTS S is a finite or infinite sequence of continuous and discrete transitions in S. The set of runs of a TTS S is denoted by $[\![S]\!]$.

A run can always be written as an alternating sequence of continuous (possibly by delay 0) and discrete transitions:

$$\rho = q_0 \xrightarrow{d_0} q_0' \xrightarrow{a_0} q_1 \xrightarrow{d_1} q_1' \xrightarrow{a_1} \cdots q_n \xrightarrow{d_n} q_n' \cdots$$

We note *Untimed*$(\rho) = q_0 \xrightarrow{a_0} q_1 \xrightarrow{a_1} \cdots$ and *Duration*$(\rho) = \sum_{i=0}^{n} d_i$, if ρ is finite and of size n, and, when ρ is infinite, *Duration*$(\rho) = \sum_{i=0}^{\infty} d_i$, if the series converges (ρ is then said to be *Zeno*) and *Duration*$(\rho) = \infty$, otherwise.

DEFINITION 1.5(TRACE).– The *trace* of a run $\rho = q_0 \xrightarrow{d_0} q_0' \xrightarrow{a_0} q_1 \cdots q_k \xrightarrow{d_k} q_k' \cdots$ in a TTS is the timed word $trace(\rho) = (a_0, \delta_0) \cdots (a_k, \delta_k) \cdots$ such that $\delta_k = \sum_{i=0}^{k} d_i$.

A timed word w, possibly infinite, is *accepted* by the TTS $S = (Q, Q_0, \Sigma, \longrightarrow)$, if there exists a run of S starting from some initial state $q_0 \in Q_0$, and whose trace is w. We could also define a set of accepting (or repeated) states in which the run has to finish (or to visit infinitely often for infinite runs). Here, we consider that this set is Q. The *timed language* $\mathcal{L}(S)$ accepted by S is the set of timed words accepted by S. In the case of finite words, as all states are accepting any prefix of an accepted timed word is also accepted, and so, we say that the corresponding timed language is *prefix-closed*.

The *untimed language* $\mathcal{L}_u(S)$ of the TTS S is the set of words accepted by S in which time actions have been abstracted: $\mathcal{L}_u(S) = \{trace(Untimed(\rho)) | \rho \in [\![S]\!]\}$.

Finally, when a TTS is defined on Σ_ε, i.e. some discrete actions are labeled by ε, its language is defined as the language of the corresponding ε-abstract TTS.

DEFINITION 1.6(ε-ABSTRACT TTS).– Let $S = (Q, Q_0, \Sigma_\varepsilon, \longrightarrow)$ be a TTS. We define a corresponding ε-*abstract* TTS $S^\varepsilon = (Q, Q_0^\varepsilon, \Sigma, \longrightarrow_\varepsilon)$ by:

– $q \xrightarrow{d}_\varepsilon q'$ with $d \geq \mathbb{R}_{\geq 0}$ iff there exists a run $\rho = q \rightarrow q'$ with $trace(Untimed(\rho)) \in \varepsilon^*$ and $Duration(\rho) = d$;

– $q \xrightarrow{a}_\varepsilon q'$ with $a \in \Sigma$ iff there exists a run $\rho = q \rightarrow q'$ with $trace(Untimed(\rho)) \subset \varepsilon^* a \varepsilon^*$ and $Duration(\rho) = 0$;

– $Q_0^\varepsilon = \{q \, | \, \exists q' \in Q_0 \, | \, \rho = q' \rightarrow q$ and $Duration(\rho) = 0 \wedge trace(Untimed(\rho)) \in \varepsilon^*\}$.

1.3. Timed models

Transition systems are very general and low-level formalism. A problem arises as their representations can be infinite, which greatly impairs our ability to perform automatic verification or control this formalism. Therefore, we will study higher level models, for which the representation is finite, and the behavior can be encoded by a (possibly infinite) transition system. This defines classes of transition systems for which the problems of interest are decidable or at least more easily expressible.

1.3.1. *Timed Automata*

Presentation

Timed Automata are basically non-deterministic finite automata equipped with real-valued clocks. They have been introduced by Alur and Dill [ALU 94] and extended with the notion of location invariant by Henzinger *et al.* [HEN 94]. The notion of time in TA relies both on the added clocks and on predicates involving these clocks.

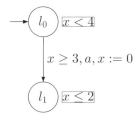

Figure 1.1. *A timed automaton*

These predicates can either be a *guard* associated with a transition and must be true for the transition to be taken, or an *invariant* associated with a location and must be true for the system to stay in that particular location.

Figure 1.1 describes a simple example of timed automaton. The initial location is l_0. The automaton has only one clock, named x, such that x is initially zero and the invariant of l_0 implies that the system can stay there during (strictly) less than four time units. As soon as three time units have elapsed, the guard of the transition between l_0 and l_1 is satisfied (and the invariant of l_1 will be satisfied if the transition is taken), so the transition can be taken. If we do so, the clock x is reset and l_1 becomes the active location.

Definitions

DEFINITION 1.7(TIMED AUTOMATON).– [HEN 94] A *Timed Automaton* is a 6-tuple $(L, l_0, X, \Sigma, E, Inv)$ where:

– L is a finite set of *locations*;

– $l_0 \in L$ is the *initial location*;

– X is a finite set of non-negative real-valued *clocks*;

– Σ is a finite set of *actions*;

– $E \subseteq L \times \mathcal{C}(X) \times \Sigma \times 2^X \times L$ is a finite set of *edges*. Let $e = (l, g, a, R, l') \in E$, then e is an edge between l and l', with the *guard* g, the action a and the set of clocks to reset R;

– $Inv \in \mathcal{C}(X)^L$ sets an *invariant* for each location.

We define the semantics of a timed automaton as a timed transition system.

DEFINITION 1.8(SEMANTICS OF A TA).– The semantics of a timed automaton $\mathcal{A}$ is a timed transition system $\mathcal{S}_\mathcal{A} = (Q, Q_0, \Sigma, \rightarrow)$ where:

– $Q = L \times (\mathbb{R}_{\geq 0})^X$;

– $Q_0 = (l_0, \mathbf{0})$;

- $\to\, \subseteq Q \times (\Sigma \cup \mathbb{R}_{\geq 0}) \times Q$ is the relation defined for $a \in \Sigma$ and $d \in \mathbb{R}_{\geq 0}$ by:
  - the *discrete* transition relation: $(l, \nu) \xrightarrow{a} (l', \nu')$ iff $\exists (l, g, a, R, l') \in E$ s.t.

$$\begin{cases} g(\nu) = \mathsf{tt}, \\ \nu' = \nu[R \mapsto 0], \\ Inv(l')(\nu') = \mathsf{tt} \end{cases}$$

  - the *continuous* transition relation: $(l, \nu) \xrightarrow{d} (l, \nu')$ iff

$$\begin{cases} \nu' = \nu + d, \\ \forall d' \in [0, d],\ Inv(l)(\nu + d') = \mathsf{tt}\,. \end{cases}$$

Decidability of classical problems

The *region graph* construction provides a universal tool for arguing about the decidability of several problems on TA [ALU 90, ALU 94]. Using this technique, it was shown, e.g. that reachability is decidable in PSPACE for TA [ALU 94] as well as for networks of TA [ACE 02], untimed language equivalence for TA is decidable in PSPACE [ALU 94], and untimed bisimilarity for TA is decidable in EXPTIME [LAR 97].

Practically more efficient algorithms are usually achieved by considering *zones* instead of regions (see e.g. [BEN 03]). Somewhat surprisingly even timed bisimilarity for TA is decidable. Using region graphs on a product construction, timed bisimilarity was shown to be decidable in EXPTIME [CER 93].

Unfortunately, timed language equivalence for TA is already undecidable [ALU 94]. In fact, even the universality problem (whether a given timed automaton generates *all* timed traces) is undecidable too.

1.3.2. *Time Petri nets*

Petri nets and time

The three main time extensions of Petri nets are *timed* Petri nets [RAM 74], *TPNs* [MER 74], and TAPNs [BOL 90, HAN 93].

In timed Petri nets, time is modeled by minimal durations (or exact when considering an "as soon as possible" execution of the net) for the firing of transitions. In TPNs, time is modeled by intervals constraining the possible firing dates of the transition. Moreover, time can be bound to timed transitions, timed places, timed arcs, or timed tokens. The resulting classes of TPNs are included in the corresponding classes of TPNs [PEZ 99].

Weak vs. strong semantics

We can further distinguish two semantics for TPN models: in weak semantics, timed actions are available in the span of the interval but can be ignored, and in strong semantics, time cannot progress if an action is possible and the value of the clock bound to it has reached the upper bound of time interval. The strong semantics permit to approach model urgency, which is an essential feature of real-time systems. Except for T-time Petri nets (where time intervals are bound to transitions) with strong semantics, the evolution of the net may also lead to the presence of so-called "dead" tokens in the net which cannot be used for any transition firing and may be sometimes difficult to interpret.

Single-server vs. multi-server semantics

We can finally distinguish the single-server semantics from multi-server semantics [BOY 01, BER 01]. The number of *clocks* to be considered is finite with the single-server semantics (one clock per transition, one per place, or one per arc), whereas in general it is not in the case of multi-server semantics.

Timed-arc Petri nets have been mainly studied with weak (lazy) multi-server semantics [HAN 93, RUI 99, FRU 00, NIE 01, RUI 00, ABD 01, ABD 07, SRB 05, BOU 08]: this means that the number of clocks is not finite but the firing of transitions may be delayed, even if this implies that some transitions are disabled because their input tokens become too old. In fact, in TAPNs, time is assigned to tokens and arcs are labeled by the intervals that restrict the age of available tokens. The reachability problem is undecidable [RUI 99] for this class of Petri nets but thanks to the weak semantics, it enjoys *monotonic* properties and falls into a class of models for which the coverability and boundedness problems are decidable [RUI 00, ABD 01, ABD 07].

Conversely, T-time Petri nets [MER 74, BER 91] and P-time Petri nets [KHA 96] have been studied only with a strong single-server semantics. They do not have the monotonic features of the weak semantics although the number of *clocks* is finite. The marking reachability and coverability problems are known to be undecidable [JON 77] but marking coverability, k-boundedness, state reachability, and liveness are decidable for *bounded* T-time Petri nets and P-time Petri nets with strong semantics.

Therefore, T-time Petri nets with a strong single-server semantics are most widely used for modeling real-time systems, and we will mainly focus on them in this book, when dealing with Petri nets. We will generally refer to them as simply TPN.

Timed-arc Petri nets are conceptually different from T-time Petri net model and since T-time Petri net and TAPNs are both the most widely used and studied for single-server and multi-server semantics, respectively, they are discussed in detail in sections 1.3.2.1 and 1.3.2.2.

1.3.2.1. *T-time Petri nets*

T-time Petri nets [MER 74] are basically Petri nets equipped with time intervals $[\alpha(t), \beta(t)]$ bound to each transition t of the net. To be fired, a transition must be enabled without interruption for a duration between $\alpha(t)$ and $\beta(t)$.

1.3.2.1.1. Definitions

DEFINITION 1.9(T-TIME PETRI NET).– A T-time Petri net is a 7-tuple $\mathcal{N} = (P, T, {}^\bullet(.), (.)^\bullet, \alpha, \beta, M_0)$, where:

 – $P = \{p_1, p_2, \ldots, p_m\}$ is a finite non-empty set of *places*;

 – $T = \{t_1, t_2, \ldots, t_n\}$ is a finite non-empty set of *transitions* $(T \cap P = \emptyset)$;

 – ${}^\bullet(.) \in (\mathbb{N}^P)^T$ is the *backward incidence* function;

 – $(.)^\bullet \in (\mathbb{N}^P)^T$ is the *forward incidence* function;

 – $M_0 \in \mathbb{N}^P$ is the *initial marking* of the net;

 – $\alpha \in (\mathbb{R}_{\geq 0})^T$ and $\beta \in (\mathbb{R}_{\geq 0} \cup \{\infty\})^T$ are functions giving for each transitions: the *earliest* and *latest* firing time $(\alpha \leq \beta)$, respectively.

A marking M of the net is an element of $\mathbb{N}^P$ such that for any $p \in P$, $M(p)$ is the number of tokens in place p.

A transition t is said to be *enabled* by the marking M, if $M \geq {}^\bullet t$, i.e., in M, the number of tokens in each input place of t is greater or equal to the valuation of the arc between that place and t. We denote this by $t \in$ enabled(M).

A transition t is said to be newly enabled by the firing of the transition t' from marking M, which we denote by $\uparrow$enabled(t, M, t'), if t is enabled by the new marking $M - {}^\bullet t' + t'^\bullet$ but was not by the marking $M - {}^\bullet t'$. Formally speaking,

$$\uparrow \text{enabled}(t, M, t') = ({}^\bullet t \leq M - {}^\bullet t' + t'^\bullet) \wedge ((t = t') \vee ({}^\bullet t > M - {}^\bullet t')).$$

Similarly, t is said to be *disabled* by the firing of t' from marking M, which we denote by disabled(t, M, t'), if t is enabled by M but is not anymore by $M - {}^\bullet t' + t'^\bullet$.

By extension, we denote by $\uparrow$ enabled(M, t') (resp. disabled(M, t')) the set of transitions newly enabled (resp. disabled) by the firing of t' from M.

As for timed automata, we define the semantics of time Petri nets as a timed transition system.

DEFINITION 1.10(SEMANTICS OF A TPN).– The semantics of a T-time Petri net $\mathcal{N}$ is a TTS $\mathcal{S}_{\mathcal{N}} = (Q, q_0, \Sigma, \rightarrow)$ where:

- $Q = \mathbb{N}^P \times (\mathbb{R}_{\geq 0})^T$;
- $q_0 = (M_0, \mathbf{0})$;
- $\Sigma = T$;
- $\rightarrow \subseteq Q \times (T \cup \mathbb{R}_{\geq 0}) \times Q$ is the relation consisting of:
    - the *continuous* relation transition defined for any $d \in \mathbb{R}_{\geq 0}$ by:

$$(M, \nu) \xrightarrow{d} (M, \nu') \text{ iff } \begin{cases} \nu' = \nu + d, \\ \forall t_k \in T, M \geq {}^\bullet t_k \Rightarrow \nu'(t_k) \leq \beta(t_k); \end{cases}$$

    - the *discrete* relation transition defined for $t_i \in T$ by:

$$(M, \nu) \xrightarrow{t_i} (M', \nu') \text{ iff } \begin{cases} M \geq {}^\bullet t_i, \\ \alpha(t_i) \leq \nu(t_i) \leq \beta(t_i), \\ M' = M - {}^\bullet t_i + t_i^\bullet, \\ \forall t_k, \nu'(t_k) = \begin{cases} 0, \text{ if } \uparrow \text{enabled}(t_k, M, t_i), \\ \nu(t_k), \text{ otherwise.} \end{cases} \end{cases}$$

When a discrete transition is possible from a state $s = (M, \nu)$ of (the semantics of) the net, we say that the corresponding transition of the net is *firable*.

DEFINITION 1.11(FIRABLE TRANSITION).– Let $s = (M, \nu)$ be a state of the semantics of a TPN. A transition t is said *firable* from s if $M \geq {}^\bullet t$ and $\alpha(t) \leq \nu(t) \leq \beta(t)$.

Note that, with this semantics, when a place contains more than necessary tokens to enable an outgoing transition, that transition is enabled only once. In particular, only one clock is implicitly associated with it, measuring the duration of the enabling. This is the *single-server semantics*. This semantics is illustrated in Figure 1.2, where we suppose that t_1 is firable. In Figure 1.2(a), t_1 and t_2 are enabled by marking M and by $M' = M - {}^\bullet t_1 + t_1^\bullet$ but not by $M - {}^\bullet t_1$. Hence, the transitions t_1 and t_2 are both *newly* enabled by the firing of t_1.

In Figure 1.2(b), t_1 and t_2 are enabled by marking M and by $M' = M - {}^\bullet t_1 + t_1^\bullet$, but also by $M - {}^\bullet t_1$. In this case, t_1 is *newly* enabled by its own firing t_1 (because it is the fired transition) but not t_2: t_2 *remains* enabled (and the associated clock keeps its value).

The semantics can be adapted to allow a transition to be enabled several times at once [BER 01]. We then consider the *multi-server semantics* and the number of clocks becomes potentially infinite.

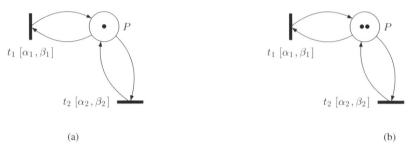

(a)   (b)

Figure 1.2. *Enabling of transitions*

DEFINITION 1.12(LABELED TIME PETRI NET).– A *Labeled Time Petri Net* $\mathcal{N}$ is a 9-tuple $\mathcal{N} = (P, T, \Sigma_\varepsilon, {}^\bullet(.), (.)^\bullet, \alpha, \beta, M_0, \Lambda)$ such that $(P, T, {}^\bullet(.), (.)^\bullet, \alpha, \beta, M_0)$ is a TPN, Σ is a finite set of *actions* and $\Lambda : T \rightarrow \Sigma_\varepsilon$ is a *labeling* function.

A non-labeled TPN can thus be seen as a labeled TPN with $\Sigma = T$ and $\Lambda(t) = t$ for all $t \in T$. Classically, by TPN we will mean a TPN labeled in this way.

Finally, Definitions 1.9, 1.10 and 1.12 could be easily extended to account for open or half-closed intervals.

1.3.2.1.2. Decidability of classical problems

Given a time Petri net $\mathcal{N}$ and its semantics $\mathcal{S}_\mathcal{N}$, several interesting problems can be studied, including:

– *state reachability*: is a given state (M, ν) reachable in $\mathcal{S}_\mathcal{N}$?

– *marking reachability*: given a marking M, is there a reachable state in $\mathcal{S}_\mathcal{N}$ of the form (M, ν) for some ν?

– *k-boundedness*: given $k \in \mathbb{N}$, is it the case that for all reachable states (M, ν) in $\mathcal{S}_\mathcal{N}$ we have $M(p) \leq k$ for all $p \in P$?

– *boundedness*: is there some $k \in \mathbb{N}$ such that the net is k-bounded?

– *liveness*: for all $t \in T$ and all reachable states (M, ν) in $\mathcal{S}_\mathcal{N}$, is it possible to reach from (M, ν) a state that enables to fire the transition t?

Marking reachability is an undecidable problem [JON 77], which implies that boundedness, state reachability and liveness are also undecidable. On the other hand, k-boundedness is decidable. In particular, it can be decided by computing a finite abstraction of the state space such as the state class graph of [BER 91], which can be efficiently computed by using *difference bound matrices* (DBM) [BER 83, DIL 89].

In the case of *bounded* TPNs, marking reachability, state reachability, and liveness are all decidable [BER 83, BER 91].

Another interesting problem is the *model-checking* problem, in particular, for real-time systems with properties expressed in a timed temporal logic such as TCTL [ALU 93].

Finally, the classical language theoretic problems include: the *emptiness* and *universality* problems, the former being equivalent to reachability and the latter being equivalent to language inclusion, and the closure properties.

We sum up the decidability results in the following table.

Problem	Timed automata	Bounded TPN (B-TPN)
Reachability emptiness	Decidable [ALU 94]	Decidable [BER 91]
Universality language inclusion	Undecidable [ALU 94]	Undecidable [BER 05]
Closures c losed	$\cap, \cup$ Not by complementary [ALU 94]	$\cap, \cup$ Not by complementary [BER 05]
Model-checking of TCTL	Decidable [ALU 94]	Decidable [CAS 04, CAS 06]

1.3.2.2. *Timed-arc petri nets*

Presentation

The last extension of Petri nets that is to be considered in this chapter is *timed-arc Petri nets* [BOL 90, HAN 93]. Here, the time entity (also called *age*) is associated with tokens. We can consider this as if every token in the net had its own private clock. The arcs from places to transitions are labeled by time intervals, which restrict the age of tokens that can be used to fire a given transition. When new tokens are produced, their age is set by default to 0. The usually considered semantics is *non-urgent* (or *weak*), which means that tokens can grow older even if this disables the firing of certain transitions which may result in the creation of *dead tokens*.

Let us consider a TAPN described in Figure 1.3. In the initial marking there is one token of age 0 in the place p_1. As the age of the token does not belong to the interval $[2, 4]$, the transition t_1 is not enabled yet, but only after two time units. Then anytime within another two units the transition can fire and produce two new tokens of age 0 into places p_2 and p_3. Note, however, that due to the non-urgent semantics it is possible that the age of the token in p_1 grows beyond 4 and hence the transition t_1 gets disabled forever. Assuming that we are in a marking with two tokens of age 0 in places p_2 and p_3. After waiting for two time units, the transition t_3 becomes enabled and if it fires it resets the age of the token in place p_3 to 0 and produces a new fresh

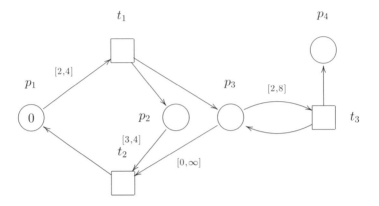

Figure 1.3. *A timed-arc Petri net*

token into place p_4. By waiting for another two time units the age of the token in the place p_2 reaches the value 4 and the tokens in the places p_3 and p_4 will be of age 2. Now, for example, the transition t_2 can fire, consuming the tokens in places p_2 and p_3 and producing a fresh one into place p_1. Another possible behavior (due to the non-urgent semantics) is that the transition t_3 keeps firing forever after arbitrary delays between two and eight time units. This shows that our TAPN is unbounded and moreover every token in place p_4 will have its own unique age. This demonstrates that unlike TA and TPN, we cannot rely only on a finite number of clocks associated with a given automaton/net.

Definitions

We first define the set $\mathcal{I}$ of *time intervals* by the following abstract syntax where a and b range over $\mathbb{N}$ such that $a < b$.

$$I ::= [a, b] \mid [a, a] \mid (a, b] \mid [a, b) \mid (a, b) \mid [a, \infty) \mid (a, \infty)$$

Let $I \in \mathcal{I}$. Given a time point $d \in \mathbb{R}_{\geq 0}$, the validity of the expression $d \in I$ is defined in the usual way, e.g., $d \in [a, b)$ iff $a \leq d < b$, and $d \in (a, \infty)$ iff $a < d$.

DEFINITION 1.13(TIMED-ARC PETRI NET).– A *(labeled)* TAPN is a tuple $N = (P, T, F, c, \Sigma, \Lambda)$ where

– P is a finite set of *places*,

– T is a finite set of *transitions* such that $T \cap P = \emptyset$,

– $F \subseteq (P \times T) \cup (T \times P)$ is a *flow relation*,

– $c : F|_{P \times T} \to \mathcal{I}$ is a function assigning a *time interval* to arcs from places to transitions,

– Σ is a set of *labels* (*actions*), and

– $\Lambda : T \to \Sigma$ a *labeling function*.

As before, we define $^{\bullet}t = \{p \mid (p, t) \in F\}$ and $t^{\bullet} = \{p \mid (t, p) \in F\}$. A *marking* M on the net N is a function

$$M : P \to \mathcal{B}(\mathbb{R}_{\geq 0})$$

where $\mathcal{B}(\mathbb{R}_{\geq 0})$ denotes the set of finite multisets on $\mathbb{R}_{\geq 0}$. Each place is thus assigned a certain number of tokens, and each token is annotated with a real number (*age*). Let $B \in \mathcal{B}(\mathbb{R}_{\geq 0})$ and $d \in \mathbb{R}_{\geq 0}$. We define $B + d$ in such a way that we add the value d to every element of B, i.e., $B + d = \{b + d \mid b \in B\}$. As *initial markings* we allow only markings with all tokens of age 0. A *marked TAPN* is a pair (N, M_0) where N is a TAPN and M_0 is an initial marking.

Let us now define the dynamics of TAPN. We introduce two types of transition rules: *firing* of a transition and *time-elapsing*. Let $N = (P, T, F, c, \Sigma, \Lambda)$ be a TAPN, M a marking and $t \in T$:

– we say that t is *enabled* by M iff $\forall p \in {}^{\bullet}t. \ \exists x \in M(p). \ x \in c(p, t)$;

– if t is enabled by M then it can *fire*, producing a marking M' such that:

$$\forall p \in P. \ M'(p) = \left(M(p) \smallsetminus C^-(p, t) \right) \cup C^+(t, p)$$

where C^- and C^+ are chosen to satisfy the following equations (note that there may be more possibilities and that all the operations are on multisets):

$$C^-(p, t) = \begin{cases} \{x\}, & \text{if } p \in {}^{\bullet}t \text{ s.t. } x \in M(p) \land x \in c(p, t) \\ \emptyset, & \text{otherwise} \end{cases}$$

$$C^+(t, p) = \begin{cases} \{0\}, & \text{if } p \in t^{\bullet} \\ \emptyset, & \text{otherwise.} \end{cases}$$

Then, we write $M[t\rangle M'$. Note that the new tokens added to the places in $t^{\bullet}$ are of the initial age 0:

– we define a *time-elapsing* transition for any $d \in \mathbb{R}_{\geq 0}$, as follows:

$$M[d\rangle M' \ \text{iff} \ \forall p \in P. \ M'(p) = M(p) + d.$$

DEFINITION 1.14(SEMANTICS OF A TAPN).– The semantics of a marked TAPN (N, M_0) where $N = (P, T, F, c, \Sigma, \Lambda)$ is the TTS $\mathcal{S}_N = (Q, q_0, \Sigma, \to)$ such that:

– $Q = P \to \mathcal{B}(\mathbb{R}_{\geq 0})$ is the set of all markings on N;

– $q_0 = M_0$; and

- $- \to \subseteq Q \times (T \cup \mathbb{R}_{\geq 0}) \times Q$ is defined by
  - $M \xrightarrow{d} M'$ whenever $M[d\rangle M'$ for some $d \in \mathbb{R}_{\geq 0}$; and
  - $M \xrightarrow{a} M'$ whenever $M[t\rangle M'$ for some $t \in T$ such that $\Lambda(t) = a$.

In standard P/T Petri nets (and TPN), there is a simple construction to ensure that a transition can be fired only if a token is present in a certain place, without removing the token. This is done by adding two arcs: one from the place to the transition and another in the opposite direction. However, a similar construction does not work in TAPN, as consuming a (timed) token resets its age. In order to recover this possibility, the so-called *read arcs* were introduced in [SRB 05]. It was later shown in [BOU 08] that this extension is not only convenient from the modeling point of view but it also extends the expressiveness of the model. Read arcs were also investigated in connection with partial order semantics for (untimed) P/T nets [VOG 02, BUS 99].

DEFINITION 1.15.– A *timed-arc Petri net with read arcs* is a tuple $N = (P, T, F, c, \Sigma, \Lambda, F*, c*)$ such that $(P, T, F, c, \Sigma, \Lambda)$ is a timed-arc Petri net, $F* \subseteq P \times T$ is a set of *read arcs*, and $c* : F* \to \mathcal{I}$ is a function which assigns a time interval to every testing arc from $F*$. We define $^*t = \{p \mid (p, t) \in F*\}$.

The dynamics of TAPN with read arcs is defined as in the case of TAPN with the only difference is that for a transition t to be enabled, it has to satisfy an extra condition, namely

$$\forall p \in {}^*t. \exists x \in M(p). x \in c*(p, t).$$

In other words, a necessary condition for a transition to fire is that all places which are connected via testing arcs to the transition contain a token satisfying the constraint on the testing arc. The transition can then fire according to the rules defined above, which means that the testing arcs do not consume any tokens and hence do not influence their age.

1.3.2.2.1. Decidability of classical problems

In TAPNs theory, researchers studied similar decidability questions as in the case of TAPNs. In particular, we can ask the *state reachability* question, i.e., is a given marking (including the exact ages of tokens) reachable from the initial marking; the *marking reachability* question, i.e. can we select some concrete ages of tokens for a given untimed marking such that the resulting marking is reachable from the initial one; the *coverability* question, i.e. can be reached a marking that covers some given marking (in other words, it contains at least all the tokens from that marking); and the *boundedness* question, i.e. is there a constant k such that all markings reachable from the initial one contain at most k tokens in total.

State and marking reachability are undecidable for (unbounded) TAPNs [RUI 99], even in the case when tokens in different places are not required to age synchronously [NIE 01]. On the other hand, coverability, boundedness, and other problems remain decidable even for unbounded TAPN [RUI 00, ABD 01, ABD 07], as TAPN are known to offer "weak" expressiveness, in the sense that TAPN cannot simulate Turing machines [BOL 89]. Coverability is decidable even for TAPN extended with read-arcs [BOU 08]. These results hold due to the monotonicity property (adding more tokens to the net does not restrict the possible executions) and the application of well-quasi-ordering (for a general introduction see [FIN 01]) and better-quasi-ordering [ABD 00] techniques, respectively.

When we consider the subclass of 1-safe TAPN, it is known that the (state and marking) reachability problem is no more difficult than in untimed 1-safe Petri nets and hence it is decidable in PSPACE [SRB 05]. This is a case for 1-safe TAPN with read-arcs also.

1.3.3. Compared expressiveness of several classes of timed models

1.3.3.1. Bisimulation and expressiveness of timed models

Timed simulation and bisimulation

DEFINITION 1.16(STRONG-TIMED SIMULATION).– Let $S_1 = (Q_1, Q_0^1, \Sigma, \longrightarrow_1)$ and $S_2 = (Q_2, Q_0^2, \Sigma, \longrightarrow_2)$ be two TTS over Σ. A binary relation $\sqsubseteq$ over $Q_1 \times Q_2$, is called *strong-timed simulation relation* of S_1 by S_2 if the following holds:

1) if $s_1 \in Q_0^1$, then there exists $s_2 \in Q_0^2$ such that $s_1 \sqsubseteq s_2$;

2) if $s_1 \xrightarrow{d}_1 s_1'$ with $d \in \mathbb{R}_{\geq 0}$ and $s_1 \sqsubseteq s_2$ then there exists $s_2 \xrightarrow{d}_2 s_2'$ such that $s_1' \sqsubseteq s_2'$;

3) if $s_1 \xrightarrow{a}_1 s_1'$ with $a \in \Sigma$ and $s_1 \sqsubseteq s_2$ then there exists $s_2 \xrightarrow{a}_2 s_2'$ such that $s_1' \sqsubseteq s_2'$.

A TTS S_2 *strongly simulates* S_1, if there exists a strong-timed simulation of S_1 by S_2, and we denote it by $S_1 \preceq_S S_2$.

DEFINITION 1.17(WEAK-TIMED SIMULATION).– Let $S_1 = (Q_1, Q_0^1, \Sigma_\varepsilon, \longrightarrow_1)$ and $S_2 = (Q_2, Q_0^2, \Sigma_\varepsilon, \longrightarrow_2)$ be two TTS over Σ_ε. A binary relation $\sqsubseteq$ over $Q_1 \times Q_2$ is called *weak-timed simulation* of S_1 by S_2 if it is a strong-timed simulation between the two ε-abstract TTS S_1^ε and S_2^ε. A TTS S_2 *weakly simulates* S_1, if there exists a weak-timed simulation of S_1 by S_2. We denote this by $S_1 \preceq_W S_2$.

DEFINITION 1.18(TIMED BISIMULATION).– Let S_1 and S_2 be two TTS and $\sqsubseteq$ a strong (resp. weak) timed simulation of S_1 by S_2. The relation $\sqsubseteq$ is a strong (resp. weak) timed bisimulation relation if its inverse relation, denoted $\sqsubseteq^{-1}$, is a strong (resp.

weak) simulation of S_2 by S_1. (Recall that $S_2 \sqsubseteq^{-1} S_1$ iff $S_1 \sqsubseteq S_2$.) We say that S_1 and S_2 are *strongly (resp. weakly) time bisimilar* if there exists a strong (resp. weak) bisimulation between S_1 and S_2. We denote this by $S_1 \approx_S S_2$ (resp. $S_1 \approx_W S_2$).

Expressiveness of timed models

Let C and C' be two classes of timed models.

DEFINITION 1.19(EXPRESSIVENESS W.R.T. AN EQUIVALENCE RELATION).– Let $\mathcal{R}$ be an equivalence relation between TTS. The class C is *more expressive* than the class C' w.r.t. $\mathcal{R}$ if for all $B' \in C'$ there exists $B \in C$ such that $B\mathcal{R}B'$. We denote this by $C' \sqsubseteq_{\mathcal{R}} C$. Moreover, if there exists $B \in C$ such that there exists no $B' \in C'$ with $B\mathcal{R}B'$, then $C' \sqsubset_{\mathcal{R}} C$ ("strictly less expressive"). If we have $C' \sqsubseteq_{\mathcal{R}} C$ and $C \sqsubseteq_{\mathcal{R}} C'$ then C and C' are equally expressive w.r.t. $\mathcal{R}$, denoted by $C =_{\mathcal{R}} C'$.

In this section, we will consider the following equivalence relations:

– timed language acceptance, and we note $\sqsubseteq_{\mathcal{L}}, \sqsubset_{\mathcal{L}}$, and $=_{\mathcal{L}}$ the corresponding relations;

– strong-timed bisimulation, and we note $\sqsubseteq_{\mathcal{S}}, \sqsubset_{\mathcal{S}}$, and $\approx_S$ the corresponding relations; and

– weak-timed bisimulation, and we note $\sqsubseteq_{\mathcal{W}}, \sqsubset_{\mathcal{W}}$, and $\approx_W$ the corresponding relations.

1.3.3.2. *Compared expressiveness of different classes of TPN*

In Figure 1.4, we give a comparison of the expressiveness of different classes of one-safe time Petri nets in terms of timed bisimulation. These results are further detailed in [BOY 08].

The considered classes are:

– one-safe nets (1-bounded);

– time Petri nets with time on places (*P-TPN*), arcs (*A-TPN*); or transitions (*T-TPN*);

– strong semantics ($\overline{P\text{-}TPN}$, $\overline{A\text{-}TPN}$, and $\overline{T\text{-}TPN}$) or weak semantics (*P-TPN*, *A-TPN*, and *T-TPN*);

– weak or strong time constraints (closed, half-open, or open intervals),

– labeled nets with ε-transitions.

Note that *A-TPN* and one-safe TAPN are the same model and $\overline{T\text{-}TPN}$ and one-safe TPN too.

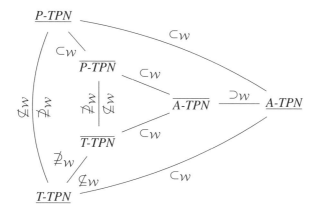

Figure 1.4. *Compared expressiveness of time Petri nets*

The *A-TPN* model generalizes all the other models, but simulating the *T-TPN* firing rule with *A-TPN* ones is not possible in practice for a human modeler [BOY 08]. Therefore, *T-TPN* are easier to use than *A-TPN* for the modeling of synchronizations.

1.3.3.3. *Compared expressiveness of TA, TPN, and TAPN*

We shall now provide an overview of the expressiveness results for the introduced models TA, TPN, and TAPN. As already mentioned, unbounded TPN and TAPN generate infinite state-spaces, and the reachability problem is undecidable for both of them. Hence in order to draw a fair comparison between the nets and TA, most of the work focuses on the relationship between *bounded* or *1-safe* nets and timed automata. There are some exceptions like the work in [CAS 06] which translates unbounded TPN into UPPAAL-like NTA extended with unbounded integer arrays.

1.3.3.3.1. From TA/NTA to TPN

A translation from diagonal-free TA without invariants and strict constraints to 1-safe TPN preserving weak-timed bisimulation was suggested by Haar *et al.* [HAA 02]. In this study, they, however, consider only weak (non-urgent) semantics for TPN. Bérard *et al.* give in [BER 05] a linear translation from diagonal-free TA with invariants to 1-safe TPN up to timed language equivalence. They also showed that TA are strictly more expressive than TPN w.r.t. weak-timed bisimilarity and in [BER 08], they identified a strict subclass of TA which was equivalent to bounded TPN w.r.t. weak-timed bisimilarity. In [BER 06], Berthomieu *et al.* suggested the extension of the TPN model with priorities and established an equivalence with NTA w.r.t. weak-timed bisimilarity. Another reduction from TA to TPN, which also includes diagonal constraints and updates to integral values, was presented by Bouyer *et al.* in [BOU 06]. The reduction preserves timed language equivalence and works in linear quadratic time, respectively, depending on what features of TA are included. However, this work does not include invariants in TA. In [BOU 06], Bouyer *et al.* also provide a translation from NTA to TPN, which preserves timed language equivalence, but introduces new deadlocks into the system behavior.

1.3.3.3.2. From TPN to TA/NTA

Haar *et al.* in [HAA 02] provided a translation from 1-safe TPN to TA preserving weak-timed bisimilarity. It improved the complexity of the previously known work on the basis of enumerative methods [BER 91, BER 83] and their translation is polynomial but only in terms of the size of the TPN reachability graph. On the other hand, they allow only non-strict intervals and consider the weak (non-urgent) semantics for TPN, while the other studies focussed on the standard strong (urgent) semantics. Another approach by Lime and Roux [LIM 03b] extends these results not only to bounded TPN but also requires first a construction of the state class graph of the given bounded TPN. An extended version of their study [LIM 06] provides an efficient reduction technique to decrease the number of clocks in the resulting timed automaton. A structural translation from TPN to NTA preserving weak-timed bisimilarity, which does not require the construction of the state class graph, was proposed by Cassez and Roux in [CAS 06]. Their reduction uses NTA extended with arrays of (unbounded) integers and enables to translate even unbounded TPN into the extended NTA. If the input net is bounded, the values in the integer arrays are bounded too, and hence automatic verification is possible. An implementation of the translation is available as a part of the TPN tool Romeo [LIM 09b] and the results seem promising as documented in several case studies [CAS 06]. A problem with this approach is a possibility of potentially higher number of clocks in the produced NTA. Recently D'Aprile *et al.* in [DAP 07] suggested an alternative technique for the translation from TPN to TA. Their method bypasses the construction of the state class graph (as used, e.g., in [HAA 02, LIM 03b]) by considering only the underlying untimed reachability graph. It preserves timed bisimulation and TCTL properties. According to the experiments carried out by the authors, it is competitive with other approaches on a number of case studies. On the other hand, it requires the underlying untimed net to be bounded, while the other approaches require only TPN boundedness. Empirical methods to deal with this limitation are outlined in the paper. Yet another approach is presented by Cortés *et al.* in [COR 02], in which the authors translated a more general model of TPN called PRES+ into UPPAAL-like timed automata, suggest several optimizations of the reduction, and provided two case studies. Their reduction works only for 1-safe nets and unfortunately there is no argument about the correctness of the translation.

1.3.3.3.3. From TA/NTA to TAPN and backwards

The first result (we are aware of), which compares the expressive power of TA and TAPN is by Sifakis and Yovine [SIF 96] from 1996. They provide a translation of 1-safe timed-arc Petri nets (with urgent behavior) into TA (with invariants) which preserves strong-timed bisimilarity but their translation causes an exponential blow up in the size. In [SRB 05], Srba established a strong relationship (up to isomorphism of timed transition systems) between NTA without invariants and a superclass of 1-safe TAPN extended with read-arcs. When we are interested only in the reachability questions, the reductions work in polynomial time. Recently Bouyer *et al.* in [BOU 08] presented a reduction from bounded TAPN (with read-arcs) to 1-safe TAPN (with read-arcs), which preserves timed language equivalence (over finite words, infinite words and non-Zeno infinite words). This demonstrates that NTA without invariants and bounded TAPN with read-arcs are timed language equivalent. The Bouyer *et al.* [BOU 08] also provide a number of expressiveness results for several subclasses of TAPN with read-arcs.

1.3.3.3.4. From TPN to TAPN and Backwards

We are aware of only a few detailed studies comparing TPN and TAPN. In [CER 99], Cerone and Maggiolio-Schettini studied several timed extensions of bounded Petri nets w.r.t. language equivalence. Regarding two classes of our main focus, they showed that TPN and TAPN are language equivalent w.r.t. weak (non-urgent) semantics and that TPN form a subclass of TAPN when considering the strong (urgent) semantics. In [BOY 00], Boyer and Vernadat showed that the inclusion of TPN in TAPN is strict (in the strong semantics). A further comparison of the different classes w.r.t. weak- timed bisimilarity is provided in [BOY 07]. We should note that all the work mentioned so far, in this section, uses the so-called single server semantics [BOY 01] for TAPN where the timing information to be remembered in every marking is constant. However, TAPN are mostly studied with the multi-server semantics where each token carries its own timing information. In this case, as concluded in [BOY 99], TPN express timed behavior and TAPN express timed behavior *and* time constraints.

1.4. Models with stopwatches

1.4.1. *Formal models for scheduling aspects*

Timed models such as timed automata [ALU 94, HEN 94] or time Petri nets [BER 91, MER 74] are usually not expressive enough to model and verify real-time applications with a pre-emptive scheduler. Thus, they need to be extended to model the interruption/resumption of tasks, while keeping track of the work already being done.

1.4.1.1. *Automata and scheduling*

Hybrid automata extend finite automata with continuous variables whose evolution rates (w.r.t. time) are given in each location by a differential equation and constrain, similar to TA, by guards and invariants. Linear hybrid automata (LHA) [ALU 95] are a syntactic subclass of hybrid automata, in which variables (in guards and invariants) and their derivatives (in each location) are constrained by convex polyhedra. For this subclass, symbolic verification semi-algorithm have been devised [ALU 96] and implemented in the tool HYTECH [HEN 97].

Stopwatch automata (SWA) [CAS 00] can be defined as timed automata in which the derivatives of clocks can be 0 in some locations. Therefore, clocks are called *stopwatches*. As for timed automata, SWA form a syntactic subclass of LHA. In [CAS 00], Cassez and Larsen proved that SWA with unobservable delays are as expressive in terms of timed languages. The reachability problem being undecidable for LHA, so is it for SWA.

In [MCM 94], McManis and Varaiya proposed an extension of TA, called suspension automata, in which continuous variables progress in a way similar to [CAS 00]. They proved the reachability problem undecidable for this model and fall back to the decidable case, similar to timed automata, by considering constant integer suspension durations. When a stopwatch is stopped and then resumed, the suspension duration is subtracted from its value. In this approach, precedence relations inducing pre-emptions must be explicitly encoded in terms of locations of the automaton, which may limit the practical expressiveness and usability of the model. For example, in the case of fixed suspension, durations cannot account for some anomalies when a task finishing early leads to a longer response time for some other task.

The approach of McManis and Varaiya is further developed by Fersman *et al.* in [FER 02, FER 03]. They relied on so-called task automata and proposed a schedulability analysis of the system through a reachability problem in the state-space of subtraction automata modeling the scheduler.

They also proved that this problem is decidable with the following additional constraints: tasks are independent and execution times are non-deterministically given by intervals [FER 02]; or tasks communicate but their execution times are constant integers [FER 03].

An interesting approach, proposed by Altisen *et al.* [ALT 99, ALT 00, ALT 02], relies on the controller synthesis paradigm. The system scheduler can indeed be seen as a controller of the system consisting of different tasks. The idea is then to obtain, by construction, the schedulability of the system by considering a discrete time and by restricting the guards of the enabled actions. These restrictions are done by added control of invariants implying a constraints approach on modeling the scheduling policy. However, this approach may be sometimes difficult to use in practice because the search for the control invariants can be hard.

1.4.1.2. *Time Petri nets and scheduling*

Several authors proposed to extend TPNs to account for suspension and resumption with memory.

Okawa and Yoneda [OKA 96] proposed an extension in which transitions are grouped together, each group having its own progress rate. These groups correspond to transitions modeling the concurrent activities and are ready to be fired simultaneously. In this case, their progress rate is divided by the sum of all the rates.

Roux and Déplanche [ROU 02] proposed an extension of TPNs (*scheduling*-TPN) to account for the scheduling of several tasks distributed over several processors. The resources (mainly processors) are bound to places. A similar approach is developed in [BUC 03, BUC 04], with resources bound to transitions. A more general stopwatch Petri net model has been proposed in [ROU 04], which extends time Petri nets with time inhibitor (hyper-)arcs. Finally an extended version of *scheduling*-TPN is presented in [LIM 09a] allowing a "fluid" modeling of tasks with the same priority for Round-Robin-type schedulers.

In this chapter, we present two of the above models: stopwatch automata and scheduling time Petri nets.

1.4.2. *Stopwatch automata*

Stopwatch automata can be seen as a straightforward extension of TA in which clocks can be frozen in some locations. Let us consider, for example, the SWA described in Figure 1.5. In location *Running* the stopwatch x_1 is active; its derivative w.r.t. time is 1. By contrast, x_1 is frozen in location *Suspended*.

DEFINITION 1.20 (STOPWATCH AUTOMATON).– A *stopwatch automaton* is a 7-tuple $(L, l_0, X, \Sigma, E, Inv, Dif)$ where:

   – $(L, l_0, X, \Sigma, E, Inv)$ is a TA;

   – $Dif \in (\{0,1\}^X)^L$ binds to each location of the *activity* of the stopwatches in that location. If $\dot{X}$ is a vector of the derivatives of all the continuous variables in X, then $\dot{X} = (Dif(l)(x))_{x \in X}$.

For the sake of simplicity, given a location l, a stopwatch x and $b \in \{0,1\}$, we denote $Dif(l)(x) = b$ by $\dot{x} = b$ when the concerned location is non-ambiguous.

DEFINITION 1.21 (SEMANTICS OF A SWA).– The semantics of a SWA $\mathcal{A} = (L, l_0, X, \Sigma, E, Inv, Dif)$ is defined by the TTS $\mathcal{S}_\mathcal{A} = (Q, Q_0, \Sigma, \rightarrow)$ where:

   – $Q = L \times (\mathbb{R}_{\geq 0})^X$;

   – $Q_0 = (l_0, \mathbf{0})$;

   – $\rightarrow \in Q \times (\Sigma \cup \mathbb{R}_{\geq 0}) \times Q$ is the relation defined for $a \in \Sigma$ and $d \in \mathbb{R}_{\geq 0}$, by:
      - the *discrete* relation transition:

$$(l, \nu) \xrightarrow{a} (l', \nu') \text{ iff } \exists (l, g, a, R, l') \in E \text{ s.t. } \begin{cases} g(\nu) = \mathsf{tt}, \\ \nu' = \nu[R \mapsto 0], \\ Inv(l')(\nu') = \mathsf{tt}; \end{cases}$$

- the *continuous* relation transition:

$$(l, \nu) \xrightarrow{d} (l, \nu') \text{ iff } \begin{cases} \nu' = \nu + \dot{X} * d, \\ \forall d' \in [0, d], Inv(l)(\nu + \dot{X} * d') = \text{tt}. \end{cases}$$

Stopwatch automataare a suitable model for systems with a pre-emptive scheduler: let us model a somewhat generic real-time task system. This model requires one automaton per task and one for each scheduler (i.e., one per processor). The result is then a synchronized product of automata, according to [ARN 94].

Figure 1.5 gives a generic automaton of modeling a task τ_i with a periodic activation of period T_i and whose execution time belongs to $[\alpha_i, \beta_i]$. This model draws its main lines from the model of extended tasks in OSEK/VDX [GRO 01]. In particular, it features a $Waiting$ location modeling, i.e. the awaiting of a message. The synchronization scheme, providing the events $release_i$! and $waitEvent_i$! and reacting to the events $sendEvent_i$!, is modeled separately as additional automata that we will omit here. This task model uses one clock o_i for the periodic activation and one stopwatch x_i, measuring the actual execution time.

Figure 1.6 presents a model approach of the fixed priority scheduler. To each event triggering a rescheduling, all tasks receive a pre-emption signal and the one with the greatest priority is started. Priorities are implicit and come from the order in which the scheduler polls the tasks when it tries to start one of them. Therefore, the structure of the scheduler depends on the number n of tasks in the system and the location $Scheduling$ must be duplicated by $(n - 1)$ times. An additional clock u is used here to enforce urgency by a $u \leq 0$ invariant in all locations but excluding $Idle$.

1.4.3. *Scheduling time Petri nets*

Scheduling time Petri nets (*scheduling*-TPN) extend time Petri nets by embedding directly into the semantics of the behavior of real-time schedulers. As seen earlier, this implies a mechanism to model the suspension and resumption with the memory of the tasks.

For each marking M of the net, we define a subset, called *active marking* and denoted by $Act(M)$, which enables the transitions for which time flows, i.e. which are not suspended. These transitions model either a running task or a service of the operating system. A transition, which is enabled by M but not by $Act(M)$ models a task that is ready but not running, possibly having been pre-empted.

The scheduler is hence considered as a controller for which the state feedback depends only on the current marking with a control law described by the Act function (Figure 1.7).

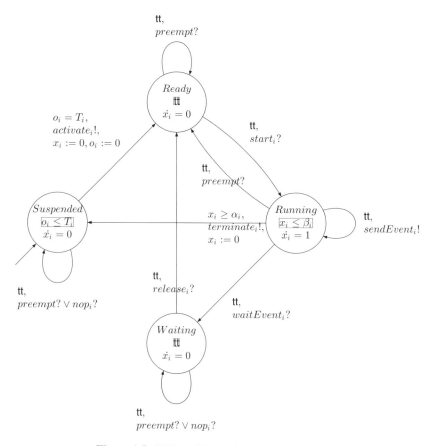

Figure 1.5. *SWA modeling of a real-time task*

The *scheduling*-TPN model is particularly well adapted to the modeling of practical real-time systems. The reader is invited to look at [LIM 03a, LIM 04] for more details on this particular topic.

Definitions

DEFINITION 1.22(*Scheduling*-TPN).– A scheduling TPN is an 8-tuple $\mathcal{N} = (P, T, {}^{\bullet}(.), (.)^{\bullet}, \alpha, \beta, M_0, Act)$, where:

– $(P, T, {}^{\bullet}(.), (.)^{\bullet}, \alpha, \beta, M_0)$ is a TPN;

– $Act \in (\mathbb{N}^P)^{\mathbb{N}^P}$ is an *active marking* function such that $\forall M \in \mathbb{N}^P, \forall p \in P, Act(M)(p) = M(p)$ or $Act(M)(p) = 0$.

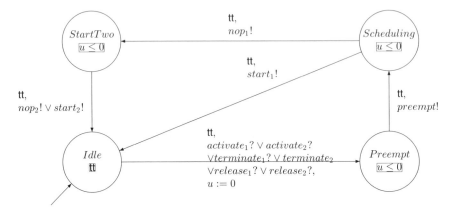

Figure 1.6. *SWA modeling of a fixed-priority preemptive scheduler for two tasks*

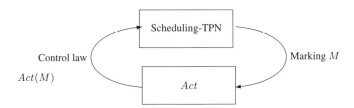

Figure 1.7. *Control (scheduling) using state feedback*

The classical notions relative to Petri nets and time Petri nets are defined similarly for *scheduling*-TPN.

In addition, we say that a transition t is *active* for the marking M, if it is enabled by $Act(M)$, i.e. $t \in \text{enabled}(Act(M))$.

Finally, we define the semantics of *scheduling*-TPN as a TTS.

DEFINITION 1.23(SEMANTICS OF A *scheduling*-TPN).– The semantics of a scheduling TPN $\mathcal{N}$ is the TTS $S_{\mathcal{N}} = (Q, q_0, \Sigma, \rightarrow)$ such that:
- $Q = \mathbb{N}^P \times (\mathbb{R}^+)^T$;
- $q_0 = (M_0, \mathbf{0})$;
- $\Sigma = T$;

$- \rightarrow \in Q \times (T \cup \mathbb{R}) \times Q$ is the transition relation:

  - *continuous* transitions defined $\forall d \in \mathbb{R}^+$ by:

$$(M, \nu) \xrightarrow{d} (M, \nu') \text{ iff } \begin{cases} \nu'(t_i) = \begin{cases} \nu(t_i), \text{ if } (Act(M) < {}^\bullet t_i) \wedge (M \geq {}^\bullet t_i) \\ \nu(t_i) + d, \text{ otherwise,} \end{cases} \\ \forall t_k \in T, M \geq {}^\bullet t_k \Rightarrow \nu'(t_k) \leq \beta(t_k); \end{cases}$$

  - *discrete* transitions defined $\forall t_i \in T$ by:

$$(M, \nu) \xrightarrow{t_i} (M', \nu') \text{ iff } \begin{cases} Act(M) \geq {}^\bullet t_i, \\ \alpha(t_i) \leq \nu(t_i) \leq \beta(t_i), \\ M' = M - {}^\bullet t_i + t_i^\bullet, \\ \forall t_k, \nu'(t_k) = \begin{cases} 0, \text{ if } \uparrow \text{enabled}(t_k, M, t_i), \\ \nu(t_k), \text{ otherwise.} \end{cases} \end{cases}$$

Active marking

The function providing the active marking defines the scheduling policy considered for the model. Moreover, the semantics of the model is independent from the actual computation of this function, which means that different scheduling policies can be defined for this model by plugging in different *Act* functions.

However, the way active marking is used in the semantics enforce some restrictions on the possible scheduling policies representable by *Act*: the active marking can only change when a discrete event occurs, modeled by the firing of a transition (for instance, the termination or arrival of a task). In particular, scheduling policies such as *least laxity first* [MOK 78] cannot be modeled by this formalism.

One of the most popular scheduling policy is using fixed priorities for the tasks. This case has been studied in [ROU 02]. The active marking can then be derived from two new parameters, bounded to places. For a given place p, we define $\gamma(p)$ to be the processor to which p is bound and $\omega(p)$ the corresponding priority. $\gamma(p)$ might have a special value ϕ which denotes that the corresponding activity is not a userspace task but a service of the operating system, and therefore, we consider it to be always active (i.e. $Act(M(p)) = M(p)$). Such places thus do not need to have a value defined for $\omega(p)$. In the figures, we will omit the values of $\gamma(p)$ and $\omega(p)$ when $\gamma(p) = \phi$.

Given γ and ω, the active marking can be calculated as follows:

1) find a set $\mathcal{P}$ of marked places, which are involved in enabling at least one transition; and

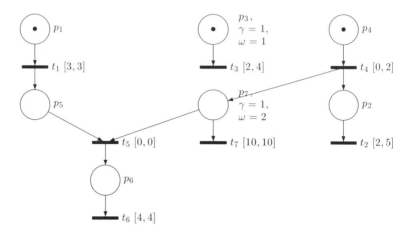

Figure 1.8. *A Scheduling-TPN*

2) for all p in $\mathcal{P}$, such that $\gamma(p) \neq \phi$, p is marked by the active marking, if it has the highest priority for its processor among all the places of $\mathcal{P}$, i.e. $Act(M)(p) = M(p)$, if $\omega(p) = \max\{\omega(p')| \, p' \in \mathcal{P}, \gamma(p') = \gamma(p)\}$ and $Act(M(p)) = 0$, otherwise.

In order to effectively calculate the active marking, we enforce the restriction that all the input places p of a given transition such that $\gamma(p) \neq \phi$ must have the same priority, thus avoiding circular priority relations. In practice, this restriction is minor and a good modeling guideline is to have at most one input place bound to a processor (for the others, $\gamma(p)$ should be ϕ), thus reflecting the fact that all the communications between different processors are operated through a service of the operating system.

Finally, to keep the active marking uniquely defined, we further forbid two places bound to the same processor with the same priority and involved in the enabling of at least one transition to be enabled simultaneously. We could alternatively make an arbitrary choice between the two (reflecting a common policy to schedule two tasks with the same priority competing for the processor) or model a round-robin policy (see [LIM 09a]).

Example

Consider a *scheduling*-TPN presented in Figure 1.8 for a particular case of the fixed-priority scheduling between places p_3 and p_7. These two places are bound to the same processor. p_7 has a greater priority than p_3. When these two places are simultaneously marked, then only p_7 will be marked active: $M(p_3) = M(p_7) = 1$, $Act(M)(p_3) = 0$ and $Act(M)(p_7) = 1$.

1.4.4. *Decidability results for stopwatch models*

The reachability problem has been proved equivalent for SWA and LHA [CAS 00]. Since it is undecidable for the latter model, so is it for the former [ALU 95, HEN 95].

Marking or state reachability as well as boundedness are undecidable for TPN [JON 77]. Therefore, they are undecidable for all stopwatch extensions of TPN.

However, these problems are decidable for bounded TPN. But they have been proved undecidable for stopwatch extensions of bounded TPN in general (and *Scheduling*-TPN in particular) in [BER 07, LIM 04]. It follows that k-boundedness is also undecidable for stopwatch TPN.

1.5. Conclusion

In this chapter, we have presented several formalisms in order to model real-time and/or embedded systems. Within a same class of models, such as the class of timed systems, for example, the different approaches have a close expressiveness and the decidability and computational complexity are similar. Therefore, the choice between those models is guided by more subjective aspects (different communities having different models of choice) or more practical aspects, such as the conciseness of the modeling of some key features for the intended application.

1.6. Bibliography

[ABD 00] ABDULLA P., NYLÉN A., "Better is better than well: on efficient verification of infinite-state systems", *Proceedings of the 15th Annual IEEE Symposium on Logic in Computer Science (LICS'00)*, pp. 132–140, Santa Barbara, CA, USA, 2000.

[ABD 01] ABDULLA P., NYLÉN A., "Timed Petri nets and BQOs", *Proceedings of the 22nd International Conference on Application and Theory of Petri Nets (ICATPN'01)*, vol. 2075 of *LNCS*, pp. 53–70, Springer-Verlag, Newcastle upon Tyne, UK, 2001.

[ABD 07] ABDULLA P., MAHATA P., MAYR R., "Dense-timed Petri nets: checking Zenoness, token liveness and boundedness", *Logical Methods in Computer Science*, vol. 3, num. 1, 1–61, 2007.

[ACE 02] ACETO L., LAROUSSINIE F., "Is your model checker on time? On the complexity of model checking for timed modal logics", *Journal of Logic and Algebraic Programming*, vol. 52–53, 7–51, 2002.

[ALT 99] ALTISEN K., GÖSSLER G., PNUELI A., SIFAKIS J., TRIPAKIS S., YOVINE S., "A framework for scheduler synthesis", *20th IEEE Real-Time Systems Symposium (RTSS'99)*, pp. 154–163, Phoenix, AZ, USA, IEEE Computer Society Press, December 1999.

[ALT 00]   ALTISEN K., GÖSSLER G., SIFAKIS J., "A methodology for the construction of scheduled systems", *6th International Symposium on Formal Techniques in Real-Time and Fault-Tolerant Systems (FTRTFT'00)*, vol. 1926 of *LNCS*, pp. 106–120, Pune, India, Springer-Verlag, September 2000.

[ALT 02]   ALTISEN K., GÖSSLER G., SIFAKIS J., "Scheduler modelling based on the controller synthesis paradigm", *Journal of Real-Time Systems*, vol. 23, 55–84, 2002 [Special issue on control-theoritical approaches to real-time computing].

[ALU 90]   ALUR R., DILL D., "Automata for Modelling Real-Time Systems", *Proceedings of the 17th International Colloquium on Algorithms, Languages and Programming (ICALP'90)*, vol. 443 of *LNCS*, pp. 322–335, Springer-Verlag, 1990.

[ALU 93]   ALUR R., COURCOUBETIS C., DILL D., "Model-checking in dense real-time", *Information and Computation*, vol. 104, 2–34, 1993.

[ALU 94]   ALUR R., DILL D., "A theory of timed automata", *Theoretical Computer Science*, vol. 126, num. 2, 183–235, 1994.

[ALU 95]   ALUR R., COURCOUBETIS C., HALBWACHS N., HENZINGER T., HO P., NICOLLIN X., OLIVERO A., SIFAKIS J., YOVINE S., "The algorithmic analysis of hybrid systems", *Theoretical Computer Science*, vol. 138, 3–34, January 1995.

[ALU 96]   ALUR R., HENZINGER T., HO P.H., "Automatic symbolic verification of embedded systems", *IEEE Transactions on Software Engineering*, vol. 22, 181–201, 1996.

[ARN 94]   ARNOLD A., *Finite Transition System*, Prentice Hall, 1994.

[BEN 03]   BENGTSSON J., YI W., "Timed automata: semantics, algorithms and tools", *Lectures on Concurrency and Petri Nets*, vol. 3098 of *LNCS*, pp. 87–124, Springer-Verlag, 2003.

[BER 05]   BÉRARD B., CASSEZ F., HADDAD S., LIME D., ROUX O.H., "Comparison of the expressiveness of timed automata and time Petri nets", *3rd International Conference on Formal Modeling and Analysis of Timed Systems (FORMATS'05)*, vol. 3829 of *LNCS*, pp. 211–225, Springer-Verlag, 2005.

[BER 08]   BÉRARD B., CASSEZ F., HADDAD S., LIME D., ROUX O.H., "When are timed automata weakly timed bisimilar to time Petri nets?", *Theoretical Computer Science*, vol. 403, num. 2–3, 202–220, 2008.

[BER 83]   BERTHOMIEU B., MENASCHE M., "An enumerative approach for analyzing Time Petri nets", *Proceedings of IFIP Congress 1983 on Information Processing*, vol. 9, pp. 41–46, Elsevier Science Publishers, Amsterdam, 1983.

[BER 91]   BERTHOMIEU B., DIAZ M., "Modeling and verification of time dependent systems using time Petri nets", *IEEE Transactions on Software Engineering*, vol. 17, num. 3, 259–273, 1991.

[BER 01]   BERTHOMIEU B., "La méthode des classes d'états pour l'analyse des réseaux temporels. Mise en œuvre, extension à la multi-sensibilisation", *Modélisation des Systèmes Réactifs (MSR'01)*, pp. 275–290, Toulouse (Fr), October 17–19, 2001.

[BER 06]   BERTHOMIEU B., PERES F., VERNADAT F., "Bridging the gap between timed automata and bounded time Petri nets", *Proceedings of the 4th International Conference on*

Formal Modeling and Analysis of Timed Systems (FORMATS'06), vol. 4202 of *LNCS*, pp. 82–97, Springer-Verlag, 2006.

[BER 07] BERTHOMIEU B., LIME D., ROUX O.H., VERNADAT F., "Reachability problems and abstract state spaces for time Petri nets with stopwatches", *Journal of Discrete Event Dynamic Systems (DEDS)*, vol. 17, num. 2, 133–158, 2007.

[BOL 89] BOLOGNESI T., CREMONESE P., The weakness of some timed models for concurrent systems, Report num. CNUCE C89-29, CNUCE—C.N.R., 1989.

[BOL 90] BOLOGNESI T., LUCIDI F., TRIGILA S., "From timed Petri nets to timed LOTOS", *Proceedings of the IFIP WG 6.1 10th International Symposium on Protocol Specification, Testing and Verification (Ottawa 1990)*, pp. 1–14, North-Holland, Amsterdam, 1990.

[BOU 06] BOUYER P., REYNIER P.A., HADDAD S., "Extended timed automata and time Petri nets", *Proceedings of the 6th International Conference on Application of Concurrency to System Design (ACSD'06)*, pp. 91–100, IEEE Computer Society, 2006.

[BOU 08] BOUYER P., HADDAD S., REYNIER P.A., "Timed Petri nets and timed automata: on the discriminating power of Zeno sequences", *Information and Computation*, vol. 206, num. 1, 73–107, 2008.

[BOY 99] BOYER M., DIAZ M., "Non equivalence between time Petri nets and time stream Petri nets", *Proceedings of the 8th International Workshop on Petri Nets and Performance Models (PNPM'99)*, pp. 198–207, IEEE Computer Society, 1999.

[BOY 00] BOYER M., VERNADAT F., Language and bisimulation relations between subclasses of timed Petri nets with strong timing semantic, Report num. No. 146, LAAS, 2000.

[BOY 01] BOYER M., DIAZ M., "Multiple enabledness of transitions in Petri nets with time", *Proceedings of the 9th International Workshop on Petri Nets and Performance Models (PNPM'01)*, pp. 219–228, IEEE Computer Society, 2001.

[BOY 07] BOYER M., ROUX O.H., "Comparison of the expressiveness of arc, place and transition time Petri Nets", *Proceedings of the 28th International Conference on Applications and Theory of Petri Nets and Other Models of Concurrency (ICATPN'07)*, vol. 4546 of *LNCS*, pp. 63–82, Springer-Verlag, 2007.

[BOY 08] BOYER M., ROUX O.H., "On the compared expressiveness of arc, place and transition time Petri Nets", *Fundamenta Informaticae*, vol. 88, num. 3, 225–249, 2008.

[BUC 03] BUCCI G., FEDELI A., SASSOLI L., VICARIO E., "Modeling flexible real time systems with preemptive time Petri nets", *15th Euromicro Conference on Real-Time Systems (ECRTS'2003)*, pp. 279–286, 2003.

[BUC 04] BUCCI G., FEDELI A., SASSOLI L., VICARIO E., "Time state space analysis of real-time preemptive systems", *IEEE Transactions on Software Engineering*, vol. 30, num. 2, 97–111, February 2004.

[BUS 99] BUSI N., PINNA G., "Process semantics for place/transition nets with inhibitor and read arcs", *Fundamenta Informaticae*, vol. 40, num. 2–3, 165–197, 1999.

[CAS 00] CASSEZ F., LARSEN K., "The impressive power of stopwatches", *11th International Conference on Concurrency Theory, (CONCUR'2000)*, num. 1877, LNCS, pp. 138–152, University Park, PA, USA, Springer-Verlag, July 2000.

[CAS 04] CASSEZ F., ROUX O., "Structural translation from time Petri nets to timed automata", *4th International Workshop on Automated Verification of Critical Systems (AVoCS 2004)*, London, UK, September 2004.

[CAS 06] CASSEZ F., ROUX O.H., "Structural translation from time Petri nets to timed automata – Model-checking time Petri nets via timed automata", *The Journal of Systems and Software*, vol. 79, num. 10, 1456–1468, 2006.

[CER 93] ČERANS K., "Decidability of bisimulation equivalences for parallel timer processes", *Proceedings of the 4th International Conference on Computer Aided Verification, (CAV'92)*, vol. 663 of *LNCS*, pp. 302–315, Springer-Verlag, 1993.

[CER 99] CERONE A., MAGGIOLIO-SCHETTINI A., "Time-based expressivity of timed Petri nets for system specification", *Theoretical Computer Science*, vol. 216, num. 1–2, 1–53, 1999.

[COR 02] CORTÉS L.A., ELES P., PENG Z., "Verification of real-time embedded systems using Petri net models and timed automata", *Proceedings of the 8th International Conference on Real-Time Computing Systems and Applications (RTCSA'02)*, pp. 191–199, 2002.

[DAP 07] D'APRILE D., DONATELLI S., SANGNIER A., SPROSTON J., "From time Petri nets to timed automata: an untimed approach", *Proceedings of 13th International Conference on Tools and Algorithms for the Construction and Analysis of Systems (TACAS'07)*, vol. 4424 of *LNCS*, pp. 216–230, Springer-Verlag, 2007.

[DIL 89] DILL D., "Timing assumptions and verification of finite-state concurrent systems", *Workshop Automatic Verification Methods for Finite-State Systems*, vol. 407, pp. 197–212, Grenoble, France, 1989.

[FER 02] FERSMAN E., PETTERSON P., YI W., "Timed automata with asynchronous processes : schedulability and decidability", *8th International Conference on Tools and Algorithms for the Construction and Analysis of Systems (TACAS'02)*, vol. 2280 of *LNCS*, pp. 67–82, Grenoble, France, Springer-Verlag, 2002.

[FER 03] FERSMAN E., MOKRUSHIN L., PETTERSSON P., YI W., "Schedulability analysis using two clocks", *9th International Conference on Tools and Algorithms for the Construction and Analysis of Systems (TACAS 2003)*, vol. 2619 of *LNCS*, pp. 224–239, Springer-Verlag, April 2003.

[FIN 01] FINKEL A., SCHNOEBELEN P., "Well-structured transition systems everywhere!", *Theoretical Computer Science*, vol. 256, num. 1–2, 63–92, 2001.

[FRU 00] DE FRUTOS ESCRIG D., RUIZ V., ALONSO O., "Decidability of properties of timed-arc Petri nets", *ICATPN'00*, vol. 1825 of *LNCS*, pp. 187–206, Aarhus, Denmark, June 2000.

[GRO 01] GROUP O., OSEK/VDX specification, http://www.osek-vdx.org, September 2001.

[HAA 02] HAAR S., KAISER L., SIMONOT-LION F., TOUSSAINT J., "Equivalence of timed state machines and safe TPN", *Proceedings of the 6th International Workshop on Discrete Event Systems (WODES'02)*, pp. 119–126, IEEE Computer Society, 2002.

[HAN 93] HANISCH H., "Analysis of place/transition nets with timed-arcs and its application to batch process control", *Proceedings of the 14th International Conference on Application and Theory of Petri Nets (ICATPN'93)*, vol. 691 of *LNCS*, pp. 282–299, 1993.

[HEN 94] HENZINGER T., NICOLLIN X., SIFAKIS J., YOVINE S., "Symbolic model checking for real-time systems", *Information and Computation*, vol. 111, num. 2, 193–244, 1994.

[HEN 95] HENZINGER T., KOPKE P., PURI A., VARAIYA P., "What's decidable about hybrid automata?", *Proceedings of the 27th Annual Symposium on Theory of Computing (STOC)*, ACM Press, pp. 373–382, 1995.

[HEN 97] HENZINGER T., HO P., WONG-TOI H., "HyTech: A Model Checker for Hybrid Systems", *Journal of Software Tools for Technology Transfer*, vol. 1, num. 1–2, 110–122, 1997.

[JON 77] JONES N., LANDWEBER L., LIEN Y., "Complexity of some problems in Petri nets", *Theoretical Computer Science*, vol. 4, 277–299, 1977.

[KHA 96] KHANSA W., DENAT J., COLLART-DUTILLEUL S., "P-time Petri nets for manufacturing systems", *International Workshop on Discrete Event Systems, WODES'96*, pp. 94–102, Edinburgh, UK, August 1996.

[LAR 97] LARSEN K.G., YI W., "Time-abstracted bisimulation: implicit specifications and decidability", *Information and Computation*, vol. 134, num. 2, 75–101, 1997.

[LIM 03a] LIME D., ROUX O., "Expressiveness and analysis of scheduling extended time Petri nets", *5th IFAC International Conference on Fieldbus Systems and their Applications, (FET 2003)*, Aveiro, Portugal, Elsevier Science, July 2003.

[LIM 03b] LIME D., ROUX O., "State class timed automaton of a time Petri net", *Proceedings of the 10th International Workshop on Petri Net and Performance Models (PNPM'03)*, pp. 124–133, Urbana-Champaign, IL, USA, 2003.

[LIM 04] LIME D., Vérification d'applications temps réel à l'aide de réseaux de Petri temporels étendus, PhD thesis, IRCCyN, December 2004.

[LIM 06] LIME D., ROUX O.H., "Model checking of time Petri nets using the state class timed automaton", *Journal of Discrete Events Dynamic Systems – Theory and Applications (DEDS)*, vol. 16, num. 2, 179–205, 2006.

[LIM 09a] LIME D., ROUX O.H., "Formal verification of real-time systems with preemptive scheduling", *Journal of Real-Time Systems*, vol. 41, num. 2, 118–151, 2009.

[LIM 09b] LIME D., ROUX O.H., SEIDNER C., TRAONOUEZ L.M., "Romeo: a parametric model-checker for Petri nets with stopwatches", in KOWALEWSKI S., PHILIPPOU A. (ed), *15th International Conference on Tools and Algorithms for the Construction and Analysis of Systems (TACAS 2009)*, vol. 5505 of *Lecture Notes in Computer Science*, pp. 54–57, York, United Kingdom, Springer, March 2009.

[MCM 94] MCMANIS J., VARAIYA P., "Suspension automata: a decidable class of hybrid automata", *6th International Conference on Computer Aided Verification (CAV'94)*, vol. 818 of *LNCS*, pp. 105–117, Stanford, CA, USA, Springer-Verlag, Junebreak 1994.

[MER 74] MERLIN P., A study of the recoverability of computing systems, PhD Thesis, Department of Information and Computer Science, University of California, Irvine, CA, 1974.

[MIL 89] MILNER R., *Communication and Concurrency*, Prentice Hall International, 1989.

[MOK 78] MOK A., DERTOUZOS M., "Multiprocessor scheduling in a hard real-time environment", *7th Texas Conference on Computing Systems*, Houston, USA, 1978.

[NIE 01] NIELSEN M., SASSONE V., SRBA J., "Properties of distributed timed-arc Petri nets", *Proceedings of the 21st International Conference on Foundations of Software Technology and Theoretical Computer Science (FSTTCS'01)*, vol. 2245 of *LNCS*, pp. 280–291, Springer-Verlag, 2001.

[OKA 96] OKAWA Y., YONEDA T., "Schedulability verification of real-time systems with extended time Petri nets", *International Journal of Mini and Microcomputers*, vol. 18, num. 3, 148–156, 1996.

[PEZ 99] PEZZE M., TOUNG M., "Time Petri nets: a primer introduction", Tutorial presented at the Multi-Workshop on Formal Methods in Performance Evaluation and Applications, Zaragoza, Spain, September 1999.

[RAM 74] RAMCHANDANI C., Analysis of asynchronous concurrent systems by timed Petri nets, PhD Thesis, Massachusetts Institute of Technology, Cambridge, MA, 1974 [Project MAC Report MAC-TR-120].

[ROU 02] ROUX O., DÉPLANCHE A., "A T-time Petri net extension for real time-task scheduling modeling", *European Journal of Automation (JESA)*, vol. 36, num. 7, 973–987, Hermès Science, 2002.

[ROU 04] ROUX O., LIME D., "Time Petri nets with inhibitor hyperarcs. Formal semantics and state space computation", *25th International Conference on Application and Theory of Petri Nets, (ICATPN'04)*, vol. 3099 of *LNCS*, pp. 371–390, Bologna, Italy, June 2004.

[RUI 99] RUIZ V.V., GOMEZ F.C., DE FRUTOS ESCRIG D., "On non-decidability of reachability for timed-arc Petri nets", *Proceedings of the 8th International Workshop on Petri Net and Performance Models (PNPM'99)*, pp. 188–196, 1999.

[RUI 00] RUIZ V.V., DE FRUTOS ESCRIG D., ALONSO O.M., "Decidability of properties of timed-arc Petri nets", *Proceedings of the 21st International Conference on Application and Theory of Petri Nets (ICATPN'00)*, vol. 1825 of *LNCS*, pp. 187–206, Springer-Verlag, 2000.

[SIF 96] SIFAKIS J., YOVINE S., "Compositional specification of timed systems", *Proceedings of the 13th Annual Symposim on Theoretical Aspects of Computer Science (STACS'96)*, vol. 1046 of *LNCS*, pp. 347–359, Springer-Verlag, 1996.

[SRB 05] SRBA J., "Timed-arc Petri nets vs. networks of timed automata", *Proceedings of the 26th International Conference on Application and Theory of Petri Nets (ICATPN 2005)*, vol. 3536 of *LNCS*, pp. 385–402, Springer-Verlag, 2005.

[VOG 02] VOGLER W., "Partial order semantics and read arcs", *Theoretical Computer Science*, vol. 286, num. 1, 33–63, 2002.

[YI 91] YI W., "CCS + Time = An interleaving model for real time systems", *Proceedings of ICALP*, pp. 217–228, 1991.

Chapter 2

Timed Model-Checking

2.1. Introduction

Reactive systems are those which handle interactions with the environment. They are frequently used in the area of transportation, communication protocols, or medical instrumentation, and often contain critical parts, where software errors can have heavy consequences. Many examples can be found in the PhD thesis of E. Fleury [FLE 02]. Even if there is a large agreement about the need for correctness of such systems, frequent accidents show that a formal verification step cannot be avoided.

Test generation is certainly the most commonly used technique. It consists of feeding input scenarios to a system and observing the output. The problem is then to guarantee a sufficient coverage of the behavior of the system, which is a difficult task. Other methods like *theorem proving* or *model-checking* ensure the completeness of the verification, but they suffer from the so-called "combinatorial explosion problem", which sets an intrinsic limit on the systems size.

Model-checking (see [CLA 08], [BAI 99] or [SCH 01] for overviews) answers to the following question: given a system and a property; does the property hold in the system? The first step consists of building formal models S and P, respectively, for the system and the property, and subsequently applying a suitable algorithm that automatically solves the problem: does S satisfy P, denoted by $S \models P$? The formalisms used for the system and the property should be the most expressive, whereas the algorithm should be the most efficient: these are of course contradictory goals, since the

Chapter written by Béatrice BÉRARD.

algorithm usually relies on an exploration of the state space of the system, which is very large.

Model-checking techniques have been extended to take into account quantitative properties of the systems, e.g. costs, probabilities, etc. The features considered here mainly concern the constraints related to time elapsing, which occur naturally in many systems. For example, communication protocols often handle *time-out* in order to guarantee the termination of user dependent operations. Other systems such as control programs contain task scheduling modules, where tasks can be suspended and resumed, and are subjected to execution deadlines. Finally, a very frequent pattern is the response time, where a precise delay is required between some signal and the following event.

We first present timed models, which handle an explicit notion of time, and timed logics, which express quantitative properties. We then explain on the basis of some examples how classical model-checking algorithms have been extended to this framework. This is an introductory text at the end of which some references can be found.

2.2. Timed models

The semantics of timed models is expressed in terms of TTSs. We define this by illustrating with some examples.

2.2.1. *Timed transition system*

The time domain is denoted by $\mathbb{T}$. It can be the set $\mathbb{N}$ of natural numbers, the set $\mathbb{Q}_{\geq 0}$ of non-negative rational numbers or the set $\mathbb{R}_{\geq 0}$ of non-negative real numbers, so, we always consider that $\mathbb{T}$ is a subset of $\mathbb{R}_{\geq 0}$.

DEFINITION 2.1.– A *Timed Transition System* over an alphabet *Act* of actions and a set **Prop** of atomic propositions is a tuple $\mathcal{T} = (S, s_0, E, L)$, where:

– S is the set of configurations;

– s_0 is the initial configuration;

– E is the transition relation, given as a subset of $S \times (Act \cup \mathbb{T}) \times S$;

– $L : S \mapsto 2^{\mathsf{Prop}}$ is a mapping which labels a configuration with a set of atomic propositions.

A transition (s, ℓ, s') in E is denoted by $s \xrightarrow{\ell} s'$ with $\xrightarrow{\ell}$ for the set of transitions with label ℓ.

Transitions $\xrightarrow{a}$ with a in *Act* correspond to usual actions and are instantaneous. Some variants use $Act_{\varepsilon} = Act \cup \{\varepsilon\}$ instead of *Act*, where the empty word ε represents a non-observable or silent action. Other models have an empty alphabet.

Transition $\xrightarrow{d}$ with $d \in \mathbb{T}$ represents a time delay of duration d. Therefore, such transitions must satisfy specific conditions that express the consistency of the system with operations on time:

– *zero delay:* $s \xrightarrow{0} s'$, if and only if $s' = s$;

– *additivity:* if $s \xrightarrow{d} s'$ and $s' \xrightarrow{d'} s''$, then $s \xrightarrow{d+d'} s''$.

Moreover, the system is sometimes required to be:

– *time deterministic:* if $s \xrightarrow{d} s_1$ and $s \xrightarrow{d} s_2$ then $s_1 = s_2$;

– *continuous:* $s \xrightarrow{d} s'$ implies for all d' and d'' such that $d = d' + d''$, there exists s'' such that $s \xrightarrow{d'} s''$ and $s'' \xrightarrow{d''} s'$.

In this presentation, an execution (or run) of $\mathcal{T}$ is an infinite path $\rho = s_0 \xrightarrow{d_1} s_0' \xrightarrow{a_1} s_1 \xrightarrow{d_2} s_1' \xrightarrow{a_2} \cdots$ starting from the initial configuration and where durations and actions strictly alternate. With an execution ρ are associated:

– the sequence $(t_i)_{i \geq 0}$ of absolute dates, naturally defined by $t_0 = 0$ and $t_i = \sum_{j=0}^{i} d_j$;

– the *timed word* $w = (a_1, t_1)(a_2, t_2) \ldots$, corresponding to the observation of actions, a_i occurring at time t_i. Thus, w is an infinite word over the alphabet $Act \times \mathbb{T}$.

The language of a TTS $\mathcal{T}$, denoted by $\mathcal{L}(\mathcal{T})$, is the set of timed words associated with executions of $\mathcal{T}$.

When the system is continuous, all intermediate configurations can be observed in a run, with the possibility of two configurations at the same time. A notion of position p of a run must then be considered (formally, a position is defined by a pair (i, δ) where $i \geq 0$ and $0 \leq \delta \leq d_{i+1}$). The relation that totally orders positions along a run ρ is denoted by $<_\rho$. For a position p in ρ, we denote by s_p the configuration associated with p and by $\rho^{\leq p}$ the prefix of ρ until p. The duration of this prefix, denoted by $Dur(\rho^{\leq p})$, is the sum of the delays occurring along $\rho^{\leq p}$.

Note that some variants consider more restrictive definitions of runs (and languages), which are said *admissible*, particularly to avoid *Zeno* runs, in which the sequence of absolute dates is convergent.

2.2.2. *Timed automata*

Since their introduction in [ALU 90, ALU 94a], which prove the first decidability (and undecidability) results, TA have been largely studied, modified, and extended. The basic model consists of a finite automaton handling variables called *clocks,* which

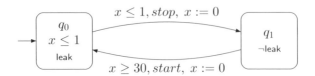

Figure 2.1. $\mathcal{A}_1$: *a timed automaton for the gas burner*

evolve at the rate of time, can be compared with constants and reset when firing transitions.

We present (in a simplified version) a classical example of a gas burner, introduced in [ALU 93b]. In the automaton described in Figure 2.1, the system can be described in two states: initial state q_0 where the burner is leaking and state q_1, where it does not leak. Leakages are detected and stopped in a time involving less than 1 second and, once it is stopped, the burner would not leak again before the expiry of 30 seconds. Clock x is used to measure the delays: the constraint $x \leq 1$ in state q_0 is called an *invariant*, the constraints $x \leq 1$ and $x \leq 30$ on the transitions are *guards* and the notation $x := 0$ corresponds to a reset of clock x.

For a set X of clocks, $\mathcal{C}(X)$ denotes the set of conjunctions of atomic constraints of the form $x \bowtie c$ where x is a clock, c is a constant (usually in $\mathbb{N}$) and $\bowtie$ is an operator in $\{<, \leq, =, \geq, >\}$.

DEFINITION 2.2.– A *timed automaton* aver an alphabet Act and a set **Prop** of atomic propositions is a tuple $\mathcal{A} = (X, Q, q_0, \Delta, Inv, \ell)$, where:

– X is a set of clocks;

– Q is a finite set of states (or control nodes);

– $q_0 \in Q$ is the initial state;

– Δ is a subset of $Q \times \mathcal{C}(X) \times Act \times 2^X \times Q$;

– $Inv : Q \mapsto \mathcal{C}(X)$ associates with each state a constraint in $\mathcal{C}(X)$, called *invariant*, using only the operators $<$ and $\leq$;

– $\ell \mapsto 2^{\mathsf{Prop}}$ is the mapping labeling states by sets of atomic propositions in **Prop**.

A transition in Δ, written as $q \xrightarrow{g,a,r} q'$, expresses a change from q to q' with action a, if guard g is satisfied. Clocks in $r \subseteq X$ are then reset, which is also written as $r := 0$, as shown in Figure 2.1 for the resetting of clock x.

The clock constraints (guards and invariants) are interpreted on clock valuations, which are mappings from X into $\mathbb{R}_{\geq 0}$, with $\mathbf{0}$ the null valuation assigning zero to all clocks in X. A valuation $v \in \mathbb{R}^X_{\geq 0}$ satisfies an atomic constraint $x \bowtie c$, denoted by $v \models g$, if $v(x) \bowtie c$.

We define:

– time elapsing from valuation v by: $(v + d)(x) = v(x) + d$ for each clock x and $d \in \mathbb{T}$, which expresses that all clocks evolve at the rate of time;

– reset from clocks in $r \subseteq X$ from valuation v by: $v[r \mapsto 0](x) = 0$, if $x \in r$ and 0, otherwise.

The semantics of a timed automaton $\mathcal{A} = (\Sigma, X, Q, q_0, \Delta, Inv, L)$ is then given as a TTS $\mathcal{T}_{\mathcal{A}} = (S, s_0, E, L)$, over $Act \cup \mathbb{T}$ and **Prop**, with:

– $S = \{(q, v) \in Q \times \mathbb{R}_{\geq 0}^X \mid v \models Inv(q)\}$. Configurations are pairs (q, v) where $q \in Q$ and v is a clock valuation satisfying the state invariant:

– the initial configuration is $s_0 = (q_0, \mathbf{0})$;

– the transitions in E are:

- either $(q, v) \xrightarrow{d} (q, v + d)$, a delay of $d \in \mathbb{T}$, possible if $v + d \models Inv(q)$;

- or $(q, v) \xrightarrow{a} (q', v')$, a discrete transition with label $a \in Act$, and $v' = v[r \mapsto 0]$, possible if there exists $q \xrightarrow{g,a,r} q'$ in Δ such that valuation v satisfies guard g;

– the labeling mapping L is defined for a configuration $(q, v) \in S$ by $L((q, v)) = \ell(q)$.

For example, the beginning of a run in the gas burner model could be:
$$(q_0, 0) \xrightarrow{0.6} (q_0, 0.6) \xrightarrow{stop} (q_1, 0) \xrightarrow{32.5} (q_1, 32.5) \xrightarrow{start} (q_0, 0) \cdots.$$

Delay transitions thus correspond to the time spent in a state and for such a transition system with time domain $\mathbb{R}_{\geq 0}$, the four properties mentioned above hold: zero delay, additivity, time determinism, and continuous delays. Most results concerning TA remain true, if rational constants may occur in the clock constraints: the basic case is obtained by multiplying all constants from the automaton by a common denominator. Adding *diagonal* constraints (of the form $x - y \bowtie c$) to $\mathcal{C}(X)$ does not increase the expressiveness but leads to exponentially more concise models [BOU 05a]. Finally, introducing accepting conditions for TA, such as Büchi or Muller conditions [ALU 94a], it yields different versions for admissible runs (and the corresponding languages) in the transition systems.

Modeling real systems often involves a component-based approach: each subsystem is given as an automaton and the complete system is then obtained as a product. For timed systems, the synchronized product of a set $\{\mathcal{A}_1, \ldots, \mathcal{A}_n\}$ of TA can also be defined. The most general definition uses a synchronization function f, which associates an action $a = f(a_1, \ldots, a_n)$ with a tuple of actions from the different components. For timed models, combinatorial explosion of the state space is due to both this composition mechanism and the addition of clocks.

A particular case of synchronized product yields exactly the set of executions consistent with several automata (and thus the intersection of accepted languages).

This operation as well as other Boolean operations have been extended to timed languages [ALU 90]. For intersection, when no convergent runs are allowed, the construction of the product $\mathcal{A}_1 \otimes \mathcal{A}_2$ is very similar to the untimed case: for two transitions $q_1 \xrightarrow{g_1,a,r_1} q_1'$ in automaton $\mathcal{A}_1$ and $q_2 \xrightarrow{g_2,a,r_2} q_1'$ in $\mathcal{A}_2$ with same action label a, the combined transition is $(q_1,q_2) \xrightarrow{g_1 \wedge g_2,a,r_1 \cup r_2} (q_1',q_2)$. The problem related to Büchi conditions is handled as in the untimed case. When *Zeno* runs must be considered, together with silent transitions (labeled by the empty word), the construction is more involved [BER 07].

2.2.3. *Other models*

Let us note first that numerous extensions of TA have been proposed: additive guards (for instance of the form $x + y \bowtie c$), non-deterministic updates of clocks, etc. (e.g., see [BOU 04b]). An important generalization consists of replacing clocks by *dynamic variables* that can evolve according to some differential equation. Adding tests and resets of these variables with linear expressions yields the model of *hybrid automata*.

The automaton associated with the gas burner example can then be extended into a hybrid automaton (Figure 2.2), by adding a variable z to measure the global duration of leaking. This variable evolves with rate 0 in state q_1, where no leaking occurs, and with rate 1 in state q_0. The notation uses the derivative with respect to time: $\dot{z} = 0$ or $\dot{z} = 1$.

This model is much more expressive and most verification questions becomes undecidable. For example, as soon as two variables with constant but different rates are used, reachability of a control state is undecidable, even if this problem is much simpler than model-checking [HEN 96, HEN 98, MAL 91].

In fact, the first definitions of timed models were proposed in the 1970s as timed extensions of Petri nets [JON 77, MER 74], which were subsequently studied in [BER 83, BER 03, LIL 99]. We do not describe these models here but, roughly speaking, the time mechanism consists of associating with each transition a time interval (min, max), the bounds representing minimal and maximal delay for the firing of the transition. A similar method was also used in various models [HEN 92,

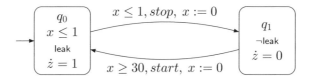

Figure 2.2. $\mathcal{A}_2$: *a hybrid automaton for the gas burner*

HEN 94a, MAL 91], and we simply present durational Kripke structures (DKS) [CAM 95, EME 92, LAR 06], for which the time domain is $\mathbb{T} = \mathbb{N}$.

Let $\mathcal{I}(\mathbb{N})$ be the set of intervals in $\mathbb{N}$, which are either closed or left closed with ∞ as upper bound.

DEFINITION 2.3.– A durational Kriple structure over a set **Prop** of atomic proposi- tions is a tuple $\mathcal{K} = (Q, q_0, \Delta, \ell)$ where:

- Q is a set of states;
- q_0 is the initial state;
- Δ is a subset of $Q \times \mathcal{I}(\mathbb{N}) \times Q$; and
- $\ell : Q \mapsto 2^{\mathsf{Prop}}$ is the labeling function.

Note that there are no action labels in such a structure. Figure 2.3, taken from [LAR 06], describes the activity of a researcher. Transitions are equipped with an interval in $\mathcal{I}(\mathbb{N})$, possibly reduced to a single value, and a duration in this interval is chosen by moving from one state to another.

Several semantics based on TTSs can be associated with this kind of model, ac- cording to the meaning given to the firing of a transition from q to q' with (integer) delay d. For instance, similar to TA, a possible interpretation is: waiting d units of time in state q and changing instantaneously for state q'.

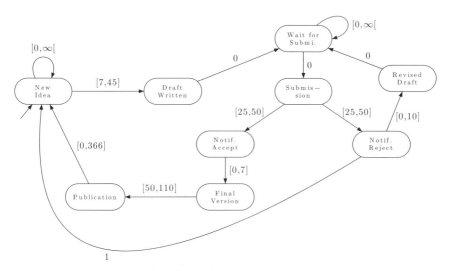

Figure 2.3. $\mathcal{A}_3$: *a durational Kripke structure*

The *jump* semantics relies on another interpretation: starting from state q at time n, we reach state q' at time $n + d$ with no intermediate times. In this case, there is no configuration for the system at the times $n + 1, \ldots, n + d - 1$. This semantics thus corresponds to costs more than durations. The associated transition system is $\mathcal{T} = (Q, q_0, E, \ell)$, with a single type of moves defined by: $q \xrightarrow{d} q'$, if there exists a transition (q, I, q') in Δ such that d belongs to interval I.

For the example described above, the beginning of a run could be:

$$NewIdea \xrightarrow{15} NewIdea \xrightarrow{10} DraftWrit. \xrightarrow{0} WaitforSub. \cdots$$

2.3. Timed logics

We now present the mechanisms for adding explicit time to temporal logics. In untimed case, two fragments of CTL* [CLA 86] are frequently used: *linear temporal logic* (LTL), for linear time [PNU 77]) and *computation tree logic* (CTL), for branching time [CLA 81, EME 82]). We recall the definition of these logics and explain how they are extended with quantitative constraints.

2.3.1. *Temporal logics* CTL *and* LTL

Let us consider again that Prop be a set of atomic propositions. The formule of LTL approach are defined by the grammar

$$\varphi, \psi ::= P \mid \neg\varphi \mid \varphi \wedge \psi \mid \mathsf{X}\varphi \mid \varphi\mathsf{U}\psi,$$

where $P \in$ Prop.

Those of CTL approach are defined by

$$\varphi, \psi ::= P \mid \neg\varphi \mid \mathsf{EX}\varphi \mid \mathsf{AX}\varphi \mid \varphi \wedge \psi \mid \mathsf{E}\varphi\mathsf{U}\psi \mid \mathsf{A}\varphi\mathsf{U}\psi,$$

where $P \in$ Prop.

Such formulae are interpreted over standard Kripke structures, i.e. without duration. Let $\mathcal{K} = (Q, q_0, \Delta, \ell)$ be such a Kripke structure, where Δ is simply a subset of $Q \times Q$.

A formula of LTL is interpreted at position i of an (infinite) run starting from the initial state $\sigma : q_0 \to q_1 \to q_2 \cdots$. For $i \geq 0$, we simply write $\sigma(i)$ for the ith state of

σ (here q_i). The semantics of LTL is then inductively defined by

$$
\begin{array}{ll}
\sigma, i \models P, & \text{if } P \text{ is in the set } \ell(\sigma(i)) \text{ of labels of } q \text{ ;} \\
\sigma, i \models \neg\varphi & \text{if } \sigma, i \text{ does not satisfy } \varphi \text{ ;} \\
\sigma, i \models \varphi \wedge \psi, & \text{if } q \text{ satisfies both } \varphi \text{ and } \psi \text{ ;} \\
\sigma, i \models \mathsf{X}\varphi & \text{if } \sigma, i+1 \models \varphi \text{ ;} \\
\sigma, i \models \varphi\mathsf{U}\psi, & \text{if there exists } j \geq i \text{ such that } \sigma, j \models \psi \\
& \text{and for all } k, \ i \leq k < j, \sigma, k \models \varphi.
\end{array}
$$

Thus, modality X, also called next, can be interpreted in a natural way by $\mathsf{X}\varphi$ holds at a position, if φ holds at the next position. The formula $\varphi\mathsf{U}\psi$ holds at a position, if there exists a position in the future where ψ holds, φ being true all along. Besides usual Boolean operators, the following abbreviations are frequently used:

– $\mathsf{F}\varphi$, defined by $\mathrm{true}\mathsf{U}\varphi$, states that from the current position, φ will hold *eventually* (formula true holds in every position);

– $\mathsf{G}\varphi$, defined by duality as $\neg\mathsf{F}(\neg\varphi)$, states that φ always holds from the current position.

A formula in CTL approach is interpreted on a state $q \in Q$ from the Kripke structure. We denote by $Exec(q)$ the execution tree from q in $\mathcal{K}$. For an execution $\sigma : q \rightarrow q_1 \rightarrow q_2 \cdots$ and for $i \geq 0$, we again denote by $\sigma(i)$ the ith state from σ and the semantics is inductively defined by

$$
\begin{array}{ll}
q \models P, & \text{if } P \text{ is in the set } \ell(q) \text{ of labels of } q \text{ ;} \\
q \models \neg\varphi, & \text{if } q \text{ does not satisfy } \varphi \text{ ;} \\
q \models \varphi \wedge \psi, & \text{if } q \text{ satisfies both } \varphi \text{ and } \psi \text{ ;} \\
q \models \mathsf{EX}\varphi, & \text{if there exists a run } \sigma \text{ in } Exec(q) \text{ such that } \sigma(1) \models \varphi \text{ ;} \\
q \models \mathsf{AX}\varphi, & \text{if each run } \sigma \text{ in } Exec(q) \text{ is such that } \sigma(1) \models \varphi \text{ ;} \\
q \models \mathsf{E}\varphi\mathsf{U}\psi, & \text{if there exists a run } \sigma \text{ in } Exec(q) \text{ and } j \geq 0 \\
& \text{such that } \sigma(j) \models \psi \text{ and for all } k, \ 0 \leq k < j, \ \sigma(k) \models \varphi \text{ ;} \\
q \models \mathsf{A}\varphi\mathsf{U}\psi, & \text{if for each run } \sigma \text{ in } Exec(q), \text{ there exists } j \geq 0 \\
& \text{such that } \sigma(j) \models \psi \text{ and for all } k, \ 0 \leq k < j, \ \sigma(k) \models \varphi.
\end{array}
$$

In these formulae, E and A are, respectively, the existential and universal quantifier on executions. Thus, state q satisfies formula $\mathsf{A}\varphi\mathsf{U}\psi$, which means that ψ will hold in future for all executions starting from q with φ true all along. Usual abbreviations are as follows:

– $\mathsf{EF}\varphi$ defined by $\mathsf{E}(\mathrm{true})\mathsf{U}\varphi$, which states that for a state q, formula φ will hold in future for at least one execution starting from q. This expresses reachability of a state satisfying φ;

– $\mathsf{AG}\varphi$ is defined by duality as $\neg\mathsf{EF}(\neg\varphi)$ and states that for a state q formula φ always holds along all executions starting from q;

– $\mathsf{AF}\varphi$, defined by $\mathsf{A}(\mathrm{true})\mathsf{U}\varphi$ expresses that for a state q, for all executions starting from q, formula φ will hold in the future. The corresponding property is said to be *inevitable*.

A Kripke structure $\mathcal{K}$ satisfies a formula φ, denoted by $\mathcal{K} \models \varphi$, if:

– $\sigma, 0$ (the initial state q_0) satisfies φ for all executions σ of $\mathcal{K}$, for a formula φ in LTL;

– the initial state q_0 satisfies φ for a formula φ in CTL.

The property "each signal is followed by an event" is expressed with two atomic propositions signal and event by the formula in LTL:

$$\mathsf{G}(\mathrm{signal} \Rightarrow \mathsf{F}\ \mathrm{event}),$$

whereas in CTL, it is written as:

$$\mathsf{AG}(\mathrm{signal} \Rightarrow \mathsf{AF}\ \mathrm{event}).$$

Although this property can be expressed in both approaches, it should be noted that LTL and CTL have incomparable expressive power [CLA 08, SCH 01].

As a final remark, a precise delay separating a signal and the corresponding event cannot be expressed in these logics, which motivates their extensions.

2.3.2. *Timed extensions*

Alur and Henzinger [ALU 91] proposed an excellent survey on this question.

2.3.2.1. *Timed CTL*

The logic TCTL [ALU 91, ALU 93a, HEN 94b] is interpreted over timed transition systems. We consider $\mathbb{T} = \mathbb{R}_{\geq 0}$ as time domain with continuous executions, which implies that the modality X is not relevant. For the subformula $\varphi\mathsf{U}\psi$, the principle consists of associating with the modality U a constraint of the form $\bowtie c$, for some comparison operator $\bowtie$ and a constant c, in order to constrain the occurrence time of formula ψ.

The syntax of TCTL is given by the following grammar:

$$\varphi, \psi ::= P \mid \neg\varphi \mid \varphi \wedge \psi \mid \mathsf{E}\varphi\mathsf{U}_{\sim c}\psi \mid \mathsf{A}\varphi\mathsf{U}_{\sim c}\psi,$$

where P is an atomic proposition in Prop, operator $\bowtie$ belongs to $\{<, >, \leq, \geq, =\}$ and c is a constant in $\mathbb{N}$.

To define the semantics of TCTL, we consider a transition system $\mathcal{T} = (S, s_0, E, L)$, over the alphabet Act and the set Prop, and denote the set of executions starting from a configuration s by $Exec(s)$. For an execution $\rho : s \xrightarrow{d_1} s_1' \xrightarrow{a_1} s_1 \xrightarrow{d_2} s_2' \xrightarrow{a_2} s_2 \cdots$ and a position p, recall that $Dur(\rho^{\leq p})$ is the sum of the delays along the prefix $\rho^{\leq p}$ of ρ.

The semantics of TCTL can then be defined in a way similar to the one of CTL. We only give the definition for the $U_{\sim c}$ modalities:

$s \models \mathsf{E}\varphi U_{\sim c}\psi$, if there exists a run $\rho \in Exec(s)$ such that $\rho \models \varphi U_{\sim c}\psi$;
$s \models \mathsf{A}\varphi U_{\sim c}\psi$, if for all runs $\rho \in Exec(s)$, $\rho \models \varphi U_{\sim c}\psi$;
with
$\rho \models \varphi U_{\sim c}\psi$,   if there exists a position p of ρ such that $Dur(\rho^{\leq p}) \sim c$,
          $s_p \models \psi$ and for all positions $p' <_\rho p$, $s_{p'} \models \varphi$.

Note that the usual modality U is obtained in this framework by $\mathsf{U}_{\geq 0}$.

A time automaton $\mathcal{A}$ satisfies a formula φ in TCTL, denoted by $\mathcal{A} \models \varphi$, if the initial configuration $s_0 = (q_0, \mathbf{0})$ of the TTS $\mathcal{T}_A$ associated with $\mathcal{A}$ satisfies φ.

It is now easy to express in this logic the response time property with a quantitative delay. With abbreviations similar to those presented above for CTL, the specification "each occurrence of a signal is followed by an event within five time units" is expressed by the following formula of TCTL:

$$\mathsf{AG}(\text{signal} \Rightarrow \mathsf{AF}_{\leq 5}\ \text{event}).$$

A variation of TCTL is obtained by keeping the usual operators but introducing constraints of the form $z \bowtie c$, where z is a formula clock, and a reset operator. In the corresponding logic TCTL$_c$ (with clocks), the response time property would be expressed by the formula

$$\mathsf{AG}(\text{signal} \Rightarrow z.\mathsf{AF}(z \leq 5 \land \text{event})),$$

where z is a formula clock. The notation $z.$ represents the reset of z, the value of which must be less than or equal to 5, when event occurs. In this case, the formulae have to be interpreted on extended configurations of the form (q, v, u) where (q, v) is a configuration of a timed automaton and u is a valuation for formula clocks.

Similarly, quantitative constraints have been added to the μ-calcul modalities [KOZ 83], producing the logic T_μ [HEN 94b] and the fragment L_ν [ACE 02, LAR 95b].

In L_ν, in addition to formula clocks, operators [a] and [succ] (as well as existential operators) are introduced and interpreted as a kind of next associated with actions and delays. The semantics is as follows:

– [a]φ holds for an extended configuration (q, v, u), if for each configuration (q', v') such that $(q, v) \xrightarrow{a} (q', v')$, (q, v', u) satisfies φ;

– [succ]φ holds for an extended configuration (q, v, u), if for each delay d, $(q, v + d, u + d)$ satisfies φ;

with an adequate definition for existential operators.

In T_μ, an operator $\rhd$ similar to some "*until* in one step" is proposed, the formula $P_1 \rhd P_2$ means that P_1 holds and will hold until the next discrete transition which makes P_2 true. Thus,

$$z.(\text{true} \rhd (P \wedge z \leq 5))$$

expresses that P will become true at the next transition, which will occur within five time units.

The logic is that TCTL itself was extended, either with parameters [BRU 03] or with modalities allowing to abstract transient states in executions [BEL 05, BEL 06]. Finally in a different direction, in order to overcome the undecidability results for hybrid automata, other extensions of TA have been proposed to associate costs with states or transitions [BOU 04a]. The logic WCTL [BRI 04] was then defined for these models, by adding cost constraints to CTL modalities.

2.3.2.2. *Timed LTL*

Timing LTL can be performed in a similar manner, yielding the logic MTL ([KOY 90]), with the syntax

$$\varphi, \psi ::= P \mid \neg\varphi \mid \varphi \wedge \psi \mid \varphi \mathsf{U}_I \psi,$$

where P is an atomic proposition and I is an interval.

In this formalism, the response time formula would become

$$\mathsf{G}(\text{signal} \Rightarrow \mathsf{F}_{[0,5]} \text{ reponse}).$$

Using formula clocks produces TPTL [ALU 94b] (see in [BOU 05b] a comparison of the expressive power of MTL and TPTL). Note that two semantics have been proposed for these linear time logics:

– the first one corresponds to the presentation described above, taking into account the continuous behavior of executions; and

– the second one is more restricted and considers only observation points corresponding to discrete transitions.

Undecidability results for MTL with continuous semantics lead to investigate several restrictions, in particular MITL [ALU 96], a syntactic restriction where intervals cannot be reduced to a single point. The second semantics is studied in [OUA 05].

2.4. Timed model-checking

The analysis of timed systems is a difficult task because of the infinite number of configurations (non-countable when the time domain is $\mathbb{R}_{\geq 0}$) in TTSs. Thus, standard model-checking techniques do not apply directly. In fact, the first decidability result for timed models was obtained by Alur and Dill [ALU 90] in the case of TA. It states that emptiness is decidable for timed languages accepted by TA with Büchi accepting conditions. A large class of positive results for timed systems relies on the technique proposed in the study [ALU 93a], including the decidability of model-checking TCTL over TA. This technique consists of constructing a finite automaton, which is time-abstract bisimilar to the originally timed automaton, thus preserving reachability of a control state.

First, we briefly recall the classical model-checking algorithms in untimed case, then we give the construction of this finite automaton, and finally we show how these techniques are combined to fit in the analysis of timed models with timed logics.

2.4.1. *Model-checking LTL and CTL (untimed case)*

The model-checking algorithm for formula φ of CTL on a Kripke structure $\mathcal{K} = (Q, q_0, \Delta, \ell)$ consists of a recursive labeling procedure [CLA 81, QUE 82] of $\mathcal{K}$. This procedure gives a Boolean lable to each state q, for each subformula ψ of φ, indicating that whether q satisfies ψ or not. It remains to evaluate the label of the states for formula φ, according to different cases [SCH 01].

Labeling(φ)

(1) $\varphi = P \in$ Prop
for all $q \in Q$,
    if P belongs to $\ell(q)$ then $q.\varphi :=$ true; otherwise $q.\varphi :=$ false;

(2) $\varphi = \neg\psi$
Labeling(ψ);
for all $q \in Q, q.\varphi := \neg q.\psi$;

(3) $\varphi = \psi_1 \wedge \psi_2$
Labeling(ψ_1); Labeling(ψ_2);
for all $q \in Q, q.\varphi := q.\psi_1 \wedge q.\psi_2$;

(4) $\varphi = \mathsf{EX}\psi$
Labeling(ψ);
for all $q \in Q, q.\varphi := \mathsf{false}$;
for all $(q, q') \in \Delta$, if $q'.\psi$ then $q.\varphi := \mathsf{true}$;

(5) $\varphi = \mathsf{AX}\psi$
Labeling(ψ);
for all $q \in Q, q.\varphi := \mathsf{true}$;
for all $(q, q') \in \Delta$, if $\neg q'.\psi$ then $q.\varphi := \mathsf{false}$;

(6) $\varphi = \mathsf{E}\psi_1 \mathsf{U}\psi_2$
Labeling(ψ_1); Labeling(ψ_2); $F := \emptyset$;
for all $q \in Q$,
    $q.\varphi := q.\psi_2$; if $q.\varphi$ then $F := F \cup \{q\}$
while $F \neq \emptyset$,
    choose $q \in F$; $F := F \setminus \{q\}$;
    for all $q' \in Q$ such that $(q', q) \in \Delta$,
        if $q'.\psi_1 \wedge \neg q'.\varphi$ then $q'.\varphi := \mathsf{true}$; $F := F \cup \{q'\}$;

(7) $\varphi = \mathsf{A}\psi_1 \mathsf{U}\psi_2$
Labeling(ψ_1); Labeling(ψ_2); $F := \emptyset$;
for all $q \in Q$,
    $q.\varphi := q.\psi_2$; $q.nb := degre(q)$; if $q.\varphi$ then $F := F \cup \{q\}$;
while $F \neq \emptyset$,
    choose $q \in F$; $F := F \setminus \{q\}$
    for all $q' \in Q$ such that $(q', q) \in \Delta$,
        $q'.nb := q'.nb - 1$;
        if $q'.nb = 0 \wedge q'.\psi_1 \wedge \neg q'.\varphi$
            then $q'.\varphi := \mathsf{true}$; $F := F \cup \{q'\}$

In this procedure, $q.\varphi$ defines the Boolean label associated with φ on state q and $q.nb$ denotes a counter associated with state q, initially equals to $degree(q)$, the number of successor states of q in transition relation. Forward or backward traversals of the structure lead to a time in $O(|\mathcal{K}|.|\varphi|)$ for this algorithm.

Model-checking **LTL** formulae [LIC 85, VAR 86] relies on a different technique based on the following result: given a formula φ in **LTL**, it is possible to build a (Büchi) automaton A_φ whose executions are exactly those satisfying φ.

This result yields first the decidability of the satisfiability problem: given a formula φ in LTL, does there exist a Kripke structure $\mathcal{K}$ such that $\mathcal{K} \models \varphi$? Indeed, after building A_φ, it remains to decide if this automaton has or not an empty set of executions. This is precisely the decidability of emptiness for languages associated with Büchi automata, which is known since [EME 85].

To solve the model-checking problem, we start from a Kripke structure $\mathcal{K}$, and an LTL formula φ and, using the previous construction, we build a Büchi automaton $A_{\neg\varphi}$ associated with the negation of φ (this automaton has a size in $O(2^{|\varphi|})$ in the worst case). Then, we build the automaton $\mathcal{K} \otimes A_{\neg\varphi}$, as a synchronized product, which accepts the intersection of languages: the executions of $\mathcal{K} \otimes A_{\neg\varphi}$ are those which are both executions of $\mathcal{K}$ and executions of $A_{\neg\varphi}$. Thus $\mathcal{K} \models \varphi \Leftrightarrow \mathcal{L}(\mathcal{K} \otimes A_{\neg\varphi}) = \emptyset$: the language accepted by this automaton is empty, if and only if there exists no execution in $\mathcal{K}$ which does not satisfy φ. As above, it remains to test emptiness. This solves the decidability of model-checking LTL, which was proved to be a PSPACE-complete problem.

It should be noted that the most complex operation is the construction of the automaton A_φ, which characterizes the formula φ. Words accepted by this automaton are sequences of elements in $\Sigma = 2^{\mathsf{Prop}}$, with the following notations, where P, P_1, and P_2 are atomic propositions in Prop:

- $\Sigma_P = \{\alpha \in \Sigma \mid P \in \alpha\}$ and $\Sigma_{\neg P} = \Sigma \setminus \Sigma_P$;
- $\Sigma_{P_1 \wedge P_2} = \Sigma_{P_1} \cap \Sigma_{P_2}$, etc.

Figure 2.4 represents a Büchi automaton for the response time formula: G(s ⇒ F e), where s and e stand for **signal** and **event** respectively. The doubly circled state corresponds to a Büchi condition: a word is accepted if the run reaches state 0 infinitely often.

2.4.2. *Region automaton*

A classical method to analyze an infinite state system is to build from it a quotient system, which can be handled by some well known technique, while retaining enough

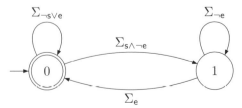

Figure 2.4. *A Büchi automaton for the response time formula*

properties of the original model. This relation between the model and its quotient may be one of the numerous equivalence or simulation relations which have been identified in the past 20 years.

Consider a timed automaton $\mathcal{A} = (X, Q, q_0, \Delta, Inv, \ell)$, over the alphabet Act and the set **Prop** of atomic propositions, with time domain $\mathbb{T} = \mathbb{R}_{\geq 0}$. Since the set of control states is finite, it can be kept unchanged, but we have to build a partition of the valuation set $\mathbb{R}_{\geq 0}^X$, such that the corresponding equivalence " $\sim$" be consistent with the constraints in $\mathcal{C}(X)$, time elapsing, and reset operations. For two valuations v and v', we write $v \leq v'$, if there exists d such that $v' = v + d$. The consistency properties can then be expressed by the following conditions (*), for two equivalent valuations $v \sim v'$:

– for each clock constraint g of the form $x \bowtie c$, we have $v \models g$ if and only if $v' \models g$;

– if $v \leq v_1$ for some valuation v_1, then there exists a valuation v'_1 such that $v' \leq v'_1$ and $v_1 \sim v'_1$; and

– for each subset r of clocks, $v[r \mapsto 0] \sim v'[r \mapsto 0]$.

Assuming such a quotient $\mathcal{R} = (\mathbb{R}_{\geq 0}^X)/_\sim$ can be built, we call *region* an element of $\mathcal{R}$. Operations " $\leq$" and reset can then be defined on $\mathcal{R}$, as well as the satisfaction relation $R \models g$ for a region R and a guard g. A synchronized product of $\mathcal{A}$ and $\mathcal{R}$ yields a new transition system, which is time abstract bisimilar (in the sense of conditions (*)) to the transition system $\mathcal{T}_\mathcal{A} = (S, s_0, E, L)$ associated with $\mathcal{A}$. We denote this system by $\mathcal{K}_\mathcal{A} = (Q \times \mathcal{R}, (q_0, \mathbf{0}), D, \hat{L})$ over $Act \cup \{\leq\}$ and **Prop**. Configurations are of the form $(q, [v])$ where $[v]$ is the equivalence class of valuation v, the labeling is defined by $\hat{L}((q, [v])) = L((q, v))$ and the transitions in D are

1) $(q, R) \xrightarrow{a} (q', R')$, if there exists a transition $q \xrightarrow{g,a,r} q' \in \Delta$ with $R \models g$ and $R' = R[r \mapsto 0]$;

2) $(q, R) \xrightarrow{\leq} (q, R')$, if $R \leq R'$.

In [ALU 90], Alur and Dill build such a relation for timed automata, with finite index. If m is the maximal constant appearing in the constraints of the automaton $\mathcal{A}$, the quotient is denoted by $\mathcal{R}_{(X,m)}$ and the equivalence relation is defined by (**) $v \sim v'$ if:

– for each clock x, either the integral parts of $v(x)$ and $v'(x)$ are equal, or $v(x) > m$ and $v'(x) > m$;

– for each clock x such that $v(x) \leq m$, $frac(v(x)) = 0$, if and only if $frac(v'(x)) = 0$, where $frac(t)$ is the fractional part of the real number t;

– for each pair (x, y) of clocks such that $v(x) \leq m$ and $v'(x) \leq m$, we have $frac(v(x)) \leq frac(v(y))$, if and only if $frac(v'(x)) \leq frac(v'(y))$.

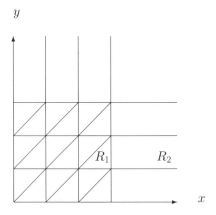

Figure 2.5. *Partition of* $\mathbb{R}^2_{\geq 0}$ *for* $m = 3$

For two clocks automaton with $m = 3$, the corresponding partition is depicted in Figure 2.5.

Regions are points with integer coordinates, open segments between such points, open triangles defined by these segments, and so on. For example, regions R_1 and R_2 in this figure can be described respectively by

$$R_1 : (2 < x < 3) \wedge (1 < y < 2) \wedge (0 < frac(y) < frac(x))$$

$$\text{and } R_2 : (x > 3) \wedge (1 < y < 2).$$

Note that there are so-called *boundary* regions inside which time cannot progress: those corresponding to horizontal and vertical lines in Figure 2.5. Such a region is characterized by the following fact: for each valuation v in R and for each positive delay $d > 0$, valuations v and $v + d$ are not equivalent. Also note that the definition of type 2 transitions in D (corresponding to time steps) can be restricted to linking a region and its immediate time successor. Except for the *final* region ($x > 3 \wedge y > 3$ in Figure 2.5), each region has a distinct immediate successor, which is the next region reached by time elapsing.

Let us observe the combinatorial explosion for the number of configurations in $\mathcal{K}_A$ due to the number of regions in $\mathcal{R}_{(X,m)}$ which is $O(|X|! \cdot m^{|X|})$.

If, instead of considering $\mathcal{C}(X)$, we consider the set of constraints $\mathcal{C}^+(X)$ where diagonal constraints have been added to $\mathcal{C}(X)$, the partition should be modified. For two clocks and $m = 2$, the corresponding partition is shown in Figure 2.6.

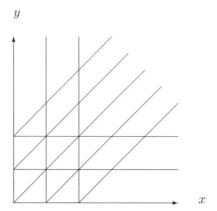

y

x

Figure 2.6. *Partition of* $\mathbb{R}^2_{\geq 0}$ *for* $m = 2$ *with diagonal constraints*

Note that in the second type of partition, each region can be described by a constraint in $\mathcal{C}^+(X)$, while in the first type, some regions cannot be described by the original set of constraints $\mathcal{C}(X)$.

The transition system $\mathcal{K}_A$ obtained by this construction is a finite automaton called *region automaton*. Conditions (*) express time abstract bisimulation and imply a natural correspondence between the runs in $\mathcal{T}_A$ and those in $\mathcal{K}_A$. When only divergent (non-Zeno) executions are considered in $\mathcal{T}_A$, additional accepting conditions, similar to fairness conditions, must be given for $\mathcal{K}_A$, for example, Muller conditions ([ALU 93a, ALU 94a]).

This construction solves, in the class of TA, the problem of reachability for a control state or, equivalently, the emptiness of associated timed languages. Alur and Dill proved that this problem is PSPACE-complete.

2.4.3. *Model-checking* **TCTL**

In this section, the time domain is $\mathbb{T} = \mathbb{R}_{\geq 0}$ for TA.

THEOREM 2.1.– *Model-checking* **TCTL** *over TA is decidable, the problem is PSPACE-complete [ALU 93a].*

We now briefly show how the marking algorithm for **CTL** is adapted to a modified region automaton.

The central property of the " $\sim$ " equivalence defined by conditions (**) above is its *consistency* with **TCTL** formula: let $\mathcal{A} = (X, Q, q_0, \Delta, Inv, \ell)$ be a timed automaton,

"$\sim$" the associated equivalence relation, $q \in Q$ a state and $v \sim v'$ two equivalent valuations. Then for each formula φ of TCTL, $(q, v) \models \varphi \Leftrightarrow (q, v') \models \varphi$.

The proof of this property relies on a notion of equivalence between runs, extending definition (**). Then, for model-checking, a construction similar to the one described above is performed, which additionally takes into account the formula φ that $\mathcal{A}$ must satisfy:

– a new clock z_φ (not in X) is added to measure delays associated with subformulas of φ. We set $X^* = X \cup \{z_\varphi\}$;

– recall that $m_\mathcal{A}$ is the maximal constant associated with $\mathcal{A}$. In order to take into account the constants appearing in the time constraints of the subformulas, we denote by m_φ, the largest of these constants and set $M = \max(m_\varphi, m_\mathcal{A})$.

Then a region automaton $\mathcal{H}_\mathcal{A}$ is built from $\mathcal{A}$ with X^* as a set of clocks and M as maximal constant. States are thus elements of $\mathcal{R}_{(X^*, M)}$ of the form $(q, [v]^*)$, where $[v]^*$ has one more component than $[v]$ corresponding to the values of z_φ. In this construction, the case of boundary regions must also be handled by modifying some transitions (omitted here).

The last step before applying the CTL-labeling algorithm is to add atomic propositions $p_{\bowtie c}$ to label the states of $\mathcal{H}_\mathcal{A}$: a state $(q, [v]^*)$ is labeled by $p_{\bowtie c}$, if the value of z_φ satisfies the constraint $z_\varphi \bowtie c$. For example, to handle a formula like $\varphi : \mathsf{AF}_{<3} P$, meaning that atomic proposition P will hold on all runs before three time units, we transform the condition for a configuration $(q, v) \models \varphi$ into $(q, [v, 0]) \models \mathsf{AF}(P \wedge p_{<3})$ in $\mathcal{H}_\mathcal{A}$. In other words, from a state where the value of z_φ is equal to 0, a state can always be reached where P holds and at the same time the value of z_φ is less than 3.

The construction is illustrated by an example from [ALU 93a]. The timed automaton $\mathcal{A}$ in Figure 2.7 has two clocks x and y, a maximal constant 1 and atomic propositions are identified to the names of states. We also choose 1 for m_φ, which allows us to deal with formulae using 0 or 1 as constants. The region automaton $\mathcal{H}_\mathcal{A}$ (Figure 2.8)

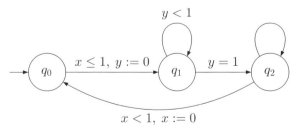

Figure 2.7. $\mathcal{A}_4$: a timed automaton

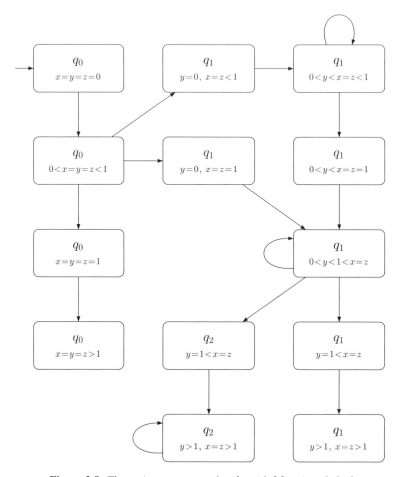

Figure 2.8. *The region automaton for $\mathcal{A}_4$ with $M = 1$ and clock z*

is thus built with $M = 1$, and the additional clock is simply denoted by z in the figure. For the sake of simplicity, the representation given here only allows us to handle one level of quantitative formula.

To conclude this section, note that this technique can be adapted to obtain the model-checking of TCTL_c or L_ν [LAR 95b].

2.4.4. *Model-checking* **MTL**

Here again the time domain is $\mathbb{R}_{\geq 0}$. For continuous semantics, it was established in [HEN 91] that model-checking **MTL** over timed automata is undecidable. On the other hand, in the restricted logic MITL, where constraints with equality are forbidden, the following was proved in [ALU 96]:

THEOREM 2.2.– *Model-checking MITL over timed automata is decidable and the problem is EXPSPACE-complete.*

In this case, the technique is adapted from LTL. First, the satisfiability problem is solved by building, for a formula φ of MITL, a timed automaton $\mathcal{A}_\varphi$ the runs of which are exactly those which satisfy φ.

For model-checking, given a timed automaton $\mathcal{A}$ and a formula φ in MITL, again a synchronized product $\mathcal{A} \otimes \mathcal{A}_{\neg\varphi}$ is built, with executions those of $\mathcal{A}$ which do not satisfy φ. It remains to check emptiness for the language associated with $\mathcal{A} \otimes \mathcal{A}_{\neg\varphi}$, which is done by the construction from [ALU 94a]. This case combines two difficult problems: construction of $\mathcal{A}_\varphi$, which is more involved than in the untimed case and emptiness check.

Recently, the different semantics associated with MTL have been re-investigated more closely [BOU 05b, OUA 05] and decidability of model-checking was obtained for MTL in the case of finite words with discrete observation points. However, the complexity is non-elementary. The authors also obtain some results for infinite words.

2.4.5. *Efficient model-checking*

The high complexity obtained for resolving these problems is an incentive to investigate restrictions, for both model and logic expressivity, to obtain more efficient verification algorithms.

For instance, the idea underlying the definition of the fragment MITL of MTL is to remove *punctual* constraints requiring that some event occurs with a precise delay. In [LAR 06], this idea is applied to the model-checking of durational Kripke structures, a simpler model than timed automata, with the fragment TCTL$_{\leq,\geq}$ from TCTL containing no equality constraints. These restrictions lead to polynomial algorithms:

– for jump semantics, the model-checking algorithm is in time $O(|\mathcal{K}|^2 \cdot |\varphi|)$. It adapts the labeling procedure of CTL model-checking, combined with shortest path or acyclic longest path algorithms;

– for continuous semantics, a more involved adaptation yields an algorithm in $O(|\mathcal{K}|^3 \cdot |\varphi|^3)$.

Other details and variants for model-checking fragments of TCTL on durational Kripke structures can be found in [LAR 06].

Another direction consists of restricting the resources used in the model. In [LAR 04], the study of TA with only one or two clocks leads to more efficient model-checking algorithms. For instance, model-checking the same fragment TCTL$_{\leq,\geq}$ is P-complete for TA with a single clock.

To conclude this section, it should be noticed that the complexity of verification for timed models can be compared with the one resulting from the standard composition [LAR 00]. As explained before, the combinatorial explosion of the product is combined by the addition of timing features.

2.4.6. *Model-checking in practice*

Another technique proposed in [AND 95] for untimed systems is *compositional model-checking*. The principle is as follows. Consider an instance of the model-checking problem of the form

$$(\mathcal{A}_1 \mid \cdots \mid \mathcal{A}_n) \models \varphi,$$

where the left-hand side is a synchronized product of n automata. A way to avoid the explicit construction of the product (leading to state explosion) consists of computing a quotient formula $\varphi/\mathcal{A}_n$ such that

$$(\mathcal{A}_1 \mid \cdots \mid \mathcal{A}_n) \models \varphi \Leftrightarrow (\mathcal{A}_1 \mid \cdots \mid \mathcal{A}_{n-1}) \models \varphi/\mathcal{A}_n,$$

and iterate this operation until reaching

$$(\mathcal{A}_1 \mid \cdots \mid \mathcal{A}_n) \models \varphi \Leftrightarrow \mathbf{1} \models \varphi/\mathcal{A}_n/\mathcal{A}_{n-1}/\cdots/\mathcal{A}_1,$$

where $\mathbf{1}$ represents a system which does nothing (the composition unity), the last step being the resolution of the constraint system.

Applying at each step reduction rules for the formulae built on the right-hand side, may yield some simpler verification procedures on particular examples. This method was extended in [LAR 95a, LAR 95c] for model-checking of L_ν over TA.

Other practical considerations for verification have lead to improved quotient constructions [ALU 92, YAN 93] or data structures for handling time zones [DIL 89, LAR 99]. Among these data structures, *Difference Bounded Matrices* have been successfully used but should be handled carefully [BOU 03].

Tools

The large ammount of work devoted by several teams on timed model-checking produced in 1995–1996, the development of *timed model checkers*, tools specifically dedicated to the verification of timed models. KRONOS [BOZ 98] implements (an optimized version) of the algorithm above for TCTL, while UPPAAL [BEN 98, LAR 97] implements on-the-fly verification of a fragment of TCTL. The tool TSMV [MAR 04] extends NuSMV [CIM 02], with the implementation of a model-checking algorithm for RTCTL [EME 92], a fragment of $TCTL_{\leq,\geq}$, for durational Kripke structures. Timed compositional model-checking is implemented in HCMC [LAR 98] and HyTech [HEN 95] provides semi-algorithms for the analysis of hybrid automata. Finally, there are two main tools for the analysis of TPNs (omitted in this presentation): TINA [BER 06] and ROMEO [GAR 05]. As soon as the prototypes appeared, numerous experiments were performed with growing success on academic toy examples and on industrial case studies. The web page of each tool contains many references to these case studies.

2.5. Conclusion

Research is still very active in the area of timed model-checking, but more generally in the verification of quantitative systems. The high complexity of most verification algorithms did not stop the development of efficient tools but it remains a limit for the verification of real systems, usually with very large size. Many current research activities are devoted to this difficult problem, either by designing pertinent abstractions or by exploiting specific patterns in the systems.

2.6. Bibliography

[ACE 02] Aceto L., Laroussinie F., "Is your model checker on time? On the complexity of model checking for timed modal logics", *Journal of Logic and Algebraic Programming*, vol.52–53, 7–51, 2002.

[ALU 90] Alur R., Dill D., "Automata for modeling real-time systems", *Proc. of ICALP'90*, vol. 443 of *Lecture Notes in Computer Sciences*, pp. 322–335, Springer, 1990.

[ALU 91] Alur R., Henzinger T., "Logics and models of real time: a survey", *Real-time: Theory in practice, Proc. REX workshop*, vol. 600 of *Lecture Notes in Computer Science*, pp. 74–106, Springer, 1991.

[ALU 92] Alur R., Courcoubetis C., Halbwachs N., Dill D.L., Wong-Toi H., "Minimization of timed transition systems", *Proc. 3rd International Conference on Concurrency Theory (CONCUR'92)*, vol. 630 of *Lecture Notes in Computer Science*, pp. 340–354, Springer, 1992.

[ALU 93a] Alur R., Courcoubetis C., Dill D., "Model-checking in dense real-time", *Information and Computation*, vol.104, num. 1, 2–34, 1993.

[ALU 93b] Alur R., Courcoubetis C., Henzinger T.A., Ho P.H., "Hybrid automata: an algorithmic approach to the specification and verification of hybrid systems", *Proceed Workshop Hybrid Systems*, vol. 736 of *Lecture Notes in Computer Science*, pp. 209–229, Springer, October 1993.

[ALU 94a] Alur R., Dill D., "A theory of timed automata", *Theoretical Computer Science*, vol.126, 183–235, 1994.

[ALU 94b] ALUR R., HENZINGER T.A., "A really temporal logic", *Journal of the ACM*, vol.41, num. 1, 181–203, 1994.

[ALU 96] ALUR R., FEDER T., HENZINGER T.A., "The benefits of relaxing punctuality", *Journal of the ACM*, vol.43, num. 1, 116–146, 1996.

[AND 95] ANDERSEN H.R., "Partial model checking", *Proceedings of the 10th IEEE Symposium on Logic in Computer Science (LICS'95)*, pp. 398–407, IEEE Computer Society Press, June 1995.

[BAI 99] BAIER C., KATOEN J.P., *Principles of Model Checking*, MIT Press, 1999.

[BEL 05] BEL MOKADEM H., BÉRARD B., BOUYER P., LAROUSSINIE F., "A new modality for almost everywhere properties in timed automata", *Proceedings of the 16th International Conference on Concurrency Theory (CONCUR'05)*, vol. 3653 of *Lecture Notes in Computer Science*, pp. 110–124, Springer, 2005.

[BEL 06] BEL MOKADEM H., BÉRARD B., BOUYER P., LAROUSSINIE F., "Timed temporal logics for abstracting transient states", *Proceedings of the 4th International Symposium on Automated Technology for Verification and Analysis (ATVA'06)*, vol. 4218 of *Lecture Notes in Computer Science*, pp. 337–351, Springer, October 2006.

[BEN 98] BENGTSSON J., LARSEN K.G., LARSSON F., PETTERSSON P., YI W., WEISE C., "New generation of UPPAAL", *Proceedings of International Workshop on Software Tools for Technology Transfer (STTT'98)*, pp. 43–52, July 1998 [Proceedings available as BRICS Notes Series NS98/4].

[BER 07] BÉRARD B., GASTIN P., PETIT A., "Timed substitutions for regular signal-event languages", *Formal Methods in System Design*, vol.31, num. 2, 101–134, Kluwer Academic Publishers, 2007.

[BER 83] BERTHOMIEU B., MENASCHE M., "An enumerative approach for analyzing time Petri nets", *Information Processing*, vol.9 of *IFIP Congress Series*, pp. 41–46, Elsevier Science Publishers, 1983.

[BER 03] BERTHOMIEU B., VERNADAT F., "State class constructions for branching analysis of time petri nets", *Proceedings of TACAS'2003*, vol. 2619 of *Lecture Notes in Computer Science*, pp. 442–457, Springer, 2003.

[BER 06] BERTHOMIEU B., VERNADAT F., "Time Petri nets analysis with TINA", *3rd International Conference on the Quantitative Evaluation of Systems (QEST'06)*, pp. 123–124, IEEE Computer Society Press, September 2006.

[BOU 03] BOUYER P., "Untameable timed automata!", *Proceedings of the 20th Annual Symposium on Theoretical Aspects of Computer Science (STACS'03)*, vol. 2607 of *Lecture Notes in Computer Science*, pp. 620–631, Springer, February 2003.

[BOU 04a] BOUYER P., BRINKSMA E., LARSEN K.G., "Staying alive as cheaply as possible", *Proceedings of the 7th International Conference on Hybrid Systems: Computation and Control (HSCC'04)*, vol. 2993 of *Lecture Notes in Computer Science*, pp. 203–218, Springer, 2004.

[BOU 04b] BOUYER P., DUFOURD C., FLEURY E., PETIT A., "Updatable timed automata", *Theoretical Computer Science*, vol.321, num. 2–3, 291–345, 2004.

[BOU 05a] BOUYER P., CHEVALIER F., "On conciseness of extensions of timed automata", *Journal of Automata, Languages and Combinatorics*, vol.10, num. 4, 393–405, 2005.

[BOU 05b] BOUYER P., CHEVALIER F., MARKEY N., "On the expressiveness of TPTL and MTL", *Proceedings of the 25th Conference on Fundations of Software Technology and Theoretical Computer Science (FSTTCS'05)*, vol. 3821 of *Lecture Notes in Computer Science*, pp. 432–443, Springer, December 2005.

[BOZ 98] BOZGA M., DAWS C., MALER O., OLIVERO A., TRIPAKIS S., YOVINE S., "Kronos: a model-checking tool for real-time systems", *Proceedings of the 10th International Conference on Computer Aided Verification (CAV'98)*, vol. 1427 of *Lecture Notes in Computer Science*, pp. 546–550, Springer, 1998.

[BRI 04] BRIHAYE T., BRUYÈRE V., RASKIN J.F., "Model-checking for weighted timed automata", *Proceedings of Joint Conference on Formal Modelling and Analysis of Timed Systems and Formal Techniques in Real-Time and Fault Tolerant System (FOR-MATS+FTRTFT'04)*, vol. 3253 of *Lecture Notes in Computer Science*, pp. 277–292, Springer, 2004.

[BRU 03] BRUYÈRE V., DALL'OLIO E., RASKIN J.F., "Durations, parametric model-checking in timed automata with Presburger arithmetic", *Proceedings of 20th Annual Symposium on Theoretical Aspects of Computer Science (STACS'03)*, vol. 2607 of *Lecture Notes in Computer Science*, pp. 687–698, Springer, 2003.

[CAM 95] CAMPOS S., CLARKE E., "Real-time symbolic model checking for discrete time models", *Theories and Experiences for Real-Time System Development*, vol. 2 of *AMAST Series in Computing*, pp. 129–145, World Scientific, 1995.

[CIM 02] CIMATTI A., CLARKE E., GIUNCHIGLIA E., GIUNCHIGLIA F., PISTORE M., ROVERI M., SEBASTIANI R., TACCHELLA A., "NuSMV Version 2: an open source tool for symbolic model checking", *Proceedings of International Conference on Computer-Aided Verification (CAV 2002)*, vol. 2404 of *Lecture Notes in Computer Science*, Springer, July 2002.

[CLA 81] CLARKE E.M., EMERSON E.A., "Design and synthesis of synchronization skeletons using branching time temporal logic", *Proceedings Logics of Programs Workshop*, vol. 131 of *Lecture Notes in Computer Sciences*, pp. 52–71, Springer Verlag, May 1981.

[CLA 86] CLARKE E.M., EMERSON E., SISTLA A., "Automatic verification of finite-state concurrent systems using temporal-logic specifications", *ACM Transactions on Programming Languages and Systems*, vol.8, 244–263, 1986.

[CLA 08] CLARKE E.M., GRUMBERG O., PELED D.A., *Model Checking*, MIT Press, 2008.

[DIL 89] DILL D.L., "Timing assumptions and verification of finite-state concurrent systems", *Proceedings of International Workshop on Automatic Verification Methods for Finite State Systems (CAV'89)*, vol. 407 of *Lecture Notes in Computer Science*, pp. 197–212, Springer, 1989.

[EME 82] EMERSON E.A., HALPERN J.Y., "Decision procedures and expressiveness in the temporal logic of branching time", *Proceedings of 14th ACM Symposium on Theory of Computing (STOC'82)*, pp. 169–180, May 1982.

[EME 85] EMERSON E.A., LEI C.L., "Modalities for model checking: branching time strikes back", *Proceedings of 12th ACM Symposium on Principles of Programming Languages (POPL'85)*, pp. 84–96, January 1985.

[EME 92] EMERSON E.A., MOK A.K., SISTLA A.P., SRINIVASAN J., "Quantitative temporal reasoning", *Real-Time Systems*, vol.4, num. 4, 331–352, 1992.

[FLE 02] FLEURY E., 'Automates temporisés avec mises à jour', Thesis ENS de Cachan, December 2002.

[GAR 05] GARDEY G., LIME D., MAGNIN M., ROUX O., "ROMÉO: A tool for analyzing time Petri nets", *17th International Conference on Computer Aided Verification (CAV'05)*, vol. 3576 of *Lecture Notes in Computer Science*, pp. 418–423, Springer, 2005.

[HEN 91] HENZINGER T.A., The temporal specification and verification of real-time systems, PhD Thesis, Technical Report STAN-CS-91-1380, Stanford University, 1991.

[HEN 92] HENZINGER T.A., MANNA Z., PNUELI A., "What good are digital clocks?", *Proceedings of 19th International Colloquium on Automata, Languages, and Programming (ICALP'92)*, vol. 623 of *Lecture Notes in Computer Science*, pp. 545–558, Springer, 1992.

[HEN 94a] HENZINGER T.A., MANNA Z., PNUELI A., "Temporal proof methodologies for timed transition systems", *Information and Computation*, vol.112, num. 2, 273–337, 1994.

[HEN 94b] HENZINGER T.A., NICOLLIN X., SIFAKIS J., YOVINE S., "Symbolic model checking for real-time systems", *Information and Computation*, vol.111, num. 2, 193–244, 1994.

[HEN 95] HENZINGER T.A., HO P., WONG-TOI H., "HYTECH: the next generation", *Proceedings of 16th IEEE Real-Time Systems Symposium (RTSS'95)*, pp. 56–65, IEEE Computer Society Press, 1995.

[HEN 96] HENZINGER T.A., "The theory of hybrid automata", *Proceedings of LICS'96*, pp. 278–292, 1996 [Invited tutorial].

[HEN 98] HENZINGER T.A., KOPKE P.W., PURI A., VARAIYA P., "What's decidable about hybrid automata?", *Journal of Computer and System Sciences*, vol.57, num. 1, 94–124, 1998.

[JON 77] JONES N., LANDWEBER L., LIEN Y., "Complexity of some problems in Petri nets", *Theoretical Computer Science*, vol.4, 277–299, 1977.

[KOY 90] KOYMANS R., "Specifying real-time properties with metric temporal logic", *Real-Time Systems*, vol.2, num. 4, 255–299, 1990.

[KOZ 83] KOZEN D.C., "Results on the propositional μ-calculus", *Theoretical Computer Science*, vol.27, num. 3, 333–354, 1983.

[LAR 95a] LAROUSSINIE F., LARSEN K.G., "Compositional model-checking of real time systems", *Proceedings of the 6th International Conference on Concurrency Theory (CONCUR'95)*, vol. 962 of *Lecture Notes in Computer Science*, pp. 27–41, 1995.

[LAR 95b] LAROUSSINIE F., LARSEN K.G., WEISE C., "From timed automata to logic – and back", *Proceedings of 20th International Symposium on Mathematical Foundations of*

Computer Science (MFCS'95), vol. 969 of *Lecture Notes in Computer Science*, pp. 529–539, Springer, 1995.

[LAR 98] LAROUSSINIE F., LARSEN K.G., "CMC: a tool for compositional model-checking of real-time systems", *Proceedings of IFIP Joint International Conference on Formal Description Techniques & Protocol Specification, Testing, and Verification (FORTE-PSTV'98)*, pp. 439–456, Kluwer Academic, November 1998.

[LAR 00] LAROUSSINIE F., SCHNOEBELEN P., "The state-explosion problem from trace to bisimulation equivalence", *Proceedings of the 3rd International Conference on Foundations of Software Science and Computation Structures (FoSSaCS 2000)*, vol. 1784 of *Lecture Notes in Computer Science*, pp. 192–207, Springer, March 2000.

[LAR 04] LAROUSSINIE F., MARKEY N., SCHNOEBELEN P., "Model checking timed automata with one or two clocks", *Proceedings of the 15th International Conference on Concurrency Theory (CONCUR'04)*, vol. 3170 of *Lecture Notes in Computer Science*, pp. 387–401, Springer, 2004.

[LAR 06] LAROUSSINIE F., MARKEY N., SCHNOEBELEN P., "Efficient timed model checking for discrete-time systems", *Theoretical Computer Science*, vol.353, num. 1–3, 249–271, March 2006.

[LAR 95c] LARSEN K.G., PETTERSSON P., YI W., "Compositional and symbolic model-checking of real-time systems", *Proceedings of 16th IEEE Real-Time Systems Symposium*, pp. 76–87, December 1995.

[LAR 97] LARSEN K.G., PETTERSSON P., YI W., "UPPAAL in a nutshell", *Journal of Software Tools for Technology Transfer (STTT)*, vol.1, num. 1–2, 134–152, 1997.

[LAR 99] LARSEN K.G., PEARSON J., WEISE C., YI W., "Clock difference diagrams", *Nordic Journal of Computing*, vol.6, num. 3, 271–298, 1999.

[LIC 85] LICHTENSTEIN O., PNUELI A., "Checking that finite state concurrent programs satisfy their linear specification", *Proceedings of 12th ACM Symposium on Principles of Programming Languages (POPL'85)*, pp. 97–107, January 1985.

[LIL 99] LILIUS J., "Efficient state space search for time Petri nets", *Electronic Notes in Theoretical Computer Science*, vol.18, pp. 113–133, 1998.

[MAL 91] MALER O., MANNA Z., PNUELI A., "From timed to hybrid systems", *Real-Time: Theory in Practice, Proc. REX Workshop*, vol. 600 of *Lecture Notes in Computer Science*, pp. 447–484, Springer, 1991.

[MAR 04] MARKEY N., SCHNOEBELEN P., "TSMV: a symbolic model checker for quantitative analysis of systems", *Proceedings of the 1st International Conference on Quantitative Evaluation of Systems (QEST'04)*, pp. 330–331, IEEE Computer Society Press, September 2004.

[MER 74] MERLIN P.M., A study of the recoverability of computing systems, PhD Thesis, UCI, Univ. California, Irvine, 1974.

[OUA 05] OUAKNINE J., WORRELL J., "On the decidability of metric temporal logic", *Proceedings of the 20th IEEE Symposium on Logic in Computer Science (LICS'05)*, pp. 188–197, 2005.

[PNU 77] PNUELI A., "The temporal logic of programs", *Proceedings of the 18th IEEE Symposium on Foundations of Computer Science (FOCS'77)*, pp. 46–57, November 1977.

[QUE 82] QUEILLE J.P., SIFAKIS J., "Specification and verification of concurrent systems in CESAR", *Proceedings of 5th International Symposium on Programming*, vol. 137 of *Lecture Notes in Computer Sciences*, pp. 337–351, Springer Verlag, April 1982.

[SCH 01] SCHNOEBELEN P., BÉRARD B., BIDOIT M., FINKEL A., LAROUSSINIE F., PETIT A., PETRUCCI L., *Systems and Software Verification – Model-Checking Techniques and Tools*, Springer, 2001.

[VAR 86] VARDI M.Y., WOLPER P., "An automata-theoretic approach to automatic program verification", *Proceedings of the 1st IEEE Symposium on Logic in Computer Science (LICS'86)*, pp. 332–344, IEEE Computer Society Press, June 1986.

[YAN 93] YANNAKAKIS M., LEE D., "An efficient algorithm for minimizing real-time transition systems", *Proceedings of 5th International Conference on Computer Aided Verification (CAV'93)*, vol. 697 of *Lecture Notes in Computer Science*, pp. 210–224, Springer, June 1993.

Chapter 3

Control of Timed Systems

In this chapter, we address the problem of controller synthesis for timed systems. By timed systems we refer to those systems which are subject to *quantitative* (hard) real-time constraints. We assume the reader is familiar with the basics of timed automata theory, or has read Chapters 1 and 2 of this book.

3.1. Introduction

It is not always possible to use *discrete time* to specify and model timing constraints. This is why *dense-time* specification formalisms, such as timed automata [ALU 94] or time Petri nets [MER 74], were introduced some years ago. Once a system is modeled by a timed automaton or a TPN, it can be checked (Chapter 2) for quantitative properties. If a property is not satisfied, we still might be able to act on the system and *control* some of its behaviors: for example, by adding a component or a *controller*. How to compute such a timed controller is the purpose of this chapter, in which we review some algorithms for controller synthesis for TA.

3.1.1. *Verification of timed systems*

A standard approach to the verification of real-time systems, called *model-checking* [SCH 99], consists of three phases: (1) build a complete model S for the system (e.g., a finite automaton); (2) specify the qualitative correctness property to be satisfied in a non-ambiguous logical language (e.g. temporal logics) as a formula ψ; and (3) check

---

Chapter written by Franck CASSEZ and Nicolas MARKEY.

algorithmically that S is a *model* of ψ, denoted by $S \models \psi$: this is the *model-checking* algorithm. Model-checking techniques for discrete event systems and qualitative properties, have been studied for quite a long time and are mature enough to have spread in industry. Nevertheless, for certain types of systems, the correctness property is formulated in terms of *quantitative* requirements that cannot be captured in a discrete time or logical time model. A typical example of such system is the *scheduling* of tasks where the durations of the tasks must be taken into account. It is sometimes possible to use discrete time as an abstraction for dense time but it may turn out to be of limited applicability: if the timing parameters of the system range from 1 to 10 000, using a discrete clock that ticks every time unit produces a prohibitive number of states, and *model-checking* algorithms (even if symbolic) will not be able to handle such state spaces. Another disadvantage of using discrete time is that it is not easy to *compose* two systems specified with different time scales. Finally, we may have some limited knowledge of the durations of the tasks in the system. To take into account this uncertainty (durations of the tasks, of the communications), we can use dense-time formalisms, for example, *TA* [ALU 94] which are finite automata extended with real-time *clocks*. Model checking algorithms for discrete event systems (finite automata, temporal logics like CTL or LTL) have been extended to timed automata and timed logics and these algorithms are implemented in a variety of tools like UPPAAL [AMN 01], KRONOS [YOV 97], CMC [LAR 98, LAR 05], PHAVER [FRE 05] (see Chapter 7 in this book) and HYTECH [HEN 97].

3.1.2. *The controller synthesis problem*

To use a *model-checking* algorithm, we must have a complete model describing all the behaviors of the system: thus we assume we have a model consisting of the *environment* of the system, the *sensors* and the *controller*. Such systems are called *closed* systems. On the contrary, in the framework of controller synthesis, we assume we have a model of the system which is *open*: if S is a model the system to be controlled, we have to find a controller C to build a closed system $C(S)$ "S controlled or supervised by C" which represents the complete model.

If the correctness property is ϕ, the *model-checking* approach answers to questions of the form "Does $C(S)$ satisfy ϕ?". Hence the *model-checking* problem can be formally defined by

$$\text{given } S, C \text{ and } \phi, \text{ does } C(S) \models \phi \text{ hold ?} \qquad \text{[MCP]}$$

The *model-checking* approach thus requires us to first build (maybe by "hand") a controller C to be able to obtain a closed system $C(S)$. This can be a very difficult task for complex systems or when the correctness property involves timing constraints. Moreover, if using our handmade controller C, ϕ does not hold on $C(S)$, we have to iterate and modify C until we finally end up with a satisfactory controller[1]. An ideal solution would be to *compute* (we say *synthesize* in the sequel) a controller (if there is one) such that the correctness property is satisfied. This is the *controller synthesis problem (CSP)* for open systems. Before building a controller we still have to check if one exists, and this is the *control problem (CP)* formally defined by

$$\text{given } S \text{ and } \phi, \text{ is there any } C \text{ such that } C(S) \models \phi \text{ ? [3.2]} \qquad \text{[CP]}$$

To solve problem [CP], we often have to narrow the class of controllers we will consider. For instance, we can look for finite state controllers (with bounded memory) or timed controllers (that can be represented by TA). In any case, once we have checked that a controller exists, another task is to build a witness, which is the *controller synthesis problem (CSP)*:

$$\text{if the answer to [CP] is "yes," build a witness controller } C. \qquad \text{[CSP]}$$

These problems have been introduced and solved for finite state systems (discrete event systems) in the pioneering work of Ramadge and Wonham [RAM 87, RAM 89]. An alternative framework to study the control problem is the framework of *game theory,* which we will introduce in the next section.

3.1.3. *From control to game*

A control problem can be formulated as a two-player *game problem* (see [ARN 03, MCN 93, RIE 03, THO 95]): the model of the system is a transition system in which one of two players, controller or environment, is responsible for state change. In this framework, the controller has to find a *strategy* to ensure a particular property whatever the environment does.

An example of a two-player game is given in Figure 3.1. In this game, round-shaped states are Player 1's states in which Player 1 chooses the next move, and the square-shaped states are Player 2's states.

Assume Player 1 plays the following strategy: when the game is in state ℓ_0, he chooses to go to ℓ_2, and when the game is in ℓ_3, he chooses to go to FINAL. If Player 1 plays this strategy, for any strategy of Player 2, the game is bound to end in FINAL. Player 1's strategy is said to be *winning*, if the objective of the game (for Player 1) is to reach FINAL (this is called a *reachability objective*).

---

1. This may take a while in the case where no such controller exists . . . .

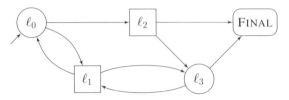

Figure 3.1. *A game example*

On the contrary, if the objective of the game for Player 1 is to avoid FINAL (this is called a *safety objective*), he still has a winning strategy: always choose to go to state ℓ_1.

Finally, if Player 1's objective is to visit ℓ_3 infinitely often (*repeated reachability objective* or *Büchi objective*), Player 1 has no winning strategy (he has to play a move and cannot refuse to play): if from ℓ_0 he chooses to go to ℓ_2, Player 2 can choose to go to FINAL; if he chooses to got to ℓ_1, Player 2 chooses to go back to ℓ_0.

The type of strategies Player 1 has to follow is also an important parameter for a game. If Player 1 wants to play one of the strategies, we have defined previously, he just has to observe the *current* state of the game. Such strategies are called *memory-less* or *positional* strategies. Player 1 could also consider waiting a bit before enforcing state FINAL and for instance choose to go to ℓ_3 the first time the game reaches ℓ_2 and the second time go to FINAL. He will then have to remember that ℓ_2 has been reached once which can be done using one bit of memory. More generally, Player 1 could choose to delay the winning moves n times (choosing to go to ℓ_3 for the first n times the game enters ℓ_2) and at the $(n + 1)$th times the game enters ℓ_2, he can choose to go to FINAL. All these strategies, when n is fixed are *bounded memory* strategies. There are also games and objectives that cannot be won with bounded memory strategies, and in this case Player 1 needs to record the entire history of the game from the beginning, to be able to choose a correct move.

To solve a control problem using a game theory approach, it suffices to let Player 1 be the controller and Player 2 be the system to be controlled (the environment). The control problem is then: is there a *winning strategy* for Player 1? A winning strategy is an actual controller to supervise the system.

3.1.4. *Game objectives*

Given a game G, a control objective ϕ, solving (G, ϕ) stands for the following control problem: "Is there a strategy C for Player 1 in G to ensure $C(G) \models \phi$?". If ϕ is a safety objective, and in this case we assume it is given as a set of states to stay in or to avoid, we have a *safety control problem (SafCP)*. If ϕ is a reachability objective, we have a *reachability control problem (RCP)*. We can define more complex objectives (repeated reachability, Büchi, or co-Büchi) or even formulate them as (timed) temporal logic formulae.

3.1.5. *Varieties of untimed games*

A game as the one described in Figure 3.1 is a *turn-based* game. As for chess or draughts board games, players' moves are alternate. A generalization of turn-based games can be obtained by tagging the states of the game with a shape, which is either circle or square: in circle-shaped states, Player 1 moves, and in square-shaped states, Player 2 moves. In this case, the type of the state determines whose turn it is, but the turn does not always change in each round. This games are called *state-based* games and can be transformed in "equivalent" turn-based games. If the two players can play at the same time as in "Scissors Paper Stone," we have a *concurrent* game. We will briefly mention timed concurrent games in section 3.10.

Turn-based (finite) games enjoy nice properties. For instance they are *determined* for a large class, say $\mathcal{B}$ (that includes Büchi objectives), of control objectives [MAR 75]. Being determined means that in each state of the game, either Player 1 can win (G, ϕ) (ϕ taken in $\mathcal{B}$), or Player 2 can win $(G, \neg\phi)$ where $\neg\phi$ is the complement of ϕ (this implies that $\mathcal{B}$ is closed under complement). Concurrent games do not have this determinacy property.

Moreover, for the types of control objectives we have mentioned earlier (safety, reachability, repeated reachability, etc.), turn-based and concurrent (untimed) games satisfy the following properties [THO 95]:

– it is decidable in polynomial time whether Player 1 has a winning strategy for (G, ϕ);

– if Player 1 has a winning strategy for (G, ϕ), he has a *memoryless* or *positional* winning strategy;

– if Player 1 has a winning strategy for (G, ϕ), there is a "most permissive" strategy which is memoryless as well.

The remainder of this chapter is organized as follows. Section 3.2 introduces the basic notions of timed games and their formal definitions, together with strategies. In section 3.3, we give algorithms to solve the safety-control problem for TA. The following sections consider more advanced topics related to the control of timed systems. Section 3.4 points out one limitation (related to the practical implementation of controllers) of the previous algorithms, and in section 3.5, we focus on the notion of *implementable* controllers. In section 3.6, we review some results on more complex control objectives. Section 3.7 addresses the problem of *optimal control* for reachability timed games. Efficient on-the-fly algorithms for controller synthesis are described in section 3.8; a good complement to this section can be found at the end of Chapter 6. Finally, section 3.10 considers an extended model of timed games introduced in section 3.2.

3.2. Timed games

The aim of this section is to define the formal framework of timed games and related notions. The definition of *timed games* used in the sequel has been introduced in [ASA 98, MAL 95]: it is an extension of TA in which the set of actions is split between both players. Besides these discrete actions, each player can also decide to wait in the current location: in this case, time will elapse until one of the player possibly decides to perform an action.

3.2.1. *Timed game automata*

DEFINITION 3.1(TIMED GAME AUTOMATON, TGA).– A *timed game automaton* (or simply *timed game*) is a 7-tuple $\mathcal{G} = (L, \ell_0, X, \Sigma_1, \Sigma_2, E, Inv)$ satisfying the following conditions:

- Σ_1 and Σ_2 are disjoint alphabets;
- $(L, \ell_0, X, \Sigma_1 \cup \Sigma_2, E, Inv)$ is a timed automaton (following Definition 2.2 of Chapter 2).

A timed game is thus a timed automaton the actions of which are associated with players: transitions that belong to the controller are called *controllable*, and the other ones belong to the environment and are called *uncontrollable*.

Informally, a *play* in a timed game proceeds as follows: it starts in an initial location ℓ_0 with all clocks set to 0, and is made of a sequence of action and delay transitions. Delay transitions are the "default" transitions, and occur as long as no player decides to (or can) play an action transition. In the special case of turn-based games, the delay in each location is decided by the player controlling that location.

EXAMPLE 3.1.– An example of a timed game is depicted on Figure 3.2 [CAS 05]. Dashed transitions are uncontrollable (labeled with Σ_2), and solid transitions are controllable ones (labeled with Σ_1). This rule will be used throughout this chapter.

In this example, all invariants are true, so that it is always possible to let time elapse. Assume that the controller decides to play action c_1 when $x = 1$. If the environment does not play action u_2 in the meantime, then the transition corresponding to action c_1 will be fired, and the game will end up in location ℓ_1 with $x = 1$. The controller will

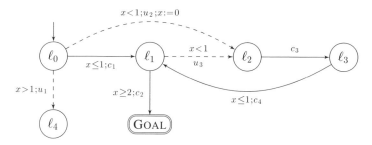

Figure 3.2. *An example of a timed game*

then have the opportunity to wait for an extra time unit, and then play action c_2, leading to his GOAL state. Notice that, when in location ℓ_1 with $x \geq 1$, the environment cannot play any action. He has to wait until the controller decides to play an action.

Of course, given the strategy "*play action c_1 when $x = 1$*" of the controller in the initial location, the environment could also have decided to play an action at an earlier time instant, for instance by playing u_2 when $x = 0.5$ (notice that u_1 is only available when $x > 1$). The play would then have moved to $(\ell_2, x = 0)$ (since the transition from ℓ_0 to ℓ_2 resets clock x).

These examples informally illustrate the intuition behind timed games. We now define the corresponding mathematical framework, which will allow us to formally check properties of those games.

In the following, we fix a game $\mathcal{G} = (L, \ell_0, X, \Sigma_1, \Sigma_2, E, Inv)$.

3.2.2. *Strategies and course of the game*

Several different semantics have been proposed for timed games: time indeed requires to fix the "rules of the game." We begin here with a natural definition of the semantics of timed games as proposed in [MAL 95]. Section 3.10 will stress the drawbacks of this semantics (especially regarding strategies consisting of "stopping time") and propose another approach to remedy this problem [ALF 03].

3.2.2.1. *The course of a timed game*

The definition of a run of a timed game is that of the underlying timed automaton; following Definition 3.1, a timed game is a timed automaton whose actions are partitioned between controllable and uncontrollable actions. Given a timed game

$\mathcal{G} = (L, \ell_0, X, \Sigma_1, \Sigma_2, E, \mathit{Inv})$, we write $\mathcal{T}_\mathcal{G}$ for the TTS, which gives the semantics of $\mathcal{G}$ (see Chapter 2). A run of the timed game $\mathcal{G}$ is a run of the TTS $\mathcal{T}_\mathcal{G}$: it is a sequence

$$\rho = s_0 \xrightarrow{d_1} s_0' \xrightarrow{a_1} s_1 \xrightarrow{d_2} s_1' \xrightarrow{a_2} \cdots \xrightarrow{d_{n-1}} s_n' \xrightarrow{a_n} s_n \cdots$$

where $a_i \in \Sigma_1 \cup \Sigma_2$, $d_i \in \mathbb{R}_{\geq 0}$, and in which configurations s_i and s_i' are pairs (ℓ, v) with $\ell \in L$ and v is a clock valuation. Delay and action transitions thus alternate (two consecutive delay transitions can be merged, and the last delay transition of a finite run can have infinite duration).

The set of runs of the timed game $\mathcal{G}$ is written $\mathrm{Exec}_\mathcal{G}$. We also define the subset of *maximal runs* as being the set of runs that cannot be extended. This includes several kinds of runs:

– runs having infinitely many action transitions;

– finite runs with infinite duration;

– finite runs with finite duration from which no delay nor action transition is possible.

We write $\mathrm{Exec}_\mathcal{G}^m$ for the set of maximal runs of $\mathcal{G}$, and $\mathrm{Exec}_\mathcal{G}^f$ for the set of its finite runs. The length of a finite run is the number of its transitions (both delay and action transitions) along that run.

3.2.2.2. *Strategies*

Strategies are the central concept in game theory. A strategy tells the player how to play, depending on the history of the game. In the case of timed games, players are allowed to wait and stay idle (this is the λ transition in the definition below). As will be seen in the sequel, both players have to agree on playing that special action in order to let time elapse. As soon as one of the players decides to play one of his available actions, time will stop elapsing and the action will be played.

DEFINITION 3.2(STRATEGY).– Let $j \in \{1, 2\}$ be a player of $\mathcal{G}$. A *strategy* for Player j is a mapping $s \colon \mathrm{Exec}_\mathcal{G}^f \to \Sigma_j \cup \{\lambda\}$ satisfying the following conditions: given a finite run ρ ending in state $q = (\ell, v)$,

– if $s(\rho) = a \in \Sigma_j$, then there must exist a transition $q \xrightarrow{a} q'$ in $\mathcal{T}_\mathcal{G}$;

– if $s(\rho) = \lambda$, then there must exist a positive delay $d > 0$ such that $q \xrightarrow{d} q'$ in $\mathcal{T}_\mathcal{G}$.

These conditions encode the fact that any action (including the λ action) proposed by a strategy must be allowed in the game $\mathcal{G}$. The set of strategies of Player j in $\mathcal{G}$ is denoted by $\mathrm{Strat}_j(\mathcal{G})$.

When a player plays according to a given strategy, he narrows the set of possible runs of the game to runs that comply with that strategy.

DEFINITION 3.3(CONTROLLED GAME).– Let $q = (\ell, v)$ be a state of $\mathcal{G}$, and s be a strategy for Player 1 (the case of Player 2 would be symmetric). The set of *finite outcomes of s from q*, denoted by $\text{Out}^f(q, s)$, is defined inductively as follows:

  – q is the only zero-length run in $\text{Out}^f(q, s)$;

  – any finite run of $\mathcal{G}$ of the form $\rho' = \rho \xrightarrow{\sigma} q'$ (hence having positive length) belongs to $\text{Out}^f(q, s)$ if, and only if, ρ belongs to $\text{Out}^f(q, s)$ and one of the following three conditions holds:

    - $\sigma \in \Sigma_2$;
    - $\sigma \in \Sigma_1$ and $\sigma = s(\rho)$;
    - $\sigma \in \mathbb{R}_{>0}$ and for any d such that $0 \leq d < \sigma$, it holds $s(\rho \xrightarrow{d} q'') = \lambda$.

The set of maximal outcomes of s from q, denoted with $\text{Out}^m(q, s)$, is the union of the following two sets of outcomes:

  – the set of maximal finite runs in $\text{Out}^f(q, s)$;

  – the set of infinite runs all of whose prefixes are in $\text{Out}^f(q, s)$.

It is understood in this definition that a player can remember the whole history of the play for applying his strategy. However, some strategies have the special feature of being independent of the history and only depending on the current state of the system. Those strategies are called *positional* or *memoryless* strategies. In those special cases, in order to alleviate notations, we will see those strategies as mapping from the set of states to the set of actions of the corresponding player. Below is an example of a positional strategy.

EXAMPLE 3.2.– We stick to the example given in Figure 3.2, and consider the following memoryless strategy $\tilde{s}$:

  – from states of the form (ℓ_0, v) with $v(x) < 1$, Player 1 (the controller) plays action λ. When $v(x) = 1$, he plays c_1. If ever $v(x) > 1$, he again decides to play λ (as this is his only allowed action). Formally, $\tilde{s}(\ell_0, x < 1 \vee x > 1) = \lambda$ and $\tilde{s}(\ell_0, x = 1) = c_1$;

  – from (ℓ_1, v), he plays λ as long as $v(x) < 2$, and c_2 when $v(x) \geq 2$, i.e. $\tilde{s}(\ell_1, x < 2) = \lambda$ and $\tilde{s}(\ell_1, x \geq 2) = c_2$;

  – from (ℓ_2, v), he plays c_3, hence $\tilde{s}(\ell_2, v) = c_3$;

  – from (ℓ_3, v), if $v(x) < 1$, he plays λ, and plays c_4 when $v(x) = 1$. When $v(x) > 1$, he has to play λ. Hence $\tilde{s}(\ell_3, x < 1 \vee x > 1) = \lambda$ and $\tilde{s}(\ell_3, x = 1) = c_4$;

  – from ℓ_4 and GOAL, Player 1 has no choice and only has to wait: $\tilde{s}(\ell_4, v) = \tilde{s}(\text{GOAL}, v) = \lambda$.

Among the outcomes of this strategy from $(\ell_0, 0)$, some directly go to ℓ_1, some others go via ℓ_2 and ℓ_3 (in case Player 2 plays u_2), but one is easily convinced that no outcome can ever reach ℓ_4, and that actually all the outcomes eventually reach GOAL.

Let Ω be a set of runs (intended to represent the set of winning plays) defining the control objective. In the following, we write $(\mathcal{G}, \Omega)$ for the game $\mathcal{G}$ under the winning objective Ω (for Player 1).

DEFINITION 3.4(WINNING STATE, WINNING STRATEGY).– Let $s \in \mathrm{Strat}_j(\mathcal{G})$ be a strategy for Player 1. We say that s is *winning* from state q for Ω, if $\mathrm{Out}^m(q, s) \subseteq \Omega$, i.e. , if all the maximal outcomes meet the objective.

A state q is *winning* for Player 1, if he has a winning strategy from q. We write $\mathrm{WinState}_1(\mathcal{G}, \Omega)$ for the set of states of $\mathcal{G}$ that are winning for Player 1.

Finally, a strategy s is said to be winning in $(\mathcal{G}, \Omega)$, if it is winning from the initial state: $\mathrm{Out}^m((\ell_0, v_0), s) \subseteq \Omega$. We write $\mathrm{WinStrat}_j(\mathcal{G}, \Omega)$ for the set of winning strategies of Player j. In the sequel, we focus on winning strategies for Player 1 (the controller). We thus write $\mathrm{WinStrat}(\mathcal{G}, \Omega)$, being understood that it refers to Player 1. We also sometimes omit to mention Ω when it is clear from the context.

EXAMPLE 3.3.– Back to the example given in Figure 3.2, location GOAL is the reachability objective of the controller. The set Ω is then the set of (maximal) runs visiting that location. The strategy $\tilde{s}$ defined above is then winning from the initial state.

3.3. Computation of winning states and strategies

Controller synthesis algorithms for timed automata are given in [ALF 01, ALF 03, ASA 98, MAL 95]. They compute fix-points (as for untimed games): the set of states which are winning in n steps is computed inductively. When n tends to infinity, all the winning states are collected. These algorithms terminate because the region equivalence relation on clock valuations introduced in Chapter 2 is also a good equivalence relation for timed games.

In this section, we use a running example depicted in Figure 3.3 where the control objective is to avoid location BAD. The results of the synthesis algorithms for this example are given at the end of this section.

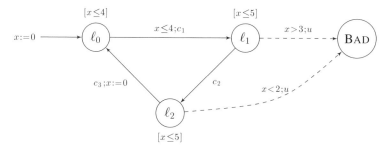

Figure 3.3. *A timed game automaton* S

3.3.1. *Controllable predecessors*

In order to implement our inductive fix-point algorithm, we define the *controllable predecessors* of a set of states: indeed, to win a game in at most $n + 1$ steps, the controller must have a strategy to force in one step, a state from which it can win in at most n steps.

Let $\mathcal{G}$ be a timed game, and $\mathcal{T}_\mathcal{G}$ the timed transition system which is the semantics of $\mathcal{G}$. For a given subset X of S (set of states of $\mathcal{T}_\mathcal{G}$), we define the sets $CPre(X)$ and $UPre(X)$ by

$$CPre(X) = \{q \in S \mid \exists c \in \Sigma_c \text{ such that } q \xrightarrow{c} q' \text{ et } q' \in X\};$$

$$UPre(X) = \{q \in S \mid \exists u \in \Sigma_u \text{ such that } q \xrightarrow{u} q' \text{ et } q' \in X\}.$$

These two sets are respectively the set from which the controller can force, with a controllable transition, the game into the set X, and the set from which the environment can force, with an uncontrollable transition, the game into the set X. To complete the definition we have to take into account the time elapsing action λ.

Figure 3.4 depicts the conditions for a state q to be a *controllable predecessor* of a set of states X: the controller must be able to *force* the game into a state of X, first by time elapsing (λ) and then by firing a controllable transition c; and from each state q_t encountered during the time elapsing phase, the environment must not be able to fire an uncontrollable transition leading outside of X (denoted $\overline{X}$).

In Figure 3.4, state q' is not a controllable predecessor of X, because during the time elapsing phase, the game reaches a state in $UPre(\overline{X})$, from where the environment can force the game in $\overline{X}$. On the contrary, q is a controllable predecessor of X.

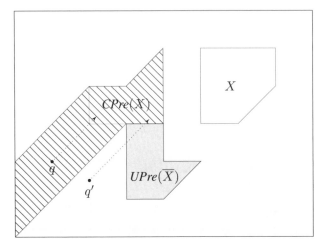

Figure 3.4. *Controllable predecessors*

DEFINITION 3.5(CONTROLLABLE PREDECESSOR).– A state q is a controllable predecessor of X iff:

1) there is some $\delta \geq 0$, such that $q \xrightarrow{\delta} q'$ and $q' \in CPre(X)$;

2) for all $0 \leq t \leq \delta$ such that $q \xrightarrow{t} q_t$, we have $q_t \notin UPre(\overline{X})$.

The set of controllable predecessors of X is denoted $\pi(X)$.

In Figure 3.4, the black lined polygon corresponds to the controllable predecessors of the set X. In the example given in Figure 3.3, the state $(\ell_1, x = 1)$ is a controllable predecessor of $(\ell_2, x = 2)$: a controller can let time elapse (1 time unit) until $(\ell_1, x = 2)$ and then fire c_2 from ℓ_1 to ℓ_2. During the time-elapsing phase, no uncontrollable transition can be fired.

REMARK 3.1.– This definition of controllable predecessors is an extension of the one given for discrete games. It does not take into account the special features of timed games, such as liveness enforced by invariants. For instance, for a reachability game with control objective GOAL, and one uncontrolable transition $(0, x \leq 1, u, \emptyset, \text{GOAL})$ with $Inv(0) \equiv x \leq 1$, the environment must play action u before the time point 1. Thus, if we take this into account, a controller could win just by waiting.

It is possible to take into account the cases where the environment is bound to play by modifying the previous definitions. The results we give in this section are still valid in this case.

3.3.2. *Symbolic operators*

The semantics of a timed game automaton is a timed transition system, and as for *model-checking* of timed automata, the set of states is infinite. Thus we must develop symbolic techniques, gathering states in *"families"* which have the same properties.

We will use the notion of equivalence, *regions*, between states introduced in section 2.4.2. To prove the correctness of this approach, we must show that two states in the same region have the same properties regarding their winning status. If this holds, we can compute the controllable predecessors of a region. The following Lemma summarizes these two claims:

LEMMA 3.1.– *if Z is a (finite) union of regions (we say a zone), then:*
$\mathbf{P_1}$: *$CPre(Z), UPre(Z)$ and $\pi(Z)$ are unions of regions (thus zones),*
$\mathbf{P_2}$: *$CPre(Z), UPre(Z)$ and $\pi(Z)$ can be effectively computed.*

Proving the previous Lemma requires the introduction of an intermediate symbolic operator that computes the states from which a set of states A can be reached by time elapsing without encountering a state in a set B. This operator is given by

$$Pre_t(A, B) = \{s \in S \mid \exists \delta \geq 0.\ s \xrightarrow{\delta} s' \wedge s' \in A \wedge$$

$$\forall 0 \leq t \leq \delta.\ [(s \xrightarrow{t} s'') \Rightarrow (s'' \notin B)]\}.$$

Taking $A = CPre(X)$ and $B = UPre(\overline{X})$ allows us to define a symbolic version of the controllable predecessors operator π using Pre_t: $\pi(X) = Pre_t(CPre(X), UPre(\overline{X}))$.

EXAMPLE 3.4.– For the automaton shown in Figure 3.3, we have $CPre(\ell_1, x \leq 3) = (\ell_0, x \leq 3)$ and if $Z = (\ell_0, x \leq 4) \cup (\ell_1, x \geq 0) \cup (\ell_2, x \geq 0)$ then $\pi(Z) = Z'$ avec $Z' = (\ell_0, x \leq 3) \cup (\ell_1, 0 \leq x \leq 3) \cup (\ell_2, x \geq 2)$.

3.3.3. *Symbolic computation of winning states*

We can now proceed to the symbolic computation of winning states of a timed game. A *symbolic state* of a TGA is given as a finite union of pairs (ℓ, Z) where ℓ is a location of the TGA and Z a zone. We assume we have to solve a safety game, and the set of bad states to avoid, is given by BAD which is a symbolic state. The set of winning states of such games is the greatest fix-point of the mapping $h: X \mapsto \overline{BAD} \cap \pi(X)$. As h is a monotonic (decreasing) mapping, this is well defined. To compute this fix-point, we start by computing $h(S)$ (where S is the set of states of the game), then $h(h(S))$,

(a) Winning States

X_i	ℓ_0	ℓ_1	ℓ_2
0	$0 \le x \le 4$	$0 \le x \le 5$	$0 \le x \le 5$
1	$0 \le x \le 4$	$0 \le x \le 3$	$2 \le x \le 5$
2	$0 \le x \le 3$	–	–

(b) Most Permissive Strategy f^*

	ℓ_0	ℓ_1	ℓ_2
λ	$x < 3$	$x < 3$	$x < 5$
c	$x \le 3$	$2 \le x$	$x \le 5$

Table 3.1. *Iterative computation of h^* for the example in Figure 3.3*

and so on. This algorithm produces a decreasing sequence of symbolic state and as there is a finite number of such states, this computation terminates in a finite number of steps. When it stabilizes, the greatest fix-point h^* of h is computed: it is a subset of $\overline{\text{BAD}}$, and from each state in h^* the controller has a strategy to stay within h^* by time elapsing and then firing a discrete transition. The set h^* is also the largest subset of $\overline{\text{BAD}}$ that the controller can enforce.

EXAMPLE 3.5.– For the example of Figure 3.3, the iterative computation of h^* is given in Table 3.1(a): the winning zone for each location ℓ_i appears in the corresponding column.

REMARK 3.2.– For reachability games, the goal is to enforce a symbolic state GOAL. Thus, the set of winning states is the least fix-point of the mapping $h: X \mapsto \text{GOAL} \cup \pi(X)$. Again, this least fix-point can be computed iteratively by computing $h(\varnothing)$, $h(h(\varnothing))$ and so on. Termination is ensured because the sequence of symbolic states which is computed is monotonic. For more complex control objectives (repeated reachability, ...), nested fix-points are required (see [MAL 95, ASA 98, ALF 01, ALF 03]).

As we can effectively decide whether the initial state of a TGA belongs to the symbolic representation h^* we can decide whether there is a winning strategy using h^* and moreover:

THEOREM 3.1([ASA 98, HEN 99B]).– *The control problems SafCP and RCP are decidable for TGA and EXPTIME-complete.*

3.3.4. *Synthesis of winning strategies*

To solve the control synthesis problem for a safety game, we can define a *most liberal* or *most permissive* strategy. Actually, this strategy is not a strategy in the sense of section 3.2.2.2, as it maps states to *sets* of controllable actions and not to a single controllable action. The most permissive strategy f^* associates with each run ρ a set of actions from $\Sigma_c \cup \{\lambda\}$ which are safe: every non-blocking strategy f (in the sense of section 3.2.2.2) such that $f(\rho) \in f^*(\rho)$ is winning and conversely a strategy f is winning only if $f(\rho) \in f^*(\rho)$. This is why f^* is called the most permissive strategy. For the synthesis problem, we have the following result:

THEOREM 3.2([ASA 98]).– *If $\mathcal{G}$ is a timed game automaton such that the initial state of $\mathcal{G}$ is winning for a safety objective, then there is a positional winning most permissive strategy f^*.*

To compute this most permissive strategy, we begin by strengthening the guards of the controllable transitions such that, from a winning state s, firing the transition with the strengthened guard leads to a winning state. This amounts to computing a most liberal pre-condition. In our case, we strengthen (the guard of) transition c_1 by $x \leq 3$, c_2 by $x \geq 2$ (which ensures that c_2 is not fired too early). The most permissive strategy is then defined by: wait in each winning state s such that there is some $\delta > 0$ and $s \xrightarrow{\delta} s'$ with s' winning; fire a controllable transition c_i, if the guard is satisfied. For the example given in Figure 3.3, the most permissive strategy is given in Table 3.1(b). Notice that to obtain a *non-Zeno* strategy, one should not choose infinitely often λ in ℓ_0 (or ℓ_1, ℓ_2), but at some point in time we should fire c_1. Using the previous method, we can compute a timed automaton C (given in Figure 3.5), which is a representation of the most permissive strategy f^*, and such that $Reach(C(G)) \subseteq \phi$ with $\phi = Reach(G) \setminus \{\text{BAD}\}$. For reachability games, computing a winning strategy may be a bit more complicated. A correct algorithm is given in [BOU 04b] for this case.

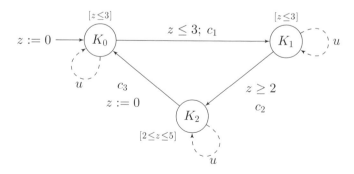

Figure 3.5. *Most permissive controller C*

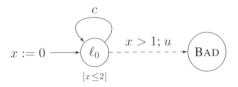

Figure 3.6. *A safety game having a winning Zeno strategy*

3.4. Zeno strategies

Fix-point algorithms presented in section 3.3 compute the set of winning states, and the corresponding winning strategies. However, we did not take into account the so-called "Zenoness" problem: it could be the case —- and is the case in the example given in Figure 3.6 where the aim is to always avoid the BADstate —- that a state is winning thanks to non-realistic strategies. In the example given in Figure 3.6, the strategy of the controller consists of firing transition c infinitely many times during the first time unit, thus preventing clock x to reach value 1. Such a controller is called a *Zeno* controller and is not realistic because physical time cannot be stopped.

Symmetrically, there is no strategy for the environment to reach the BAD state in this game, since any strategy of the environment has to "wait" as long as $x \leq 1$. Hence the controller can fire transition c at dates $(1 - 1/n)$, which yields an infinite run never reaching BAD.

As will be seen in section 3.10, a (rather technical) solution exists to rule out those non-realistic strategies. More generally, control problems (in particular for safety games) have been extended to generate *implementable* controllers (thus in particular non-Zeno). This extension is presented in the following section.

3.5. Implementability

Variants of the safety control problem SafCP have been proposed in many papers [HEN 99a, HEN 99b, ASA 98, MAL 95].

In [CAS 02], we can find a classification of these problems according to the following criteria:

– discrete time control: can we control the system with a controller that reacts every β time units? This is the *known sampling rate* (KSR) *control problem*. A more general question is asking for the computation of a value β such that the system is controllable. This is the *unknown sampling rate* (USR) *control problem*;

– dense-time control: in this setting the controller can either (*i*) control time elapsing, which is the setting of the seminal papers [MAL 95, ASA 98]; in this case this is the *unknown switch condition* (USC) *control problem*; or (*ii*) cannot control time elapsing and in this case this is the *known switch condition* (KSC) *control problem*.

The decidability status of the standard safety control problem SafCP also depends on the expressive power of the formalism used to specify timed games. Before giving the decidability status of the previous problems, we review some well-known classes of extensions of TA.

3.5.1. *Hybrid automata*

The more general class that is usually considered for the control problem SafCP is the class of *linear hybrid automata* (LHA) [HEN 96]. The reader is referred to Chapter 7 for a detailed presentation of LHA. This class extends TA in the following manner: (*i*) the evolution rate of the variables[2] are given by intervals of the form $1 \leq \dot{x} \leq 3$; (*ii*) guards and resets are linear functions like $2x + 3y \leq 4$ and $x := 3y - 7z$.

An interesting subclass of LHA is the class of *rectangular automata* (RA) [HEN 99b]. For RA, the guards and resets cannot involve two distinct variables: they are of the form $x \geq 1 \wedge y < 2$ and for resets $x :=]2,3]$ to assign a value v with $2 < v \leq 3$ to x. This class has interesting and surprising decidability results: the reachability problem is decidable for RA [HEN 99b]. A subclass of RA is the class of *initialized rectangular automata* (IRA): if a derivative of a variable changes on a transition from ℓ to ℓ', then the variable must be reset on this transition.

The reachability problem is decidable for RA but for any subclass it becomes undecidable [HEN 98]. Another interesting class of hybrid systems with good decidability properties, is the class of *O-minimal Automata*, (OminA) [LAF 00]: in this model, the dynamics can be nonlinear (exponential or any o-minimal theory) but all the variables must be reset when firing a discrete transition.

Decidability results for the safety control problem on LHA are summarized in Table 3.2: the meaning of abbreviations are: KSC = *known switch conditions controller*, USC = *unknown switch conditions controller*, KSR = *known sampling rate controller*, and USR = *unknown sampling rate controller*. $\sqrt{}$ = decidable, $\times$ = undecidable.

A recent result by Patricia Bouyer, Thomas Brihaye and Fabrice Chevalier [BOU 06b] is the decidability of the reachability control problem, USC variant, for o-minimal automata.

---

2. We note $\dot{x}$ the derivative of x.

System given by:	KSC	USC	KSR	USR
Timed auto.	√ [MAL 95]	√ [MAL 95]	√ [HOF 92]	× [CAS 02]
Initialized rect. auto.	√ [HEN 99a]	× [HEN 98]	√ [HEN 99b]	× [CAS 02]
Rect. auto.	× [HEN 99a]	× [HEN 99a]	√ [HEN 99b]	× [CAS 02]

Table 3.2. *Safety control problem: decidability results*

3.5.2. *On the existence of non-implementable continuous controllers*

In [CAS 02], it is proved that the USR-CP is undecidable, even for the class of TA. Another result of the paper is that there are systems that can be controlled with a dense-time controller (USC), but by no sampling controller (USR). We have given an example of such a system, given by the timed automaton of Figure 3.7. This timed automaton can be controlled with a non-Zeno controller. In this example, all the transitions are controllable. To avoid location BAD, it suffices to avoid firing a d-transition. This can be achieved by computing a most permissive controller: this controller C only requires to leave ℓ_2 when $x < 1$, and thus we add the invariant $[x < 1]$ to location ℓ_2. The controller C has to do the sequence of actions $(a.b.c)^\omega$, but the time elapsed between the $(n + 1)$th a and the $(n + 1)$th b must be smaller than for the previous round n. More precisely, if the time elapsed between the nth a and the nth b is δ_n, the controller has to ensure that $\sum_{i=1}^{+\infty} \delta_i \leq K$ where $K \leq 1$. Because of this, no sampling controller can control the system: given a sampling rate β, after a finite number of rounds m, the sum $\sum_{i=1}^{m} \delta_i$ is beyond 1. The controller C is non-Zeno (and non-blocking) because the nth a action occurs at time n. This shows dense-time controllability does not imply sampling controllability. In other words, if the answer to the USC-CP is "yes", the most permissive controller is not always *implementable* on a digital controller.

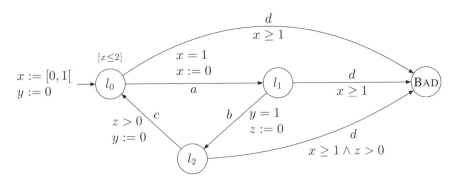

Figure 3.7. *A system that cannot be controlled with a sampling controller*

3.5.3. *Recent results and open problems*

The main undecidability result of [CAS 02] can be extended to intervals of the form $[\alpha, \beta]$, i.e. we impose that a controllable action occurs within $[\alpha, \beta]$ after the preceding controllable action. The proof of this result is given in [DOY 07].

The previous result shows that the notion of *implementable controllers* is important and must be addressed in the control problem. This aspects of the control problem have been extensively studied by Jean-François Raskin and co-authors in [DEW 05a, DEW 05b, DEW 04a, DEW 04b] and a synthesis of this work (in French) is given in [ALT 05].

An open problem is the direct synthesis of implementable or robust controllers which would extend the corresponding results on robust *model-checking* [BOU 06f, BOU 08b].

3.6. **Specification of control objectives**

In the previous section, we considered safety (or reachability) control objectives. In this section, we model the systems by TA and focus on more general types of control objectives.

In [ALF 01], the authors give an algorithm to deal with general ω-regular control objectives. They consider ω-regular objectives on TGA with a "surprise" semantics (see section 3.10 in this chapter). They show that the CP with this "surprise" semantics is EXPTIME-complete. It is to be noticed that those control objectives are often called *internal* in the sense that they refer to the state properties (and clocks) of the system to be controlled. The safety and reachability properties that we have considered previously are examples of internal property. In the case of timed systems, they only refer to the untimed sequences of states of the system and thus have a restrictive expressiveness: it is possible to specify a property like "from a state satisfying p we must reach a state satisfying q" but nothing like "from a state satisfying p we must reach a state satisfying q within d time units" (*bounded liveness*). In [FAE 02a], the authors show that the control problem is 2EXPTIME-complete for specifications given by LTL formulae.[3]

A control objective is a property of a closed system, and it is natural to write properties using temporal logics or automata, i.e. to give the set of timed words the

---

3. This result does not contradict the complexity result of [ALF 03] because the specification is given as an LTL formula and not by the automaton that recognizes the valid sequences.

controlled system has to generate. The language[4] $\mathcal{L}(A)$ accepted by a TA is a set of behaviors (timed words) and this can be considered to be a control objective: in this sense, this is an *external* control objective. Notice that it can either specify good or bad behaviors. Let us assume that we have two timed automata: A_d which defines the desired (permitted) behaviors of the system, and A_u which defines the undesired behaviors. Let S be the system we want to control. The *external specification control problem* (ESCP) is the following:

is there any C s.t. (1) $\mathcal{L}(C(S)) \cap \mathcal{L}(A_u) = \varnothing$ *et* (2) $\mathcal{L}(C(S)) \subseteq \mathcal{L}(A_d)$?   [ESCP]

In [DSO 02], the authors prove that:

1) the sub-problems ESCP.(1) and ESCP.(2) are undecidable when A_d and A_u are non-deterministic TA;

2) these problems become decidable if A_d and A_u are deterministic; deterministic TA can be complemented and in this case the ESCP can be reduced to a (internal) safety control problem;

3) the control problem ESCP.(2) is decidable and 2EXPTIME-complete, if the resources (number of clocks, granularity, and constants used in the specification) of the controller are bounded, and this even if A_u is non-deterministic. ESCP.(1) remains undecidable even for bounded resources.

Expressing control objectives using timed automata is a very powerful tool and there is a gap between the control objectives we considered previously (safety or reachability) and these very general class of ω-regular properties. Temporal logics are a less powerful yet often sufficient specification formalism for most properties needed in practice.

In [BOU 06a], the authors consider a timed extension of LTL namely MTL [KOY 90]. The control problem is undecidable for MTL specifications but become decidable, if the resources of the controller are bounded (it is still non-primitive recursive). In [FAE 02b], the authors consider TCTL specifications without equality and prove that the control problem (for timed automata) can be decided in exponential time for this type of specifications.

In [BOU 05b], control objectives are specified using the (timed) temporal logic L_ν (more precisely a fragment L_ν^{det} of L_ν), which is a fragment of the timed μ-calculus: it allows to specify *bounded safety* properties.

What is interesting is that the CP for L_ν^{det} control objectives can be reduced to *model-checking* problem and the later problem is EXPTIME-complete.

Finally, there is a nice logic, which was specifically designed to specify properties of open (discrete) systems: *alternating-time temporal logic* (ATL) [ALU 02]. This

---

4. We consider languages over infinite words, e.g. ω-regular languages.

logic is an extension of CTL where the path quantifiers are replaced by "strategies quantifiers." It is possible to write a property like "Player 1 has a strategy to reach a state from which Player 2 will not be able to reach a winning state."

Several recent papers have extended the definitions of this logics to timed systems. We can then write a property specifying that a winning state must be reached "within five-time units". The extended logic has been studied for TA operating in discrete time [LAR 06], and PTIME algorithms are proposed for model-checking the extended logic. For TA in dense time, some results are available [BRI 07, HEN 06a] but the semantics of TGA s a bit different from the one we have introduced so far (see section 3.10).

3.7. Optimal control

If we consider the reachability *reachability control problem* (RCP), we want to synthesize a controller that enforces a particular state or location q. Once solved, we can ask for the controller to be *optimal*, e.g., the state q is reached as soon as possible with the controller. This version of optimal control called *time-optimal control* was solved in [ASA 99].

3.7.1. *TA with costs*

A few years later in 2001, timed automata were extended with *costs* or *prices*: this extension was called *priced timed automata* (PTA) in [BEH 01b, BEH 01a] and *weighted timed automata* (WTA) in [ALU 01] (both models are exactly the same thing but they were proposed independently at the same time by two different groups).

The notion of cost or price generalizes the notion of elapsed time: the cost is a linear function of the elapsed time in each location, and is an integer value on each discrete transition. In the example given in Figure 3.8, the costs in the PTA $\mathcal{A}$ are given by the keyword **cost**.

When the cost is associated with a location, it stands for the *cost per time unit* when time elapses in this location. When it is associated with a discrete transition, it stands for the cost of *firing* the transition. Let us assume that δ time units elapse in location ℓ_0, and then c_1 is fired. The invariant on ℓ_1 prevents time from elapsing in ℓ_1. This location is a choice location in which we immediately go either to ℓ_2 or ℓ_3. Assume that we choose ℓ_2 and let δ' time units elapse before firing c_2. In this case, the total cost of this execution is $5 \cdot \delta + 10 \cdot \delta' + 1$. In PTA, all the transitions are controllable.

The optimal-cost computation problem for PTA consists of computing the minimal cost to reach a particular location. The (smart) solutions to the optimal-cost computation problem for PTA were simultaneously proposed in [ALU 01, BEH 01b]. Notice

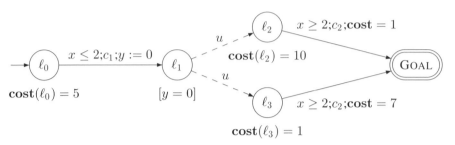

Figure 3.8. *A PTGA $\mathcal{A}$*

that in PTA, there is only one player and this is not the cost-optimal control problem. A symbolic algorithm [BEH 01a] has been implemented in an extended version of UPPAAL called UPPAAL CORA [BEH 07b].

If we consider PTA and a dual problem, i.e. keeping the system in a set of states, we can define an optimal problem as well: here the model has *costs* and *rewards*, and the aim is to minimize the limit of the ration cost/reward on infinite runs. This latter problem was solved in [BOU 08a, BOU 04a].

A step further consists of defining a logic which can refer to cost values: such a logic, WCTL, has been defined in [BRI 04], and extends TCTL with cost variables. Inside this logic, it is possible to write a formula which states "it is possible to reach a state q and this at a cost which is less than K." The model-checking problem for WCTL against timed automata was proved undecidable (even if the time domain is discrete). Nevertheless, for a subset of WCTL, there are some classes of TA for which model-checking is decidable. Recently in [BOU 07], the authors have proved that WCTL was decidable for o-minimal PTA. The formal definition of a priced timed game automaton (PTGA) is the following:

DEFINITION 3.6(PTGA).– A *priced timed game automaton* is a pair $(\mathcal{G}, \mathbf{cost})$ where $\mathcal{G} = (L, \ell_0, X, \Sigma_1, \Sigma_2, E, Inv)$ is a TGA and $\mathbf{cost}$ is a *cost mapping* such that: $\mathbf{cost}$: $L \cup E \to \mathbb{N}$, i.e. $\mathbf{cost}$ associates with each location a cost per time unit and a firing cost with each discrete transition. Let $\mathcal{T_G} = (Q, Q_0, \Sigma_1, \Sigma_2, \Gamma, \delta)$ be the semantics of $\mathcal{G}$. If ρ is the run of $\mathcal{T_G}$ defined by

$$\rho = (\ell_0, v_0) \xrightarrow{(\delta_1, e_1)} (\ell_1, v_1) \xrightarrow{(\delta_2, e_2)} \dots \xrightarrow{(\delta_n, e_n)} (\ell_n, v_n),$$

we can define the *cost* of ρ by

$$\mathbf{Cost}(\rho) = \sum_{i=0}^{n-1} \left(\mathbf{cost}(\ell_i) \times \delta_{i+1} + \mathbf{cost}(\ell_i \xrightarrow{e_i} \ell_{i+1}) \right).$$

The cost of a run is thus the sum of the discrete costs and the delay costs.

3.7.2. *Optimal cost in timed games*

We can now formulate the optimal-cost problem for timed games. In this case, we start with a model which is a *Priced Timed Game Automaton*, i.e. a TGA enriched with costs. We consider here reachability games: the aim is to reach a location at an optimal cost, and this optimal cost is the best the controller can ensure, whatever the adversary (environment) does. The automaton $\mathcal{A}$ of Figure. 3.8 is an example of a PTGA. Uncontrollable transitions are labeled by u. Notice that in this game, there is a controller which can enforce location GOAL: fire c_1 and then whatever the environment chooses in ℓ_1, fire c_2. In the sequel, we assume that the reachability control problem has been solved and the answer was "yes", i.e. there is a controller which can enforce GOAL. Our problem is now to compute the optimal cost.

This optimal cost is defined as the minimum value the controller can guarantee whatever the environment does. For example, in the PTGA $\mathcal{A}$ of Figure 3.8, there are two families of runs: the runs in which the environment chooses to go from ℓ_1 to ℓ_2 and the runs in which it chooses to go from ℓ_1 to ℓ_3. The only real decision the controller has to make is to choose how long to wait in ℓ_0 before firing c_1 (indeed when in ℓ_2 or ℓ_3 it chooses to fire c_2 as soon as $x \geq 2$.) Let δ be the amount of time the controller chooses to wait for in ℓ_0. The costs that can result from this choice depend on the choice of the environment: if it chooses $\ell_i, i = 2, 3$, the cost is respectively $\alpha_2(\delta) = 5 \cdot \delta + 10 \cdot (2 - \delta) + 1$ and $\alpha_3(\delta) = 5 \cdot \delta + 1 \cdot (2 - \delta) + 7$. Once the controller has fired c_1, the environment will try to maximize the cost of the current run: it will choose $\ell_i, i = 2, 3$ such that $\alpha_i(\delta)$ is maximal. The aim of the controller is to minimize this maximum over all paths.

Thus the optimal cost for the PTGA $\mathcal{A}$ is defined by

$$\mathbf{OptCost} = \inf_{0 \leq \delta \leq 2} \max(5 \cdot \delta + 10 \cdot (2 - \delta) + 1, 5 \cdot \delta + 1 \cdot (2 - \delta) + 7).$$

For $\mathcal{A}$, this value is 43/3, which means c_1 should be fired at the date 4/3. The problem of computing this optimal cost automatically is the *optimal cost reachability control problem* (OC-RCP).

Of course, we can generalize the definition of the optimal cost given for $\mathcal{A}$ to PTGA. With the model of PTGA we have introduced, the *time optimal control* problem is a particular version: in each location, the cost rate is 1 and each discrete transition has a null cost.

Let $\mathsf{WinStrat}(q, \mathcal{G})$ be the set of winning strategies from q in $\mathcal{G}$. Given a strategy s for the controller, we can define the cost of s from a state q of $\mathcal{T}_\mathcal{G}$ by

$$\mathbf{Cost}(q, s) = \sup \left\{ \mathbf{Cost}(\rho) \mid \rho \in \mathsf{Out}^m(q, f) \right\}.$$

DEFINITION 3.7(OPTIMAL COST).– Let $(\mathcal{G}, \mathbf{cost})$ be a PTGA. We consider the RCP for $\mathcal{G}$ and the goal location is GOAL. The *set of possible costs*, $\mathbf{Cost}(q)$, from q in $\mathcal{G}$ when playing s is defined by

$$\mathbf{Cost}(q) = \{\mathbf{Cost}(q, s) \mid s \in \mathsf{WinStrat}(q, \mathcal{G})\}.$$

The *optimal cost from* q is $\mathbf{OptCost}(q) = \inf \mathbf{Cost}(q)$. The *optimal cost for* $\mathcal{G}$, $\mathbf{OptCost}(\mathcal{G})$, is $\sup_{q \in Q_0} \mathbf{OptCost}(q)$.

REMARK 3.3.– Notice that we consider the supremum from the initial states of $\mathcal{G}$ and this means that we consider that the choice of the initial state is not controllable. If there is a single initial state (such as in the following examples), we have $\mathbf{OptCost}(\mathcal{G}) = \mathbf{OptCost}(q_0)$.

The *cost optimal reachability control problem* (CO-RCP) asks the following:

Given $(\mathcal{G}, \mathbf{cost})$, compute $\mathbf{OptCost}(\mathcal{G})$.   [CO-RCP]

3.7.3. *Computation of the optimal cost*

A first step towards a solution of the optimal cost reachability control problem was given for *acyclic* timed games in [LAT 02]. As the PTGA does not have any cycle, the computation of the optimal cost can be reduced to a linear optimization problem.

If we consider PTGA which can contain cycles, it is not obvious that the algorithm proposed in [LAT 02] can be tuned to accommodate cycles. A solution to the OC-RCP was simultaneously given by Alur *et al.* [ALU 04] and Bouyer *et al.* [BOU 04c, BOU 05a]. Alur *et al.* [ALU 04] give some complexity results (lower bound) and in [BOU 04c] gives decidability results for PTGA as well as structural properties of the class of strategies (or controllers) that can win this type of games. The algorithm of [BOU 04c] was implemented in HYTECH [HEN 97] and this is described in [BOU 05a].

We detail here the algorithm of [BOU 04c] to solve the OC-RCP. The idea we propose to solve the optimal cost problem[5] for PTGA is the following: the OC-RCP can be rephrased as: "What is the minimum amount of resources (time, petrol,

---

5. As emphasized earlier, we assume there is a strategy to win the game, i.e. to force GOAL. This ensures that the optimal cost exists and is a finite number.

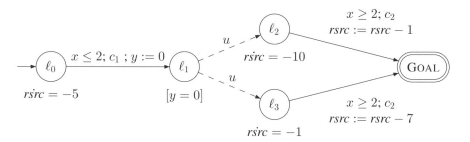

Figure 3.9. *The LHA H_A built from A*

etc.) I should start with, to be able to enforce GOAL, and when GOAL is reached I have not run out of resources?" Thus to solve the OC-RCP we can proceed as follows:

1) we start with a PTGA A similar to the one given in Figure 3.8;

2) then we build a game H_A, which is a timed game with a special variable *rsrc*: we end up with a timed game which is a special kind of linear hybrid automata (LHA). This variable stores the amount of resources which is left at each point in the game. Its value will then decrease in a location ℓ of H_A with a rate which is the opposite of the rate of the cost in the corresponding location in A.

Applied to A of Figure 3.8, this construction gives the automaton H_A in Figure 3.9 (the notation *rsrc* stands for the first derivative of *rsrc*). The OC-RCP for PTGA can then be reduced to a (standard) reachability control problem for a *linear hybrid game*[6] (LHG): the control objective is to enforce GOAL and a value of *rsrc* which is larger or equal than 0, i.e. the control objective is $(\text{GOAL}, rsrc \geq 0)$. We know how the set of winning states for this type of (linear hybrid) games should be computed, and if the algorithm terminates we obtain a set of pairs of the form (ℓ, Z) where ℓ is a location and Z a polyhedron. In particular, we may obtain a set of pairs (ℓ_0, Z) giving the set of winning states (values of the variables) in the initial location. By definition of the algorithm to solve LHGs, Z is the maximal winning zone, i.e. if one starts outside Z, the game cannot be won.

The projection of the winning set Z in ℓ_0 on the variable *rsrc* gives the set of values of *rsrc* from which we can win the game, i.e. enforce $(\text{GOAL}, rsrc \geq 0)$. We can prove that this set is of the form $rsrc \bowtie k$ with $\bowtie \{>, \geq\}$ and this means that the optimal cost is k.

---

6. See section 7.5.1.

Decidability of the OC-RCP for PTGA is also reduced to the decidability of the RCP for the class of LHA that is obtained when we use our translation. The results obtained by this approach are:

– for bounded PTGA (all the clocks are bounded) such that on each cycle, the cost is at least $\beta > 0$ (we call this class of PTGA, *cost non-Zeno PTGA*), the classical backward algorithm that computes the winning states of the associated linear hybrid game terminates;

– the optimal cost can be obtained by computing the projection of the set of initial winning states on the variable *rsrc*. When the previous algorithm terminates, this set is always of the form *rsrc* $\bowtie k$ with $\bowtie \{>, \geq\}$ and k is the optimal cost. We can decide whether there is a strategy that guarantees the optimal cost, i.e. an optimal strategy: if the initial winning interval is of the form *rsrc* $\geq k$ the answer is "yes," otherwise it is of the form *rsrc* $> k$ and there is a family of strategies that can ensure a cost $k + \varepsilon$ for any $\varepsilon > 0$. Still there is no optimal strategy;

– optimal strategies when they exist, may need cost information, i.e. the accumulated amount of resources consumed since the game started. In this sense, the clocks of the PTGA are not always sufficient to decide what to do to ensure winning at optimal cost, and we may need the cost information.

3.7.4. *Recent results and open problems*

Since these results were published, some new results about optimal cost for PTGA were obtained:

– in [BRI 05], the authors prove that the *Cost non-Zeno* the optimal cost computation problem is undecidable. This shows that the assumption we had made to prove termination of our algorithm is necessary. This proof was refined in [BOU 06c] and the most recent result is that for PTGA with three clocks the optimal cost computation problem is undecidable;

– in [BOU 06e], the authors prove that for turn-based PTGA with one clock, the optimal cost can be computed (3EXPTIME);

– finally, in [BOU 07], there is a proof that the optimal cost is computable for o-minimal automata.

An interesting open problem is the cost optimal safety control problem where the goal is to minimize the cost over infinite runs. This can be viewed as the generalization of the result in [BOU 08a, BOU 04a] (costs and rewards) to timed games with costs and rewards.

3.8. Efficient algorithms for controller synthesis

In the past 10 years, a lot of progress has been made in the design of efficient tools for the analysis (model-checking) of timed systems. Tools like KRONOS [YOV 97] or

UPPAAL [AMN 07, AMN 01] have become very efficient and widely used to check properties of TA but still no real efficient counterpart had been designed for timed games.

One of the main reasons behind the efficiency of tools like UPPAAL is the *on-the-fly* generation of the state space (this is also due to the use of efficient data structures in the implementation of the algorithms). Notice that *on-the-fly* algorithms were already crucial for model-checkers for finite communicating systems like SPIN [HOL 07].

The algorithm for computing controllers for safety timed games described in section 3.3.3 is based on *backwards* fix-point computations of the set of winning states [MAL 95, ASA 98, ALF 01]. We call this algorithm a *backward algorithm*. A drawback of a backward algorithm is that it does not take into account the fact that a state is reachable from the initial state or not. Backward computation may thus yield an enormous set of winning (symbolic) states most of which could be non-unreachable. Moreover, at each iteration, we compute the: pi operator for these unreachable states.

A more difficult problem is that for simple extensions of TA, it is very difficult and sometimes impossible to compute the controllable predecessor operator π. For example, if transitions are of the form $i := 2j + k$ (which is allowed in UPPAAL), computing the controllable predecessors of the symbolic state $(\ell, j \geq 0 \wedge k \geq 0)$ means collecting all the values of i such that $i = 2j + k$. This computation can be very expensive. In practice, if we start from a given initial state and given j and k, there might be a few reachable (admissible) values for j and k and consequently a few for i. Or at least, for each new value of i which is reached, we know the values of j and k that were used to obtain i.

A first step towards a solution is to compute the set of reachable states R. Then for each step of the iterative algorithm using π for computing winning states, take the intersection on the winning states and R. Even if these sets are represented with efficient data structures this can be very expensive and imply the computation of the whole state space of the system which may be unnecessary to check whether a winning strategy exists.

3.8.1. *On-the-fly algorithms*

To obtain a real *on-the-fly* algorithm for computing winning states, we should not have to compute the set R of reachable states before we compute the winning set of states but rather explore the symbolic state space as needed.

Regarding timed games, in [ALT 99, ALT 02], Karine Altisen and Stavros Tripakis proposed a (partially) on-the-fly method for solving timed games. This algorithm consists of first computing an abstraction of the region graph (which can be huge) and second using an *on-the-fly* algorithm on the abstraction. In this sense, this is not a real *on-the-fly* algorithm on the timed automaton as we first have to compute a finite abstraction of the set of reachable states.

To design a truly *on-the-fly* algorithm for the computation of winning states for reachability TGA, we start from the *on-the-fly* algorithm suggested by Liu and Smolka in [LIU 98] for linear-time model-checking of finite-state systems.

To obtain an on-the-fly algorithm for TGA, we can first extend the algorithm suggested by Liu and Smolka in [LIU 98] to the RCP for finite automata.

The idea for this on-the-fly algorithm for a finite game $\mathcal{A}$ is the following. We assume that some variables store two sets of transitions: ToExplore store the transitions that have been explored and ToBackPropagate store the transitions the target states of which has been declared winning. Moreover, the set of explored states R of $\mathcal{A}$ is also stored. For each state s of $\mathcal{A}$ already explored, we keep track of its *status*, which is either *winning* (this is the initial value for state s in GOAL) or *unknown* (this is the initial value for the other states).

To perform a step of the on-the-fly algorithm, we pick a transition (s, a, s') in one of the two sets ToExplore or ToBackPropagate and we do step (A1) for a transition from ToExplore and (A2) for a transition from ToBackPropagate:

– **(A1)** we explore (s, a, s'):

  – if s' is encountered for the first time, we add the outgoing transitions of s' to ToExplore; if s' is a winning state in GOAL, we update the status of s' to *winning* and otherwise set it to *unknown*;

  – if the status of s' is *winning*, we add (s, a, s') to the set ToBackPropagate; otherwise we just keep track of the fact that "the status of s depends on the status of s' via transition (s, a, s')";

– **(A2)** we backpropagate some information for the transition (s, a, s'). Actually, if it is in ToBackPropagate, this must be because the status of s' became *winning* recently, and we have to update the status of s accordingly:

  – either a is a controllable action, and in this case we update a counter $c(s)$. The meaning of $c(s)$ is "$c(s)$ is the number of controllable transitions from s leading to a winning state";

  – or a is uncontrollable and we increment a counter $u(s)$. The meaning of $u(s)$ is: "$u(s)$ is the number of uncontrollable transitions from s leading to a winning state";

– once $c(s)$ or $u(s)$ has been updated, the status of s may change. Let $U(s)$ be the total number of uncontrollable transitions originating from s in $\mathcal{A}$. If $c(s) \geq 1$ and $u(s) = U(s)$, s can be declared a *winning* state. The status of the states which depend on s has to be re-considered. Thus, we add to ToBackPropagate all the transitions (s'', a, s) such that the status of s'' depends on s via (s'', a, s).

An on-the-fly algorithm for reachability, games will process the sets ToExplore and ToBackPropagate in a random order. As soon as the status of the initial state of $\mathcal{A}$ is *winning*, we can stop the algorithm and the answer to the RCP is "yes" (moreover a winning strategy can be computed). This algorithm is linear in the size of $\mathcal{A}$. Indeed, each transition is processed at most twice: once in ToExplore and once in ToBackPropagate. To design the on-the-fly version for timed games, we consider *symbolic* states or zones which are unions of regions. Given a TGA and a symbolic state (ℓ, Z) we do a forward exploration of each transition from location ℓ to ℓ' by computing the discrete successors of Z and the time successors (constrained by ℓ' invariant). The status of the symbolic is then updated as for the untimed case. The on-the-fly algorithm for timed games together with the correctness proof are given in [CAS 05]. Actually, for timed games, the algorithm we give is not linear in the size of the region graph! We use zones to store symbolic states, and a region may be included in several zones. Our algorithm is thus not optimal as there is an algorithm which is linear in the size of the region graph [ALT 99]. However, this algorithm is really on-the-fly, and in practice gives good results, as witnessed by the experiments carried out with the games version of UPPAAL called UPPAAL-TIGA [BEH 07a], which is presented in Chapter 6.

3.8.2. *Recent results and open problems*

Using the previous algorithm, it is possible to compute *time optimal* controllers (cost associated with locations are all 1 and cost associated with discrete transitions are all 0). It suffices to give an upper bound on the maximum time to reach GOAL (see [CAS 05] for details). There is also a "safety games" version of the previous algorithm. In [CAS 07b], this on-the-fly algorithm has been adapted to games under *partial observation* (see section 3.9). An overview of the on-the-fly algorithms for timed games is given in [CAS 07a].

Some open problems still remain:

– on-the-fly algorithm could be extended to more general control objectives like repeated reachability (Büchi objective). This is really useful for timed games as Büchi objectives allow to enforce a controller to be non-Zeno;

– another direction is to extend the previous algorithm and find good data structures to solve the optimal cost reachability control problem (see section 3.7).

3.9. Partial observation

In the previous sections, we (tacitly) assumed that the controller had perfect knowledge of the environment, and that it could observe all the actions and states of the system. In practice, it might not always be the case: in some cases, the controller can only observe some of the actions of the environment (which are said to be *observable*), and can only have partial knowledge about the current state of the environment. However, we would like to be able, as much as possible, to control the environment: this problem is known as *control under partial observation* (referred to as PO in the following).

In this case, we keep assuming that the set of events is partitioned into two sets – controllable (Σ_c) and uncontrollable (Σ_u) – but only a subset Σ_u^o of Σ_u is *observable*. The controller is only able to observe a timed trace $(a_0, t_0)(a_1, t_1) \cdots (a_n, t_n)$ in $((\Sigma_c \cup \Sigma_u^o) \times \mathbb{R}_{\geq 0})^*$, and based on this information, it must decide which actions to play.

As regards strategies, we say that a strategy f is *trace-based*, if for any two runs ρ and ρ' yielding the same observation,[7] we have $f(\rho) = f(\rho')$.

The control problem under partial observation (PO-CP) aims at deciding whether there exists a winning *trace-based* strategy f (i.e., a *trace-based controller*, TBC). The PO-CP problem is then the following:

given a partially observable system S and an objective ϕ, does there   [PO-CP]
exists a TBC C such that $(S \parallel C) \models \phi$?

A survey on partial observation in timed systems is given in [BOU 05c]. In case the specification is given as a deterministic timed automaton, the PO-CP is undecidable [BOU 03]. Even if we restrict to the *safety* fragment, and if we are only interested in synthesizing non-Zeno controllers (non-Zeno-PO-SCP), the problem remains undecidable [BOU 06d].

However, by fixing in advance the resources available to the controller, the proof of [DSO 02] on control with external specifications (see section 3.6) can be extended to the partial observation setting. The result is then the following: if the resources available to the controller are fixed and if the control objective ϕ is given as a deterministic finite automaton, then the PO-CP is EXPTIME-complete [BOU 03].

Recent works [CHA 06, DEW 06] focus on partial observation of the *states* of a finite-state system. A timed extension of those works is given in [CAS 07b].

---

7. That is having the same projection on $((\Sigma_c \cup \Sigma_u^o) \times \mathbb{R}_{\geq 0})^*$.

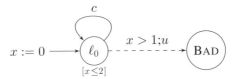

Figure 3.10. *A (safety) game in which winning requires Zenoness*

3.10. Changing game rules...

As mentioned above when defining TGAs, several semantics have been defined for timed games. We present below an alternative semantics, based on [ALF 03], and whose main advantage is that it can handle Zeno strategies.

Informally,[8] the main difference in the rules is the following: instead of choosing between waiting and performing an action, each player concurrently choose an action and *how long* they want to wait before performing that action. The rest is identical: the player with the shortest delay is selected, and his action is performed after delaying for the amount of time this player had chosen.

Though this might look like a minor change, this semantics has one important advantage: at each step, we know which player has chosen the shortest delay. That way, along Zeno runs, we are able to detect which player has been unfair by choosing converging delays. The other player is declared the winner in this case.[9]

Let us go back to our example given in section 3.4; see Figure 3.10. Consider the following strategy: in state (ℓ_0, x) with $x < 1$, the controller proposes a positive delay δ such that, after this delay, the value of x is of the form $(1 - 1/n)$ (this is always possible when $x < 1$). Using this value, the controller decides to perform action c. With our new semantics, this strategy is not winning: it suffices for the environment to play the strategy *"wait until $x = 1$ and perform action u"* to win, since the controller will be disqualified.

Unfortunately, this setting has drawbacks. For instance, even for simple reachability objectives, winning strategies might need memory: from state $(\ell_0, 0)$ of the game depicted on Figure 3.11(a), the controller has to play c_1 at date 0 (in order to satisfy the reachability condition). The play will then come back to the same state $(\ell_0, 0)$ after the second move. If the controller is memoryless, he will keep applying this strategy, which results in a Zeno run.

---

8. We do not give the precise definition of these games in this chapter, and refer the eager reader to [ALF 03, BRI 07, HEN 06b], where the details can be found.

9. It could be the case that both players are disqualified. There is no winner in this case.

(a) strategy requiring memory   (b) "surprise" strategy

Figure 3.11. *Examples of timed games*

Even though the players cannot rely on Zeno behaviors to win, there are examples where it is necessary to apply a "Zeno strategy" for a finite number of steps. Figure 3.11(b) depicts such an example: the objective in this game being to reach state ℓ_1, the controller will play action c at dates $1/2$, $3/4$, $7/8$, etc., always letting $1/2^{n+1}$ time units elapse between the nth and $(n + 1)$st step. This strategy is Zeno, but it is intended to be applied only for a finite number of times. Plays that are winning for the environment under that strategy are plays in which the environment itself always plays smaller delays. In that case, the environment loses.

Under such rules, most of the results presented in this chapter still hold. In particular, the notion of *controllable predecessors* can be extended to this setting, and zone-based arguments are still valid; that way, fix-point techniques can be developed, still resulting in exponential time algorithms.

Recent extensions of these models have been proposed, where all the players can act upon the action to be performed even if they do not choose the smallest delay. Those games extend classical *concurrent games* [ALU 02] with clocks: in this setting, each player will not only tell his preferred delay and action, but also the actions he would like to perform is a smaller delay were to be chosen by some other player. The resulting action would then depend on all the choices of all the players, even if their preferred delays were too large. In [BRI 07], the techniques and results presented above have been adapted to this framework.

3.11. Bibliography

[ALF 01] DE ALFARO L., HENZINGER T.A., MAJUMDAR R., "Symbolic algorithms for infinite-state games", *Proceedings of the 12th International Conference on Concurrency Theory (CONCUR'01)*, vol. 2154 of *Lecture Notes in Computer Science*, pp. 536–550, Springer, 2001.

[ALF 03] DE ALFARO L., FAËLLA M., HENZINGER T.A., MAJUMDAR R., STOELINGA M., "The element of surprise in timed games", *Proceedings of the 14th International Conference on Concurrency Theory (CONCUR'03)*, vol. 2761 of *Lecture Notes in Computer Science*, pp. 142–156, Springer, 2003.

[ALT 99] ALTISEN K., TRIPAKIS S., "On-the-fly controller synthesis for discrete and dense-time systems", *Proceedings of the World Congress on Formal Methods in the Development of Computing System (FM'99)*, vol. 1708 of *Lecture Notes in Computer Science*, pp. 233–252, Springer, 1999.

[ALT 02] ALTISEN K., TRIPAKIS S., "Tools for controller synthesis of timed systems", *Proceedings of 2nd Workshop on Real-Time Tools (RT-TOOLS'02)*, Uppsala University, Sweden 2002, [Proceeding published as Technical Report 2002-025].

[ALT 05] ALTISEN K., MARKEY N., REYNIER P.A., TRIPAKIS S., "Implémentabilité des automates temporisés", *Actes du 5ème Colloque sur la Modélisation des Systèmes Réactifs (MSR'05)*, pp. 395–406, Autrans, France, Hermès, October 2005.

[ALU 94] ALUR R., DILL D., "A theory of timed automata", *Theoretical Computer Science*, vol. 126, num. 2, 183–235, 1994.

[ALU 01] ALUR R., LA TORRE S., PAPPAS G.J., "Optimal paths in weighted timed automata", *Proceedings of the 4th International Workshop Hybrid Systems, Computation and Control (HSCC'01)*, vol. 2034 of *Lecture Notes in Computer Science*, pp. 49–62, Springer, 2001.

[ALU 02] ALUR R., HENZINGER T.A., KUPFERMAN O., "Alternating-time temporal logic", *Journal of the ACM*, vol. 49, 672–713, 2002.

[ALU 04] ALUR R., BERNADSKY M., MADHUSUDAN P., "Optimal reachability in weighted timed games", *Proceedings of the 31st International Colloquium on Automata, Languages and Programming (ICALP'04)*, vol. 3142 of *Lecture Notes in Computer Science*, pp. 122–133, Springer, 2004.

[AMN 01] AMNELL T., BEHRMANN G., BENGTSSON J., D'ARGENIO P.R., DAVID A., FEHNKER A., HUNE T., JEANNET B., LARSEN K.G., MÖLLER O., PETTERSSON P., WEISE C., YI W., "UPPAAL – now, next, and future", *Proceedings of Modelling and Verification of Parallel Processes (MOVEP2k)*, vol. 2067 of *Lecture Notes in Computer Science*, pp. 99–124, Springer, 2001.

[AMN 07] AMNELL T., BEHRMANN G., BENGTSSON J., D'ARGENIO P.R., DAVID A., FEHNKER A., HUNE T., JEANNET B., LARSEN K.G., MÖLLER O., PETTERSSON P., WEISE C., YI W., "UPPAAL", 2007, http://www.uppaal.com.

[ARN 03] ARNOLD A., VINCENT A., WALUKIEWICZ I., "Games for synthesis of controllers with partial observation", *Theoretical Computer Science*, vol. 1, num. 303, 7–34, 2003.

[ASA 98] ASARIN E., MALER O., PNUELI A., SIFAKIS J., "Controller synthesis for timed Automata", *Proceedings of IFAC Symposium on System Structure and Control*, pp. 469–474, Elsevier Science, 1998.

[ASA 99] ASARIN E., MALER O., "As soon as possible: time optimal control for timed automata", *Proceedings of the 2nd International Workshop on Hybrid Systems, Computation and Control (HSCC'99)*, vol. 1569 of *Lecture Notes in Computer Science*, pp. 19–30, Springer, 1999.

[BEH 01a] BEHRMANN G., FEHNKER A., HUNE T., LARSEN K.G., PETTERSSON P., ROMIJN J., VAANDRAGER F., "Efficient guiding towards cost-optimality in UPPAAL",

Proceedings of the 7th International Conference on Tools and Algorithms for the Construction and Analysis of Systems (TACAS'01), vol. 2031 of *Lecture Notes in Computer Science*, pp. 174–188, Springer, 2001.

[BEH 01b] BEHRMANN G., FEHNKER A., HUNE T., LARSEN K.G., PETTERSSON P., ROMIJN J., VAANDRAGER F., "Minimum-cost reachability for priced timed automata", *Proceedings of the 4th International Workshop Hybrid Systems, Computation and Control (HSCC'01)*, vol. 2034 of *Lecture Notes in Computer Science*, pp. 147–161, Springer, 2001.

[BEH 07a] BEHRMANN G., COUGNARD A., DAVID A., FLEURY E., LARSEN K.G., LIME D., "UPPAAL-TiGA", 2007, http://www.cs.aau.dk/~adavid/tiga/.

[BEH 07b] BEHRMANN G., LARSEN K.G., RASMUSSEN J.I., "UPPAAL-CORA", 2007, http://www.cs.aau.dk/~behrmann/cora/.

[BOU 03] BOUYER P., D'SOUZA D., MADHUSUDAN P., PETIT A., "Timed control with partial observability", *Proceedings of the 15th International Conference on Computer Aided Verification (CAV'03)*, vol. 2725 of *Lecture Notes in Computer Science*, pp. 180–192, Boulder, USA, Springer, July 2003.

[BOU 04a] BOUYER P., BRINKSMA E., LARSEN K.G., "Staying alive as cheaply as possible", *Proceedings of the 7th International Conference Hybrid Systems, Computation and Control (HSCC'04)*, vol. 2993 of *Lecture Notes in Computer Science*, pp. 203–218, Philadelphia, USA, Springer, March 2004.

[BOU 04b] BOUYER P., CASSEZ F., FLEURY E., LARSEN K.G., "Optimal strategies in priced timed game automata," BRICS Reports Series num. RS-04-0, BRICS, Aalborg, Denmark, February 2004, ISSN 0909-0878.

[BOU 04c] BOUYER P., CASSEZ F., FLEURY E., LARSEN K.G., "Optimal strategies in priced timed game automata", *Proceedings of the 24th Conference on Foundations of Software Technology and Theoretical Computer Science (FSTTCS'04)*, vol. 3328 of *Lecture Notes in Computer Science*, pp. 148–160, Chennai, India, Springer, December 2004.

[BOU 05a] BOUYER P., CASSEZ F., FLEURY E., LARSEN K.G., "Synthesis of optimal strategies using HyTech", *Proceedings of the Workshop on Games in Design and Verification (GDV'04)*, vol. 119 of *Electronic Notes in Theoretical Computer Science*, pp. 11–31, Boston, USA, Elsevier Science, February 2005.

[BOU 05b] BOUYER P., CASSEZ F., LAROUSSINIE F., "Modal logics for timed control", *Proceedings of 16th International Conference on Concurrency Theory (CONCUR'05)*, vol. 3653 of *Lecture Notes in Computer Science*, pp. 81–94, San Francisco, USA, Springer, 2005.

[BOU 05c] BOUYER P., CHEVALIER F., KRICHEN M., TRIPAKIS S., "Observation partielle des systèmes temporisés", *Actes du 5ème Colloque sur la Modélisation des Systèmes Réactifs (MSR'05)*, pp. 381–393, Autrans, France, Hermès, October 2005.

[BOU 06a] BOUYER P., BOZZELLI L., CHEVALIER F., "Controller synthesis for MTL specifications", *Proceedings of 17th International Conference on Concurrency Theory (CONCUR'06)*, vol. 4137 of *Lecture Notes in Computer Science*, pp. 450–464, Bonn, Germany, Springer, August 2006.

[BOU 06b] BOUYER P., BRIHAYE T., CHEVALIER F., "Control in o-minimal hybrid systems", *Proceedings of 21st IEEE Symposium on Logic in Computer Science (LICS'06)*, pp. 367–378, Seattle, USA, IEEE Computer Society Press, August 2006.

[BOU 06c] BOUYER P., BRIHAYE T., MARKEY N., "Improved undecidability results on weighted timed automata", *Information Processing Letters*, vol. 98, num. 5, 188–194, June 2006.

[BOU 06d] BOUYER P., CHEVALIER F., "On the control of timed and hybrid systems", *EATCS Bulletin*, vol. 89, pp. 79–96, European Association for Theoretical Computer Science, June 2006.

[BOU 06e] BOUYER P., LARSEN K.G., MARKEY N., RASMUSSEN J.I., "Almost optimal strategies in one-clock priced timed automata", *Proceedings of 26th Conference on Foundations of Software Technology and Theoretical Computer Science (FSTTCS'06)*, vol. 4337 of *Lecture Notes in Computer Science*, pp. 345–356, Kolkatta, India, Springer, December 2006.

[BOU 06f] BOUYER P., MARKEY N., REYNIER P.A., "Robust model-checking of linear-time properties in timed automata", *Proceedings of the 7th Latin American Symposium on Theoretical Informatics (LATIN'06)*, vol. 3887 of *Lecture Notes in Computer Science*, pp. 238–249, Valdivia, Chile, Springer, March 2006.

[BOU 07] BOUYER P., BRIHAYE T., CHEVALIER F., "Weighted O-minimal hybrid systems are more decidable than weighted timed automata!", *Proceedings of Symposium on Logical Foundations of Computer Science (LFCS'07)*, Lecture Notes in Computer Science, New-York, USA, Springer, June 2007.

[BOU 08a] BOUYER P., BRINKSMA E., LARSEN K.G., "Optimal infinite scheduling for multi-priced timed automata", *Formal Methods in System Design*, vol. 32, num. 1, 2–23, February 2008.

[BOU 08b] BOUYER P., MARKEY N., REYNIER P.A., "Robust analysis of timed automata *via* channel machines", *Proceedings of the 11th International Conference on Foundations of Software Science and Computation Structures (FoSSaCS'08)*, vol. 4962 of *Lecture Notes in Computer Science*, pp. 157–171, Budapest, Hungary, Springer, March 2008.

[BRI 04] BRIHAYE T., BRUYÈRE V., RASKIN J.F., "Model-checking for weighted timed automata", *Proceedings of the Joint International Conferences on Formal Modelling and Analysis of Timed Systems (FORMATS'04) and Formal Techniques in Real-Time and Fault-Tolerant Systems (FTRTFT'04)*, vol. 3253 of *Lecture Notes in Computer Science*, pp. 277–292, Springer, 2004.

[BRI 05] BRIHAYE T., BRUYÈRE V., RASKIN J.F., "On optimal timed strategies", *Proceedings of the 3rd International Conference on Formal Modelling and Analysis of Timed Systems (FORMATS'05)*, vol. 3829 of *Lecture Notes in Computer Science*, pp. 49–64, Springer, 2005.

[BRI 07] BRIHAYE T., LAROUSSINIE F., MARKEY N., OREIBY G., "Timed concurrent game structures", *International Conference on Concurrency Theory (CONCUR'07)*, vol. 4703 of *Lecture Notes in Computer Science*, pp. 445–459, Springer, 2007.

[CAS 02] CASSEZ F., HENZINGER T.A., RASKIN J.F., "A comparison of control problems for timed and hybrid systems", *Proceedings of the 5th International Workshop on Hybrid Systems, Computation and Control (HSCC'02)*, vol. 2289 of *Lecture Notes in Computer Science*, pp. 134–148, Springer, 2002.

[CAS 05] CASSEZ F., DAVID A., FLEURY E., LARSEN K.G., LIME D., "Efficient on-the-fly algorithms for the analysis of timed games", *Proceedings of the 16th International Conference on Concurrency Theory (CONCUR'05)*, vol. 3653 of *Lecture Notes in Computer Science*, pp. 66–80, San Francisco, USA, Springer, August 2005.

[CAS 07a] CASSEZ F., "Efficient on-the-fly algorithms for partially observable timed games", *Proceedings of the 5th International Conference on Formal Modeling and Analysis of Timed Systems (FORMATS'07)*, vol. 4763 of *Lecture Notes in Computer Science*, pp. 5–24, Springer, 2007.

[CAS 07b] CASSEZ F., DAVID A., LARSEN K.G., LIME D., RASKIN J.F., "Timed control with observation based and stuttering invariant strategies", *Proceedings of the 5th International Symposium on Automated Technology for Verification and Analysis (ATVA'07)*, vol. 4762 of *Lecture Notes in Computer Science*, pp. 307–321, Springer, 2007.

[CHA 06] CHATTERJEE K., DOYEN L., HENZINGER T.A., RASKIN J.F., "Algorithms for omega-regular games with imperfect information", *Proceedings of the 20th International Workshop on Computer Science Logic (CSL'06)*, pp. 287–302, 2006.

[DEW 04a] DE WULF M., DOYEN L., MARKEY N., RASKIN J.F., "Robustness and implementability of timed automata", *Proceedings of the Joint International Conferences on Formal Modelling and Analysis of Timed Systems (FORMATS'04) and Formal Techniques in Real-Time and Fault-Tolerant Systems (FTRTFT'04)*, vol. 3253 of *Lecture Notes in Computer Science*, pp. 118–133, Springer, 2004.

[DEW 04b] DE WULF M., DOYEN L., RASKIN J.F., "Almost ASAP semantics: from timed models to Timed Implementations", *Proceedings of the 7th International Workshop on Hybrid Systems, Computation and Control (HSCC'04)*, vol. 2993 of *Lecture Notes in Computer Science*, pp. 296–310, Springer, 2004.

[DEW 05a] DE WULF M., DOYEN L., RASKIN J.F., "Almost ASAP semantics: from timed models to timed implementations", *Formal Aspects of Computing*, vol. 17, num. 3, pp. 319–341, Springer, 2005.

[DEW 05b] DE WULF M., DOYEN L., RASKIN J.F., "Systematic implementation of real-time models", *Proceedings of the International Symposium on Formal Methods Europe (FM'05)*, vol. 3582 of *Lecture Notes in Computer Science*, pp. 139–156, Springer, 2005.

[DEW 06] DE WULF M., DOYEN L., RASKIN J., "A lattice theory for solving games of imperfect information", *Proceedings of the 9th International Workshop Hybrid Systems, Computation and Control (HSCC'06)*, pp. 153–168, 2006.

[DOY 07] DOYEN L., "Robust parametric reachability for timed automata", *Information Processing Letters*, vol. 102, num. 5, pp. 208–213, Elsevier Science, 2007.

[DSO 02] D'SOUZA D., MADHUSUDAN P., "Timed control synthesis for external specifications", *Proceedings of 19th International Symposium on Theoretical Aspects of Computer Science (STACS'02)*, vol. 2285 of *Lecture Notes in Computer Science*, pp. 571–582, Springer, 2002.

[FAE 02a] FAËLLA M., LA TORRE S., MURANO A., "Automata-theoretic decision of timed games", *Proceedings of the 3rd International Workshop on Verification, Model Checking, and Abstract Interpretation (VMCAI'02)*, vol. 2294 of *Lecture Notes in Computer Science*, pp. 240–254, Venice, Italy, Springer, January 2002.

[FAE 02b] FAËLLA M., LA TORRE S., MURANO A., "Dense real-time games", *Proceedings of 17th IEEE Symposium on Logic in Computer Science (LICS'02)*, pp. 167–176, IEEE Computer Society Press, 2002.

[FRE 05] FREHSE G., "PHAVer: Algorithmic verification of hybrid systems past HyTech", *HSCC'05*, vol. 3414 of *LNCS*, pp. 258–273, Springer, 2005.

[HEN 96] HENZINGER T.A., "The theory of hybrid automata", *Proceedings of the 11th IEEE Symposium on Logic in Computer Science (LICS'96)*, pp. 278–292, 1996.

[HEN 97] HENZINGER T.A., HO P.H., WONG-TOI H., "HYTECH: a model-checker for hybrid systems", *Journal on Software Tools for Technology Transfer*, vol. 1, num. 1–2, pp. 110–122, 1997.

[HEN 98] HENZINGER T.A., KOPKE P.W., PURI A., VARAIYA P., "What's decidable about hybrid automata?", *Journal of Computer and System Sciences*, vol. 57, pp. 94–124, Elsevier Science, 1998.

[HEN 99a] HENZINGER T.A., HOROWITZ B., MAJUMDAR R., "Rectangular hybrid games", *Proceedings of 10th International Conference on Concurrency Theory (CONCUR'99)*, vol. 1664 of *Lecture Notes in Computer Science*, pp. 320–335, Springer, 1999.

[HEN 99b] HENZINGER T.A., KOPKE P.W., "Discrete-time control for rectangular hybrid automata", *Theoretical Computer Science*, vol. 221, 369–392, 1999.

[HEN 06a] HENZINGER T.A., PRABHU V.S., "Timed alternating-time temporal logic", *Proceedings of 4th International Conferences on Formal Modelling and Analysis of Timed Systems, (FORMATS'06)*, vol. 4202 of *Lecture Notes in Computer Science*, pp. 1–17, Springer, September 2006.

[HEN 06b] HENZINGER T.A., PRABHU V.S., "Timed alternating-time temporal logic", *Proceedings of the 4th International Conferences on Formal Modelling and Analysis of Timed Systems, (FORMATS'06)*, vol. 4202 of *Lecture Notes in Computer Science*, pp. 1–17, Springer, September 2006.

[HOF 92] HOFFMANN G., WONG-TOI H., "The input-output control of real-time discrete-event systems", *Proceedings of the 13th Annual Real-time Systems Symposium*, pp. 256–265, IEEE Computer Society Press, 1992.

[HOL 07] HOLTZMANN G., "SPIN", 2007, http://spinroot.com.

[KOY 90] KOYMANS R., "Specifying real-time properties with metric temporal logic", *Real-Time Systems*, vol. 2, num. 4, 255–299, 1990.

[LAF 00] LAFFERRIERE G., PAPPAS G., SASTRY S., "O-minimal hybrid systems", *Mathematics of Control Signals and Systems*, vol. 13, num. 1, 1–21, 2000.

[LAR 98] LAROUSSINIE F., LARSEN K.G., "CMC: a tool for compositional model-checking of real-time systems", *Proceedings of the IFIP Joint International Conference on Formal Description Techniques & Protocol Specification, Testing, and Verification (FORTE-PSTV'98)*, pp. 439–456, Kluwer Academic, 1998.

[LAR 05] LAROUSSINIE F., "CMC", 2005, http://www.lsv.ens-cachan.fr/~fl/cmcweb.html.

[LAR 06] LAROUSSINIE F., MARKEY N., OREIBY G., "Model checking timed ATL for durational concurrent game structures", *Proceedings of the 4th International Conference on Formal Modelling and Analysis of Timed Systems (FORMATS'06)*, vol. 4202 of *Lecture Notes in Computer Science*, pp. 245–259, Paris, France, Springer, September 2006.

[LAT 02] LA TORRE S., MUKHOPADHYAY S., MURANO A., "Optimal-reachability and control for acyclic weighted timed automata", *Proceedings of 2nd IFIP International Conference on Theoretical Computer Science (TCS'02)*, vol. 223 of *IFIP Conference Proceedings*, pp. 485–497, Kluwer, 2002.

[LIU 98] LIU X., SMOLKA S.A., "Simple linear-time algorithm for minimal fixed points", *Proceedings of the 26th International Conference on Automata, Languages and Programming (ICALP'98)*, vol. 1443 of *Lecture Notes in Computer Science*, pp. 53–66, Aalborg, Denmark, Springer, 1998.

[MAL 95] MALER O., PNUELI A., SIFAKIS J., "On the synthesis of discrete controllers for timed systems", *Proceedings of the 12th Symposium on Theoretical Aspects of Computer Science (STACS'95)*, vol. 900 of *Lecture Notes in Computer Science*, pp. 229–242, Springer, 1995.

[MAR 75] MARTIN D.A., "Borel determinacy", *Annals of Mathematics*, vol. 102, num. 2, 363–371, 1975.

[MCN 93] MCNAUGHTON R., "Infinite games played on finite graphs", *Annals of Pure and Applied Logic*, vol. 65, num. 2, 149–184, Elsevier Science, 1993.

[MER 74] MERLIN P., A study of the recoverability of computing systems, PhD thesis, Department of Information and Computer Science, University of California, Irvine, CA, 1974.

[RAM 87] RAMADGE P.J., WONHAM W.M., "Supervisory control of a class of discrete event processes", *SIAM Journal of Control and Optimization*, vol. 25, num. 1, 1202–1218, 1987.

[RAM 89] RAMADGE P.J., WONHAM W.M., "The control of discrete event systems", *Proceedings of the IEEE*, vol. 77, num. 1, pp. 81–98, 1989.

[RIE 03] RIEDWEG S., PINCHINAT S., "Quantified Mu-calculus for control synthesis", *Proceedings of the 28th International Symposium on Mathematical Foundations of Computer Science (MFCS'03)*, vol. 2747 of *Lecture Notes in Computer Science*, pp. 642–651, Springer, 2003.

[SCH 99] SCHNOEBELEN P., BÉRARD B., BIDOIT M., LAROUSSINIE F., PETIT A., *Vérification de logiciels : Techniques et outils de model-checking*, Vuibert, Paris, 1999.

[THO 95] THOMAS W., "On the synthesis of strategies in infinite games", *Proceedings of the 12th Annual Symposium on Theoretical Aspects of Computer Science (STACS'95)*, vol. 900 of *Lecture Notes in Computer Science*, pp. 1–13, Springer, 1995.

[YOV 97] YOVINE S., "KRONOS: A verification tool for real-time systems", *Journal of Software Tools for Technology Transfer*, vol. 1, num. 1–2, 123–133, Springer, 1997.

Chapter 4

Fault Diagnosis of Timed Systems

In this chapter, we review the main results pertaining to the problem of fault diagnosis of timed automata. Timed automata are introduced in Chapters 1 and 2 in this book, and the reader not familiar with this model is invited to read them first.

4.1. Introduction

Many computerized systems (sometimes embedded) supervise/control devices or appliances the failure of which can be life-threatening (airplanes, railways, nuclear plants, medical devices etc.) or extremely expensive (Ariane 5 rocket, telephone networks etc.).

For more than two decades, researchers have tried to develop tools and algorithms to increase the dependability of computerized systems. All verification techniques can be gathered under the generic name of *formal methods*, the most famous and successful one certainly being *model checking* [SCH 99], which consists of building a mathematical model of a system S, and then checking that it satisfies a given property ϕ. It is sometimes even possible to *synthesize* a *controller* C (see Chapter 3) for S, in order to ensure that the controlled system $C(S)$ satisfies a property ϕ.

The model checking and controller synthesis techniques assume that we can build a complete model of the system (and the controller), and everything is observable (controller synthesis under partial observation can also be solved for some particular

Chapter written by Franck CASSEZ and Stavros TRIPAKIS.

properties for timed automata). Also it might be that no controller exists or it is not possible to compute one, to ensure that a system $C(S)$ satisfies a property ϕ.

Still we might be able to detect when property ϕ is violated. An alternative approach to verification is thus to try and detect erroneous or *faulty* behavior, and in case a fault occurs, to trigger a fault handler (shut down the system, restart from a particular state etc.).

The notion of *fault diagnosis* for discrete event systems (DES) was formalized in the mid-1990s in [SAM 95, SAM 96]. The two previous papers introduced the formal definitions of fault diagnosis for DES and have been followed by numerous papers on the subject. The framework of fault diagnosis for DES is the following:

– we assume that a formal model S of the system to monitor is available. The *faults* are specified in S by special events $f_1, \ldots, f_n$. Thus, we have a formal model of S with the faults, but the faults cannot be observed at runtime (sensors can only observe a subset of the events of the system, and faults are not observable); formally the events in S are partitioned into a set of observable events and a set of unobservable events (which includes $f_1, \ldots, f_n$);

– fault diagnosis consists of detecting faulty behaviors – which are behaviors in which a fault event occurs – by observing only the observable events (and of course assuming that we have a complete knowledge of the formal model of S). A fault should be detected in a bounded amount of time after it occurred and the bounded fault diagnosis problem asks the following: "Is it possible to detect a fault f_i within a maximum of Δ time units after it occurred?". For DES, one time unit corresponds to firing a discrete transition.

When timing constraints are part of the system description, S can be modeled as a timed automaton [ALU 94a]. The fault diagnosis problem for timed automata has been introduced in [TRI 02] and further studied in [BOU 05]. Some open problems still remain and are listed in section 4.6.

In section 4.2, we briefly recall the basic notions of timed languages and timed automata. For a detailed introduction to these concepts we refer the reader to Chapters 1 and 2 in this book.

In section 4.3, we define the notion of *diagnoser* which is an observer the purpose of which is to detect faults. We also introduce the fault diagnosis problems studied in the following sections, together with a necessary and sufficient condition for *diagnosability*.

Section 4.4 is devoted to fault diagnosis of DES. The algorithms presented in this section are extended to timed automata in section 4.5.

4.2. Notations

$\mathbb{B} = \{\top, \bot\}$ is the set of Boolean values, $\mathbb{N}$ is the set of natural numbers, $\mathbb{Z}$ is the set of integers and $\mathbb{Q}$ is the set of rational numbers. $\mathbb{R}$ is the set of real numbers and $\mathbb{R}_{\geq 0}$ is the set of non-negative real numbers. Let X be a finite set of variables called *clocks*. A *clock valuation* is a mapping $v : X \to \mathbb{R}_{\geq 0}$. $\mathbb{R}^X_{\geq 0}$ is the set of clock valuations over X. We write $\mathbf{0}_X$ for the *zero* valuation where all the clocks in X are set to 0 (we use $\mathbf{0}$ when X is clear from the context). Given $\delta \in \mathbb{R}$, $v + \delta$ denotes the valuation defined by $(v + \delta)(x) = v(x) + \delta$. We let $\mathcal{C}(X)$ be the set of *convex constraints* on X, i.e., the set of conjunctions of constraints of the form $x \bowtie c$ with $c \in \mathbb{Z}$ and $\bowtie \in \{\leq, <, =, >, \geq\}$. Given a constraint $g \in \mathcal{C}(X)$ and a valuation v, we write $v \models g$ if g is satisfied by the valuation v. Given a set $R \subseteq X$ and a valuation v of the clocks in X, $v[R]$ is the valuation defined by $v[R](x) = v(x)$ if $x \notin R$ and $v[R](x) = 0$ otherwise.

4.2.1. *Timed words and timed languages*

Let Σ be a finite alphabet. The set of finite (resp. infinite) words over Σ is Σ^* (resp. Σ^ω) and we let $\Sigma^\infty = \Sigma^* \cup \Sigma^\omega$. A *language* L is any subset of Σ^∞. A finite (resp. infinite) *timed word* over Σ is a word in $(\mathbb{R}_{\geq 0}.\Sigma)^*.\mathbb{R}_{\geq 0}$ (resp. $(\mathbb{R}_{\geq 0}.\Sigma)^\omega$). In this chapter, we write timed words as $0.4\ a\ 1.0\ b\ 2.7\ c \cdots$ where the real values are the durations elapsed between two letters: thus c occurs at global time 4.1. We let *Duration(w)* be the duration of a timed word w which is defined to be the sum of the durations ($\mathbb{R}_{\geq 0}$) which appear in w; if this sum is infinite, the duration is ∞. Note that the duration of an infinite word can be finite, and such words which contain an infinite number of letters, are called *Zeno* words. We let *Unt(w)* be the *untimed* version of w obtained by erasing all the durations in w. An example of untiming is $Unt(0.4\ a\ 1.0\ b\ 2.7\ c) = abc$.

$TW^*(\Sigma)$ is the set of finite timed words over Σ, $TW^\omega(\Sigma)$, the set of infinite timed words and $TW^\infty(\Sigma) = TW^*(\Sigma) \cup TW^\omega(\Sigma)$. A *timed language* is any subset of $TW^\infty(\Sigma)$.

Let $\pi_{/\Sigma'}$ be the projection of timed words of $TW^\infty(\Sigma)$ over timed words of $TW^\infty(\Sigma')$. When projecting a timed word w on a sub-alphabet $\Sigma' \subseteq \Sigma$, the durations elapsed between two events are set accordingly: for instance $\pi_{/\{a,c\}}(0.4\ a\ 1.0\ b\ 2.7\ c) = 0.4\ a\ 3.7\ c$ (note that projection erases some letters but updates the time elapsed between two letters). Given a timed language L, we let $Unt(L) = \{Unt(w) \mid w \in L\}$. Given $\Sigma' \subseteq \Sigma$, $\pi_{/\Sigma'}(L) = \{\pi_{/\Sigma'}(w) \mid w \in L\}$.

4.2.2. *Timed automata*

Timed automata are finite automata extended with real-valued clocks to specify timing constraints between occurrences of events. For a detailed presentation of the fundamental results for timed automata, the reader is referred to the seminal paper of Alur and Dill [ALU 94a]. In this chapter, we consider timed automata with a *silent* or *invisible* action, denoted by τ, and we let $\Sigma_\tau = \Sigma \cup \{\tau\}$.

DEFINITION 4.1(TIMED AUTOMATON, TA).– A *Timed Automaton* A is a tuple $(L, l_0, X, \Sigma_\tau, E, Inv, F, R)$ where:

   – L is a finite set of *locations*;

   – l_0 is the *initial location*;

   – X is a finite set of *clocks*;

   – Σ is a finite set of *actions*;

   – $E \subseteq L \times \mathcal{C}(X) \times \Sigma_\tau \times 2^X \times L$ is a finite set of *transitions*; in a transition (ℓ, g, a, r, ℓ'), g is the *guard*, a the *action*, and r the *reset* set;

   – $Inv \in \mathcal{C}(X)^L$ associates with each location an *invariant*; as usual we require the invariants to be conjunctions of constraints of the form $x \preceq c$ with $\preceq \in \{<, \leq\}$;

   – $F \subseteq L$ and $R \subseteq L$ are respectively the *final* and *repeated* sets of locations. $\qquad\square$

In the following, we often omit the sets R and F in TA and this implicitly means $F = L$ and $R = \emptyset$.

The semantics of a timed automaton is a timed transition system as described in Chapters 1 and 2 . A *run* ρ of A from (q_0, v_0) is a sequence of the form:

$$\rho = (q_0, v_0) \xrightarrow{\delta_0} (q_0, v_0 + \delta_0) \xrightarrow{a_1} (q_1, v_1) \cdots \xrightarrow{a_n} (q_n, v_n) \xrightarrow{\delta_n} (q_n, v_n + \delta_n) \cdots$$

where $q_i \in L$, $v_i : X \to \mathbb{R}_{\geq 0}$ is a clock valuation, $a_i \in \Sigma$ and $\delta_i \in \mathbb{R}_{\geq 0}$. The set of finite (resp. infinite) runs in A from a state s is denoted $Runs^*(s, A)$ (resp. $Runs^\omega(s, A)$) and we let $Runs^*(A) = Runs^*((l_0, \mathbf{0}), A)$ and $Runs^\omega(A) = Runs^\omega((l_0, \mathbf{0}), A)$. The set of runs of A is $Runs(A) = Runs^*(A) \cup Runs^\omega(A)$. If ρ is finite and ends in s_n, we define $last(\rho) = s_n$. Because of the denseness of the time domain, the unfolding of A as a graph is infinite (uncountable number of states and delay edges).

The *trace*, $tr(\rho)$, of a run ρ is the timed word $\delta_0 a_0 \delta_1 a_1 \cdots a_n \delta_n \cdots$. The duration of the run ρ is $Duration(\rho) = Duration(tr(\rho))$. For $V \subseteq Runs(A)$, we let $Tr(V) = \{tr(\rho) \mid \varrho \in V\}$, which is the set of traces of the runs in V.

A finite (resp. infinite) timed word w is *accepted* by A if $w = \pi_{/\Sigma}(tr(\rho))$ for some finite run ρ of A that ends in an F-location (resp. a infinite run that reaches infinitely often an R-location). $\mathcal{L}^*(A)$ (resp. $\mathcal{L}^\omega(A)$) is the set of traces of finite (resp. infinite) timed words accepted by A, and $\mathcal{L}(A) = \mathcal{L}^*(A) \cup \mathcal{L}^\omega(A)$ is the set of timed words accepted by A.

4.2.3. *Region graph of a TA*

The *region graph* $RG(A)$ of a TA (A) is a finite quotient of the infinite graph of A, which is time-abstract bisimilar to A [ALU 94a] (see Chapter 2 for a formal definition of the region graph). It is a finite automaton on the alphabet $E' = E \cup \{\tau\}$. The states of $RG(A)$ are pairs (ℓ, r) where $\ell \in L$ is a location of A and r is a *region* of $\mathbb{R}^X_{\geq 0}$. More generally, the edges of the graph are tuples (s, t, s') where s, s' are states of $RG(A)$ and $t \in E'$. Genuine unobservable moves of A labeled τ are labeled by tuples of the form $(s, (g, \tau, R), s')$ in $RG(A)$. An edge (g, λ, R) in the region graph corresponds to a discrete transition of A with guard g, action λ and reset set R. A τ move in $RG(A)$ stands for a delay move to the time-successor region. The initial state of $RG(A)$ is $(l_0, \mathbf{0})$. A final (resp. repeated) state of $RG(A)$ is a state (ℓ, r) with $\ell \in F$ (resp. $\ell \in R$). A fundamental property of the region graph [ALU 94a] is:

THEOREM 4.1([ALU 94A]).– $\mathcal{L}(RG(A)) = Unt(\mathcal{L}(A))$.

In other words:

1) if w is accepted by $RG(A)$, then there is a timed word v with $Unt(v) = w$ s.t. v is accepted by A.

2) if v is accepted by A, then $Unt(w)$ is accepted by $RG(A)$.

The (maximum) size of the region graph is exponential in the number of clocks and in the maximum constant of the automaton A (see [ALU 94a]): $|RG(A)| = |L| \cdot |X|! \cdot 2^{|X|} \cdot K^{|X|}$ where K is the largest constant used in A.

4.2.4. *Product of TA*

The product of TA is defined in a standard way, keeping in mind that the τ actions do not synchronize.

DEFINITION 4.2(PRODUCT OF TA).– Let $A_i = (L_i, l_0^i, X_i, \Sigma_\tau^i, E_i, Inv_i)$, $i \in \{1, 2\}$, be two TA s.t. $X_1 \cap X_2 = \varnothing$. The *product* of A_1 and A_2 is the TA $A_1 \times A_2 = (L, l_0, X, \Sigma_\tau, E, Inv)$ given by:

- $L = L_1 \times L_2$;
- $l_0 = (l_0^1, l_0^2)$;
- $\Sigma = \Sigma^1 \cup \Sigma^2$;
- $X = X_1 \cup X_2$; and

- $E \subseteq L \times \mathcal{C}(X) \times \Sigma_\tau \times 2^X \times L$ and $((\ell_1, \ell_2), g_{1,2}, \sigma, r, (\ell'_1, \ell'_2)) \in E$ if:
  - either $\sigma \in (\Sigma_1 \cap \Sigma_2) \setminus \{\tau\}$, and (i) $(\ell_k, g_k, \sigma, r_k, \ell'_k) \in E_k$ for $k = 1$ and $k = 2$; (ii) $g_{1,2} = g_1 \wedge g_2$, and (iii) $r = r_1 \cup r_2$;
  - or for $k = 1$ or $k = 2$, $\sigma \in (\Sigma_k \setminus \Sigma_{3-k}) \cup \{\tau\}$, and (i) $(\ell_k, g_k, \sigma, r_k, \ell'_k) \in E_k$; (ii) $g_{1,2} = g_k$, and (iii) $r = r_k$;
- and finally $Inv(\ell_1, \ell_2) = Inv(\ell_1) \wedge Inv(\ell_2)$. $\square$

4.2.5. *Timed automata with faults*

To model timed systems with faults, we use timed automata on the alphabet $\Sigma_{\tau,f} = \Sigma_\tau \cup \{f\}$ where f is the *faulty* (unobservable) event. We only consider one type of fault here, but the results we give are valid for various types of faults $\{f_1, f_2, \cdots, f_n\}$: indeed solving the various types of diagnosability problem amounts to solving n one-type diagnosability problems [YOO 02]. Other unobservable events are abstracted as a τ action (one τ suffices as these events are all unobservable).

The system we want to supervise is given by a timed automaton $A = (L, l_0, X, \Sigma_{\tau,f}, E, Inv)$. Figure 4.1 gives an example of such a system (α is a positive integer parameter). Invariants in the automaton $\mathcal{A}(\alpha)$ are written within square brackets as in $[x \leq 3]$.

Let $\Delta \in \mathbb{N}$. A run ρ of A such that

$$\rho = (\ell_0, v_0) \xrightarrow{\delta_0} (\ell_0, v_0 + \delta_0) \xrightarrow{a_1} (\ell_1, v_1) \cdots$$
$$\cdots \xrightarrow{a_{n-1}} (\ell_n, v_n) \xrightarrow{\delta_n} (\ell_n, v_n + \delta_n) \cdots$$

is Δ-faulty, if: (1) there is an index i s.t. $a_i = f$; and (2) the duration of the run $\rho' = (\ell_i, v_i) \xrightarrow{\delta_i} \cdots \xrightarrow{\delta_n} (\ell_n, v_n + \delta_n) \cdots$ is larger than Δ. We let *Faulty*$_{\geq \Delta}(A)$ be

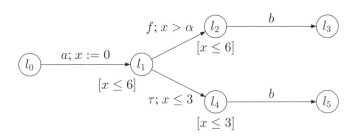

Figure 4.1. *Automaton* $\mathcal{A}(\alpha)$

the set of Δ-faulty runs of A. Note that by definition, if $\Delta' \geq \Delta$ then $Faulty_{\geq\Delta'}(A) \subseteq Faulty_{\geq\Delta}(A)$. We let $Faulty(A) = \cup_{\Delta \geq 0} Faulty_{\geq\Delta}(A) = Faulty_{\geq 0}(A)$ be the set of faulty runs of A, and $NonFaulty(A) = Runs(A) \setminus Faulty(A)$ be the set of non-faulty runs of A. Finally, we let

$$Faulty^{tr}_{\geq\Delta}(A) = Tr(Faulty_{\geq\Delta}(A)) \quad and \quad NonFaulty^{tr}(A) = Tr(NonFaulty(A))$$

which are respectively the traces of Δ-faulty and non-faulty runs of A.

4.3. Fault diagnosis problems

In this section, we give the definition of a *diagnoser*. We then introduce the formal definitions of the fault diagnosis problems for which we are interested in. We end this section by giving a necessary and sufficient condition for *diagnosability* that we use in the following sections.

4.3.1. *Diagnoser*

The purpose of fault diagnosis is to detect a fault as early as possible. Faults (f event) are unobservable and only the events in Σ can be observed as well as the time-elapsed between these events. Whenever the system generates a timed word w, the observer can only see $\pi_{/\Sigma}(w)$. If an observer can detect faults in this way it is called a *diagnoser*. A diagnoser must detect a fault within a given delay $\Delta \in \mathbb{N}$.

DEFINITION 4.3((Σ, Δ)-DIAGNOSER).– Let A be a timed automaton over the alphabet $\Sigma_{\tau,f}$ and $\Delta \in \mathbb{N}$. A (Σ, Δ)-*diagnoser* for A is a mapping $D : TW^*(\Sigma) \to \{0, 1\}$ such that:
  – for each $\varrho \in NonFaulty(A)$, $D(\pi_{/\Sigma}(tr(\rho))) = 0$,
  – for each $\varrho \in Faulty_{\geq\Delta}(A)$, $D(\pi_{/\Sigma}(tr(\rho))) = 1$. □

A is (Σ, Δ)-*diagnosable*, if there exists a (Σ, Δ)-diagnoser for A. A is Σ-*diagnosable*, if there is some $\Delta \in \mathbb{N}$ s.t. A is (Σ, Δ)-diagnosable. In the following, we often omit the parameter Σ when it is clear from the context.

REMARK 4.1.– Nothing is required for the Δ'-faulty words with $\Delta' < \Delta$. Thus a diagnoser could change its mind and answers 1 for a Δ'-faulty word, and 0 for a Δ''-faulty word with $\Delta' < \Delta'' < \Delta$.

EXAMPLE 4.1.– The timed automaton $\mathcal{A}(3)$ in Figure 4.1 taken from [TRI 02] is three-diagnosable. For the timed words of the form $t.a.\delta.b.t'$ with $\delta \leq 3$, no fault has occurred, whereas when $\delta > 3$ a fault must have occurred. A diagnoser can then be easily constructed. As we have to wait for a "b" action to detect a fault, D cannot detect a fault in strictly less than three-time units. If $\alpha = 2$, in $\mathcal{A}(2)$ there are two runs (we write (ℓ, v) a state with v the value of clock x)

$$\rho_1(\delta) = (l_0, 0) \xrightarrow{a} (l_1, 0) \xrightarrow{2.5} (l_1, 2.5) \xrightarrow{f} (l_2, 2.5)$$
$$\xrightarrow{0.2} (l_2, 2.7) \xrightarrow{b} (l_3, 2.7) \xrightarrow{\delta} (l_2, 2.7 + \delta)$$

$$\rho_2(\delta) = (l_0, 0) \xrightarrow{a} (l_1, 0) \xrightarrow{2.5} (l_1, 2.5) \xrightarrow{\tau} (l_4, 2.5)$$
$$\xrightarrow{0.2} (l_4, 2.7) \xrightarrow{b} (l_5, 2.7) \xrightarrow{\delta} (l_5, 2.7 + \delta)$$

that satisfy $\pi_{/\Sigma}(tr(\rho_1(\delta))) = \pi_{/\Sigma}(tr(\rho_2(\delta)))$, and this for every $\delta \geq 0$. For each $\Delta \in \mathbb{N}$, there are two runs $\rho_1(\Delta)$ and $\rho_2(\Delta)$ that produce the same observations and thus no diagnoser can exist. $\mathcal{A}(2)$ is not diagnosable.

4.3.2. The problems

The classical fault diagnosis problems, we are interested in, are the following:

PROBLEM 4.1((Σ, Δ)-DIAGNOSABILITY).–
   INPUT: A timed automaton $A = (L, \ell_0, X, \Sigma_{\tau,f}, E, Inv)$ and $\Delta \in \mathbb{N}$.
   PROBLEM: Is A (Σ, Δ)-diagnosable?

PROBLEM 4.2(Σ-DIAGNOSABILITY).–
   INPUT: A timed automaton $A = (L, \ell_0, X, \Sigma_{\tau,f}, E, Inv)$.
   PROBLEM: Is A Σ-diagnosable?

PROBLEM 4.3(MAXIMUM DELAY TO ANNOUNCE A FAULT).–
   INPUT: A timed automaton $A = (L, \ell_0, X, \Sigma_{\tau,f}, E, Inv)$.
   PROBLEM: If A is Σ-diagnosable, what is the minimum Δ s.t. A is (Σ, Δ)-diagnosable ?

PROBLEM 4.4(DIAGNOSER SYNTHESIS).–
   INPUT: A timed automaton $A = (L, \ell_0, X, \Sigma_{\tau,f}, E, Inv)$.
   PROBLEM: If A is (Σ, Δ)-diagnosable, compute a witness (Σ, Δ)-diagnoser D.

4.3.3. Necessary and sufficient condition for diagnosability

According to Definition 4.3, A is Σ-diagnosable, if and only if, there is some $\Delta \in \mathbb{N}$ s.t. A is (Σ, Δ)-diagnosable. Thus:

A **is not** Σ-diagnosable $\quad\Longleftrightarrow\quad$ $\forall \Delta \in \mathbb{N}$, A is not (Σ, Δ)-diagnosable.

Moreover, a trace-based definition of (Σ, Δ)-diagnosability can be stated as: A is (Σ, Δ)-diagnosable, if and only if

$$\pi_{/\Sigma}(Faulty^{tr}_{\geq \Delta}(A)) \cap \pi_{/\Sigma}(NonFaulty^{tr}(A)) = \varnothing. \qquad [4.1]$$

Indeed, if equation [4.1] is satisfied, we can define a diagnoser D by: $D(\rho) = 1$, if and only if $\pi_{/\Sigma}(tr(\rho)) \in \pi_{/\Sigma}(Faulty^{tr}_{\geq \Delta}(A))$. If equation [4.1] is not satisfied, we can find two runs ρ_1 and ρ_2 with $\rho_1 \in Faulty_{> \Delta}(A)$, $\rho_2 \in NonFaulty(A)$ and such that $\pi_{/\Sigma}(tr(\rho_1)) = \pi_{/\Sigma}(tr(\rho_2))$. Thus, no (Σ, Δ)-diagnoser can exist because it should announce at the same time 1 and 0. This gives a necessary and sufficient condition for non-diagnosability and thus diagnosability

$$A \text{ is not diagnosable} \Longleftrightarrow \forall \Delta \in \mathbb{N}, \begin{cases} \exists \rho_1 \in Faulty_{\geq \Delta}(A) \\ \exists \rho_2 \in NonFaulty(A) \\ \quad such\ that\ \pi_{/\Sigma}(tr(\rho_1)) = \pi_{/\Sigma}(tr(\rho_2)). \end{cases} \qquad [4.2]$$

In the next section, we show how to solve Problems [4.1–4.4] for discrete event systems. In section 4.5, we extend the solutions for systems given by timed automata.

4.4. Fault diagnosis for discrete event systems

In this section, we review the main results about diagnosability of DES introduced in [SAM 95, SAM 96], and give an alternative proof of Theorem 4.3 which originally appeared in [CAS 08]. In this framework, we assume to have a formal model of the system to observe. This model defines the runs of the system including faulty runs.

4.4.1. Discrete event systems for fault diagnosis

We consider here that the DES is given by a finite automaton (with no clock) $A = (Q, q_0, \Sigma_{\tau, f}, \rightarrow)$ where Q is a finite set of states and $\rightarrow \subseteq Q \times \Sigma_{\tau, f} \times Q$. A finite automaton is a particular TA with $X = \varnothing$. Consequently, guards and invariants are vacuously true and time-elapsing transitions do not exist. Notice that the language accepted by such DES is prefix closed.[1]

A run from ℓ_0 of the finite automaton A is thus a sequence of the form

$$\varrho \;=\; \ell_0 \xrightarrow{a_1} \ell_1 \xrightarrow{a_2} \ell_2 \quad\cdots\quad \ell_j \quad\cdots\quad \xrightarrow{a_n} \ell_n \cdots ,$$

where for each $i \geq 0$, $(\ell_i, a_{i+1}, \ell_{i+1}) \in E$. In this case, the duration of a run ϱ is the number of steps (including τ-steps) of ϱ: if ϱ is finite and ends in ℓ_n, $Duration(\varrho) = n$ and otherwise $Duration(\varrho) = \infty$.

Definitions of traces and languages, and k-faulty runs given in section 4.3 extend straightforwardly using the duration function defined above.

REMARK 4.2.– Using a timed automaton where discrete actions are separated by one time unit is not equivalent to using a finite automaton when solving a fault diagnosis problem. For example, a timed automaton can generate the timed words $1.f.1.a$ and $1.\tau.1.\tau.1.a$. In this case, it is 1-diagnosable: after reading the timed word $2.a$ we announce a fault. If we do not see the one-time unit durations, the timed words $f.a$ and $\tau^2.a$ give the same observation. And thus it is not diagnosable, if we cannot measure time. Using a timed automaton where discrete actions are separated by one-time unit gives to the diagnoser the ability to count/measure time and this is not equivalent to the fault diagnosis problem for untimed systems.

Moreover, we assume that the automaton A is such that every faulty run of length n can be extended to a run of length $n + 1$; this assumption simplifies the proofs and if A does not satisfy it, it is easy to add τ loops to deadlock states of A to ensure it holds. It does not modify the observation made by the external observer and thus does not modify the diagnosability status of A.

4.4.2. *Checking Δ-diagnosability and diagnosability*

4.4.2.1. *Checking Δ-diagnosability*

To check problem [4.1], we have to decide whether there is a $(\Delta + 1)$-faulty run ρ_1 and a non-faulty run ρ_2 that give the same observations when projected on Σ.

An easy way to do this is to build a finite automaton $\mathcal{B}$, which accepts exactly those runs, and check whether $\mathcal{L}(\mathcal{B})$ is empty or not.

---

1. L is prefix closed, if $\forall w \in \Sigma^*$, if there is some $w' \in \Sigma^\infty$ s.t. $w.w' \in L$ then $w \in L$.

Let $A_1 = (Q \times \{-1, 0, 1, \cdots, \Delta, \Delta + 1\}, (q_0, -1), \Sigma_\tau, \rightarrow_1)$ be the automaton with $\rightarrow_1$ defined by

- $(q, n) \xrightarrow{\lambda}_1 (q', n)$, if $q \xrightarrow{\lambda} q'$ and $n = -1$ and $\lambda \in \Sigma \cup \{\tau\}$;
- $(q, n) \xrightarrow{\lambda}_1 (q', \min(n+1, \Delta+1))$, if $q \xrightarrow{\lambda} q'$ and $n \geq 0$ and $\lambda \in \Sigma \cup \{\tau\}$;
- $(q, n) \xrightarrow{\tau}_1 (q', \min(n+1, \Delta+1)$ if $q \xrightarrow{f} q'$.

Let $A_2 = (Q, q_0, \Sigma_\tau, \rightarrow_2)$ with $q \xrightarrow{\lambda}_2 q'$, if $q \xrightarrow{\lambda} q'$ and $\lambda \in \Sigma \cup \{\tau\}$. Define $\mathcal{B} = A_1 \times A_2$ with the final states $F_\mathcal{B}$ of $\mathcal{B}$ given by: $F_\mathcal{B} = \{((\ell, \Delta+1), \ell') \mid (\ell, \ell') \in Q \times Q\}$. We let $R_\mathcal{B} = \varnothing$. It is straightforward to see that

THEOREM 4.2.– *A is Δ-diagnosable if and only if $\mathcal{L}^*(\mathcal{B}) = \varnothing$.*

As language emptiness for $\mathcal{B}$ amounts to reachability checking, it can be done in linear time in the size of $\mathcal{B}$. Still strictly speaking, the automaton $\mathcal{B}$ has size $(\Delta + 2) \cdot |A|^2$ which is exponential in the size of the inputs of the problem A and Δ because Δ is given in binary. Thus, problem [4.1] can be solved in EXPTIME. However, as storing Δ requires only polynomial space problem [4.1] is in PSPACE.

4.4.2.2. *Checking diagnosability*

To check whether A is diagnosable, we build a synchronized product $A_1 \times A_2$, s.t. A_1 behaves exactly as A but records in its state whether a fault has occurred, and A_2 behaves like A without the faulty runs as before. It is then as if $\Lambda = 0$ in the previous construction. More precisely, we have $A_1 = (Q \times \{0, 1\}, (q_0, 0), \Sigma_\tau, \rightarrow_1)$ with

- $(q, n) \xrightarrow{l}_1 (q', n)$, if $q \xrightarrow{l} q'$ and $l \in \Sigma \cup \{\tau\}$;
- $(q, n) \xrightarrow{\tau}_1 (q', 1)$, if $q \xrightarrow{f} q'$, (n is set to 1 after a fault);

and $A_2 = (Q, q_0, \Sigma_\tau, \rightarrow_2)$ with $q \xrightarrow{l}_2 q'$ since $q \xrightarrow{l} q'$ and $l \in \Sigma \cup \{\tau\}$. Let $A_1 \times A_2$ be the synchronized product of A_1 and A_2 (recall they only synchronize on common actions except τ, see Definition 4.2).

Let us assume that we have a predicate $A_1 Move(t)$ (resp. $A_2 Move$), which is true when A_1 (resp. A_2) participates in a transition t of the product $A_1 \times A_2$. For instance for A_1 moves, and $t : (s_1, s_2) \xrightarrow{\lambda} (s'_1, s'_2)$, $A_1 Move(t)$ is true, if either $\lambda \in \Sigma$ or $s_1 \xrightarrow{\tau} s'_1$ and $s_2 = s'_2$. Given a run $\rho \in Runs(A_1 \times A_2)$, we let $\rho_{|1}$ be the run of A_1, which consists of the sequence of transitions $t_1 t_2 \cdots t_k$ that satisfy $A_1 Move(\cdot)$, and $\rho_{|2}$ be the run of A_2 which consists of the sequence of transitions $t'_1 t'_2 \cdots t'_l$ that satisfy $A_2 Move(\cdot)$. By definition of $A_1 \times A_2$, we have $\pi_{/\Sigma}(tr(\rho_{|1})) = \pi_{/\Sigma}(tr(\rho_{|2}))$.

Let $Runs_{\geq k}(A_1 \times A_2)$ be the set of runs in $A_1 \times A_2$ s.t. a (faulty) state $((q_1, 1), q_2)$ is followed by at least k A_1-actions. Then, we have the following lemmas:

LEMMA 4.1.– *Let $\rho \in Runs_{\geq k}(A_1 \times A_2)$. Then $\rho_{|1} \in Faulty_{\geq k}(A)$ and $\rho_{|2} \in NonFaulty(A)$. Moreover, $\pi_{/\Sigma}(tr(\rho_{|1})) = \pi_{/\Sigma}(tr(\rho_{|2}))$.*

LEMMA 4.2.– *Let $\rho_1 \in Faulty_{\geq k}(A)$ and $\rho_2 \in NonFaulty(A)$ s.t. $\pi_{/\Sigma}(tr(\rho_1)) = \pi_{/\Sigma}(tr(\rho_2))$. Then there is some $\rho \in Runs_{\geq k}(A_1 \times A_2)$ s.t. $\rho_{|1} = \rho_1$ and $\rho_{|2} = \rho_2$.*

PROOF 4.1.– By definition of $A_1 \times A_2$, it suffices to notice that a run in $Runs_{\geq k}(A_1 \times A_2)$ can be split into a run of A_1 and a run of A_2 having the same projection on Σ. □

To check problem [4.2], we build an extended automaton $\mathcal{B}$ s.t. $\mathcal{B}$ accepts an infinite word, if and only if A is not diagnosable.

$\mathcal{B}$ is the extended version of $A_1 \times A_2$ built as follows: we add a Boolean variable z that is set to 0 in the initial state of $\mathcal{B}$. An extended state of $\mathcal{B}$ is a pair (s, z) with s a state of $A_1 \times A_2$. Whenever A_1 participates in an $A_1 \times A_2$-action, z is re-set to 1, and when only A_2 makes a move in $A_1 \times A_2$, z is set 0. We denote $\longrightarrow_\mathcal{B}$ the new transition relation between extended states. The Büchi automaton $\mathcal{B}$ is the tuple $((Q \times \{0, 1\}) \times Q \times \{0, 1\}, ((q_0, 0), q_0, 0), \Sigma^\tau, \longrightarrow_\mathcal{B}, \varnothing, R_\mathcal{B})$ defined by

– $(s, z) \xrightarrow{\lambda}_\mathcal{B} (s', z')$, if (i) there exists a transition $t : s \xrightarrow{\lambda}_{1,2} s'$ in $A_1 \times A_2$, and (ii) $z' = 1$, if $A_1Move(t)$ and $z' = 0$ otherwise;

– $R_\mathcal{B} = \{((q, 1), q', 1) \mid (q, q') \in Q \times Q\}$ and $F_\mathcal{B} = \varnothing$.

$\mathcal{B}$ accepts a language of infinite words $\mathcal{L}(\mathcal{B}) = \mathcal{L}^\omega(\mathcal{B}) \subseteq \Sigma^\omega$ and the following theorem holds:

THEOREM 4.3.– $\mathcal{L}^\omega(\mathcal{B}) \neq \varnothing \iff A$ *is not Σ-diagnosable.*

PROOF 4.2.– Proof of $\Longrightarrow$. Let us assume $\mathcal{L}^\omega(\mathcal{B}) \neq \varnothing$ and let $\rho \in \mathcal{L}^\omega(\mathcal{B})$: ρ has infinitely many faulty states and infinitely many A_1 actions because of the definition of $R_\mathcal{B}$ which implies that $z = 1$ infinitely often. Let $k \in \mathbb{N}$ and $\rho[i_k]$ be a finite prefix of ρ that contains more than k A_1 actions after the first faulty state in ρ (for any k this i_k exists because ρ contains infinitely many A_1 actions). $\rho[i_k] \in Runs_{\geq k}(A_1 \times A_2)$ and by Lemma 4.1, it follows that $\rho[i_k]_{|1} \in Faulty_{\geq k}(A)$ and $\rho[i_k]_{|2} \in NonFaulty(A)$ and $\pi_{/\Sigma}(tr(\rho[i_k]_{|1})) = \pi_{/\Sigma}(tr(\rho[i_k]_{|2}))$. Thus equation [4.2] is satisfied for any $k \in \mathbb{N}$ and A is not diagnosable.

Proof of $\Longleftarrow$. Conversely, assuming A is not Σ-diagnosable. Then by equation [4.2] and Lemma 4.2, for any $k \in \mathbb{N}$, there is a run $\rho_k \in Runs_{\geq k}(A_1 \times A_2)$. Consider the tree, which is the unfolding of $A_1 \times A_2$. Restricting this tree to branches where there is only a finite number of consecutive τ-actions fired by A_2. This is not a real restriction, because after a finite number of such moves, A_2 will enter an already visited state. In this tree, there is an infinite number of paths $(\rho_k, k \in \mathbb{N})$, which contain a faulty state of $A_1 \times A_2$. Thus, an infinite number of them must contain the same first faulty state. Without loss of generality, we can assume that all the ρ_k have the same first faulty state $((q_1, 1), q_2)$. It follows that $((q_1, 1), q_2)$ is the source of a tree having an infinite number of nodes and thus, by König's Lemma, the source of an infinite branch. On this infinite branch, we have only a bounded number of consecutive τ actions fired by A_2, and thus it must contain an infinite number of A_1 moves. We then have an infinite path containing infinitely many A_1 moves the source of which is a faulty state which implies that $\mathcal{L}^\omega(\mathcal{B}) \neq \varnothing$. $\qquad\square$

REMARK 4.3.– The set $R_\mathcal{B}$ involves z because A_1 has to move infinitely often. This corresponds to logical time divergence. Without this condition, it could be that A_1 refuses to proceed, and thus prevents the logical time to progress. If A_2 then fires an infinite number of transitions τ, the automaton would be declared not diagnosable. Still they could be no arbitrary large faulty run on A and this does not match definition 4.2.

Theorem 4.3 gives a procedure to check whether an automaton A is Σ-diagnosable or not and thus to decide problem [4.2].

COROLLARY 4.1.– *problem [4.2] can be checked in polynomial time $O(|A|^2)$.*

PROOF 4.3.– Büchi emptiness can be decided in polynomial (linear) time. For an automaton H with n states and m transitions, deciding whether $\mathcal{L}^\omega(H) = \varnothing$ can de done in $O(n + m)$. As the size of $\mathcal{B}$ is $4 \times |Q|^2$, problem [4.2] can be checked in $O(|Q|^2)$. $\qquad\square$

In the case of a finite number of *failure types*, it suffices to design $A_1 \times A_2$ for each type of faults [YOO 02] and check for diagnosability. Thus, checking diagnosability with multiple type of faults is also polynomial.

Polynomial algorithms for checking diagnosability (problem [4.2]) were already reported in [JIA 01, YOO 02]. In these two papers, the plant cannot have unobservable loops, i.e. loops that consist of τ actions. Our algorithm does not have this limitation (we may even have to add τ loops to ensure that each faulty run can be extended). Note also that in [JIA 01, YOO 02], the product construction is symmetric in the sense that

A_2 is a copy of A as well. Our A_2 does not contain the f transitions, which makes no difference complexity-wise, but in practice this can be useful to reduce the size of the product.

Moreover, reducing problem [4.2] to emptiness checking of Büchi automata is interesting in many respects:

– the proof of Theorem 4.3 is easy and short; algorithms for checking Büchi emptiness are well known and correctness follows easily as well;

– this also implies that standard tools from the *model-checking/verification* community can be used to check for diagnosability. There are very efficient tools to check for Büchi emptiness (e.g. SPIN [HOL 05]). Numerous algorithms, like *on-the-fly* algorithms [COU 05] have been designed to improve memory/time consumption (see [SCH 05] for an overview). Also when the DES is not diagnosable a counter-example is provided by these tools. The input languages (e.g. PROMELA for SPIN) that can be used to specify the DES are more expressive than the specification languages of some dedicated tools[2] like DESUMA/UMDES [RIC 06] (notice that the comparison with DESUMA/UMDES concerns only the diagnosability algorithms; DESUMA/UMDES can perform a lot more than only checking diagnosability).

From Theorem 4.3, we can also conclude that diagnosability amounts to bounded diagnosability: indeed if A is diagnosable, there can be no accepting cycles of faulty states in $\mathcal{B}$; in this case, there cannot be a faulty run of length more than $2 \cdot |Q|^2$ in $\mathcal{B}$. Thus, problem [4.2] reduces to a particular instance of problem [4.1] as was already stated in [YOO 02]:

THEOREM 4.4.– *A is Σ-diagnosable, if and only if A is $(\Sigma, 2 \cdot |Q|^2)$-diagnosable.*

This appeals from some final remarks on the algorithms we should choose to check diagnosability: for the particular case of $\Delta = 2 \cdot |A|^2$, solving problem [4.1] (a reachability problem) can be done in time $2 \cdot |A|^2 \cdot |A|^2$, i.e., $O(|A|^4)$, whereas solving problem [4.2] directly as a Büchi emptiness problem can be done in $O(|A|^2)$. Thus, the extra cost of using a reachability algorithm vs. a Büchi emptiness checking algorithm is still reasonable.

4.4.3. *Computation of the maximum delay*

To compute the least k s.t. A is (Σ, k)-diagnosable, we can proceed as follows: if A is Σ-diagnosable, there cannot be any run in $\mathcal{B}$ which is (1) faulty and (2) contains an infinite number of A_1 moves. Thus, any run of $\mathcal{B}$ starting in a faulty state is followed

---

2. UMDES was the only publicly available tool which could be found by a Google search.

by a bounded number of A_1 moves: if not, there would be a faulty run with an infinite number of A_1 moves and A would not be diagnosable. Let k be the maximum number of A_1 transitions that can follow a faulty state of $\mathcal{B}$. Then A is $(\Sigma, k+1)$-diagnosable: otherwise, there would a faulty run with $k+1$ actions of A_1. Moreover, A is not (Σ, k)-diagnosable because there is a faulty run in $\mathcal{B}$ which has k A_1 steps; the definition of A_2 and $\mathcal{B}$ implies (Lemma 4.1) that A has a k-faulty run and a non-faulty run with the same observation. Altogether this means that the maximum delay to detect faults is $k+1$. Let $Max_d(A)$ be the value of this maximum delay. Computing $Max_d(A)$ amounts to finding the maximum number of A_1 actions that can follow a faulty (reachable) state of $\mathcal{B}$. This can be computed in polynomial time. Solving problem [4.3] can also be done by a binary search solving iteratively Δ-diagnosability problems starting with $\Delta = 2 \cdot |A|^2$. As there are at most $O(\log |A|)$ Δ-diagnosability problems to solve we obtain

THEOREM 4.5.– *Problem [4.3] can be solved in polynomial time $O(\log |A| \cdot |A|^4)$.*

Using a different approach, problem [4.3] was reported to be solvable in $O(|A|^3)$ in [YOO 03]. The algorithm is based on the computation of longest paths in a weighted automaton built from $A_1 \times A_1 \times A_2$.

4.4.4. *Synthesis of a diagnoser*

To compute a witness diagnoser when A is Σ-diagnosable, we just have to determinize A_1. To do this, we use the classical *subset construction*. Let F be the set of faulty states of A_1, i.e. $F = Q \times \{1\}$.

Define $E_a(q)$ to be the set of states q', s.t. there is a path in A_1 from q to q' involving only a finite number of τ steps followed by a:

$$E_a(q) = \{q'' \mid q \xrightarrow{\tau*} q' \xrightarrow{a} q''\}. \qquad\qquad [E]$$

We then define the deterministic automaton $Det(A_1) = (S, s_0, \Sigma, \delta', F', \varnothing)$ by
- $S = 2^Q$;
- $s_0 = \{q' \in Q \times \{0,1\} \mid (q_0, 0) \xrightarrow{\tau*} q'\}$;
- for $s \in S$, $a \in \Sigma$, $\delta'(s, a) = \cup_{x \in s} E_a(x)$;
- $F' = \{s \in S \mid s \subseteq F\}$.

$Det(A_1)$ is deterministic by construction. Let w be a word in $\pi_{/\Sigma}(\mathcal{L}^*(A))$, $last(w)$ is thus determined in a unique way.

To obtain a $(\Sigma, Max_d(A))$-diagnoser D for A, we let $D(w) = 1$, if $last(w) \in F'$ and 0 otherwise. This diagnoser detects faults at most $Max_d(A)$ discrete steps after they occurred. It has size exponential in the size of A.

THEOREM 4.6.– *Problem [4.4] can be solved in time $O(2^{|A|})$.*

4.5. Fault diagnosis for timed systems

In this section, we show how to decide wether a systems given as a timed automaton is diagnosable or not. For the synthesis problem, we take into account the *resources* (clocks and integer constants) that a diagnoser can use. Indeed, there is one major difference between the fault diagnosis problems in discrete time and dense time: if a timed automaton is diagnosable, there is not always a diagnoser, which is a (deterministic) timed automaton. This is in contrast to the discrete time case where a finite automaton diagnoser (at most of exponential size) can be built when a system is diagnosable. The results of sections 4.5.1–4.5.4 are based on [TRI 02] and the results of section 4.5.5 on [BOU 05, CHE 04].

Throughout this section, we assume $A = (L, l_0, X, \Sigma_{\tau,f}, E, Inv)$ is a timed automaton with faults.

4.5.1. *Checking Δ-diagnosability*

Let t be a fresh clock not in X. Let $A_1(\Delta) = ((L \times \{0, 1\}) \cup \{Bad\}, (l_0, 0), X \cup \{t\}, \Sigma_\tau, E_1, Inv_1)$ where Bad is a fresh location not in L, and

- $((\ell, n), g, \lambda, r, (\ell', n)) \in E_1$, if $(\ell, g, \lambda, r, \ell') \in E$, $\lambda \in \Sigma \cup \{\tau\}$;
- $((\ell, 0), g, \tau, r \cup \{t\}, (\ell', 1)) \in E_1$, if $(\ell, g, f, r, \ell') \in E$;
- $Inv_1((\ell, 0)) = Inv(\ell)$, $Inv_1((\ell, 1)) = Inv(\ell) \wedge t \leq \Delta$ and $Inv_1(Bad) = \top$;
- for $\ell \in L$, $((\ell, 1), t \geq \Delta, \tau, \varnothing, Bad) \in E_1$

and $A_2 = (L, l_0, X_2, \Sigma_\tau, E_2, Inv_2)$ with:

- $X_2 = \{x_2 \mid x \in X\}$ (clocks of A are renamed);
- $(\ell, g_2, \lambda, r_2, \ell') \in E_2$ if $(\ell, g, \lambda, r, \ell') \in E$, $\lambda \in \Sigma \cup \{\tau\}$ with: g_2 is g where each clock x is replaced by its counterpart x_2; r_2 is r with the same renaming;
- $Inv_2(\ell)$ is $Inv(\ell)$ with the renaming of x by x_2.

Consider $A_1(\Delta) \times A_2$. A faulty state of $A_1(\Delta) \times A_2$ is a state of the form $(((\ell, 1), v), (\ell', v'))$, i.e. where the state of A_1 is faulty. Let $Runs_{\geq \Delta}(A_1(\Delta) \times A_2)$ be the runs of $A_1(\Delta) \times A_2$ s.t. a faulty state of A_1 is encountered and s.t. at least Δ time units have elapsed after this state. Then there are two runs, one Δ-faulty and one non-faulty which give the same observation. Moreover, because t is reset exactly when the first fault occurs, we have $t \geq \Delta$. Conversely, if a state of the form $(((\ell, 1), v), (\ell', v'))$ with $v(t) \geq \Delta$ is reachable, then there are two runs, one Δ-faulty and one non-faulty which give the same observation. Location Bad in A_1 is thus reachable exactly, if A is not Δ-diagnosable. Let $\mathcal{D}$ be $A_1(\Delta) \times A_2$ with the final set of locations $F_{\mathcal{D}} = \{Bad\}$ and $R_{\mathcal{D}} = \varnothing$.

THEOREM 4.7([TRI 02]).– *A is Δ-diagnosable if and only if $\mathcal{L}^*(\mathcal{D}) = \varnothing$.*

Checking reachability of a location for timed automata is PSPACE-complete [ALU 94a]. More precisely, it can be done in linear time on the region graph. The size of the region graph of $\mathcal{D}$ is $(2 \cdot |L|^2 + |L|) \cdot (2|X| + 1)! \cdot 2^{2|X|+1} \cdot K^{2|X|} \cdot \Delta$, where K is the maximal constant appearing in A. It follows that

COROLLARY 4.2.– *Problem [4.1] can be solved in PSPACE for TA.*

4.5.2. *Checking diagnosability*

As for the untimed case, we build an automaton $\mathcal{D}$, which is a special version of $A_1(\Delta) \times A_2$. Assume A_1 is defined as before omitting the clock t and the location Bad. In the timed case, we have to take care of the following real-time related problems [TRI 02]:

– some runs of A_2 might prevent time from elapsing from a given point in time. In this case, equation [4.1] cannot be satisfied but this is for a spurious reason: for Δ to be large enough, there will be no Δ faulty run in $A_1 \times A_2$ because A_2 will block the time. In this case, we can claim that A is diagnosable but it is not realistic;

– a more tricky thing may happen: A_1 could produce a Zeno run[3] after a fault occurred. This could happen by firing infinitely many τ transitions in a bounded amount of time. If we declare that A is not diagnosable but the only witness run is a Zeno run, it does not have any physical meaning. Thus, to declare that A is not diagnosable, we should find a non-Zeno witness run which is realizable, and for which time diverges.

To cope with the previous dense time-related problems, we have to ensure that the following two conditions are met:

C_1: A_2 is *timelock-free*, i.e., A_2 cannot prevent time from elapsing; this implies that every finite non-faulty run of A_2 can be extended in a time divergent run. We

---

3. A Zeno run is a run with infinitely many discrete steps the duration of which is bounded.

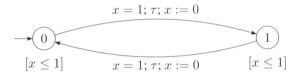

Figure 4.2. *Timed automaton $Div(x)$*

can assume that A_2 satisfies this property or check it on A_2 before checking diagnosability;

C_2: for A to be non-diagnosable, we must find an infinite run in $A_1 \times A_2$ for which time diverges.

C_2 can be enforced by adding a third timed automaton $Div(x)$ and synchronizing it with $A_1 \times A_2$. Let x be a fresh clock not in X. Let $Div(x) = (\{0, 1\}, 0, \{x\}, E, Inv)$ be the TA given in Figure 4.2.

If we use $F = \varnothing$ and $R = \{1\}$ for $Div(x)$, any infinite accepted run is time divergent. Let $\mathcal{D} = (A_1 \times A_2) \times Div(x)$ with the sets $F_{\mathcal{D}} = \varnothing$ and $R_{\mathcal{D}}$ is the set of states where A_1 is in a faulty state and $Div(x)$ is in location 1. The following theorem is the counterpart of Theorem 4.3 for timed automata:

THEOREM 4.8([TRI 02]).– *A is diagnosable, if and only if $\mathcal{L}^\omega(\mathcal{D}) = \varnothing$.*

PROOF 4.4.– Proof of $\Longrightarrow$. Assume $\mathcal{L}^\omega(\mathcal{D}) \neq \varnothing$. Let $\rho \in \mathcal{L}^\omega(\mathcal{D})$. Because of the definition of $R_{\mathcal{D}}$, ρ is a time divergent run: $\forall \alpha \in \mathbb{N}$, there is a prefix $\rho[\alpha]$ of ρ such that $Duration(\rho[\alpha]) \geq \alpha$. Using Lemma 4.1 (extended for timed automata), there exist two runs $\rho_{\alpha,1} = \rho[\alpha]_{|1}$ and $\rho_{\alpha,2} = \rho[\alpha]_{|2}$ such that $\pi_{/\Sigma}(tr(\rho_{\alpha,1})) = \pi_{/\Sigma}(tr(\rho_{\alpha,2}))$ and $\rho_{\alpha,1} \in Faulty_{\geq\alpha}(A)$, $\rho_{\alpha,2} \in NonFaulty(A)$. For every α, equation [4.2] is satisfied and thus A is not Σ-diagnosable.

Proof of $\Longleftarrow$. Let us assume that A is not Σ-diagnosable. Then, from equation [4.2], for every $\alpha \in \mathbb{N}$, there are two runs $\rho_1 \in Faulty_{\geq\alpha}(A)$, $\rho_2 \in NonFaulty(A)$, $\pi_{/\Sigma}(tr(\rho_1)) = \pi_{/\Sigma}(tr(\rho_2))$. From Lemma 4.2 (again extended to finite automata), the following property (P) holds: for every α, there exists[4] a run $\rho[\alpha] \in Runs_{\geq\alpha}((A_1 \times A_2) \times Div(x))$ such that $\rho[\alpha]_{|1} = \rho_1$ and $\rho[\alpha]_{|2} = \rho_2$. To replay the proof of Theorem 4.3, we use a property of the region graph introduced in Chapter 2. Let $RG(\mathcal{D})$ be the region graph of $\mathcal{D}$. This graph is finite and satisfies: ρ is a run of $RG(\mathcal{D})$ if

---

4. $Div(x)$ does not constraint A_1 nor A_2 and every run of $A_1 \times A_2$ can be interleaved with a run of $Div(x)$ to form a run of $(A_1 \times A_2) \times Div(x)$.

and only if there is a *timed version* of ρ, $\widetilde{\rho}$ which is a run of $\mathcal{D}$. Property (P) above, implies that faulty behaviors of arbitrary length exist in the region graph $RG(\mathcal{D})$. As this graph is finite, from König's Lemma, there is an infinite run[5] in $RG(\mathcal{D})$ from a faulty state. Hence, there is a timed version of this run which is an infinite execution in $\mathcal{D}$. And thus $\mathcal{L}^{\omega}(\mathcal{D}) \neq \varnothing$. □

Deciding whether $\mathcal{L}^{\omega}(A) \neq \varnothing$ for timed automata is PSPACE-complete [ALU 94a]. Thus deciding diagnosability is in PSPACE.

The reachability problem for TA can be reduced to a diagnosability problem [TRI 02]. Let A be a TA on alphabet Σ and *End* a particular location of A. We want to check whether *End* is reachable in A. It suffices to build A' on the alphabet $\Sigma_{\tau, f}$ by adding to A the following transitions: $(End, \top, \lambda, \varnothing, End)$ for $\lambda \in \{\tau, f\}$. Then: A' is not diagnosable if and only if *End* is reachable in A. It follows that:

THEOREM 4.9([TRI 02]).– *Problem [4.2] is PSPACE-complete for TA.*

4.5.3. *Computation of the maximal delay*

To compute the maximum delay, we can proceed as for the untimed case. assume we have checked that A is Σ-diagnosable. We can then check wether A is (Σ, Δ)-diagnosable starting with $\Delta = 1 = 2^0$, and then $\Delta = 2^k$, increasing k, until A is $(\Sigma, 2^k)$-diagnosable (which is bound to happen as we have previously checked that A is Σ-diagnosable). Let k_0 be the smallest k such that A is $(\Sigma, 2^{k_0})$-diagnosable. We can then do a binary search for the maximal delay k in the interval $[2^{k_0 - 1} + 1, 2^{k_0}]$.

Nevertheless, we can be more effective because we draw another conclusion from the proof of Theorem 4.8: if a TA A is diagnosable, there cannot be any cycle with faulty states in the region graph of $A_1 \times A_2 \times Div(x)$. Indeed, otherwise, by Theorem 4.1, there would be a non-Zeno word in $A_1 \times A_2 \times Div(x)$ itself.[6] Let $\alpha(A)$ denote the size of the region graph $RG(A_1 \times A_2 \times Div(x))$. If A is diagnosable, then (P_1): a faulty state in $RG(A_1 \times A_2 \times Div(x))$ can be followed by at most $\alpha(A)$ (faulty) states. Notice that a faulty state cannot be followed by a state (s, r) where r is an unbounded region of A, as this would give rise to a non-Zeno word in $A_1 \times A_2 \times Div(x)$. Hence (P_2): all the regions following a faulty state in $RG(A_1 \times A_2 \times Div(x))$ are bounded. As the amount of time, which can elapse within a region is less than one-time unit,[7]

---

5. The reason is the same as for the proof of Theorem 4.3.

6. Note that, this is true because we add the automaton $Div(x)$. Otherwise, an infinite run in the region graph of a TA does not imply a time divergent run in the TA A itself.

7. We assume the constants are integers.

this implies that the duration of the longest faulty run in $A_1 \times A_2 \times Div(x)$ is less than $\alpha(A)$. Actually as every other region is a *singular region*,[8] it must be less than $(\alpha(A)/2) + 1$. Thus, we obtain the following result:

THEOREM 4.10.– *A is diagnosable, if and only if A is $(\alpha(A)/2 + 1)$-diagnosable.*

As diagnosability can be reduced to Δ-diagnosability for timed automata.

COROLLARY 4.3.– *Problem [4.1] is PSPACE-complete for TA.*

PROOF 4.5.– The size of the binary encoding of $(\alpha(A)/2 + 1)$ is polynomial in the size of A. □

Although problems [4.1] and [4.2] are PSPACE-complete for timed automata, the price to pay to solve problem [4.2] as a reachability problem is much higher than solving it as a Büchi emptiness problem: indeed the size of the region graph of $A_1(\alpha(A)/2+1) \times A_2$ is the square of the size of the region graph of $A_1 \times A_2 \times Div(x)$ which is already exponential in the size of A. Time-wise this means a blow up from 2^n to 2^{n^2}, which is not negligible as in the discrete case.

4.5.4. *Synthesis of a diagnoser*

In case A is Σ-diagnosable, we define a diagnoser as a mapping that performs a state estimate of A after a timed word w is read by A. Indeed, we cannot determinize A (as for the untimed case) because timed automata cannot always be determinized [ALU 94a]. Moreover, testing whether a timed automaton is determinizable is undecidable [FIN 05, TRI 06].

Note that for classes of determinizable timed automata like ERA (see [ALU 94b]), we can do the same construction as for the untimed case.

Nevertheless, there are some non-deterministic timed automata, which do not admit any deterministic timed automaton as a diagnoser. An example automaton, C, is given in Figure 4.3. The faulty runs of C are of the form $\delta.a.t$ with $\delta \in \mathbb{N}$ and $t \geq 0$, and the non-faulty runs are of the form $\delta.a.t$ with $\delta \notin \mathbb{N}$. Equation [4.1] is thus satisfied for every delay Δ and C is diagnosable. We can build a 0-diagnoser for C, which is the mapping $D : TW^*(\{a\}) \rightarrow \{0,1\}$ given by $D(\delta.a.t) = 1$, if $\delta \in \mathbb{N}$ and $D(\delta.a.t) = 0$ otherwise. But there is no deterministic timed automaton which can accept the language $\delta.a$ with $\delta \in \mathbb{N}$ (see [BER 98]). To build a diagnoser in the general

---

8. A singular region is a region in which time-elapsing is not possible, e.g. defined by $x = 0 \wedge y \geq 1$.

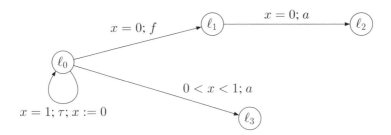

Figure 4.3. *Automaton C (taken from [BOU 05])*

case, we proceed as follows. The first stage is to add to the states of A a bit, which indicates whether a fault occurred or not. This amounts to building A_1 as defined earlier in this section. Then A has two types of states: faulty states with the bit set to 1 and non-faulty states with the bit set to 0. We then define a mapping D, which computes the (symbolic) set of states A can be in after reading a timed word w. This set of states is updated after each occurrence of a new event (δ, a). If the set of states A can be in after reading a timed word w contains only faulty states, then we can announce a fault. If it contains both faulty and non-faulty states, it is too early to decide wether a fault has really occurred.

The formal construction of such a mapping is detailed in [TRI 02]. A diagnoser in the general case is thus an algorithm (a Turing machine), which computes sets of symbolic states. The worst case is obtained when each state is a node of the region graph. Thus, computing the set of states A can be done in time exponential in the size of A.

If we have to compute this set of states in real time, this can be prohibitive. It is thus sensible to address the problem of diagnosability with timed automata, where we compute off-line a diagnoser, which is a timed automaton. This is the purpose of our study in the next section.

4.5.5. *Fault diagnosis with deterministic timed automata*

The fault diagnosis problem with deterministic timed automata (DTA) was introduced and solved in [BOU 05, CHE 04]. A closely related problem was studied in [KRI 04b] for the synthesis of *timed testers*, which are deterministic timed automata.

We recall that a timed automaton A is deterministic if there is no τ labeled transition in A, and if, whenever (ℓ, g, a, r, ℓ') and $(\ell, g', a, r', \ell'')$ are transitions of A, $g \wedge g' \equiv \perp$. A is *complete* if from each state (ℓ, v), and for each action a, there is a transition (ℓ, g, a, r, ℓ') such that $v \models g$. Let $\mathcal{C}$ be a class of deterministic timed automata. We note DTA is the class of deterministic timed automata.

In the following, DTA diagnosers are used as language acceptors and we do not need any invariants on locations. We let $Inv_\top$ (abusing notations) be the invariant, which assigns $\top$ to any location of a DTA.

DEFINITION 4.4($\mathcal{C}$-DIAGNOSER).– Let A be a timed automaton over $\Sigma_{\tau,f}$ and $\Delta \in \mathbb{N}$. A (Σ, Δ)-$\mathcal{C}$-diagnoser for A is a complete and deterministic timed automaton $\Theta = (N, n_0, C, \Sigma, E_\Theta, Inv_\top, F_\Theta, \varnothing)$ in the class $\mathcal{C}$ such that

– for each $\rho \in NonFaulty(A)$, $last(\pi_{/\Sigma}(tr(\rho))) \notin F_\Theta$;
– for each $\rho \in Faulty_{\geq\Delta}(A)$, $last(\pi_{/\Sigma}(tr(\rho))) \in F_\Theta$.   □

In other words, Θ accepts the Δ-faulty words, but not the non-faulty words. A is (Σ, Δ)-$\mathcal{C}$-diagnosable, if there is a (Σ, Δ)-$\mathcal{C}$-diagnoser for A. A is Σ-$\mathcal{C}$-diagnosable, if there exists a $\Delta \in \mathbb{N}$ such that A is (Σ, Δ)-$\mathcal{C}$-diagnosable. The fault diagnosis problem using a diagnoser in $\mathcal{C}$ can be formally stated as follows:

PROBLEM 4.5($\mathcal{C}$-DIAGNOSABILITY).–
INPUT: A TA $A = (L, \ell_0, X, \Sigma_{\tau,f}, E, Inv)$.
PROBLEM: Is A Σ-$\mathcal{C}$-diagnosable?

In this problem, we are looking for a delay Δ and a deterministic timed automaton in the class $\mathcal{C}$, which accepts the Δ-faulty words.

EXAMPLE 4.2.– The timed automaton $\mathcal{A}(3)$ of Figure 4.1 is 3-diagnosable and there is a deterministic timed automaton which is a 3-diagnoser. An example is the automaton of Figure 4.4: when location 3 is reached, we announce a fault. Actually, this automaton is in location 3, if and only if a fault occurred less than three-time units ago and was followed by a b. $\mathcal{A}(3)$ fires a transition on the occurrences of observable events (a and b) in a deterministic manner. When it enters location 3 a fault has certainly occurred. Thus $\mathcal{A}(3)$ is 3-DTA diagnosable.

Problem [4.5] in its general version is still open. A solution for a simpler version has been proposed in [BOU 05] when the resources of the automata of the class $\mathcal{C}$ are fixed and when the maximum delay Δ to announce a fault is given. The resources of a timed automaton are: the number of clocks it can use, the constants the clocks can be compared against; this includes the maximal constant and the granularity of the constants. For instance, the resources of a class of timed automata can be given as a triple $(\{x\}, 2, \frac{1}{3})$ with the meaning:

– only one clock (the name x is unimportant) can be used to measure time;

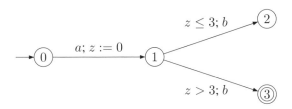

Figure 4.4. *A DTA diagnoser for* $\mathcal{A}(3)$

– the maximal constant that can be used is 2; and

– x can only be compared against multiples of $\frac{1}{3}$ in the interval $[-2, 2]$.

EXAMPLE 4.3.– The automaton $\mathcal{A}(3)$ is diagnosable with the resource $(\{z\}, 3, 1)$.

Let $\mu = (Y, \max, \frac{1}{m})$ be a resource,[9] with Y a finite set of clocks (disjoint from X), $\max \in \mathbb{N}$ and $m \in \mathbb{N}^*$. A timed automaton *of resource* μ is an automaton, which uses clocks in Y, those clocks are compared to constants the absolute values of which are less than $\max$ and which are multiples of $\frac{1}{m}$. We let DTA$_\mu$ be the set of determiistic timed automata of resource μ. In the following, we use the term "regions of μ" for the set of regions of granularity μ and also the clock constraints, which define these regions. The DTA diagnosis problem with fixed resource μ is the following:

PROBLEM 4.6(DTA$_\mu$-DIAGNOSABILITY).–
INPUT: A TA $A = (L, \ell_0, X, \Sigma_{\tau,f}, E, Inv)$ and a resource μ.
PROBLEM: Is A Σ-DTA$_\mu$-diagnosable?

The previous problem is still open: the maximum delay (Δ) to announce a fault is not an input of this problem. A simpler problem is thus:

PROBLEM 4.7(Δ-DTA$_\mu$-DIAGNOSABILITY).–
INPUT: A TA $A = (L, \ell_0, X, \Sigma_{\tau,f}, E, Inv)$ and a delay $\Delta \in \mathbb{N}$.
PROBLEM: Is A (Σ, Δ)-DTA$_\mu$-diagnosable?

A solution to problem [4.7] has been proposed in [BOU 05]. Before giving the sketch of this solution, we focus on the following problem:

PROBLEM 4.8(CHECKING DTA-DIAGNOSABILITY).–
INPUT: A TA $A = (L, \ell_0, X, \Sigma_{\tau,f}, E, Inv)$, a DTA $\Theta = (N, n_0, C, \Sigma, E_\Theta, Inv_\top, F_\Theta,$

---

9. Such a triple is also called a *granularity* in the literature.

$\varnothing$) and $\Delta \in \mathbb{N}$.
PROBLEM: Is Θ a (Σ, Δ)- diagnoser for A?

To solve the previous problem, we consider the automaton A_1 described in section 4.5.1. We let $A(\Delta) = A_1(\Delta)$. In $A(\Delta)$, we can distinguish the Δ-faulty locations, $L_{\Delta f} = \{Bad\}$, and the non-faulty locations, $L_{\neg f}$, of the form $(\ell, 0)$.

To check that Θ is a (Σ, Δ)-diagnoser for A amounts to verifying that each reachable state $((q, v), (n, v'))$ of $A(\Delta) \times \Theta$ satisfies

1) $q \in L_{\Delta f} \implies n \in F_{\Theta}$;
2) $n \in F_{\Theta} \implies q \notin L_{\neg f}$ (i.e., $q = (\ell, k)$ and $k = 1$).

This can be done in PSPACE using the region graph of $A(\Delta) \times \Theta$.

REMARK 4.4.– In $A(\Delta)$, a Δ-faulty run does not necessarily ends in Bad. However, if it ends in $((\ell, 1), v)$, we must have $v(t) = \Delta$, and thus Bad is reachable in one (immediate) discrete step. In the synchronized product $A(\Delta) \times \Theta$, Θ cannot change its location on this last move of $A(\Delta)$, and this is why condition 1 as described above is sufficient.

We can now consider a more liberal version of problem [4.8]: let $\Theta^- = (N, n_0, C, \Sigma, E_{\Theta}, Inv_{\top})$ be a DTA, for which the accepting locations can be chosen. Is there a set $F_{\Theta} \subseteq N$ such that A is (Σ, Δ)-diagnosable with $\Theta = (N, n_0, C, \Sigma, E_{\Theta}, Inv_{\top}, F_{\Theta}, \varnothing)$?

EXAMPLE 4.4.– As pointed out previously, the automaton of Figure 4.4 can be configured to be a diagnoser for $\mathcal{A}(3)$: it suffices to set the accepting locations to $\{3\}$. In the example given in Figure 4.5, we want to diagnose the faults of automaton J of Figure 4.5(a). The automaton O^- of Figure 4.5(b) cannot be configured to diagnose J. Indeed, it cannot make any difference between the runs with traces $\delta.a$ with

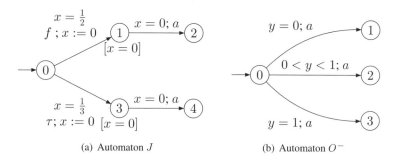

(a) Automaton J (b) Automaton O^-

Figure 4.5. *Automata J and O^-*

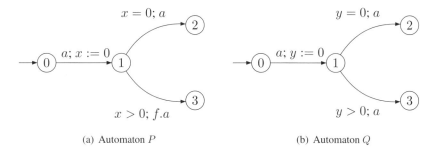

(a) Automaton P (b) Automaton Q

Figure 4.6. *Automata P and Q*

$0 < \delta < 1$ and thus cannot distinguish faulty and non-faulty runs in J. Notice that J is diagnosable in the sense of Definition 4.3, and there is even a DTA, which correctly diagnoses J: we just have to take an automaton of resource $(\{y\}, 1, \frac{1}{2})$.

As witnessed in the previous example, to decide whether a given automaton can be configured to be a diagnoser, we have to check whether it is not too "coarse": it must accept all the Δ-faulty words without accepting a non-faulty word.

Given a run ρ of a DTA H such that

$$\rho = (n_0, \mathbf{0}) \xrightarrow{\delta_0} (n_0, v_0') \xrightarrow{a_1} (n_1, v_1) \cdots (n_{k_1}, v_{k-1}') \xrightarrow{a_k} (n_k, v_k) \xrightarrow{\delta_k} (n_k, v_k'),$$

we let *Symbtr*(ρ) be the *symbolic trace* of ρ: *Symbtr*(ρ) is the[10] sequence (g_i, a_i, R_i) of symbolic labels of the transitions of H fired in the run ρ. Let *Det*$(RG(H))$ be the automaton obtained by determinization of the region graph $RG(H)$ (i.e., we interpret the transitions τ and the transitions (g, τ, R) of $RG(H)$ as invisible). By definition of the region graph $RG(H)$, if ρ is a run of H then *Symbtr*(ρ) is a run of *Det*$(RG(H))$. Conversely, for each word w of *Det*$(RG(H))$, there is a timed word v which is accepted by H such that *Symbtr*$(v) = w$. Actually, the automaton H cannot make any difference (considering the reachable locations) between two-timed words v_1 and v_2, which have the same symbolic trace.

EXAMPLE 4.5.– Consider the automaton given in Figure 4.6(a) taken from [BOU 05] and the candidate diagnoser Q of Figure 4.6(b). The transition $f.a$ in P indicates that a is fired immediately after f. The automaton Q can be configured to diagnose P: it suffices to set localition 3 as accepting. The automaton Q has resource $(\{y\}, 0, 1)$ and Q is thus a 0-diagnoser for P.

---

10. We restrict ourselves to deterministic timed automata and thus there is only one sequence of transitions.

Formally, an automaton Θ^- can be configured to be a diagnoser for A, if and only if the following conditions, (K), is satisfied: we cannot find two runs $\rho_1 \in Faulty_{\geq \Delta}(A)$, $\rho_2 \in NonFaulty(A)$, such that $\pi_{/\Sigma}(tr(\rho_1))$ and $\pi_{/\Sigma}(tr(\rho_2))$ produce the same symbolic trace when "read" by Θ^-. To check (K), we proceed as follows: let $RG_1 = RG(A(\Delta) \times \Theta^-)$ be the region graph of $A(\Delta) \times \Theta^-$. We "project" the labels of this region graph on Θ^-: each label different from τ (time elapsing to the next region) is of the form $(g_1 \wedge g_2, a, R_1 \cup R_2)$ where (g_2, a, R_2) is a symbolic label of Θ^-. The projection consists of replacing the labels $(g_1 \wedge g_2, a, R_1 \cup R_2)$ by (g_2, a, R_2). Let RG_2 be the graph obtained after these replacements. The next step consists of determinizing RG_2 to obtain $Det(RG_2)$ (the transitions τ and (g, τ, R) are the invisible transitions). In $Det(RG_2)$, the nodes are of the form $\{((q_1, \ell), r_1), \cdots, ((q_n, \ell), r_n)\}$ with ℓ a location of Θ^- because Θ^- is deterministic. We can thus use an equivalent form (S, ℓ) with $S = \{(q_1, r_1), \cdots, (q_n, r_n)\}$ and each q_i is a location of L and each r_i a region of RG_1. We let $Bad(\ell)$ be the set of nodes $(\{(q_1, r_1), \cdots, (q_n, r_n)\}, \ell)$ such that there exist two indices i, j with $q_i \in L_{\Delta f}$ and $q_j \in L_{\neg f}$.

EXAMPLE 4.6.– For the automata P and Q described in Figure 4.6, the graphs RG_1 and RG_2 are given in Figure 4.7. We assume $\Delta = 0$ and thus $P(\Delta) = P$ and the Δ-faulty location in P is 3. In the region graphs, r_0 is the initial region with $x = y = 0$ and r_1 is $x = y > 0$. There is no location ℓ in Q such that $Bad(\ell) \neq \varnothing$ because only $(3, 3)$ is Δ-faulty.

Checking whether a set F_Θ exists to make Θ^- a diagnoser amounts to checking whether there is a location $\ell \in N$ such that $Bad(\ell) \neq \varnothing$. If the answer is "yes" then N cannot be partioned so that Θ^- is a diagnoser for A. If the answer is "no" it suffices to set F_Θ to the set of locations ℓ such that, in the region graph, (S, ℓ) contains a location q_i which is in $L_{\Delta f}$. The complexity of this algorithm is doubly exponential in the size of A (one exponential for the region graph, and another for the determinization step).

EXAMPLE 4.7.– On the example of automaton Q, we set 3 to be accepting and Q is a diagnoser for P, and this can be figured out using RG_2 of Figure 4.7.

To solve problem [4.8], the algorithm given in [BOU 05] uses a construction similar to the one we have introduced.

THEOREM 4.11([BOU 05]).– *Problem [4.7] is 2EXPTIME-complete for DTA*

PROOF 4.6.– The 2EXPTIME easiness proof is done by reducing problem [4.7] to a safety game problem. 2EXPTIME hardness consists of reducing the acceptance problem of an alternating Turing machine of exponential space to problem [4.7]. In the sequel, we give the sketch of the 2EXPTIME easiness proof. For the hardness proof

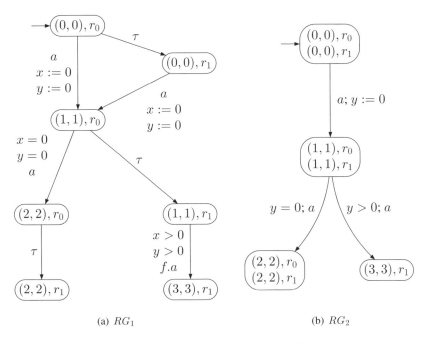

(a) RG_1 (b) RG_2

Figure 4.7. *Region graphs RG_1 and RG_2*

(very technical) and further details the reader is referred to [CHE 04] (in French). Let $A = (L, \ell_0, X, \Sigma_{\tau, f}, E, Inv)$ be a TA and let $A_1(\Delta)$ be the automaton defined in section 4.5.1. Again we use the notation $A(\Delta)$ for $A_1(\Delta)$. As we do not know the structure of a DTA which could diagnose A, we start with the most powerful TA w.r.t. to the given fixed resource μ.

Given a resource $\mu = (Y, \max, \frac{1}{m})$ $(X \cap Y = \varnothing)$, a *minimal guard* for μ is a guard, which defines a region of μ. We can define the *universal automaton* $\mathcal{U} = (\{0\}, \{0\}, Y, \Sigma, E_\mu, Inv_\mu)$ by:

– $Inv_\mu(0) = \top$,

– $(0, g, a, R, 0) \in E_\mu$ for each (g, a, R) s.t. $a \in \Sigma$, $R \subseteq Y$, and g is a minimal guard for μ.

$\mathcal{U}$ is finite because E_μ is finite. Nevertheless $\mathcal{U}$ is not deterministic because it can choose to reset different sets of clocks Y for a pair "guard,letter" (g, a). To diagnose A, we have to find when a set of clocks has to be reset. This can provide enough information to distinguish Δ-faulty words from non-faulty words.

Thus, we first define the automaton $A(\Delta) \times \mathcal{U}$. Second, we build the region graph $RG(A(\Delta) \times \mathcal{U})$ and compute its projection A' on $\mathcal{U}$ (using the same procedure as the one defined for problem [4.8]). Finally, we compute the determinization of A' and we obtain the automaton $H_{A,\Delta,\mu}$. The bad locations of $H_{A,\Delta,\mu}$ are the nodes, which contain both location Bad and another location. We let $Bad(H_{A,\Delta,\mu})$ be the set of bad locations. Next, we define a game from $H_{A,\Delta,\mu}$ using the following transformation. Each transition of $H_{A,\Delta,\mu}$ of the form

is split into two consecutive transitions

Notice that R is a set of clocks of $\mathcal{U}$ because we have projected the labels on $\mathcal{U}$ in the first step.

This transformation produces a turn-based game $G_{A,\Delta,\mu}$ where the set of states are partitioned as follows: Player 1's states (round shape) of type S; Player 2's states (square shape), of the form (S, g, a). The Bad states of $G_{A,\Delta,\mu}$ are the states in $Bad(H_{A,\Delta,\mu})$. The objective of Player 2 is "avoid states Bad." The key step in the proof is then to prove that: Player 2 has a *winning* strategy, if and only if there is a DTA diagnoser for A in DTA_μ. As the game $G_{A,\Delta,\mu}$ is a finite turn-based game, if Player 2 can win, there is a *positional* winning strategy: the choice of actions for Player 2 depends only on the current state (square) of the game. There is even a so-called *most permissive positional strategy*: this strategy gives, for each state, the *set* of actions Player 2 can play to win the game. Thus, we have an algorithm to decide Problem [4.7]: (1) we can check wether there is strategy for Player 2 to win the game $G_{A,\Delta,\mu}$; and (2) if the answer is "yes," compute the most permissive strategy. The previous algorithm runs in 2EXPTIME because (i) the game $G_{A,\Delta,\mu}$ has size doubly exponential in the size of A and (ii) solving a safety finite game can be done in linear time in the size of the game. □

EXAMPLE 4.8.– The previous construction is exemplified in Figure 4.8. The automaton to diagnose P is given in Figure 4.6. We look for DTA of resource $\mu = (\{y\}, 0, 1)$ to diagnose the faults within $\Delta = 0$ time units. As shown before, it suffices to use automaton Q and reset y when the first a occurs; if the second a occurs when $y > 0$ we announce a fault. The game $G_{P,0,\mu}$ obtained using the previous algorithm is given in Figure 4.8. In this graph, r_0 is the region $x = y = 0$, r_1 is $x = y > 0$, r_2 is $y = 0 \land x > 0$, and r_3 is $x = 0 \land y > 0$.

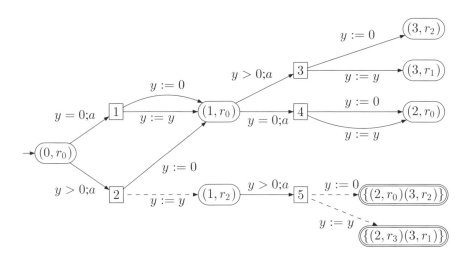

Figure 4.8. *The game* $G_{P,0,\mu}$

The states to avoid for Player 2 (who plays from square-shaped states) are double circled: they contain a faulty state 3 and a non-faulty state 2. In order to win, Player 2
must avoid state $(1, r_2)$, and thus must reset y when a occurs from states $\boxed{2}$. The
winning choices for Player 2 are the plain arrows whereas the losing ones are dashed
arrows. The accepting states where a fault can be announced are $(3, r_2)$ and $(3, r_1)$,
respectively: in state $\boxed{4}$, we can choose either to reset y or not, as no fault has
occurred.

Another interesting class of deterministic timed automata is the class of *event
recording automata* (ERA) introduced in [ALU 94b]. An ERA imposes that clocks
be associated with events. Thus, for each event $a \in \Sigma$, there is a clock x_a, which
is reset exactly when a occurs. It this measures the time since the last occurrence of
a (or since the system started, if no a occurred). The class ERA enjoys nice properties: in particular, every ERA A can be determined in an ERA $Det(A)$, which accepts the same language. Another result of [BOU 05] thus concerns ERA and proves
that solving the diagnosis problem with ERA diagnosers is less expensive than for
DTA:

THEOREM 4.12([BOU 05]).– *Problem [4.7] is PSPACE-complete for ERA.*

As the diagnosis problem is already PSPACE-complete, the previous result gives
an optimal algorithm.

4.6. Other results and open problems

The previous results extend for *multiple types of faults*. In this case, we want to diagnose several faults $f_1, f_2, \ldots, f_k$. It thus suffices to consider the diagnosis problem for each fault f_i (considering that the other faults $f_j, j \neq i$ are replaced by τ). The fault diagnosis problem is closely related to conformance testing. The relationships between these problems are investigated in [KRI 04a, KRI 04b].

Altisen *et al.* [ALT 06] and Jiang and Kumar [JIA 06] consider the diagnosis problem with *digital clocks*. In this framework, the diagnoser cannot measure time but can only count the number of ticks generated by a *clock*. The setting is thus a (nondeterministic) timed automaton A to be diagnosed, and a timed automaton *Clock*, which generates *tick* events (we assume *tick* is not an event of A). The system to be observed produces timed words w, which are generated by the product $A \times Clock$, but the diagnoser can only observe the untimed version, $Unt(w)$ of w. Thus, the timing information about the events of A can only be inferred from the ordering of the events of A and the *tick* event. Given A and *Clock*, checking whether $A \times Clock$ is diagnosable is PSPACE [ALT 06].

Finally, here are some open problems about fault diagnosis of timed systems:

– diagnosability with DTA with no fixed resource or with fixed resource but no bound Δ on the maximal delay; the corresponding problems are problems [4.5] and [4.6];

– for the digital clock diagnosis problem, the problem of deciding the existence of a digital clock (timed automaton) *Clock* such that $A \times Clock$ is diagnosable.

4.7. Bibliography

[ALT 06] ALTISEN K., CASSEZ F., TRIPAKIS S., "Monitoring and fault-diagnosis with digital clocks", *Proceedings of the 6th International Conference on Application of Concurrency to System Design (ACSD'06)*, pp. 101–110, IEEE Computer Society, June 2006.

[ALU 94a] ALUR R., DILL D., "A theory of timed automata", *Theoretical Computer Science*, vol. 126, 183–235, 1994.

[ALU 94b] ALUR R., FIX L., HENZINGER T.A., "A determinizable class of timed automata", *Proceedings of the 6th International Conference on Computer Aided Verification (CAV'94)*, vol. 818 of *Lecture Notes in Computer Science*, pp. 1–13, Springer, 1994.

[BER 98] BÉRARD B., DIEKERT V., GASTIN P., PETIT A., "Characterization of the expressive power of silent transitions in timed automata", *Fundamenta Informaticae*, vol. 36, num. 2–3, 145–182, 1998.

[BOU 05] BOUYER P., CHEVALIER F., D'SOUZA D., "Fault diagnosis using timed automata", *Proceedings of the 8th International Conference on Foundations of Software*

Science and Computation Structures (FoSSaCS'05), vol. 3441 of *Lecture Notes in Computer Science*, pp. 219–233, Springer, April 2005.

[CAS 08] CASSEZ F., TRIPAKIS S., "Fault diagnosis with static or dynamic diagnosers", *Fundamenta Informaticae*, vol. 88, num. 4, 497–540, November 2008.

[CHE 04] CHEVALIER F., Détection d'erreurs dans les systèmes temporisés, University Report, DEA Algorithmique, Paris, France, September 2004.

[COU 05] COUVREUR J.M., DURET-LUTZ A., POITRENAUD D., "On-the-Fly Emptiness Checks for Generalized Büchi Automata", GODE FROID P. (ed.), *Proceedings of SPIN*, vol. 3639 of *Lecture Notes in Computer Science*, pp. 169–184, Springer, 2005.

[FIN 05] FINKEL O., "On decision problems for timed automata", *Bulletin of the European Association for Theoretical Computer Science*, vol. 87, 185–190, 2005.

[HOL 05] HOLZMANN G.J., "Software model checking with SPIN", *Advances in Computers*, vol. 65, 78–109, 2005.

[JIA 01] JIANG S., HUANG Z., CHANDRA V., KUMAR R., "A polynomial algorithm for testing diagnosability of discrete event systems", *IEEE Transactions on Automatic Control*, vol. 46, num. 8, 1318–1321, August 2001.

[JIA 06] JIANG S., KUMAR R., "Diagnosis of dense-time systems using digital clocks", *Proceedings of the American Control Conference (ACC'06)*, IEEE Computer Society, June 2006.

[KRI 04a] KRICHEN M., TRIPAKIS S., "Black-box conformance testing for real-time systems", *Proceedings of the 11th International SPIN Workshop on Model Checking of Software (SPIN'04)*, vol. 2989 of *Lecture Notes in Computer Science*, pp. 109–126, Springer, 2004.

[KRI 04b] KRICHEN M., TRIPAKIS S., "Real-time testing with timed automata testers and coverage criteria", *Proceedings of Formal Techniques, Modelling and Analysis of Timed and Fault Tolerant Systems (FORMATS-FTRTFT'04)*, vol. 3253 of *Lecture Notes in Computer Science*, pp. 134–151, Springer, 2004.

[RIC 06] RICKER L., LAFORTUNE S., GENC S., "DESUMA: A tool integrating GIDDES and UMDES", *Proceedings of the 8th Workshop on Discrete Event Systems (WODES'08)*, Ann Arbor, MI, USA, IEEE Computer Society, July 2006.

[SAM 95] SAMPATH M., SENGUPTA R., LAFORTUNE S., SINNAMOHIDEEN K., TENEKETZIS D., "Diagnosability of discrete event systems", *IEEE Transactions on Automatic Control*, vol. 40, num. 9, 1555–1575, September 1995.

[SAM 96] SAMPATH M., SENGUPTA R., LAFORTUNE S., SINNAMOHIDEEN K., TENEKETZIS D., "Failure diagnosis using discrete-event models", *IEEE Transactions on Control Systems technology*, vol. 4, num. 2, 105–124, March 1996.

[SCH 99] SCHNOEBELEN P., BÉRARD B., BIDOIT M., LAROUSSINIE F., PETIT A., *Vérification de logiciels : Techniques et outils de model-checking*, Vuibert, Paris, 1999.

[SCH 05] SCHWOON S., ESPARZA J., "A note on on-the-fly verification algorithms", HALBWACHS N., ZUCK L.D. (ed.), *TACAS*, vol. 3440 of *Lecture Notes in Computer Science*, pp. 174-190, Springer, 2005.

[TRI 02] TRIPAKIS S., "Fault diagnosis for timed automata", *Proceedings of the International Conference on Formal Techniques in Real Time and Fault Tolerant Systems (FTRTFT'02)*, vol. 2469 of *Lecture Notes in Computer Science*, pp. 205–224, Springer, 2002.

[TRI 06] TRIPAKIS S., "Folk theorems on the determinization and minimization of timed automata", *Information Processing Letters*, vol. 99, num. 6, 222–226, Elsevier, 2006.

[YOO 02] YOO T.S., LAFORTUNE S., "Polynomial-time verification of diagnosability of partially-observed discrete-event systems", *IEEE Transactions on Automatic Control*, vol. 47, num. 9, 1491–1495, September 2002.

[YOO 03] YOO T.S., GARCIA H., "Computation of fault detection delay in discrete-event systems", *Proceedings of the 14th International Workshop on Principles of Diagnosis, DX'03*, pp. 207–212, Washington, DC, USA, June 2003.

Chapter 5

Quantitative Verification of Markov Chains

5.1. Introduction

Hardware and software systems are more and more pervasive in every day life and, therefore, there is an obvious demand for these systems to meet the functional and performance requirements that the users expect. Automatic verification methods are a possible, and doable, way to increase our level of confidence in the systems that we design and produce, both in terms of functionality (what the system does) and performance (how long does it take). Verification methods that take into account the randomness of systems work with a model of the system which is a stochastic process. In order to limit the complexity of the verification process, these stochastic processes are often either discrete time Markov chains (DTMC) or continuous time Markov chains (CTMC), usually automatically generated by some higher level formalism such as stochastic Petri nets or stochastic process algebras.

Historically, the functional verification and the evaluation of performance of an application have been considered as two distinct steps of the system development and verification process: each step had its own model and associated verification techniques. In the past 15 years, we have instead witnessed the flourishing of a discipline that aims at taking into consideration both aspects simultaneously, and is often referred to as probabilistic verification or, more appropriately, of verification of probabilistic systems. The moving force of the discipline is the need of being able to evaluate the probability of a property expressed as a logic formula. To show why this is an important need, we recall a classical example from system reliability.

Chapter written by Susanna DONATELLI and Serge HADDAD.

Consider a system in which the states can be partitioned in three classes: W is the state in which the system works properly, D is the state in which the system is still working, although in a degraded mode, and F is the state in which the system is not working (failure states). The system can evolve from W state to D or F state, and from D to F state. A classical reliability measure for such a system is the probability of being in an F state within a given time interval I. The classical performance and reliability methods can be easily applied to compute such probability.

On the other hand, if we ask for a slightly more refined question, such as the probability of failing within I, *given that the system has not passed through a degraded mode of operation*, then we need to express and compute the probability of reaching an F state within I, passing only through W state. A temporal logic (as CSL for example) has temporal operators that allow a simple, and semantically well-founded definition for the above property. In this particular case, the formula is $P_{\leq p}(W \, \mathcal{U}^I F)$, where p is the upper limit of the probability of such an event as fixed by the designer.

This chapter presents two main themes of probabilistic verification: the temporal logics to express probabilistic verification properties and the techniques to verify such properties for Markov chains.

The first part of the chapter recalls the basic elements of stochastic processes and Markov chains, the second part is devoted to the quantitative verification of discrete time Markov chains, followed by the quantitative verification of continuous time Markov chains. The chapter concludes with an overview of the literature on various techniques for probabilistic verification as well as on a number of extensions to the basic temporal logics presented in the chapter.

5.2. Performance evaluation of Markov models

5.2.1. *A stochastic model for discrete events systems*

In this section, we assume that the reader is familiar with the basic probability concepts. For more details the interested reader may consult [FEL 68, FEL 71, TRI 82].

Notations

– $\Pr(E)$ is the probability of event E, while $\Pr(A \mid B)$ is the probability of A given B;

– the term *almost*, in an expression like *almost everywhere* or *almost surely*, means with probability 1;

– $\mathbb{R}$ (resp. $\mathbb{R}^+, \mathbb{R}^{+*}$) denotes the real numbers (resp. non-negative and strictly positive reals). If x is a real, then $\lfloor x \rfloor$ denotes its integer part;

– if $E \subseteq \mathbb{R}$ then $Inf(E)$ (resp. $Sup(E)$) denotes the lower (resp. upper) bound of E.

Given a discrete event system, its execution is characterized by a sequence, possibly infinite, of events $\{e_1, e_2, \ldots\}$ and associated interval of time between successive events in the sequence. Only the events can change the state of the system.

Formally, the stochastic behavior of a DES is defined by two families of random variables:

– $X_0, \ldots, X_n, \ldots$ defined over the (discrete) state space of the system, denoted as S. In the following, unless otherwise specified, we assume that S is finite. X_0 is the system initial state and X_n ($n > 0$) is the state after the nth event. The occurrence of an event does not necessarily modify the state of the system, and therefore X_{n+1} may be equal to X_n;

– $T_0, \ldots, T_n, \ldots$ defined over $\mathbb{R}^+$, where T_0 is the time interval before the first event and T_n ($n > 0$) is the time interval between the nth and the $(n + 1)$th event. Please note that this interval may be null (e.g., a sequence of assignment instructions can be considered as instantaneous with respect to a complex database transaction involving some input/output activity).

If the initial distribution of variable x_0 is concentrated on a single state s, we say that the process starts in s (i.e., $\Pr(x_0 = s) = 1$).

A priori there is no restriction whatsoever on the two families of random variables, but, for the stochastic processes that we shall study in the following, we assume that a discrete event system cannot execute an infinite number of actions in a finite amount of time. That is to say:

$$\sum_{n=0}^{\infty} t_n = \infty \text{ almost surely.} \tag{5.1}$$

The above property allows to define the state of the system at a given time instant. let $n(\tau)$ be the random variable defined by

$$n(\tau) =_{def} min(\{n \mid \sum_{k=0}^{n} t_k > \tau\}),$$

according to equation [5.1], $n(\tau)$ is defined *almost everywhere*. As exemplified in Figure 5.1, $n(\tau)$ can have jumps of size bigger than one. The state $y(\tau)$ of the system at time τ, is then simply $x_{n(\tau)}$. it is important to remark that $y(\tau)$ it is not equivalent to the stochastic process, but it allows, in most cases, to apply standard solution methods.

The diagram in Figure 5.1 represents a possible *execution* of the process and shows the interpretation of each random variable defined above. In the execution, the process is initially in state s_4, where it stays until, at time τ_0, it moves to state s_6. At time $\tau_0 + \tau_1$, the system visits, in zero time, the states s_3 and s_{12}, ending up in state s_7,

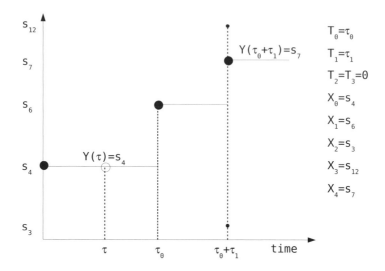

Figure 5.1. *An execution of the stochastic process*

where it stays for a certain amount of time. The use of $y(\tau)$ in continuous time, hides the vanishing states s_3 and s_{12} visited by the process.

The performance evaluation of a discrete event system can be based on two complementary approaches:

– analysis under transient behavior, that is to say, the computation of performance measures which are function of the time passed since the start of the system. This type of analysis is well suited for studying the system behavior in the initialization phase, or for studying systems with final states. Classical applications of transient analysis can be found in the studies aimed at assessing the dependability and reliability of systems [LAP 95, MEY 80, TRI 92];

– analysis in steady state, that is to say, the computation of performance measures which takes into account only the stationary behavior of the system, that may be reached after a transient initial phase.

The analysis in steady state makes sense only if such a stationary behavior exists, a condition that can be expressed as follows, denoting $\pi(\tau)$ the distribution of $y(\tau)$:

$$\lim_{\tau \to \infty} \pi(\tau) = \pi,$$ [5.2]

where π is also a distribution, called the *stationary distribution*.

The transient and stationary distributions are the basis for the computation of *performance indices*. Examples of indices are the steady state probability that a server is up and running, the probability that at time τ a connection has been established, and the mean number of clients waiting for a service. To abstract from the definition of the single performance index, we can introduce the concept of *reward function*, a function f defined on the set of states of the discrete event system and with value onto $\mathbb{R}$. Given a distribution π, the quantity $\sum_{s \in s} \pi(s) \cdot f(s)$ represents the measure of the performance index defined by f.

If f takes values over $\{0, 1\}$, we can consider f as the definition of an *atomic proposition* which is satisfied in state s, if $f(s) = 1$ and false otherwise. in the following we shall indicate with $\mathcal{P}$ the set of atomic propositions and with $s \vDash \phi$, with s a state and ϕ an atomic proposition, the fact that s verifies (or satisfies) ϕ. in this context, if π is a distribution, the quantity $\sum_{s \vDash \phi} \pi(s)$ represents the measure of the index defined by f.

5.2.2. *Discrete time Markov chains*

Presentation

A discrete time Markov chain is a stochastic process with the following characteristics:

– the time interval between the time instants t_n is a constant whose value is 1;

– the next state depends only on the current state, and the transition probability among states remains constant over time[1]

$$\Pr(X_{n+1} = s_j \mid X_0 = s_{i_0}, ..., X_n = s_i) =$$

$$\Pr(X_{n+1} = s_j \mid X_n = s_i) = p_{ij} =_{def} \mathbf{P}[i, j]$$

and we shall freely mix the two notations p_{ij} and $\mathbf{P}[i, j]$ for the transition probability.

Transient and steady state behavior of a DTMC

We now recall a number of classical results on the analysis of DTMC: the results will be explained in an intuitive manner, a full mathematical treatment of the topic being out of the scope of this chapter.

The transient analysis is rather simple: the change of state takes place at time instants $\{1, 2, \ldots\}$, and given an initial distribution π_0 and the transition probability

---

1. Which justifies the definition of a *homogenous* Markov chain.

matrix $\mathbf{P}$, we have that π_n, the distribution of X_n (i.e., the state of the chain at time n) can be expressed as $\pi_n = \pi_0 \cdot \mathbf{P}^n$, which is computed using a basic recurrence scheme.

To analyze the asymptotic behavior of a DTMC, we need to investigate a bit further the DTMC behavior, in particular we shall classify states as follows:

– a state s is said to be *transient*, if the probability of visiting s more than once is strictly less than 1. As a consequence, the probability of $\Pr(X_n = s)$ goes to zero as n tends to infinity. A state is said to be *recurrent*, if it is not transient;

– a recurrent state s is said to be *null recurrent*, if the mean time between two successive visits to s is infinite. Intuitively, a null-recurrent state will be visited at intervals whose mean duration goes to infinity and therefore the probability of visiting s will also tend toward 0;

– a recurrent state s is *not null recurrent* if the mean time between two successive visit to s is finite. If a steady state distribution exists, then it is concentrated on the set of non-null recurrent states.

We now explain in detail the steady-state analysis procedure for the case of DTMCs with a finite state space. The first step consists of building the following graph:

– the set of nodes is the set of states of the chain;

– there is an arc from s_i to s_j if $p_{ij} > 0$.

On the graph, we compute the strongly connected components (SCCs). If an SCC has an exit arc, then all the states of the SCC are transient. All the arcs of a bottom SCC (BSCC), which are components without an exit arc, are non-null recurrent. In the particular case of a sink, SCC composed by a single state s (i.e. $\mathbf{P}[s, s] = 1$), we say that s is an *absorbing* state.

If the graph is strongly connected (there is a single SCC), then the chain is said to be *irreducible*. In the more general case instead each sink SCC constitutes an irreducible subchain.

Even if we consider an irreducible chain, the existence of a steady-state distribution is not guaranteed. Indeed a chain with two states s_0 and s_1, with an initial distribution concentrated in a single state and transition probabilities $p_{0,1} = p_{1,0} = 1$, keeps switching between the two states at each instant of time and, therefore, it does not converge to any stationary distribution. An irreducible chain is said to be *periodic* of period $k > 1$, if its states can be partitioned into subsets $S_0, S_1, \ldots, S_{k-1}$ such that, from the states in S_i the chain moves, in one step only to states which are in $S_{(i+1) \mod k}$. It is possible to compute the periodicity of a chain with a linear time algorithm (in the size of the graph) that we describe in the following using the graph given in Figure 5.2.

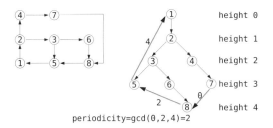

Figure 5.2. *Example of the computation of a DTMC periodicity*

The algorithm first computes a directed tree that covers all nodes of the chain, using a breadth-first strategy, that allows us to label each node with its 'height" h. The next steps associate with each arc (u, v) of the graph a weight $w(u, v) = h(u) - h(v) + 1$: as a result all the arcs that are part of the covering tree have a null weight. The periodicity of the graph is then the greatest common divisor (gcd) of the arcs of non-null weight. The formal proof of correctness, that we do not develop here is based on the two following observations. Periodicity is the gcd of the length of the elementary circuits of the graphs, and this length is equal to the sum of the weight of the arcs of the circuit.

An irreducible, aperiodic chain (also called *ergodic*) has a stationary distribution, and such a distribution is *independent from the initial distribution*. The computation of the steady state distribution is then rather easy, since $\pi_{n+1} = \pi_n \cdot \mathbf{P}$. Taking the limit as n goes to infinity (which is mathematically sound) we get $\pi = \pi \cdot \mathbf{P}$. Moreover, π is the single distribution which is a solution for:

$$\mathbf{X} = \mathbf{X} \cdot \mathbf{P}. \qquad [5.3]$$

Please note that an initial distribution which is the solution of the above equation, is *invariant*: whatever the instant of time at which the chain is observed the distribution will be equal to the initial distribution. Equation [5.3] can be solved with a direct method, once we add the normalization equation $\mathbf{X} \cdot \mathbf{1}^T = 1$ where $\mathbf{1}^T$ denotes the column vector of all 1. If the size of the system is large, iterative methods are more effective. The simplest one iterates over $\mathbf{X} \leftarrow \mathbf{X} \cdot \mathbf{P}$ [STE 94].

We now consider a more general case, with the single remaining assumption that the BSCC (denoted as $\{\mathcal{C}_1, \ldots, \mathcal{C}_k\}$) are aperiodic with stationary distribution $\{\pi_1, \ldots, \pi_k\}$. In this case also, the chain has a stationary distribution (which now depends on the initial distribution), given by $\pi = \sum_{i=1}^{k} \Pr(\text{of reaching } \mathcal{C}_i) \cdot \pi_i$. To compute the probability of reaching a BSCC we condition on being in a initial state: $\Pr(\text{of reaching } \mathcal{C}_i) = \sum_{s \in S} \pi_0(s) \cdot \pi'_{\mathcal{C}_i}(s)$ where $\pi'_{\mathcal{C}_i}(s) = \Pr(\text{of reaching } \mathcal{C}_i \mid X_0 = s)$. If $\mathbf{P}_{T,T}$ is the submatrix of the transition matrix limited to transient states, and if $\mathbf{P}_{T,i}$ is the submatrix from transient states towards the states of $\mathcal{C}_i$, then

$\pi'_{C_i} = (\sum_{n \geq 0} (\mathbf{P}_{T,T})^n) \cdot \mathbf{P}_{T,i} \cdot \mathbf{1}^T = (\mathbf{I} - \mathbf{P}_{T,T})^{-1} \cdot \mathbf{P}_{T,i} \cdot \mathbf{1}^T$. The first equality is obtained by conditioning on the length of all possible paths that leads to C_i, while the second one is immediate.

5.2.3. Continuous time Markov chain

Presentation

A continuous time Markov chain has the following characteristics:

– the time interval between the time instants T_n is a random variable distributed as a negative exponential, whose rate depends only on the state X_n. That is to say:

$$\Pr(T_n \leq \tau \mid X_0 = s_{i_0}, ..., X_n = s_i, T_0 \leq \tau_0, ..., T_{n-1} \leq \tau_{n-1}) =$$

$$\Pr(T_n \leq \tau \mid X_n = s_i) = 1 - e^{\lambda_i \cdot \tau}$$

– the next state depends only on the current state, and the transition probabilities remain constant[2] over time:

$$\Pr(X_{n+1} = s_j \mid X_0 = s_{i_0}, ..., X_n = s_i, T_0 \leq \tau_0, ..., T_{n-1} \leq \tau_{n-1}) =$$

$$\Pr(X_{n+1} = s_j \mid X_n - s_i) = p_{ij} =_{def} \mathbf{P}[i,j]$$

The DTMC defined by $\mathbf{P}$ is called *embedded chain*. It observes the change of state, independently of the time-elapsed in the state. A CTMC state is said to be absorbing, if it is absorbing in the embedded DTMC.

Transient and stationary behavior of a CTMC

In a continuous time Markov chain, at any time the evolution of a DES is completely determined by its current state, due to the memoryless property of the exponential distribution.

In particular, the process is fully characterized by the initial distribution $\pi(0)$, matrix $\mathbf{P}$ and by the rates λ_i. Let $\pi(\tau)$ be the distribution of $Y(\tau)$ and write $\pi_k(\tau) = \pi(t)(s_k)$. If δ is small enough, the probability of more than one event occurring in the interval τ and $\tau + \delta$ is very small and can be neglected, and the probability of a change from state k to state k' is approximately equal to $\lambda_k \cdot \delta \cdot p_{kk'}$ (by definition of exponential distribution).

$$\pi_k(\tau + \delta) \approx \pi_k(\tau) \cdot (1 - \lambda_k \cdot \delta) + \sum_{k' \neq k} \pi_{k'}(\tau) \cdot \lambda_{k'} \cdot \delta \cdot p_{k'k}$$

---

2. Also in this case, we say that the chain is *homogenous*.

From which we derive

$$\frac{\pi_k(\tau + \delta) - \pi_k(\tau)}{\delta} \approx \pi_k(\tau) \cdot (-\lambda_k) + \sum_{k' \neq k} \pi_{k'}(\tau) \cdot \lambda_{k'} \cdot p_{k'k}$$

and finally

$$\frac{d\pi_k}{d\tau} = \pi_k(\tau) \cdot (-\lambda_k) + \sum_{k' \neq k} \pi_{k'}(\tau) \cdot \lambda_{k'} \cdot p_{k'k}.$$

Let us define matrix $\mathbf{Q}$ as: $q_{kk'} = \lambda_k \cdot p_{kk'}$ for $k \neq k'$ and $q_{kk} = -\lambda_k (= -\sum_{k' \neq k} q_{kk'})$. We can the rewrite the previous equation as:

$$\frac{d\boldsymbol{\pi}}{d\tau} = \boldsymbol{\pi} \cdot \mathbf{Q} \qquad [5.4]$$

Matrix $\mathbf{Q}$ is called *infinitesimal generator* of the CTMC.

According to equation [5.4], the infinitesimal generator completely specifies the evolution of the system. Although this equation clearly establish the memoryless property of the CTMC, it does not give any direct mean of computing the transient behavior of a CTMC. A possible method, called *uniformization*, has been defined in [JEN 53], and it is based upon the construction of a second Markov chain, which is equivalent to the first one from a probabilistic point of view. This chain is built as follows. Let us choose a value $\mu \geq Sup(\{\lambda_i\})$, and assume that this is the parameter of the exponential distribution of the time until the next change of state, whatever the current state is (from which the term *uniform*). The change of state is defined by the transition matrix $\mathbf{P}^\mu$ defined by: $\forall i \neq j, \mathbf{P}^\mu[s_i, s_j] = (\mu)^{-1} \cdot \lambda_i \cdot \mathbf{P}[s_i, s_j]$. The computation of the infinitesimal generator of such a chain shows immediately that it is equal to the infinitesimal generator of the first CTMC, which implies that, if we disregard transitions, the two CTMCs describe the same stochastic process. We can then compute the transient distribution $\boldsymbol{\pi}(\tau)$ as follows. We first compute the probability of being in state s at time τ, knowing that there have been n changes of state in the interval $[0, \tau]$. This probability can be computed through the embedded Markov chain, and precisely as $\boldsymbol{\pi}(0) \cdot (\mathbf{P}^\mu)^n$. We can then "condition" it through the probability of having n changes of state, knowing that the time between two successive changes follows an exponential distribution. This probability is given by $e^{-\mu \cdot \tau} \cdot (\mu \cdot \tau)^n / n!$, from which we obtain

$$\boldsymbol{\pi}(\tau) = \boldsymbol{\pi}(0) \cdot (e^{-\mu \cdot \tau} \sum_{n \geq 0} \frac{(\mu \cdot \tau)^n (\mathbf{P}^\mu)^n}{n!}).$$

Although there is an infinite sum, in practice the sum converges rather quickly, and the sum can be stopped once the precision required is greater than $e^{-\mu \cdot \tau} \cdot (\mu \cdot \tau)^n / n!$.

We now consider the asymptotic behavior of a CTMC. Again, the simplest way is to study the embedded chain, which, as observed when explaining uniformization, is not unique. Let us build a DTMC as follows. Choose $\mu > Sup(\{\lambda_i\})$, since the inequality is strict, it is true that, for each state s, $\mathbf{P}^\mu[s,s] > 0$ and therefore each BSCC of this chain is ergodic. As a consequence, a single stationary distribution exists, that measures the steady state probability of the occurrence of a state. Since the uniform chain has the same mean sojourn time in each state, equal to $(1/\mu)$, this also gives the stationary distribution of the CTMC.

In the particular case (rather frequent) in which the embedded chain is ergodic, this distribution can be computed through the solution of the equation $\mathbf{X} = \mathbf{X} \cdot \mathbf{P}^\mu$, and $\mathbf{P}^\mu = \mathbf{I} + (1/\mu)\mathbf{Q}$. Therefore, the distribution is a unique solution of the equation

$$\mathbf{X} \cdot \mathbf{Q} = 0 \quad \text{and} \quad \mathbf{X} \cdot \mathbf{1}^T = 1. \qquad [5.5]$$

By analogy, we then say that the CTMC is ergodic.

5.3. Verification of discrete time Markov chain

5.3.1. *Temporal logics for Markov chains*

We consider a "probabilistic" extension of the CTL^* logic, that is named $PCTL^*$. The syntax of this logic is defined inductively upon state formulae and paths formulae.

DEFINITION 5.1.– Let $\mathcal{P}$ be the set of atomic propositions.
A $PCTL^*$ state formula (relative to $\mathcal{P}$) is defined by:

E_1: If $\phi \in \mathcal{P}$ then ϕ is a $PCTL^*$ state formula;

E_2: If ϕ and ψ are $PCTL^*$ state formulae then $\neg\phi$ and $\phi \wedge \psi$ are $PCTL^*$ state formulae;

E_3: If φ is a $PCTL^*$ path formula, $a \in [0,1]$ is a rational number, and $\bowtie \in \{=,\neq, <,\leq,>,\geq\}$ then $P_{\bowtie a}\varphi$ is a $PCTL^*$ state formula.

A path formula of $PCTL^*$ (relative to $\mathcal{P}$) is defined by:

C_1: A $PCTL^*$ state formula is a $PCTL^*$ path formula;

C_2: if φ and θ are $PCTL^*$ path formulae, then $\neg\varphi$ and $\varphi \wedge \theta$ are $PCTL^*$ path formulae;

C_3: if φ and θ are $PCTL^*$ path formulae, then $\mathcal{X}\varphi$ and $\varphi\mathcal{U}\theta$ are $PCTL^*$ path formulae.

Two subsets of the $PCTL^*$ formulae are of particular interest. The first subset is called $PCTL$ (by analogy with CTL) and it is built using only the rules E_1, E_2, E_3, C_3'

where C_3' is defined as "If ϕ and ψ are $PCTL$ state formulae, the $\mathcal{X}\phi$ and $\phi\mathcal{U}\psi$ are $PCTL$ path formulae". The second subset is called $PLTL$ (by analogy with LTL) and it is built only on the rules E_1, E_3, C_1', C_2, C_3 where C_1' is "If $\varphi \in \mathcal{P}$ the φ is a $PLTL$ state formula".

We now explain how to evaluate the truth value of a $PCTL$, $PLTL$, or $PCTL^*$ formula.

The semantics of formulae is given in the following. We consider a Markov chain $\mathcal{M}$ whose states are labeled by a subset of atomic propositions. We indicate with s a state of the chain and with $\sigma = s_0, s_1, \ldots$ an infinite path in the graph associated to the chain. We denote σ_i the suffix $s_i, s_{i+1}, \ldots$, and $\mathcal{M}, s \models \phi$ the satisfaction of state formula ϕ by state s and $\sigma \models \varphi$ the satisfaction of path formula φ by path σ.

DEFINITION 5.2.– Let $\mathcal{M}$ be a Markov chain, s a state of the chain, and σ a path of the chain.

The satisfaction of the state formula ϕ by s is inductively defined by:

- if $\phi \in \mathcal{P}$ then $\mathcal{M}, s \models \phi$, iff s is labelled by ϕ;
- if $\phi \equiv \neg\psi$ then $\mathcal{M}, s \models \phi$, iff $\mathcal{M}, s \not\models \psi$;
- $\phi \equiv \psi_1 \wedge \psi_2$ then $\mathcal{M}, s \models \phi$, iff $\mathcal{M}, s \models \psi_1$ and $\mathcal{M}, s \models \psi_2$;
- if $\phi \equiv P_{\bowtie a}\varphi$ then $\mathcal{M}, s \models \phi$, iff $\Pr(\{\sigma \models \varphi\} \mid s_0 = s) \bowtie a$.

The satisfaction of a path formula φ by σ is inductively defined by

- if φ is a state formula, then $\sigma \models \varphi$ iff $\mathcal{M}, s_0 \models \phi$;
- if $\varphi \equiv \neg\theta$ then $\sigma \models \varphi$, iff $\sigma \not\models \theta$;
- if $\varphi \equiv \theta_1 \wedge \theta_2$ then $\sigma \models \varphi$, iff $\sigma \models \theta_1$ and $\sigma \models \theta_2$;
- if $\varphi \equiv \mathcal{X}\theta$ then $\sigma \models \varphi$, iff $\sigma_1 \models \theta$;
- if $\varphi \equiv \theta_1\mathcal{U}\theta_2$ then $\sigma \models \varphi$, iff $\exists i \; \sigma_i \models \theta_2$ and $\forall j < i \; \sigma_j \models \theta_1$.

This semantics assume implicitly that the set of paths that verify a formula is measurable. This hypothesis is justifiable, as can be proved through basic results of measure theory, but this goes beyond the scope of this chapter.

5.3.2. *Verification of PCTL formulae*

Given a DTMC and a $PCTL$ formula ϕ the verification algorithm proceeds by evaluating bottom up the subformulae of the syntactic tree of ϕ, from the leaves up to the root. At each step the algorithm evaluates a subformula considering as atomic propositions the operands of the most external operator (of the subformula associated to the tree node considered).

Considering the syntax of $PCTL$ the formulae to be considered are $\neg\psi, \psi \wedge \chi, P_{\bowtie a}\mathcal{X}\psi, P_{\bowtie a}\psi\mathcal{U}\chi$, where ψ and χ are (formulae transformed into) atomic propositions. We now provide an informal explanation of the algorithm and its correctness.

$\boxed{\phi = \neg\psi}$ The algorithm labels with ϕ each state not labelled with ψ.

$\boxed{\phi = \psi \wedge \chi}$ The algorithm labels with ϕ each state labelled with ψ et χ.

$\boxed{\phi = P_{\bowtie a}\mathcal{X}\psi}$ The algorithm computes the probability p_s of reaching in a single step a state labeled with ψ, with $p_s \equiv \sum_{s'\models\psi} \mathbf{P}[s, s']$ where $\mathbf{P}$ is the transition matrix of the DTMC. State s is then labeled with ϕ iff $p_s \bowtie a$.

$\boxed{\phi = P_{\bowtie a}\psi\mathcal{U}\chi}$ The algorithm computes the probability of reaching a state labeled by χ, passing only through states labelled by ψ. Let p_s be such a probability. If $s \models \chi$ then $p_s = 1$; if $s \not\models \chi$ and $s \not\models \psi$ then $p_s = 0$. In all other cases, p_s is computed on a transformed DTMC: all the states described above are made absorbing, and then the probability of reaching χ from s in the new chain. Since each χ state is a BSCC, such a probability can be computed as explained in section 5.2.2, and illustrated in Figure 5.3. State s is then labeled with ϕ, iff $p_s \bowtie a$.

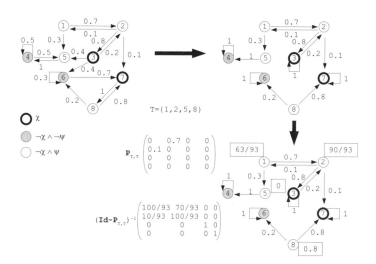

Figure 5.3. *Calculate the $P_{\bowtie a}\psi\mathcal{U}\chi$*

5.3.3. *Aggregation of Markov chains*

In order to establish the correction of the verification algorithm of PLTL, we recall the notions of aggregation in Markov chains. The aggregation of finite Markov chains is an efficient method when one is faced with huge chains [KEM 60]. Its principle is simple: substitute a chain with an "equivalent" chain where each state of the lumped chain is a set of states of the initial chain. There are different versions of aggregation depending on whether the aggregation is sound for every initial distribution (*strong aggregation*) or for at least one distribution (*weak aggregation*). We simultaneously introduce aggregation for DTMCs and CTMCs. We note π_0 the initial distribution of the chain and X_n (resp. X_t) the random variable describing the state of the DTMC (resp. CTMC) at time n (resp. t) (variables called Y at the beginning of this chapter). $\mathbf{P}$ is the transition matrix of the DTMC and $\mathbf{Q}$ is the infinitesimal generator of the CTMC.

DEFINITION 5.3.– Let $\mathcal{M}$ be a DTMC (resp. a CTMC) and $\{X_n\}_{n\in\mathbb{N}}$ (resp. $\{X_t\}_{t\in\mathbb{R}^+}$) the family of corresponding random variables. Let $\{S_i\}_{i\in I}$ be a partition of the state space. Define the random variable Y_n for $n \in \mathbb{N}$ (resp. Y_t for $t \in \mathbb{R}^+$) by $Y_n = i$ iff $X_n \in S_i$ (resp. $Y_t = i$ iff $X_t \in S_i$). Then:

– $\mathbf{P}$ (resp. $\mathbf{Q}$) is *strongly lumpable* w.r.t. $\{S_i\}_{i\in I}$
iff there exists a transition matrix $\mathbf{P}^{lp}$ (resp. an infinitesimal generator $\mathbf{Q}^{lp}$) s.t
$\forall\pi_0 \{Y_n\}_{n\in\mathbb{N}}$ (resp. $\{Y_t\}_{t\in\mathbb{R}^+}$) is a DTMC (resp. CTMC)
with transition matrix $\mathbf{P}^{lp}$ (resp. with infinitesimal generator $\mathbf{Q}^{lp}$);

– $\mathbf{P}$ (resp. $\mathbf{Q}$) is *weakly lumpable* w.r.t. $\{S_i\}_{i\in I}$
iff $\exists\pi_0 \{Y_n\}_{n\in\mathbb{N}}$ (resp. $\{Y_t\}_{t\in\mathbb{R}^+}$) is a DTMC (resp. CTMC).

While a characterization of the strong aggregation by examination of the transition matrix or the infinitesimal generator is easy, the search of a weak aggregation is much harder [LED 60]. So we introduce exact aggregation, a simple case of weak aggregation.

DEFINITION 5.4.– Let $\mathcal{M}$ be a DTMC (resp. a CTMC) and $\{X_n\}_{n\in\mathbb{N}}$ (resp. $\{X_t\}_{t\in\mathbb{R}^+}$) the family of corresponding random variables. Let $\{S_i\}_{i\in I}$ be a partition of the state space. Define the random variable Y_n for $n \in \mathbb{N}$ (resp. Y_t for $t \in \mathbb{R}^+$) by $Y_n = i$ iff $X_n \in S_i$ (resp. $Y_t = i$ iff $X_t \in S_i$). Then:

– an initial distribution π_0 is *equiprobable* w.r.t. $\{S_i\}_{i\in I}$
if $\forall i \in I, \forall s, s' \in S_i, \pi_0(s) = \pi_0(s')$;

– $\mathbf{P}$ (resp. $\mathbf{Q}$) is *exactly lumpable* w.r.t. $\{S_i\}_{i\in I}$
iff there exists a transition matrix $\mathbf{P}^{lp}$ (resp. an infinitesimal generator $\mathbf{Q}^{lp}$) s.t.
$\forall\pi_0$ equiprobable $\{Y_n\}_{n\in\mathbb{N}}$ (resp. $\{Y_t\}_{t\in\mathbb{R}^+}$) is a DTMC (resp. CTMC)

with transition matrix $\mathbf{P}^{lp}$ (resp. with infinitesimal generator $\mathbf{Q}^{lp}$) and π_n (resp. π_t) is equiprobable w.r.t. $\{S_i\}_{i \in I}$.

Exact and strong aggregations have simple characterizations [SCH 84] stated in the next proposition.

PROPOSITION 5.1.– *Let $\mathcal{M}$ be a DTMC (resp. a CTMC) and $\mathbf{P}$ (resp. $\mathbf{Q}$) the corresponding transition matrix (resp. the corresponding infinitesimal generator). Then*

  – $\mathbf{P}$ *(resp. $\mathbf{Q}$) is strongly lumpable w.r.t. $\{S_i\}_{i \in I}$ iff*
$\forall i, j \in I \; \forall s, s' \in S_i \; \sum_{s'' \in S_j} \mathbf{P}[s, s''] = \sum_{s'' \in S_j} \mathbf{P}[s', s'']$
(resp. $\sum_{s'' \in S_j} \mathbf{Q}[s, s''] = \sum_{s'' \in S_j} \mathbf{Q}[s', s'']$)
  – $\mathbf{P}$ *(resp. $\mathbf{Q}$) is exactly lumpable w.r.t. $\{S_i\}_{i \in I}$ iff*
$\forall i, j \in I \; \forall s, s' \in S_i \; \sum_{s'' \in S_j} \mathbf{P}[s'', s] = \sum_{s'' \in S_j} \mathbf{P}[s'', s']$
(resp. $\sum_{s'' \in S_j} \mathbf{Q}[s'', s] = \sum_{s'' \in S_j} \mathbf{Q}[s'', s']$).

PROOF 5.1.– We prove the first point and leave the similar proof of the second point to the reader.

Assume that the condition is fulfilled, let π_n the distribution of X_n at time n.
Define $\mathbf{P}^{lp}[i, j] = \sum_{s' \in S_j} \mathbf{P}[s, s']$ for an arbitrary $s \in S_i$ (well defined using the condition). Then
$\sum_{s \in S_i} \pi_{n+1}(s) = \sum_{s \in S_i} \sum_j \sum_{s' \in S_j} \pi_n(s')\mathbf{P}[s', s] =$
$\sum_j \sum_{s' \in S_j} \pi_n(s') \sum_{s \in S_i} \mathbf{P}[s', s] = \sum_j (\sum_{s' \in S_j} \pi_n(s'))\mathbf{P}^{lp}[j, i]$
This establishes that the condition is sufficient.

Assume now that the condition is not fulfilled,
$\exists i, j \in I \; \exists s, s' \in S_i \; \sum_{s'' \in S_j} \mathbf{P}[s, s''] \neq \sum_{s'' \in S_j} \mathbf{P}[s', s'']$
Let $\pi_{0,s}$ and $\pi_{0,s'}$ be the initial point distributions for s and s'. These two distributions lead to the same Y_0. Then
$\sum_{s'' \in S_j} \pi_{1,s}(s'') = \sum_{s'' \in S_j} \mathbf{P}[s, s''] \neq \sum_{s'' \in S_j} \mathbf{P}[s', s''] = \sum_{s'' \in S_j} \pi_{1,s'}(s')$.
This proves that matrix $\mathbf{P}^{lp}$ cannot exist. □

Figure 5.4 illustrates the concept strong aggregation in case of a DTMC.

When the condition of strong aggregation is fulfilled, the transition matrix (resp. the infinitesimal generator) of the lumped chain can be directly computed from the transition matrix (resp. from the infinitesimal generator) of the initial chain as stated by the next proposition (immediate consequence of the proof of Proposition 5.1).

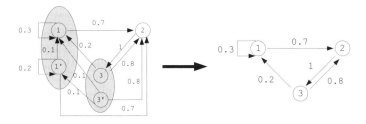

Figure 5.4. *An example of strong aggregation in a DTMC*

PROPOSITION 5.2.– *Let $\mathcal{M}$ be a DTMC (resp. a CTMC) strongly lumpable w.r.t. $\{S_i\}_{i\in I}$. Let $\mathbf{P}^{lp}$ (resp. $\mathbf{Q}^{lp}$) be the transition matrix (resp. the infinitesimal generator) associated with the lumped chain then*

$$\forall i, j \in I, \forall s \in S_i, \mathbf{P}^{lp}[i,j] = \sum_{s' \in S_j} \mathbf{P}[s,s'] \ (resp. \ \mathbf{Q}^{lp}[i,j] = \sum_{s' \in S_j} \mathbf{Q}[s,s']).$$

As for strong aggregation, in case of exact aggregation the transition matrix (resp. the infinitesimal generator) of the lumped chain can be directly computed from the transition matrix (resp. from the infinitesimal generator) of the initial chain. Observe that starting with an initial distribution equidistributed over the states of every subset of the partition, at any time the distribution is equidistributed. Consequently, if the DTMC (resp. the CTMC) is ergodic, its stationnary distribution is equidistributed over the states of every subset of the partition. Otherwise stated, knowing the transition matrix (resp. the infinitesimal generator) of the lumped chain, one can compute its stationary distribution, and deduce (by *local* equidistribution) the stationary distribution of the initial chain. This last step is impossible with strong aggregation, which does not ensure equiprobability of states inside a subset.

PROPOSITION 5.3.– *Let $\mathcal{M}$ be a DTMC (resp. a CTMC) which is exactly lumpable w.r.t. $\{S_i\}_{i\in I}$. Let $\mathbf{P}^{lp}$ (resp. $\mathbf{Q}^{lp}$) be the transition matrix (resp. the infinitesimal generator) associated with the lumped chain, then*

$- \ \forall i, j \in I, \forall s \in S_j \ \mathbf{P}^{lp}[i,j] = (\sum_{s' \in S_i} \mathbf{P}[s',s]) \times (|S_j|/|S_i|)$
(resp. $\mathbf{Q}^{lp}[i,j] = (\sum_{s' \in S_i} \mathbf{Q}[s',s]) \times (|S_j|/|S_i|)$*);*

$-$ *if* $\forall i \in I, \forall s, s' \in S_i, \pi_0(s) = \pi_0(s')$ *then*
$\forall n \in \mathbb{N}$ *(resp.* $\forall t \in \mathbb{R}^+$*),* $\forall i \in I, \forall s, s' \in S_i, \pi_n(s) = \pi_n(s')$ *(resp.* $\pi_t(s) = \pi_t(s')$*), where π_n (resp. π_t) is the probability distribution at time n (resp. t);*

$-$ *if* $\mathbf{P}$ *(resp.* $\mathbf{Q}$*) is ergodic and π is its stationary distribution then*
$\forall i \in I, \forall s, s' \in S_i, \pi(s) = \pi(s').$

5.3.4. *Verification of PLTL formulae*

Given a DTMC $\mathcal{M}$ and a $PLTL$ formula ϕ, by definition ϕ is either an atomic proposition, or $P_{\bowtie a}\varphi$ where φ is a path formula built on the operators $\mathcal{X}, \mathcal{U}$, and on atomic propositions. The first case is straightforward, while we describe the second case in the following section.

As in the previous case, the evaluation proceeds by evaluating the subformulae of φ in the order given by a bottom-up visit of the syntactical tree of the formula. Here after each subformula, evaluation transforms both the formula and the DTMC such that at the end, the formula becomes an atomic proposition whose evaluation is straightforward. The evaluated subformula φ' is substituted by the atomic proposition $[\varphi']$ in the formula itself.

The transformation of the DTMC is more complex. We describe it as follows: for the most complex case of a subformula $\varphi' \equiv \psi \mathcal{U}\chi$. Every state s such that $0 < \Pr(\sigma \models \varphi' \mid s_0 = s) < 1$ of the original DTMC is duplicated into s^y, labeled by the propositions labeling s and $[\varphi']$ and s^n labeled by the propositions labeling s. All other states are labeled according to the value of the same probability formula, either 0 or 1. The above probabilities are computed with the same procedure as for $PCTL$. S_o will denote the states that are not duplicated.

The transition probability matrix of the new DTMC is defined as follows:
– the transition probability between states of S_0 is left unchanged as well;
– for all duplicated states, let $py(s) = \Pr(\sigma \models \varphi' \mid s_0 = s)$ and $pn(s) = 1 - py(s)$. The probability to move from a state s' of the original chain to a state s^y (resp. s^n) is the probability of moving from s' to s in the original chain, multiplied by $py(s)$ (resp. $pn(s)$);
– from states s^y (resp. s^n) the chain can only move toward duplicated states s'^y (resp. s'^n) or toward states s' of the original chain such that $py(s') = 1$ (resp. $pn(s') = 1$). The associated transition probabilities are defined by $\mathbf{P}'[s^y, s'^y] = \mathbf{P}[s, s']py(s')/py(s)$ and $P'[s^y, s'] = P[s, s']/py(s)$, similarly for the states s^n.

To complete the definition of the transformed chain, we need to define the initial probability of a state s^y (resp. s^n) given that the system starts in state s. This conditional probability is given by $py(s)$ (resp. $pn(s)$). Consequently, $\pi'_0(s^y) = py(s)\pi_0(s)$ and $\pi'_0(s^n) = pn(s)\pi_0(s)$.

Observe that $\mathbf{P}'$ is indeed a transition matrix. We prove it only for a relevant case.
$$\sum_{s' \in S_o} \mathbf{P}'[s^y, s'] + \sum_{s' \in S \setminus S_o} \mathbf{P}'[s^y, s'^y] =$$
$$\tfrac{1}{py(s)} \left(\sum_{s' \in S_o, py(s')=1} \mathbf{P}[s, s'] + \sum_{s' \in S \setminus S_o} \mathbf{P}[s, s']py(s') \right).$$
Examining a step of the chain, we observe that the expression between parentheses is the probability $py(s)$.

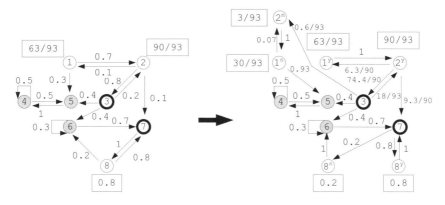

Figure 5.5. *CTMC transformation for PLTL*

We show the DTMC transformation caused by subformula $\psi \mathcal{U} \chi$ in Figure 5.5.

The correction of this construction is established using the following lemmas. We note $\mathcal{M}'$ the transformed chain. A path is said *normal* if it meets infinitely often S_o.

LEMMA 5.1.– *The set of normal paths has measure 1 in $\mathcal{M}$ and in $\mathcal{M}'$.*

PROOF 5.2.– Let us recall that a random path has a probability 1 to meet a sink SCC and to visit infinitely often its states. Examine the different cases of a sink SCC in $\mathcal{M}$ ou $\mathcal{M}'$:

– there exists a state of the SCC fulfilling χ or $\neg\chi \wedge \neg\psi$; this state belonging to S_o will be visited infinitely often;

– all states of the SCC fulfill $\neg\chi \wedge \psi$. In $\mathcal{M}$, this leads to $pn(s) = 1$ for every state s in this SCC. Suppose that in $\mathcal{M}'$ the SCC includes a duplicate state s. Then necessarily there is a path from s to a state s' which fulfills χ. Hence, this SCC could not be a sink one. □

Let φ'' be a subformula of φ where φ' occurs. Let us note $\varphi''(\varphi' \leftarrow [\varphi'])$, the formula φ'' in which φ' has been substituted by the atomic proposition $[\varphi']$.

LEMMA 5.2.– *For every subformula φ'' of φ where φ' occurs, one has for every random path σ of $\mathcal{M}'$, $\Pr(\sigma \models \varphi''(\varphi' \leftarrow [\varphi']) \Leftrightarrow \varphi'') = 1$*

PROOF 5.3.– The base case corresponds to $\varphi'' = \varphi'$, and this is a consequence of the previous lemma since for a normal path σ, $\sigma \models \varphi'$ iff $\sigma \models [\varphi']$. We prove the lemma by induction on the size of the formula observing in the case of temporal operators that a suffix of a normal path is a normal path.   □

Observe that the previous lemma applies to the case $\varphi'' = \varphi$.

Notations. Define the abstraction mapping abs from states of $\mathcal{M}'$ s.t. $\mathrm{abs}(s^y) = \mathrm{abs}(s^n) = s$ and $\mathrm{abs}(s) = s$ for every $s \in S_o$. Define the stochastic process $\mathcal{M}^{\mathrm{abs}}$ whose state space is the one of $\mathcal{M}$ obtained by the abstraction abs applied on $\mathcal{M}'$. The following lemma is the key point for the correction of the algorithm.

LEMMA 5.3.– *The stochastic process $\mathcal{M}^{\mathrm{abs}}$ is a weak aggregation of the process $\mathcal{M}'$ (w.r.t. the initial distribution π_0') and it is identical to the Markov chain $\mathcal{M}$.*

PROOF 5.4.– Let us note π_n (resp. π_n') the distribution of $\mathcal{M}$ (resp. $\mathcal{M}'$) at time n. We prove by recurrence on n that
$\forall s \in S_o \ \pi_n(s) = \pi_n'(s)$ and $\forall s \in S \setminus S_o \ \pi_n'(s^y) = \pi_n(s)py(s) \wedge \pi_n'(s^n) = \pi_n(s)pn(s)$

For $n = 0$, this is due to the definition of π_0'. Assume that the equations are fulfilled for n. Let us prove it for $n + 1$. We only handle the case of a state s^y and let to the reader the other cases.
$\pi_{n+1}'(s^y) = \sum_{s' \in S_o} \pi_n'(s') \mathbf{P}'[s, s^y] + \sum_{s'^y \in S_o} \pi_n'(s'^y) \mathbf{P}'[s'^y, s^y]$
$= \sum_{s' \in S_o} \pi_n(s') \mathbf{P}[s', s]py(s) + \sum_{s'^y | s' \in S \setminus S_o} \pi_n(s')py(s') \mathbf{P}'[s', s] \frac{py(s)}{py(s')}$
$= py(s) \left(\sum_{s' \in S_o} \pi_n(s') \mathbf{P}[s', s] + \sum_{s' \in S \setminus S_o} \pi_n(s') \mathbf{P}'[s', s] \right) = py(s)\pi_{n+1}(s)$

The result is then immediate since in $\mathcal{M}^{\mathrm{abs}}$, $\forall s \in S \setminus S_o \ \pi_n^{\mathrm{abs}}(s) = \pi_n'(s^y) + \pi_n'(s^n)$.
□

We now establish the correction of the algorithm.

THEOREM 5.1.– *Let σ (resp. σ') be a random path of $\mathcal{M}$ (resp. $\mathcal{M}'$). Then*
$$\mathrm{Pr}_{\mathcal{M}}(\sigma \models \varphi) = \mathrm{Pr}_{\mathcal{M}'}(\sigma' \models \varphi(\varphi' \leftarrow [\varphi'])).$$

PROOF 5.5.– $\mathrm{Pr}_{\mathcal{M}}(\sigma \models \varphi) = \mathrm{Pr}_{\mathcal{M}^{\mathrm{abs}}}(\sigma^{\mathrm{abs}} \models \varphi)$
(Lemma 5.3)
$= \mathrm{Pr}_{\mathcal{M}'}(\sigma' \models \varphi)$
Indeed the truth value of φ for a path σ' depends only on its abstraction σ^{abs}.
$= \mathrm{Pr}_{\mathcal{M}'}(\sigma' \models \varphi(\varphi' \leftarrow [\varphi']))$
(Lemma 5.2)
    □

5.3.5. *Verification of* $PCTL^*$

Given a DTMC and a formula ϕ of $PCTL^*$, the verification algorithm proceeds again through a bottom-up visit of the syntactical tree of the formula ϕ by evaluating the subtrees of ϕ that correspond to $PLTL$ formulae, substituting each verified subformula with an atomic proposition. In each step of the algorithm what needs to be evaluated is a formula of $PLTL$.

5.4. Verification of continuous time Markov chain

Performance evaluation of systems is usually defined in a continuous context. We open this section with a discussion on the limits of classical performance indices, that justify the introduction of a temporal logics for performance evaluation.

5.4.1. *Limitations of standard performance indices*

The classical performance evaluation indices, recalled in section 5.2.1, provide a set of important information to a system designer, but they do not capture all performance aspects of a system. As an example, we consider some performance indices aimed at assessing the dependability of a system:

– *instantaneous availability* is related to transient behavior: it represents the probability at time τ of service availability;

– *steady-state availability* is related to steady-state behavior: it represents the probability of service availability in steady-state;

– *interval availability*: this represents the probability of having the service always available between time τ and τ';

– *steady-state interval availability*: this is the steady-state probability that the service is continuously available between two instants of time. Because we are considering the steady-state behavior, such probability does not depend on the specific points in time, but only on the duration of the interval limited by the two points;

– *steady-state simultaneous availability and reactivity*: this is the steady-state probability that, upon a request, the system is continuously working until the service is completed and the response time does not exceed a predefined threshold.

While the first two properties can be directly and easily computed from both the transient and steady-state probabilities, the computation of the other properties is more involved. It is feasible to devise, for each property, an ad-hoc computation for the probability of interest, but it is more convenient to define a general logic that can express complex performance properties, and for which a general algorithm can be designed.

5.4.2. *A temporal logics for continuous time Markov chains*

The temporal logics "continuous stochastic logic" (CSL) that we are going to define is an adaptation of the "computation tree logic" (CTL) ([EME 80] to CTMC. The logics allow to express formulae that *evaluates over states*, and that are built with the following syntax (in the definition, we follow the approach proposed in [BAI 03a]).

DEFINITION 5.5.– A CSL formula is inductively defined by:

– if $\phi \in \mathcal{P}$ then ϕ is a CSL formula;

– if ϕ et ψ are CSL formula then $\neg\phi$ and $\phi \wedge \psi$ are CSL formulae;

– if ϕ is a CSL formula, $a \in [0, 1]$ is a real number, $\bowtie \in \{<, \leq, >, \geq\}$ then $S_{\bowtie a}\phi$ is a CSL formula;

– if ϕ and ψ are CSL formulae, $a \in [0, 1]$ is a real number, $\bowtie \in \{<, \leq, >, \geq\}$ and I is an interval of $\mathbb{R}_{\geq 0}$ then $P_{\bowtie a}\mathcal{X}^I\phi$ and $P_{\bowtie a}\phi\mathcal{U}^I\psi$ are CSL formulae.

The first two definitions are standard CTL formulae, and we do not explain them here in more details. The formula $S_{\bowtie a}\phi$ is satisfied by a state s of the CTMC, if given that the initial state of the chain is s, the cumulative steady-state probability p of the states that satisfy ϕ, verifies $p \bowtie a$. This evaluation is well defined, since, in a finite CTMC, a steady-state distribution always exists. If the CTMC is ergodic the evaluation of the formula does not depend on the specific state s.

An execution of a stochastic process satisfies $\mathcal{X}^I\phi$, if the first change of state takes place within the interval I and leads to a state that verifies ϕ. A state s satisfies $P_{\bowtie a}\mathcal{X}^I\phi$, if the probability p of the executions of the stochastic process that start in s and satisfy $\mathcal{X}^I\phi$ verifies $p \bowtie a$.

An execution of a stochastic process satisfies $\phi\mathcal{U}^I\psi$, if there exists a time instant $\tau \in I$ such that ψ is true at τ and for all proceeding time instants ϕ is true. A state s satisfies $P_{\bowtie a}\phi\mathcal{U}^I\psi$, if the probability p of the executions that starts in s and satisfy $\phi\mathcal{U}^I\psi$ verifies $p \bowtie a$.

Using CSL, the availability and dependability properties informally defined before can be expressed in more formal terms as:

– *instantaneous availability* guarantee of 99%:

$$P_{\geq 0.99}true\mathcal{U}^{[\tau,\tau]}disp$$

where $disp$ is an atomic proposition, which indicates that the service is available;

– *steady-state availability* guarantee of 99%:

$$S_{\geq 0.99}disp$$

– *interval availability* guarantee of 99%:

$$P_{<0.01} true \mathcal{U}^{[\tau,\tau']} \neg disp$$

– *steady-state interval availability* guarantee of 99%:

$$S_{<0.01} true \mathcal{U}^{[\tau,\tau']} \neg disp$$

– *steady-state simultaneous availability and reactivity* guarantee of 99% with latency of at most three-time units

$$S_{\geq 0.99}(req \Rightarrow P_{\geq 0.99}(disp \mathcal{U}^{[0,3]} ack)),$$

where req is the atomic proposition that indicates that a request has been received, and ack is an atomic proposition that indicates that the service has been delivered. Note that the two 99% requirements do not have the same meaning. The condition on the internal operator is a condition on the executions that starts in a particular state, while the condition on the outer operator is a global requirement on all the states of the chain, weighted by their steady-state probabilities.

5.4.3. *Verification algorithm*

Given a CTMC and a CSL formula ϕ, the algorithm evaluates the formula starting from the inner formulae and proceeding from inner to outer formulae, following bottom-up the syntactical tree of the formula ϕ and labeling each state with the sub-formulae satisfied in that state. At each step, the algorithm evaluates a formula by considering as atomic propositions the operands of the most external operator. Therefore, the algorithm can be explained considering one operator at a time.

$\boxed{\phi = \neg \psi}$ The algorithm labels with ϕ each state which is not labeled with ψ.

$\boxed{\phi = \psi \wedge \chi}$ The algorithm labels with ϕ every state labeled with both ψ and χ.

$\boxed{\phi = S_{\bowtie a} \psi}$ The algorithm computes the steady-state distribution of the CTMC with initial probability concentrated in s (the stochastic process starts in s) as explained in section 5.2.3. The probability of all states labeled with ψ are then summed up and the algorithm labels with ϕ the state s if the sum, let it be p, verifies $p \bowtie a$. Note that for all the states of a BSCC a single computation is needed: indeed either all states of the BSCC satisfy ϕ or none of them does. Similarly, if the CTMC has a single stationary distribution, then the truth value of the formula does not depend on the state.

$\boxed{\phi = P_{\bowtie a} \mathcal{X}^I \psi}$ The occurrence of a transition in a state s in within the interval I and the fact that the state reached upon the transition satisfies ψ are two independent events, and therefore the probability of the paths that satisfy the formula can be computed as the product of the probabilities of the two events. Let $I = [\tau, \tau']$; we assume a closed interval, without loss of generality (since we are in a continuous domain the fact of including or not the bounds of the interval in the computation does not influence the result). Let $\mathbf{Q}$ the infinitesimal generator of the CTMC, and $\mathbf{P}$ the matrix of the embedded DTMC. The probability of the first event is $e^{\tau \mathbf{Q}[s,s]} - e^{\tau' \mathbf{Q}[s,s]}$, while the probability of the second even is $\sum_{s' \models \psi} \mathbf{P}[s, s']$.

$\boxed{\phi = P_{\bowtie a} \psi \mathcal{U}^I \chi}$ The evaluation of this formula requires transient analysis of a CTMC obtained from the original CTMC by some simple transformations. If X is a CTMC, then we shall indicate with X^ϕ the chain obtained by making absorbing all states of X that verify ϕ. In order to simplify the presentation, we consider the various type of intervals as separate cases:

– $\phi = P_{\bowtie a} \psi \mathcal{U}^{[0,\infty[} \chi$. In this case, the executions of the chain on which we cumulate the probability should never leave the states that verify ψ, until a state that verifies χ is reached, without any constraint in time. temps. In other words, we are interested in the behavior of the chain from its initial state until it enters a state that satisfies $\neg\psi \vee \chi$. Let us consider the chain $X^{\neg\psi \vee \chi}$. If a BSCC of this chain contains a state, which verifies χ then the probability that we are interested in is 1 for all states of the BSCC (since all states of a BSCC are recurrent), if no such a state exists in the BSCC, then the probability is 0. Let us call "good" a BSCC associated with a probability 1. This probability depends only on the embedded chain of $X^{\neg\psi \vee \chi}$ and its computation has already been described in section 5.2.2;

– $\phi = P_{\bowtie a} \psi \mathcal{U}^{[0,\tau]} \chi$. In this case, the execution of the process must visit only states that verify ψ until a state that satisfies χ s reached, and this event should happen at time τ at the latest. In other words, the probability is cumulated along the paths until a state that verifies $\neg\psi \vee \chi$ is reached. Therefore, we need to compute the following probability $\Pr(X^{\neg\psi \vee \chi}(\tau) \models \chi \mid X^{\neg\psi \vee \chi}(0) = s)$;

– $\phi = P_{\bowtie a} \psi \mathcal{U}^{[\tau,\tau]} \chi$. In this case, the execution of the process must stay in within states that verify ψ during the interval $[0, \tau]$ and it must verify χ at time τ. The case of a change of state at τ is not considered since the probability of this event is zero. The probability to be computed is equal to $\Pr(X^{\neg\psi}(\tau) \models \psi \wedge \chi \mid X^{\neg\psi}(0) = s)$;

– $\phi = P_{\bowtie a} \psi \mathcal{U}^{[\tau,\infty[} \chi$. In this case, the execution of the process must stay in within states that verify ψ during the interval $[0, \tau]$ and then starting from the state s reached at time τ it must verify the formula $\psi \mathcal{U}^{[0,\infty[} \chi$. Therefore, the probability to be computed is $\sum_{s' \models \psi} \Pr(X^{\neg\psi}(\tau) = s' \mid X^{\neg\psi}(0) = s) \cdot \pi(s')$ where $\pi(s')$ is computed using the procedure for the first case;

– $\phi = P_{\bowtie a} \psi \mathcal{U}^{[\tau,\tau']} \chi$. A similar reasoning as for the previous case leads to the following formula:

$$\sum_{s' \models \psi} \Pr(X^{\neg\psi}(\tau) = s' \mid X^{\neg\psi}(0) = s) \cdot \Pr(X^{\neg\psi \vee \chi}(\tau' - \tau) \models \chi \mid X^{\neg\psi \vee \chi}(0) = s')$$

5.5. State of the art in the quantitative evaluation of Markov chains

The field of Markov chain verification has started on the verification of DTMCs. The first approach for the verification of LTL over DTMCs (proposed in [VAR 85]) is conceptually very simple: the formula is translated into a Büchi automata, the non-determinism is then removed and a Rabin automata is produced. The synchronized product of this automata with the DTMC produces another DTMC, for which, using a variation of the technique explained in section 5.2, it is possible to compute the required probability. The complexity of the computation is doubly exponential in the size of the formula. An improvement in complexity is given by the algorithm in [COU 95]: a new DTMC is built iteratively from the initial DTMC, and the iteration is driven by the operators of the formula. This is the algorithm that we presented in section 5.3.4. The resulting algorithm is exponential in the size of the formula, and the authors show that the algorithm has optimal complexity. A third algorithm, proposed in [COU 03], also translates the formula into a Büchi automata. Due to the particular construction followed by the algorithm, it is then possible to compute the probability associated with the formula directly on the synchronized product of the automata and of the formula. This algorithm has an optimal complexity as well, and moreover, it provides better performance than the previous one in many practical cases.

A classical technique for evaluating the performance of a system consists of associating "rewards" with states and/or transitions of the chain, and in computing the mean reward or the cumulated reward at time t. Rewards are taken into account by the $PRCTL$ logics, which has been defined in [AND 03], where an evaluation algorithm is also presented.

The first relevant work on the verification of CTMCs appeared in [AZI 96, AZI 00], where it is shown that CSL verification is decidable. The verification algorithm is extremely complex because it does not perform the implicit approximations, which we have done in the CSL verification algorithm presented in this chapter.

We should note that the verification algorithm may become impractical for large Markov chains. A possible way to solve the problem is to take advantage of a modular specification of the system, substituting a module with a smaller one, which is nevertheless equivalent with respect to the verification of the given formula. This approach has been introduced first in [BAI 03a], and it has been later generalized by Baier *et al.* in [BAI 03b], where various definitions of equivalence are considered.

The CSL logics introduced in section 5.4.2 has two main limitation. On one side, the path formulae are defined only in terms of atomic propositions associated to states, and not in terms of the actions/transitions in the path. On the other side the temporal constraints on path formulae are bound to be intervals, which generates a number of limitations to the expressivity of the temporal constraints in the formula. The first limitation has been eliminated in [BAI 04]: the $asCSL$ logics substitutes to the temporal operators, a regular expression over states and actions. A different approach is presented instead in [DON 07]: the CSL^{TA} logics there introduced defines the formulae with the support of a one-clock, deterministic, timed automata. CSL^{TA} strictly extends CSL, and it is at least as expressive as $asCSL$. Moreover, the verification algorithm is not based on the construction of a number of modified CTMCs, but on the definition of a Markov renewal process, and on the computation of the discrete embedded Markov chain of the process.

A totally different approach to limit the complexity of the verification task has been proposed in [YOU 06]. If $P_{\leq a}\phi$ is the formula to be verified, we can generate a number of random executions, and we can then compute the percentage of the executions that do satisfy ϕ; according to standard probability results, this percentage tends to the probability to be computed. This method is very efficient when the verification of the formula requires only executions that have an upper bound in time.

5.6. Bibliography

[AND 03] ANDOVA S., HERMANNS H., KATOEN J.P., "Discrete-time rewards model-checked", *Proceedings of Formal Modelling and Analysis of Timed Systems (FORMATS 2003)*, vol. 2791 of *Lecture Notes in Computer Science*, pp. 88–103, Marseille, France, Springer-Verlag, 2003.

[AZI 96] AZIZ A., SANWAL K., V.SINGHAL, BRAYTON R., "Verifying continuous-time Markov chains", *8th Int. Conf. on Computer Aided Verification (CAV'96)*, vol. 1102 of *Lecture Notes in Computer Science*, pp. 269–276, New Brunswick, NJ, USA, Springer-Verlag, 1996.

[AZI 00] AZIZ A., SANWAL K., V.SINGHAL, BRAYTON R., "Model chcking continuous-time Markov chains", *ACM Transactions on Computational Logic*, vol. 1, num. 1, 162–170, 2000.

[BAI 03a] BAIER C., HAVERKORT B., HERMANNS H., KATOEN J.P., "Model-checking algorithms for continuous time Markov chains", *IEEE Transactions on Software Engineering*, vol. 29, num. 7, 524–541, July 2003.

[BAI 03b] BAIER C., HERMANNS H., KATOEN J.P., WOLF V., "Comparative branching-time semantics for Markov chains", *Concurrency Theory (CONCUR 2003)*, vol. 2761 of *Lecture Notes in Computer Science* , pp. 492–507, Marseille, France, Springer-Verlag, 2003.

[BAI 04] BAIER C., CLOTH L., HAVERKORT B., KUNTZ M., SIEGLE M., "Model checking action- and state-labelled Markov chains", *Proceedings of DSN'04*, pp. 701–710, IEEE, 2004.

[COU 95] COURCOUBETIS C., YANNAKAKIS M., "The complexity of probabilistic verification", *Journal of the ACM*, vol. 42, num. 4, 857–907, July 1995.

[COU 03] COUVREUR J.M., SAHEB N., SUTRE G., "An optimal automata approach to LTL model checking of probabilistic systems", *Proceedings of 10th International Conference on Logic for Programming, Artificial Intelligence, and Reasoning (LPAR'2003)*, vol. 2850 of *LNAI*, pp. 361–375, Almaty, Kazakhstan, Springer-Verlag, September 2003.

[DON 07] DONATELLI S., HADDAD S., SPROSTON J., "CSL^{TA}: an expressive logic for continuous-time Markov chains", *Proceedings of the 4th International Conference on Quantitative Evaluation of Systems (QEST'07)*, pp. 31–40, Edinburgh, Scotland, IEEE Computer Society Press, September 2007.

[EME 80] EMERSON E.A., CLARKE E.M., "Characterizing correctness properties of parallel programs using fixpoints", *Proceedings of the 7th International Colloquium on Automata, Languages and Programming, (ICALP)*, pp. 169–181, Noordweijkerhout, The Netherlands, 1980.

[FEL 68] FELLER W., *An introduction to probability theory and its applications. Volume I*, John Wiley & Sons, 1968.

[FEL 71] FELLER W., *An introduction to probability theory and its applications. Volume II*, second edition, John Wiley & Sons, 1971.

[JEN 53] JENSEN A., "Markov chains as an aid in the study of Markov processes", *Skand. Aktuarietidskrift*, vol. 3, 87–91, 1953.

[KEM 60] KEMENY J., SNELL J., *Finite Markov Chains*, D. Van Nostrand-Reinhold, New York, NY, 1960.

[LAP 95] LAPRIE J. (ed.), *Guide de la sûreté de fonctionnement*, Cépaduès, Toulouse, France, 1995.

[LED 60] LEDOUX J., *Weak lumpability of finite Markov chains and positive invariance of cones*. Research report INRIA-IRISA num. 2801, 1960.

[MEY 80] MEYER J., "On evaluating the performability of degradable computing systems", *IEEE Transactions on Computers*, vol. 29, num. 8, p. 720–731, August 1980.

[SCH 84] SCHWEITZER P.J., "Aggregation methods for large Markov chains", *Proceedings of the International Workshop on Computer Performance and Reliability*, pp. 275–286, North-Holland, 1984.

[STE 94] STEWART W.J., *Introduction to the Numerical Solution of Markov Chains*, Princeton University Press, USA, 1994.

[TRI 82] TRIVEDI K.S., *Probability & Statistics with Reliability, Queueing, and Computer Science Applications*, Prentice Hall, Englewood Cliffs, NJ, USA, 1982.

[TRI 92] TRIVEDI K.S., MUPPALA J.K., WOOLE S.P., HAVERKORT B.R., "Composite performance and dependability analysis", *Performance Evaluation*, vol. 14, num. 3–4, 197–215, February 1992.

[VAR 85] VARDI M., "Automatic verification of probabilistic concurrent finite-state programs", *FOCS 1985*, pp. 327–338, 1985.

[YOU 06] YOUNES H., KWIATKOWSKA M., NORMAN G., PARKER D., "Numerical vs. statistical probabilistic model checking", *International Journal on Software Tools for Technology Transfer (STTT)*, vol. 8, num. 3, 216–228, 2006.

Chapter 6

Tools for Model-Checking Timed Systems

6.1. Introduction

In this chapter, we present different tools for verification of timed systems. UP-PAAL [LAR 97a, BEH 04b] is a tool for model-checking real-time systems developed jointly by Uppsala and Aalborg Universities. The first version of UPPAAL was released in 1995 [LAR 97a] and has been in constant development since then [BEN 98, AMN 01, BEH 01a, BEH 02, DAV 02, DAV 03, DAV 06]. It has been applied successfully to case studies ranging from communication protocol to multimedia applications [HAV 97, LON 97, DAR 97, BOW 98, HUN 00, IVE 00, DAV 00, LIN 01]. The tool is designed to verify systems that can be modeled as networks of timed automata [ALU 90a, ALU 90b, HEN 92, ALU 94] extended with integer variables, structured data types, user defined functions, and channel synchronization. UPPAAL-CORA is a specialized version of UPPAAL that implements guided and minimal cost reachability algorithms [BEH 01b, BEH 01c, LAR 01]. It is suitable in particular to cost-optimal schedulability problems [BEH 05a, BEH 05b]. UPPAAL-TIGA [BEH 07] is a specialization of UPPAAL designed to verify systems modeled as timed game automata where a controller plays against an environment. The tool synthesizes code represented as a strategy to reach control objectives [DEA 01, ASA 98, MAL 95, TRI 99]. The tool is based on a recent on-the-fly algorithm [CAS 05] and has already been applied to an industrial case study [JES 07]. The tool can also handle timed games with partial observability [CAS 07] and has been extended more recently to

Chapter written by Alexandre DAVID, Gerd BEHRMANN, Peter BULYCHEV, Joakim BYG, Thomas CHATAIN, Kim G. LARSEN, Paul PETTERSSON, Jacob Illum RASMUSSEN, Jiří SRBA, Wang YI, Kenneth Y. JOERGENSEN, Didier LIME, Morgan MAGNIN, Olivier H. ROUX and Louis-Marie TRAONOUEZ .

check for simulation of timed automata and timed game automata. TAPAAL [BYG 09] is an editor, simulator, and verifier for timed-arc Petri nets and for the verification task it translates nets into networks of timed automata and uses the UPPAAL engine for the actual verification. It is developed at the Aalborg University.

ROMÉO [GAR 05b, LIM 09] is a tool for model-checking time Petri-nets [ZUB 80, ZUB 85, RAZ 85, ABD 01a, ABD 01b] and Petri nets with stopwatches [ROU 04]. It is developed by IRCCyN in Nantes. Since its first version in 2001, the software has benefited from regular improvements, both theoretical and experimental. Theoretical researches aim to widen the classes of models and properties on which the tool can perform model-checking. From an experimental point of view, developments focus on the use of up-to-date efficient libraries (e.g. the Parma Polyhedra Library [BAG 02]). The first releases of ROMÉO were mostly based on translations to other tools. The tool not only allows state space computation of TPN and on-the-fly model-checking of reachability properties, but it also performs translations from TPNs to Timed Automata TA that preserve the behavioral semantics (timed bisimilarity) of the TPNs. Recent research stresses on the emergence of autonomous model-checking algorithms. ROMÉO now provides an integrated TCTL model-checker and has gained in expressivity with the addition of parameters. Although there exist other tools to compute the state-space of stopwatch models, Romeo is the first one that performs TCTL model-checking on stopwatch models [MAG 08]. Moreover, it is the first tool that performs TCTL model-checking on timed parametric models [TRA 08]. Indeed, Romeo now features an efficient model-checking of TPNs using the Uppaal DBM Library, the model-checking of stopwatch Petri nets and parametric stopwatch Petri nets using the Parma Polyhedra Library and a graphical editor and simulator of these models. Furthermore, its audience has led to several industrial contracts, such as *DGA*, *SODIUS*, *Dassault Aviation*, and *EADS*.

In this chapter, we present the architecture of the tools, the basic model-checking algorithms, and the main techniques developed over past years to improve performance both in time and space.

6.2. UPPAAL

6.2.1. *Timed automata and symbolic exploration*

UPPAAL is based on an extension of timed automata. A timed automaton is a finite-state machine extended with clock variables. It uses a dense-time model where a clock variable evaluates to a real number. All the clocks progress synchronously. A system is modeled as a network of such timed automata in parallel. Furthermore, the model is extended with (bounded) integer variables. The query language used to specify properties to be checked is a subset of timed computation tree logic [ALU 90a, HEN 94, BAI 08].

A state of the system is defined by the locations of all automata, the clock values, and the values of the integer variables. The system changes state by firing a transition. A transition may consist of one edge in any of the automata that can take such an edge, or several edges when a synchronization is involved (hand-shake or broadcast synchronization).

A timed automaton is a finite directed graph annotated with conditions over and resets of non-negative real valued clocks. We recall here the definition of a timed automaton (Definition 6.1). We omit here F and R.

DEFINITION 6.1(TIMED AUTOMATON).– A *timed automaton* $\mathcal{A}$ is a tuple $(L, l_0, X, \Sigma_\varepsilon, E, Inv)$ where: L is a finite set of *locations*; $l_0 \in L$ is the *initial location*; X is a finite set of positive real-valued *clocks*; $\Sigma_\varepsilon = \Sigma \cup \{\varepsilon\}$ is a finite set of *actions* and ε is the *silent* action; $E \subseteq L \times \mathcal{C}(X) \times \Sigma_\varepsilon \times 2^X \times L$ is a finite set of *edges*, $e = \langle l, \gamma, a, R, l' \rangle \in E$ represents an edge from the location l to the location l' with the guard γ, the label a and the reset set $R \subseteq X$; $Inv \in \mathcal{C}(X)^L$ assigns an *invariant* to any location. We restrict the invariants to conjuncts of terms of the form $x \preceq r$ for $x \in X$ and $r \in \mathbb{N}$ and $\preceq \in \{<, \leq\}$.

We recall that a clock valuation (1.2) ν over a set of variables X is an element of $\mathbb{R}_{\geq 0}^X$. For $\nu \in \mathbb{R}_{\geq 0}^X$ and $d \in \mathbb{R}_{\geq 0}$, $\nu + d$ denotes the valuation defined by $(\nu + d)(x) = \nu(x) + d$, and for $X' \subseteq X$, $\nu[X' \mapsto 0]$ denotes the valuation ν' with $\nu'(x) = 0$ for $x \in X'$ and $\nu'(x) = \nu(x)$ otherwise. We give now the semantics of a timed automaton (Definition 6.2).

DEFINITION 6.2(SEMANTICS OF A TIMED AUTOMATON).– The semantics of a timed automaton $\mathcal{A} = (L, l_0, C, \Sigma_\varepsilon, E, Act, Inv)$ is a timed transition system $S_{\mathcal{A}} = (Q, q_0, \Sigma_\varepsilon, \rightarrow)$ with $Q = L \times (\mathbb{R}_{\leq 0})^X$, $q_0 = (l_0, \mathbf{0})$ is the initial state, and $\rightarrow$ is defined by: *i)* the discrete transitions relation $(l, v) \xrightarrow{a} (l', v')$ iff $\exists (l, \gamma, a, R, l') \in E$ s.t. $\gamma(v) = \mathtt{tt}$, $v' = v[R \mapsto 0]$ and $Inv(l')(v') = \mathtt{tt}$; *ii)* the continuous transition relation

$(l, v) \xrightarrow{\epsilon(t)} (l', v')$ iff $l = l'$, $v' = v + t$ and $\forall 0 \leq t' \leq t$, $Inv(l)(v + t') = \mathtt{tt}$.

The problem when exploring is that the semantics of timed automata results in an infinite transition system. There exists an exact finite state abstraction based on convex polyhedra in $\mathbb{R}^X$ called zones [YI 94, LAR 95] (a zone can be represented by a conjunction in $\mathcal{C}(X)$). This abstraction leads to the following symbolic semantics of timed automata.

DEFINITION 6.3(SYMBOLIC SEMANTICS OF TA).– Let $Z_0 = Inv(l_0) \wedge \bigwedge_{x,y \in X} x = y = 0$ be the initial zone. The symbolic semantics of a timed automaton $(L, l_0, X, \Sigma_\varepsilon, E, Inv)$ over X is defined as a transition system $\langle \mathcal{S}, \int_0, \Rightarrow \rangle$ called the *symbolic reachability graph*, where $S \subseteq L \times \mathcal{C}(X)$ is the set of symbolic states, $f_0 = (l_0, Z_0)$ is the initial state, $\Rightarrow$ is the transition relation and is defined by the following rules:

- $(l, Z) \stackrel{\delta}{\Rightarrow} (l, \mathrm{widen}(m, (Z \wedge Inv(l))^{\uparrow} \wedge Inv(l)))$, and
- $(l, Z) \stackrel{e}{\Rightarrow} (l', r(\gamma \wedge Z \wedge Inv(l)) \wedge Inv(l'))$ if $e = (l, \gamma, a, R, l') \in E$,

where $Z^{\uparrow} = \{u + d \mid u \in Z \wedge d \in \mathbb{R}_{\geq 0}\}$ (the *future* operation), and $r(Z) = \{[x \mapsto 0]u \mid x \in R, u \in Z\}$ (the *reset* operation). The function widen : $\mathbf{N} \times \mathcal{C}(X) \to \mathcal{C}(X)$ widens the clock constraints with respect to the maximum constant m of the timed automaton. This operation is also called normalization [YI 94] or extrapolation.

The relation $\stackrel{\delta}{\Rightarrow}$ represents the delay transitions and $\stackrel{e}{\Rightarrow}$ the edge transitions. The classical representation of a zone is the difference bound matrix [ROK 93, WON 94, BEN 02].

In UPPAAL, timed automata are composed into a *network of timed automata* over a common set of clocks and actions, consisting of n timed automata $\mathcal{A}_i = (L_i, l_i^0, X, \Sigma_\varepsilon, E_i, Inv_i)$, $1 \leq i \leq n$. A location vector is a vector $\bar{l} = (l_1, \ldots, l_n)$. We compose the invariant functions into a common function over location vectors $I(\bar{l}) = \wedge_i Inv_i(l_i)$. We write $\bar{l}[l_i'/l_i]$ to denote the vector where the ith element l_i of $\bar{l}$ is replaced by l_i'. In the following section, we define the semantics of a network of timed automata (NTA).

DEFINITION 6.4(SEMANTICS OF NTA).– Let $\mathcal{A}_i = (L_i, l_i^0, X, \Sigma_\varepsilon, E_i, Inv_i)$ be a network of n -timed automata. Let $\bar{l}_0 = (l_1^0, \ldots, l_n^0)$ be the initial location vector. The semantics is defined as a transition system $\langle S, s_0, \to \rangle$, where $S = (L_1 \times \cdots \times L_n) \times \mathbb{R}^X$ is the set of states, $s_0 = (\bar{l}_0, u_0)$ is the initial state, and $\to \subseteq S \times S$ is the transition relation defined by

- $(\bar{l}, u) \stackrel{d}{\to} (\bar{l}, u + d)$ if $\forall d' : 0 \leq d' \leq d \implies u + d' \in I(\bar{l})$;

- $(\bar{l}, u) \stackrel{a}{\to} (\bar{l}[l_i'/l_i], u')$ if there exists $l_i \xrightarrow{\epsilon, \gamma, R_i} l_i'$ s.t. $u \in \gamma$, $u' = [R_i \mapsto 0]u$ and $u' \in I(\bar{l}[l_i'/l_i])$;

- $(\bar{l}, u) \stackrel{a}{\to} (\bar{l}[l_j'/l_j, l_i'/l_i], u')$ if there exist $l_i \xrightarrow{\gamma_i, c?, R_i} l_i'$ and $l_j \xrightarrow{\gamma_j, c!, R_j} l_j'$ s.t. $u \in (\gamma_i \wedge \gamma_j)$, $u' = [R_i \cup R_j \mapsto 0]u$ and $u' \in I(\bar{l}[l_j'/l_j, l_i'/l_i])$.

The symbolic semantics of timed automata is naturally extended to networks of timed automata. We omit conditions on S that define location vectors of 2^L as valid, that is, the locations may not belong to the same automaton. In addition, we omit for the sake of simplicity the integer variables that UPPAAL supports. The definitions would be extended by adding a set of integers and actions over these integers that would be part of the state. Further extensions supported by UPPAAL are:

– *broadcast channels:* if a channel *c* is declared *broadcast* then one process taking the action *c!* synchronizes with all other processes that have enabled edges that can take the action *c?*;

– *urgent channels:* if a channel is declared *urgent* then time cannot elapse in a given state if a transition involving an urgent channel is possible;

– *urgent locations:* a state having an urgent location in its location vector cannot delay;

– *committed locations:* a state having a committed location in its location vector cannot delay and must take a transition that leaves a committed location or deadlock.

Other syntactic constructions are defined on top as a convenience for the user. These include arrays of integer variables, clocks, or channels, user-defined functions, and structured data types. For a more complete reference see the updated version of [BEH 04b] available on *www.uppaal.org*.

UPPAAL implements a symbolic exploration algorithm based on the symbolic semantics of timed automata. In the reachability 6.2.4 or liveness 6.2.5 algorithms, UP-PAAL computes successor states symbolically in the following way: when a transition is taken, the next state is delayed infinitely (if possible) and the invariant of the state is applied. This computes all the (timed) successors w.r.t. a given transition. Thus, in the algorithms, computing successors will refer to trying all possible actions followed by delay.

6.2.1.1. *Example*

We give as an example the well-known Fischer's mutual exclusion algorithm [ABA 92, KRI 96] with two processes for the sake of simplicity. The protocol scales with any number of processes, each having its own identifier (in the example only 1 and 2). Figure 6.1 shows the model of the protocol. The processes want to avoid being

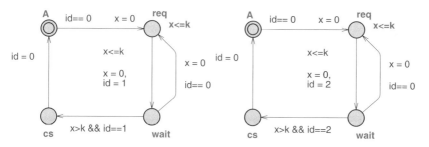

Figure 6.1. *Timed automata model of Fischer's mutual exclusion protocol*

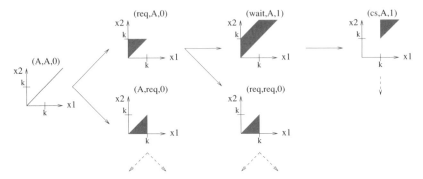

Figure 6.2. *Symbolic exploration of Fischer's mutual exclusion protocol*

in their critical sections (cs) at the same time. The protocol is using a shared identifier (id) to choose which process should access the critical section and a clock to force the processes to wait at least k time units before entering cs. Processes may retry and go back to req. Figure 6.2 shows the symbolic exploration of the model. The locations and the integer variable as a tuple and the zone are shown graphically in this figure. Resetting a clock corresponds to projecting the zone on the axis corresponding to that clock. Delaying corresponds to removing the upper bounds on the zone (but keeping the diagonal constraints). Applying a guard corresponds to intersecting a zone with the zone corresponding to the set of states described by the guard, or constraining the zone by the constraint of the guard. The (symbolic) initial state is delayed from the origin and the symbolic successors are computed from there. Either the first process goes to req or the second does, performing a reset of its clock, followed by a delay bounded by the invariant in req. From (req,A,0), either the first process continues or the second tries to go to req. If the first process moves then again we have a reset followed by a delay but no invariant this time. From (wait,A,1), we apply the constraint of the guard to the zone and we obtain the states that can reach (cs,A,1). The exploration continues from there.

6.2.2. *Queries*

The properties that can be checked by UPPAAL, as illustrated in Figure 6.3 are defined in a subset of TCTL and are of the form:

- $A[]$ ϕ "always globally ϕ",
- $E <>$ ϕ "exists eventually ϕ",
- $A <>$ ϕ "always eventually ϕ",
- $E[]$ ϕ "exists globally ϕ", or
- $\phi -->$ ψ "ϕ always leads to ψ", equivalent to $A[](\phi \to A <> \psi)$,

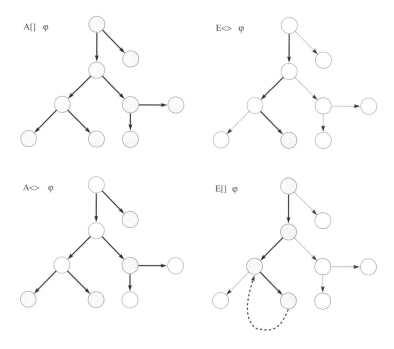

Figure 6.3. UPPAAL *basic queries*

where ϕ and ψ are Boolean expressions over locations, variables and clocks. These queries are defined on paths: A applies for all paths and E for one existing path. "[]" queries all states along paths and $<>$ queries one state along paths. Figure 6.3 shows traces of states and paths for which CTL formulae hold. The filled states are those for which a given ϕ holds. Bold edges are used to show the paths the formulae evaluate on. The time part (**TCTL**) comes from the clock constraints used in ϕ (and ψ).

The formulae $A[] \ \phi$ and $E <> \ \phi$ are *reachability* properties and are symmetric: $A[] \ \phi = \neg E <> \ \neg\phi$. The $A[] \ \phi$ properties are also called safety properties because they check for a formula to hold for all the states. If such a property is not satisfied then $E <> \ \neg\phi$ characterizes counter-example paths. The reachability algorithm checks for $E <> \ \phi$.

The formulae $A <> \ \phi$ and $E[] \ \phi$ are *liveness* properties and are symmetric as well: $A <> \ \phi = \neg E[] \ \neg\phi$. These properties involve a loop detection algorithm because $E[] \ \phi$ holds for an infinite trace where every state satisfies ϕ. As the (symbolic) state-space is finite, we are looking for loops. The liveness algorithm checks for $E[] \ \phi$.

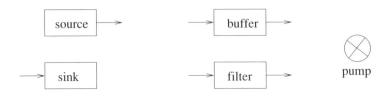

Figure 6.4. *Filter components in* UPPAAL

6.2.3. *Architecture of the tool*

The tool is separated into two main components: the graphical user interface (GUI) – the client – and the model-checker engine – the server. The GUI is written in Java and is easily deployed on different platforms whereas the engine is recompiled for every platform. We refer here to the architecture of the engine [DAV 03], the performance critical part of the tool. The data structures of the engine are designed around a data flow centric architecture that forms a *pipeline*. The data going through the filters are states or states and a transition.

The different components, as shown in Figure 6.4, are sources where states are created (typically the initial state), sinks where states disappear (typically checking an expression), buffers where states are pushed to and pulled from, and filters where states are pushed to and forwarded to the next component after processing. In addition, a pump shows where the main loop of the reachability or liveness algorithm executes.

The benefits of using pipeline components are *flexibility*, *code reuse*, and *efficiency*. The flexibility comes from the possibility to exchange a component for another to configure the pipeline to use, e.g., different storage structures to implement an exact exploration, an under-approximation or an over-approximation. Such dynamic configurations allows us to skip completely some stages in the pipeline, if they are not necessary, e.g., storing traces. The code reuse comes from the reuse of the components across different algorithms, e.g. the reachability and the liveness pipeline.

The common components that are used in the reachability 6.2.4 and the liveness 6.2.5 pipelines are:

– *transition:* that computes which transitions can be taken from a given states,

– *successor:* that fires a transition from a given state,

– *delay:* that computes the delay of state (if possible) bounded by its invariant,

– *extrapolation + Active clock reduction:* that applies the extrapolation according to the maximal (clock) constants of the model and at the same time active clock reduction. It appears that having locally $-\infty$ for the maximal constant of a given clock has the same effect as to free the constraints of that clock with the extrapolation algorithm.

6.2.4. *Reachability pipeline*

The reachability algorithm is storing its states inside a so-called *PWList* data structure [BEH 03b], which is unifying the traditional passed and waiting queues of model-checkers. Let us consider symbolic states to be of the form (l, Z) where l is the location vector and Z a zone. For simplicity, we omit the integer variables. A traditional reachability algorithm would look similar to the one depicted in Figure 6.5. Such an algorithm uses two main structures, namely the *passed* list to store previously explored states and the *waiting* list to store states to be explored. The algorithm starts with the initial state where $I(l_0)$ refers to its invariant. The expression $\forall(l', Z') : (l, Z) \to (l', Z')$ refers to computing all successors (l', Z') of (l, Z). The algorithm basically loops over the states in the waiting list, tests if the goal state has been found, computes the successors, and pushes the ones that are new to the waiting list. When this algorithm is implemented we have to put states in two hash tables (for efficient look-up) and make two inclusion checkings, i.e., we need to see if a state is included either in the passed or in the waiting list before adding it. The second inclusion check is implicit in the algorithm when a state is added to the waiting list. Inclusion checking is crucial in improving performance (to avoid redundant exploration) but it costs $O(n^2)$ where n is the number of clocks.

$waiting = \{(l_0, Z_0 \land I(l_0))\}$
$passed = \varnothing$
while $waiting \neq \varnothing$ **do**
  $(l, Z) =$ select state from $waiting$
  $waiting = waiting \setminus \{(l, Z)\}$
  if $goal(l, Z)$ **then return true**
  if $\forall(l, Y) \in passed : Z \nsubseteq Y$ **then**
    $passed = passed \cup \{(l, Z)\}$
    $\forall(l', Z') : (l, Z) \to (l', Z')$ **do**
      if $\forall(l', Y') \in waiting : Z' \nsubseteq Y'$ **then**
        $waiting = waiting \cup \{(l', Z')\}$
      endif
    done
  endif
done
return false

Figure 6.5. *Traditional reachability algorithm*

In contrast to having these two structures, a unified structure contains all the states but some of them are colored-waiting whereas others are colored-passed (the implementation behind is using a colored-state set). We note by (P, W), the unified structure. P denotes all states (that are considered as passed) and W marks the subset of them that are waiting. A PW-List is described as a pair $(P, W) \in 2^S \times 2^S$, where S is the set of symbolic states, $W \subseteq P$, and the two functions $put : 2^S \times 2^S \times S \to 2^S \times 2^S$ and $get : 2^S \times 2^S \to 2^S \times 2^S \times S$, such that:

- $get(P, W) = (P, W \setminus \{(l, Z)\}, (l, Z))$ for some $(l, Z) \in W$;
- $put(P, W, (l, Z)) =$
$$\begin{cases} (P \setminus I, W \cup \{(l, Z)\}) & \text{if } \forall (l, Y) \in P : Z \not\subseteq Y \\ (P, W) & \text{otherwise,} \end{cases}$$
where $I = \{(l, Y) \in P \mid Y \subset Z\}$.

The get function removes states from W and leaves them in P. The put function removes the states of P that are included in the new state (the set I) and add this new state to W. Removing states from P implicitly removes them from W too because $W \subseteq P$. Similarly, states added to W are also added to P.

Figure 6.6 shows the simplified algorithm using the PW-List structure. Now there is no redundancy in the state-set and states are not between sets but merely re-colored. In addition, we need only one hash table and we have one inclusion check. In practice, we only need a list of references to keep track of the subset W.

The reachability pipeline of UPPAAL is based on the algorithm given in Figure 6.6 with the *PWList* structure at its center. The pipeline is depicted in Figure 6.7. The pipeline computes symbolic successors, which is separated into computing transitions, firing them, delaying, and extrapolating. Expressions are evaluated at the end of the pipeline. The attentive reader notices that checking the goal in the implementation is not at the same place as in the algorithm. We do this after computing every successor.

$(P, W) = \{(l_0, Z_0 \wedge I(l_0)), (l_0, Z_0 \wedge I(l_0))\}$
while $W \neq \varnothing$ **do**
  $(P, W, (l, Z)) = \text{get(P, W)}$
  if $goal(l, Z)$ **then return true**
  $\forall (l', Z') : (l, Z) \to (l', Z')$ **do**
    $(P, W) = put(P, W, (l', Z'))$ **done**
done
return false

Figure 6.6. UPPAAL *reachability algorithm*

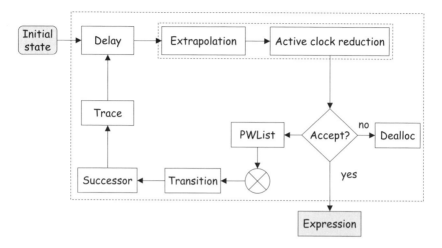

Figure 6.7. *The reachability pipeline of* UPPAAL

This way, we avoid going through the waiting list before finding out that the searched state is there and we can terminate earlier. The initial state (corresponding to the zero-point) is inserted in the pipeline at the delay stage and then treated as a successor.

6.2.5. *Liveness pipeline*

The liveness algorithm is given in Figure 6.8. The algorithm keeps track of a set of passed states P that verify $A <> \phi$ and a stack Stk of states that verify $\neg\phi$. The other states are not yet explored. The delay operation is special here and is restricted to states verifying $\neg\phi$. The goal of the algorithm is to find a loop of states that verify $\neg\phi$. Such a loop would be a counter-example to $A <> \phi$. If the algorithm finds a state for which there is an unbounded delay or a deadlock then this is also a counter-example. The reader notices that the recursive call is made with the proper action α in practice to keep track of the current path.

The liveness pipeline based on the algorithm of Figure 6.8 is given in Figure 6.9. Here, the recursive call is unfolded with a waiting list that keeps track of transitions that need to be fired. As the algorithm shows, when the *Search* function returns, states are moved from the stack Stk to the set of passed states P. The main loop (the pump) explores and moves these states. The successor transitions are pushed to the waiting list. The source states are pushed to the stack if they are not explored, and they are also checked for unbounded delay or deadlock. If a state exits the pipeline, it is the entry to an infinite path, counter-example of $A <> \phi$.

```
proc Eventually(S_0, φ)
   Stk = ∅
   P = ∅
   Search(delay(S_0, ¬φ))
   exit(true)
end

proc Search(S)
   if loop(S, Stk) then
      exit(false)
   fi
   S = S ∧ ¬φ
   push(Stk, S)
   if unbounded(S) ∨ deadlock(S) then
      exit(false)
   fi
   if ∀S' ∈ P : S ⊈ S' then
      foreach S' : S →α S' do
         Search(delay(S', ¬φ))
      od
   fi
   P = P ∪ {pop(Stk)}
end
```

Figure 6.8. UPPAAL *liveness algorithm*

6.2.6. *Leadsto pipeline*

The leadsto pipeline is checking $A[](\phi \rightarrow A <> \psi)$ properties. The algorithm here is to launch a liveness check from all states that satisfy ϕ. This is implemented as a composition of the two previous pipelines as illustrated in Figure 6.10. The reachability and liveness pipelines can be used as filter components themselves. States satisfying ϕ are pushed to the liveness pipeline, which is fed by the expression ψ. A state that exits the liveness pipeline is an entry to an infinite path, counter-example of $A <>; \psi$.

6.2.7. *Active clock reduction*

Active clock reduction is a technique to remove irrelevant clock constraints to states. If a clock is reset before being tested later then its value is irrelevant before the reset.

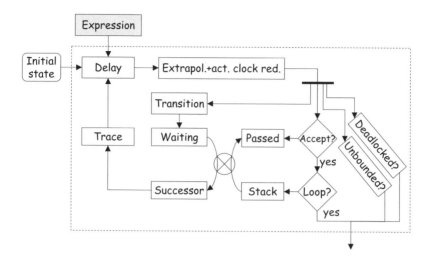

Figure 6.9. *The liveness pipeline of* UPPAAL

DEFINITION 6.5(INACTIVE CLOCK).– A clock x is *inactive* at a state S, if on all paths from S, x is always reset before being tested. In practice, the reduction is done in two steps: (i) there is a static analysis for every process that computes the set of active clocks for every location; and (ii) during the verification the set of active clocks for a given state is obtained by computing the union of active clocks for the locations in the current location vector. Only clock constraints for the active clocks are saved in zones.

6.2.8. *Space reduction techniques*

6.2.8.1. *Avoid storing all states*

One reduction technique (available with the -S1 option of the model-checker) is to avoid storing all states. It turns out that, in order to ensure termination, we only

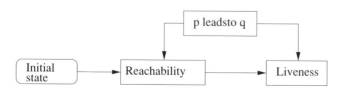

Figure 6.10. *The leadsto pipeline of* UPPAAL

need to store states that contain loop entries (in the *passed* list). Another more aggressive heuristic (option -S2) has been developed to store even fewer states while still ensuring termination [BEH 03a].

6.2.8.2. *Sharing data*

States are tuples of the form (L, V, Z) where L is a location vector, V is a variable vector, and Z is a zone (DBM in practice). Although states are uniquely stored (if they are not included into a larger one w.r.t. their zones), it appears that the individual components L, V, and Z of the states are repeated among all the states. The reason behind it is that when changing state, a system often keeps either its location vector, variables, or zone. Therefore, we can share these individual parts among all states. In practice, this gives typically 80% reduction in memory [BEH 03b].

6.2.8.3. *Minimal graph*

We need to tighten the constraints of our DBMs to be able to check for inclusion (in $O(n^2)$, n being the number of clocks). The inclusion check is done by comparing all constraints c_{ij} and c'_{ij} by pairs. The tightening is done by running a shortest paths algorithm, typically Floyd's [FLO 62]. This tightening results in a unique representation of a given zone, the canonical form of DBMs. This is useful for storing DBMs uniquely but it consumes space in $O(n^2)$. Figure 6.11 shows what the shortest paths algorithm does (shortest paths closure from (a) to (b)), if we see a DBM as a graph with vertices being clocks and the edges from x_j to x_i being weighted by the constraints $x_i - x_j \le c_i j$, which represents a distance. In [LAR 97b], a reduction was presented that reduces the number of necessary constraints to represent a zone. Applying this algorithm (shortest paths reduction from (b) to (c)) results in a minimal graph in the sense that the number of edges is minimal. This cost $O(n^3)$ in time. Although we still have $O(n^2)$ edges in the worst case, in practice we get $O(n)$ in average. UP-PAAL stores this reduced number of edges and can restore the full DBM, i.e., the full graph, by running its shortest paths algorithm on it (and we get back to (b)).

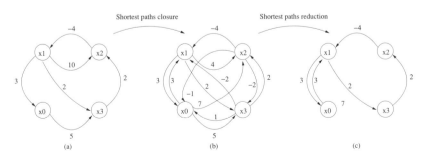

Figure 6.11. *Shortest paths closure and reduction*

In a nutshell, the shortest paths reduction algorithm works in two main steps: (i) it computes equivalence classes of the clocks, which is done by detecting zero cycles; and (ii) it chooses one representant per equivalence class and removes redundant edges between them.

We note that computing the shortest paths algorithm costs $O(n^3)$ in time so it is vital for performance to avoid doing it, if possible. It turns out that most operations on DBMs (delay, intersection, etc.) can be done on a canonical DBM in such a way that they preserve canonicity at no additional cost. We also note that we still do not know of any efficient way of applying these operations directly on the minimal graph. However, if the constraints of a (canonical) DBM are less or equal than the constraints (that are present) of a minimal graph then we can deduct that the DBM is included.

6.2.8.4. *Symmetry reduction*

UPPAAL implements the algorithm presented in [HEN 03]. This algorithm finds equivalence classes of states w.r.t. symmetry (also known as orbits) and chooses representative states by sorting the states (in the same equivalence class). The algorithm is implemented with the help of the *scalar* type that defines a set (of some size) of different but unordered scalar numbers. Figure 6.12 shows the experimental performance gains obtained by Fischer's protocol.

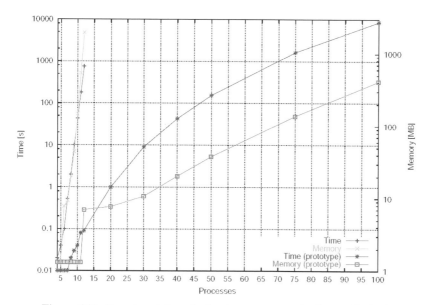

Figure 6.12. *Experimental results for the symmetry reduction on Fischer's protocol*

6.2.9. *Approximation techniques*

Sometimes systems are still too complex to be verified exactly. For these cases, it is useful to apply approximation techniques.

6.2.9.1. *Over-approximation: convex-hull*

UPPAAL implements the convex-hull over-approximation technique [BAL 96] that consists of computing the convex-hull of some zones instead of keeping all of them. Figure 6.13 illustrates the following example: in some automaton there are two paths that lead to the state $S3$, thus giving two different zones that are depicted graphically. The technique stores the convex union of these two zones (in fact, the smallest zone that contains both of these). Even though we are adding more states, the technique is still useful for safety properties.

6.2.9.2. *Under-approximation: bit-state hashing*

UPPAAL implements the bit-state hashing under-approximation technique [HOL 91, HOL 98]. This techniques consists of storing only one bit per state instead of its full location vector, variables, and zone. This is done by allocating a big hash table of size N (bits) initially filled with zeros and setting the $hash(state)\%N$ bit to one when states are visited (hash function applied to a state modulo N). There will be collisions that may conclude that a state was visited although it was not and avoid exploring it further. The technique is still useful for reachability properties.

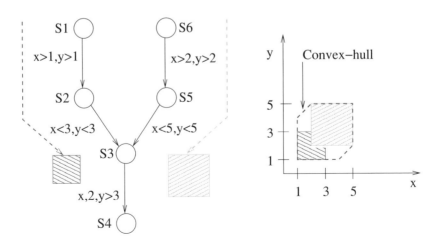

Figure 6.13. *Example of convex-hull*

6.2.10. *Extensions*

6.2.10.1. *Robust reachability*

Traditionally, the verification is done considering all clocks perfect but in practice this is not the case and clocks are known to drift slightly over time. Specialized algorithms are needed to compute *robust* reachability analysis w.r.t. such drifts. One robust reachability algorithm is available in the recent development snapshot versions of the tool. The algorithm of [DAW 06] is implemented and is accessible via properties of the form $E <> * \phi$ and $A[] * \phi$.

6.2.10.2. *Merging DBMs*

The convex-hull technique is an over-approximation technique that reduces the number of zones dramatically. UPPAAL offers an *exact* technique [DAV 05] to merge DBMs on-the-fly. This technique replaces two or more DBMs by their convex-hull union when the union is exact in the sense that no extra states are added. States are merged in the passed list but also in the waiting list if possible. We note that although the data structure we are using unifies waiting and passed states, we do not want to mix them when we merge to avoid duplicate exploration of states. This option is active by default in the development snapshot.

6.2.10.3. *Stopwatches*

Reachability analysis of timed automata augmented with stopwatches is undecidable but there is an efficient over-approximation technique to check such automata [CAS 00]. The technique consists of modifying the delay operator of DBMs such that clocks that are stopped keep their upper bounds. Syntactically, the user adds to the invariant of a state expressions of the type $x' == expr$ where $expr$ evaluates to 0 or 1. This technique has proven useful in modeling schedulability problems since we want to check safety properties, e.g., deadlines are never missed. This extension is available in the development snapshot.

6.2.10.4. *Supremum values*

When analyzing systems for worst case execution or response time, typically on models that schedule processes, it is useful to know maximal value of clocks that measure execution or response time. The development version of UPPAAL supports a special kind of property, namely, *sup: expr_list* where *expr_list* is a list of expressions that evaluate either to clocks or to integer values. The tool explores all the states and computes the maximal reached values for the integer variables or the maximal upper bound for the clocks.

6.2.10.5. *Other extensions*

UPPAAL implements the generalized sweep line method [KRI 02]. The user needs to define progress measures to take advantage of it. Different extrapolation algorithms [BEH 04a] have been implemented. These approximations take advantage of maximal upper bounds as before but also maximal lower bounds. A distributed version of UPPAAL has been developed [BEH 00] that runs on clusters. From the model point-of-view, an acceleration technique has been developed that improves reachability analysis on the models containing cycles [HEN 02].

6.3. UPPAAL-CORA

When computing traces that satisfy reachability properties, UPPAAL provides an algorithm for computing the time-wise shortest trace that satisfies the reachability property. This feature can be exploited for solving a number of general scheduling problems such as the famous traveling salesman problem.

UPPAAL-CORA is an extension of UPPAAL that performs minimum cost reachability analysis for timed automata models augmented with costs. These models, called priced timed automata, have been independently proposed and their reachability problems proven to be a decidable in [BEH 01b] and [ALU 01]. UPPAAL-CORA has been successfully applied to a number of scheduling case studies such as lacquor scheduling and aircraft landing [BEH 05a, BEH 05b].

6.3.1. *Priced timed automata*

A priced timed automaton is defined similarly to a timed automaton (Definition 6.1) except that it is augmented with a cost function $\mathsf{Cost} : (L \cup E) \to \mathbb{N}$ that assigns a non-negative integral value to locations and edges. If we consider a network of priced timed automata, the semantics of the cost function is such that when delaying in a state, the cost grows by a rate given by the sum of the costs of the locations, and when taking a transition the cost grows by the sum of the costs of the edges involved. We note that costs grow monotonically.

To efficiently analyze priced timed automata using symbolic semantics, UPPAAL-CORA uses the notion of priced zones, indicated by $\mathcal{Z}$, [LAR 01]. Priced zones are convex abstractions over clock valuations similarly to regular zones together with an affine cost function over the zone. The cost function in UPPAAL-CORA is implemented as a linear combination of the integral coefficients associated with the clocks of a zone. The use of priced zones complicates the computations of discrete and delay successors of symbolic states as these operations need zones to be split into sets of smaller disjoint zones in order to maintain the affinity of the cost function. This results in a significantly larger number of symbolic states that need to be explored. For a thorough description of the algorithms for computing delay and successors of symbolic states with priced zones, we refer to [LAR 01].

$$(P, W) = \{(l_0, \mathcal{Z}_0 \land I(l_0)), (l_0, \mathcal{Z}_0 \land I(l_0))\}$$
$cost = \infty$
while $W \neq \varnothing$ **do**
  $(P, W, (l, \mathcal{Z})) = $ get(P, W)
  if $goal(l, \mathcal{Z})$ **and** $mincost(\mathcal{Z}) < cost$ **then**
    $cost = mincost(\mathcal{Z})$
    continue
  endif
  if $mincost(\mathcal{Z}) + remain(l, \mathcal{Z}) < cost$
    $\forall(l', \mathcal{Z}') : (l, \mathcal{Z}) \rightarrow (l', \mathcal{Z}')$ **do**
      $(P, W) = put(P, W, (l', \mathcal{Z}'))$
    done
  endif
done
return $cost$

Figure 6.14. UPPAAL-CORA *minimum cost branch-and-bound reachability algorithm*

Figure 6.14 depicts the UPPAAL-CORA minimum cost reachability algorithm which outputs the minimum cost of satisfying a reachability property or ∞, if the property is unsatisfiable. The algorithm is a variation of the classical branch-and-bound algorithm fitted to the UPPAAL framework. The algorithm maintains a cost variable to keep track of the best solution found so far. The value of the cost variable is updated every time a better solution is found. The bounding of the algorithm is achieved by not exploring the successors of states, which cannot improve on the best solution. This allows us for a heuristic search algorithm, UPPAAL-CORA lets the user to define remaining costs for states, i.e. a lower bound estimates on the cost required to satisfy the reachability property. If the remaining estimate is misused by not providing a valid lower bound estimate, the algorithm does not guarantee correctness.

The pipeline for UPPAAL-CORA is similar to the one of UPPAAL for the reachability algorithm depicted in Figure 6.7. The difference is that the pipeline does not terminate upon finding a solution to the reachability problem but continues until there are no more states in the waiting list and reports the value of the cost variable as the solution to the reachability problem. Furthermore, there is no extrapolation operator defined for UPPAAL-CORA. The reader may then question why the algorithm terminates. Indeed, the guaranteed termination follows from two facts: first, it is well known that any timed automaton can be converted to a bounded timed automaton with upper bound invariants on all clocks. This means that the number of zones is finite. Second, given that the cost assignments of a priced timed automaton are integral, it is a known fact that cost functions over bounded zones are well-quasi-ordered, meaning that for a given zone, there cannot exist an infinite sequence costs functions without one eventually included in a previous one of the sequence [LAR 01]. These facts combined guarantee the termination of the algorithm.

The minimum cost algorithm utilizes the PW-List data structure used in UPPAAL. In order to correctly use the PW-List data structure, the inclusion check needs to be modified to handle the cost information contained in priced zones. Obviously, it not enough for a priced zone Z to include another priced zone Z', the cost function of Z further needs to be consistently smaller than Z' in order for Z to include Z'. In UPPAAL-CORA, this check is implemented by solving the linear program given by minimizing the difference between the cost functions of Z' and Z over the zone of Z'. If the solution is positive, we know that Z includes Z'. Moreover, the bounding of states with costs greater than the best found solution so far (potentially including a remaining estimate) is also implemented as part of the insertion into the PW-List.

One of the key aspects of the UPPAAL-CORA algorithm is solving the linear programs arising from inclusion checks on priced zones and computation of minimum costs of priced zones. Since zones have the property that they can be described solely by difference constraints, the linear programs can exploit this structure. It turns out that the minimization problem is basically the dual problem of the min-cost flow problem which is well known to have more efficient algorithms than general linear programming problems, [AHU 93, RAS 06]. Thus, UPPAAL-CORA converts every priced zone minimization problem to the related min-cost flow problem and solves this instead. This approach greatly increases the running time of the tool.

6.3.2. Example

Figure 6.15 depicts an example of how the cost rates of location and costs of edges are used in UPPAAL-CORA. Note that cost is a built-in variable and does not need to be declared. The cost increases continuously with a rate of 1 in A and 2 in B. In addition, taking the transition to C adds a rate of 3 to the cost. The automaton could take immediately the transition to B but then it would have to wait in B where the cost rate is higher than in A. Moreover, the automaton must delay at least one unit of time in B because of y. The reader can convince herself that the minimal cost to reach C is 6, waiting one unit of time both in A and B.

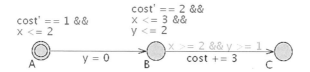

Figure 6.15. *An example of a* UPPAAL-CORA *model*

6.4. UPPAAL-TIGA

6.4.1. *Timed game automata*

UPPAAL-TIGA implements the first efficient truly on-the-fly algorithm for solving timed games [CAS 05]. It is an extension of [LIU 98] with time. Our input models are specified as networks of timed game automata [MAL 95] , where edges are marked either controllable or uncontrollable (see Figure 6.16). This defines a two players game with on one side the *controller* and on the other side the *environment*. Winning conditions of the game are specified through TCTL formulae. The tool is designed to generate strategies for a controller to reach an objective or to maintain safety whatever the environment (playing as an opponent) does.

As an example, let us consider the timed game automaton described in Figure 6.16. It has one clock x and two types of edges: controllable (c_i) and uncontrollable (u_i).

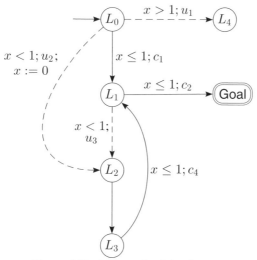

Figure 6.16. *An example of timed game automaton*

The reachability game consists of finding a strategy for the controller to reach the state Goal, no matter which uncontrollable transitions (u_i) the opponent takes. For all initial states of the form (l_0, x) with $x \leq 1$, there is such a strategy. This strategy consists of:

 – taking c_1 immediately in all states (l_0, x) with $x \leq 1$;

 – taking c_2 immediately in all states (l_1, x) with $x \leq 2$;

 – taking c_3 immediately in all states (l_2, x);

 – and delaying in all states (l_3, x) with $x < 1$ until the value of x is 1 at which point the edge c_4 is taken.

DEFINITION 6.6(NETWORK OF TIMED GAME AUTOMATA (NTGA)).– An NTGA is an NTA G with the set of transitions E_i of each automaton $\mathcal{A}_{\rangle}$ partitioned into *controllable* (E_i^c) and *uncontrollable* (E_i^u) actions. We denote $E^c \stackrel{\text{def}}{=} \bigcup_{i \in \{1,...,n\}} E_i^c$ and $E^u \stackrel{\text{def}}{=} \bigcup_{i \in \{1,...,n\}} E_i^u$. In addition, invariants are restricted to $Inv_i : L_i \rightarrow \mathcal{C}'(X_i)$ where $\mathcal{C}'$ is the subset of $\mathcal{C}$ using constraints of the form $x \leq k$.

Given an NTGA G and a control property, the *reachability (resp. safety) control problem* consists of finding a *strategy* f for the controller such that all the runs of G supervised by f satisfy the formula. The different control properties handled by UPPAAL-TIGA are:

 – *control: $A[\phi \, \mathcal{U} \, \psi]$*, i.e., reach ψ while avoiding $\neg\phi$,

 – *control: $A <> \psi$*, i.e., reach ψ, shortcut for $A[\, true \, \mathcal{U} \, \psi]$,

 – *control: $A[\phi \, \mathcal{W} \, \psi]$*, i.e., *possibly* reach ψ while avoiding $\neg\phi$, and

 – *control: $A[]\, \phi$*, i.e., avoid $\neg\phi$, shortcut for $A[\phi \, \mathcal{W} \, false]$.

The formal definition of the control problems is based on the definitions of *strategies* and *outcomes*. In any given situation, the strategies suggest to do a particular action after a given delay. A strategy [MAL 95] is described by a function that during the course of the game constantly gives information as to what the players want to do, under the form of a pair $(e, \delta) \in (E \times \mathbb{R}_{\geq 0}) \cup \{(\bot, \infty)\}$. $(\bot, \infty)$ means that the strategy wants to delay forever.

The environment has priority when choosing its actions. In addition, it can decide not to take action, unless it is forced to do so. Uncontrollable actions can be forced to happen only in states q where an invariant requires to take action and no controllable transition is possible and there is a possible uncontrollable transition (from the location involving that invariant). For more details on the different cases where so-called "forced" actions occur, we refer the reader to the manual of UPPAAL-TIGA available from *http://www.cs.aau.dk/~adavid/tiga/*. The implemented semantics is slightly different from [CAS 05] – the game could be won only through controllable actions, which means that there was no "forced" action.

Initialisation:
    $Passed \leftarrow \{S_0\}$;
    $Waiting \leftarrow \{(S_0, \alpha, S') \mid S' = Post_\alpha(S_0)^\nearrow\}$;
    $Win[S_0] \leftarrow \emptyset$;
    $Depend[S_0] \leftarrow \emptyset$;

Main:
while $((Waiting \neq \emptyset) \wedge (s_0 \notin Win[S_0]))$ **do**
    $e = (S, \alpha, S') \leftarrow pop(Waiting)$;
    if $S' \notin Passed$ **then**
        $Passed \leftarrow Passed \cup \{S'\}$;
        $Depend[S'] \leftarrow \{(S, \alpha, S')\}$;
        $Win[S'] \leftarrow S' \cap G$;
        $Waiting \leftarrow Waiting \cup \{(S', \alpha, S'') \mid S'' = Post_\alpha(S')^\nearrow\}$;
        if $Win[S'] \neq \emptyset$ **then** $Waiting \leftarrow Waiting \cup \{e\}$;
    otherwise (* reevaluate *)
        $Win^* \leftarrow Pred_t(Win[S] \cup \bigcup_{S \xrightarrow{c} T} Pred_c(Win[T]),$
                            $\bigcup_{S \xrightarrow{u} T} Pred_u(T \setminus Win[T])) \cap S$;
        if $(Win[S] \subsetneq Win^*)$ **then**
            $Waiting \leftarrow Waiting \cup Depend[S]$; $Win[S] \leftarrow Win^*$;
        if $Win[S'] \subsetneq S'$ **then** $Depend[S'] \leftarrow Depend[S'] \cup \{e\}$;
    endif
endwhile

Figure 6.17. *SOTFTR: symbolic on-the-fly algorithm for timed reachability games*

6.4.2. *Reachability pipeline*

We adapt the reachability algorithm of [CAS 05] based on transition as depicted in Figure 6.17 to an algorithm based on states for the reachability pipeline of UPPAAL-TIGA given in Figure 6.18. Upon close look at the algorithm, it appears that we need only the destination state S' to explore forward and the source state S to explore backward. Following this remark, the waiting queue in the pipeline contains states and a direction for the exploration. The state-graph stores in addition the winning and losing subsets. Although the algorithm does not show it, we can keep track of the losing states as well. The upper part of the pipeline is computing successors similarly to the reachability pipeline of UPPAAL. The bottom part is back-propagating information (winning or losing states).

The implementation in Figure 6.18 works as follows: when popping a state s that needs to be explored forward (source of a transition), the successors s' are computed

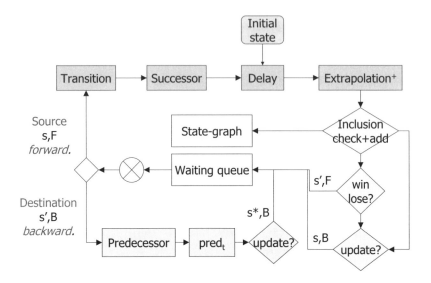

Figure 6.18. *The reachability pipeline of* UPPAAL-TIGA

and checked against the state-graph. Further successors will be computed (s', F), if s' is not included in the graph and s' is not winning (because then the game ends). In addition, we need to back-propagate an update to the source (s, B), if s' turned out to be winning. When popping a state s' to be explored backward, we need to go back to all sources that lead to s'. To do that, we compute the $pred_t$ operation [CAS 05] (temporal predecessors of winning states while avoiding losing states) and we back-propagate the winning subsets to the sources $(s*, B)$ for those sources that have new winning subsets.

We note that the given algorithm only computes the set of winning states but not a *strategy*. Strategies are computed on the fly by adding the mapping state-to-action when a given state is winning and taking this action leads to another winning state. In addition, if the winning part derives from a delay then the mapping adds the delay action instead. The only important point is to keep previously assigned states and not change their mappings when more winning states are discovered on the fly. This is to guarantee progress on the already known paths and avoid being caught in a loop.

6.4.3. *Time optimality*

Time optimality for reachability games consists of computing the best (optimal) time the controller can guarantee to reach a winning state: if t^* is the optimal-time, the controller has a strategy that guarantees to reach a winning state within t^* time units whatever the opponent is doing, and moreover, the controller has no strategy to guarantee this for any $t < t^*$. This problem is solved [CAS 05] by adding a new clock z to the original TGA and the invariant $Inv(\ell) \equiv z \leq T$ for all locations ℓ, where T is upper bound to reach the winning state. Furthermore, z is unconstrained in the initial state. The algorithm is then to compute the fix-point of all winning states and use z to deduct the optimal time. In practice, we compute iteratively the upper bound on-the-fly to prune the state-space when a solution is found and then we continue the search to refine the current optimal. The optimal time is given in the initial state by the interval between the max of z on the zero-axis and T. When pruning and updating T, the algorithm effectively converges to T being the upper bound and the max of z being zero.

Timed optimality queries are defined by *control_t*(u,g): A[ϕ $\mathcal{U}$ ψ], which is, only for reachability. The additional expression u defines an upper bound to prune the search, corresponding to T in the algorithm. This upper bound is updated on-the-fly. The expression g gives a lower bound from the current state in the search to the (goal) winning state. States that are at time $t + g > u$ are pruned. Here t is the elapsed time from the initial state. In case of doubt, it is always possible to assign u to a large value and g to zero, but meaningful values will help the search greatly.

6.4.4. *Cooperative strategies*

In games, where there is no winning strategy it may be useful to know what is the maximal set of states for which there is a winning strategy and how the environment can "help" the controller to reach such states. We call such strategies cooperative [DAV 08]. By "helping", we mean either the environment takes friendly uncontrollable actions or it lets the controller take action instead of preventing it. The result of the search is then a partition between (i) states that have a winning strategy, (ii) states that need cooperation of the environment, and (iii) states for which there is no hope of winning.

The algorithm is using the previous reachability analysis algorithm as a component. The algorithm is shown in Figure 6.19. The main idea is to compute the fix-point of the original model (and construct the strategy on-the-fly) and then recompute a fix-point of the modified model where we consider all transitions controllable, i.e. the environment is helping, *but very importantly*, we complete the previously obtained strategy. By completing, we mean adding more states to the previous mapping but we keep the previously assigned states. These additional actions are part of the cooperative strategy, the original actions define the winning sub-strategy, and for all other states there is no hope of winning. The algorithm computes these two fix-points, although the first one may terminate early, if we know that there is a winning strategy from the initial state, which we test. If the set of winning states is not reachable at

$fixpoint(G,l_0, Z_0)$
if $win(l_0, Z_0)$ **then return true**
if $\neg reached(Win)$ **then return false**
$fixpoint(G[c/u],l_0, Z_0)$
return true

Figure 6.19. UPPAAL-TIGA *cooperative reachability algorithm*

all, then there is no hope. In fact, there is a cooperative strategy, *iff* a winning state is reachable (in the worst case the environment always cooperate).

Cooperative strategies are queried with $E <> \Phi$ where Φ is an ordinary UPPAAL-TIGA formula (including *control*). The algorithm is generalized to safety as well, where the environment needs to avoid losing states.

6.4.5. *Timed games with Büchi objectives*

In games with Büchi objectives, at least one of the goal states must be often visited infinitely. The obtained strategy guarantees this while maintaining some other (optional) safety property. The algorithm is based on the symbolic on-the-fly timed reachability algorithm of [CAS 05] (SOTFTR) with a few notable changes as follows:

– the set Win (or winning states) contains only the states that can reach $Goal$ (the set of goal states) but not the $Goal$ itself (unless these states can themselves reach some goal states) contrary to the original algorithm where $Goal$ was always included in Win;

– the algorithm does not stop exploring states even if they are goal states;

– the algorithm is not on-the-fly any more in the sense that it needs to complete the search (forward and backward).

Figure 6.20 shows the simplified algorithm using parts of the original algorithm with the aforementioned changes. The first step is to run the original algorithm that returns the set of winning states. The input $Goal$ is the set of all goal states. The second step is to compute the fixed point of the set of goal states that are also winning, i.e., that can reach other goal states. Upon update of the set, we back-propagate again the set of goal states to compute which states are winning. We note that the call to SOTFTR in the loop executes only the back-propagation part. In addition, in order to be declared winning, a goal state must reach another goal state by a discrete transition. Delaying is not enough, e.g., if $x \geq 0$ is asked with x being a clock we still need discrete transitions to be taken (this is the current semantics but it may change in the future).

The complexity of this algorithm is quadratic in size S of the underlying untimed game (based on the region graph) of the game, which is in line with the results on

Initialization:
$G = Goal$
$Win = SOTFTR(G)$

Main:
while $G \neq G \cap Win$ **do**
$G = G \cap Win$
$Win = SOTFTR(G)$
done

Figure 6.20. *Simplified algorithm for solving timed games with Büchi objectives*

untimed games [CHA 06b]. It is straightforward to extend this algorithm to be on-the-fly. In essence, we add to the main while loop condition $\neg(\forall S \in Passed, Goal[S] = Win[S] \wedge q_0 \in Win[S_0])$. Also, we stop the SOTFTR procedure with this condition. This basically means that if all the goal states we have explored so far and the initial state are winning, we can stop because they can all enforce some of these goal states we have already explored.

The syntax for these properties is of the form (i) `control: A[] ( p and A<> q )` and (ii) `control: A[] A<> q`, where p is the safety predicate and q the Büchi control objective.

A major application is to generate non-Zeno strategies. If we add the automaton of Figure 6.21(a) to some system (the guard $y == 1$ is unimportant and the constant can be tuned to the particular model), then we can ask UPPAAL-TIGA to reach the $NonZeno$ state as a Büchi objective in addition to some other safety property we

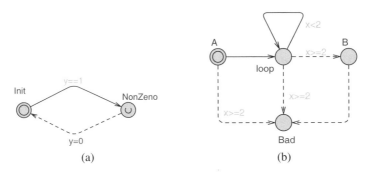

(a)   (b)

Figure 6.21. *(a) Monitor automaton to avoid Zeno behavior. (b) Example exhibiting Zeno behavior*

want the original system to satisfy. In the example shown in Figure 6.21(b), the control objective is to avoid the Bad state. There is a winning strategy that consists of looping without delaying in the $loop$ state. However, this strategy is Zeno. If we add the automaton of Figure 6.21(a) and update the query to make $NonZeno$ a repeated location, there will be no such strategy any more. In addition, if we fix the model and we add the reset x=0 to the loop transition, the Zeno strategy is still possible with a classical safety objective. With the Büchi objective however, we get a non-Zeno strategy.

6.4.6. *Timed games with partial observability*

UPPAAL-TIGA supports timed games with partial observability. Theoretical results on decidability are known on control of systems for event-based partial observation [LAM 00, BOU 03] and state-based partial observation [ARN 03, CHA 06a]. In this section, we summarize the algorithm proposed in [CAS 07] where we consider the problem of controller synthesis for timed games under state-based partial observation. Given a timed game automaton and a finite collection of *observations* (state predicates), we compute, if there exists a strategy such that a controller seeing only these observations can guarantee a safety or reachability control objective. In addition, these strategies are *stuttering invariant* in the sense that repeated identical observations will not change the strategy. The game is played as follows: initially and whenever the observation of the system state changes, Player 1 (the controller) proposes to take an action or to delay. The proposed action may be taken whenever and as long as it is enabled in the system until the observation changes. Delay means that the player is waiting for a change of observation. Then Player 2 (the environment) decides the evolution of the system according the rules:

1) if Player 1 chooses a discrete action then Player 2 can choose to play this action or another of its (enabled and uncontrollable) actions or let time pass while the action of Player 1 is not enabled – as long as the observation does not change,

2) if Player 1 chooses to delay then player 2 can choose to play its own (enabled and uncontrollable) actions or let time pass – as long as the observation does not change,

3) Player 1 can choose again what to do as soon as the observation changes.

The first rule entails that actions of the controller are urgent and that the environment has priority. Also, the controller does not know *a priori* whether his proposed action has effectively been taken or not.

The property supported are the same reachability and safety property as with perfect information but extended with observation. In practice, the query language is

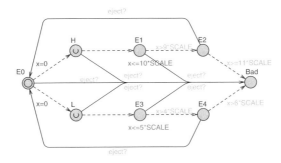

Figure 6.22. *Timed game for sorting heavy and light bricks*

extended by prefixing a list of observations to the ordinary control queries. The supported queries are:

- `- { o1, o2,...} control: A[ p U q ]`: must reach q while maintaining p,
- `- { o1, o2,...} control: A[ p W q ]`: may reach q while maintaining p,
- `- { o1, o2,...} control: A<> q`: must reach q,
- `- { o1, o2,...} control: A[] p`: maintain p.

The expressions `p`, `q`, `o1`, `o2`, ..., are state predicates. This extension has been used in the context of testing [DAV 09].

Figure 6.22 illustrates an example of a game played with imperfect information. The goal is to sort heavy and light boxes and avoid the bad state *Bad*. To do so, the controller must eject the box at the right moment. The controller can reset its own clock y or synchronize on the eject channel. However, the controller can only observe the states H, L, one of $E1$, $E2$, $E3$, or $E4$ (E), *Bad*, and if $y \in [0, 1/2)$. In addition, if the controller ejects the box at the wrong moment then the *Bad* state is reached. Figure 6.23 shows the obtained strategy (here determined and reduced). The generated controller is discretizing time with the only clock it can control by doing a series of reset/delay to measure time. The length of the chain depends on observing a light or heavy box. The states are partitioned as a function of the observations. In Figure 6.22, we note that the model is parameterized the variable SCALE to encode $[0, 1)$ or $[0, 1/2)$ while keeping the same query. The language limits the use of constraints to integers, so we scale the timing constraints of the model instead. Interestingly, the property is not satisfied, if the accuracy on y is too low (i.e. $y \in [0, 1)$) but it is satisfied, if we have a finer observation (i.e. $y \in [0, 1/2)$). The query for this example is:

```
{ Box.E1 or Box.E2 or Box.E3 or Box.E4, Box.H, Box.L,
Controller.y >= 0 and Controller.y < 1 } control: A[] not Box.Bad
```

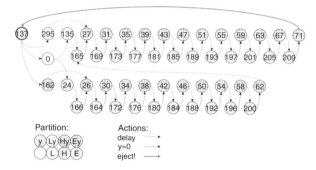

Figure 6.23. *Generated strategy to sort light and heavy boxes*

6.4.6.1. *Algorithm*

To solve such games with partial observation, we extend the timed game structure of UPPAAL-TIGA with two disjoint alphabets of actions σ_1 and σ_2 for the set of actions of the Players 1 and 2. The algorithm given in Figure 6.24 is similar in its main structure to the previous algorithm for solving timed games with perfect information of Figure 6.17. It has two phases of exploring the states forward and then back-propagating winning or losing information. The main differences are that we are exploring *sets* of symbolic states (W). Furthermore, the successor states depend on the observations because the algorithm needs to compute a local fix-point at every step to find out which states (and thus construct a set of them) leave the current observation. This is what $W' = \text{Next}_\alpha(W)$ is doing. The observation sets (of states) are given by $\gamma(o)$. In addition, the back-propagation is simpler than before because we do not need to use the $pred_t$ operator. Another remark is that it is possible that when computing the successors for a given action, there is a way to either deadlock or loop in the same observation. This is a *sink* for the current set of states (and action) and it is considered to be losing. We refer to [CAS 07] for a more complete description of the theory and the algorithm.

6.4.6.2. *Implementation*

The pipeline architecture is depicted in Figure 6.25. The pipeline has different levels, the top level working on sets of (symbolic) states. Sets are explored forward or backward. The forward exploration is the most complex part since it needs to constrain the successor computation w.r.t. observations. As mentioned in the algorithm description, we have a local reachability filter (a compound filter) that has a second level where the exploration is done at the state level. The action filter described in Figure 6.25 has another internal level that decomposes into computing the successor (basically the chain transition – successor – delay – extrapolation) and takes care of

Initialization:
$Passed \leftarrow \{\{s_0\}\}$;
$Waiting \leftarrow \{(\{s_0\}, \alpha, W') \mid \alpha \in \Sigma_1, o \in \mathcal{O}, \ W' = \mathsf{Next}_\alpha(\{s_0\}) \cap o \wedge W' \neq \emptyset\}$;
$Win[\{s_0\}] \leftarrow (\{s_0\} \subseteq \gamma(\mathsf{Goal}) \ ? \ 1 : 0)$;
$Losing[\{s_0\}] \leftarrow (\{s_0\} \not\subseteq \gamma(\mathsf{Goal}) \wedge (Waiting = \emptyset \vee \forall \alpha \in \Sigma_1, \mathsf{Sink}_\alpha(s_0) \neq \emptyset) \ ? \ 1 : 0)$;
$Depend[\{s_0\}] \leftarrow \emptyset$;

Main:
while $((Waiting \neq \emptyset) \wedge Win[\{s_0\}] \neq 1 \wedge Losing[\{s_0\}] \neq 1))$ **do**
    $e = (W, \alpha, W') \leftarrow pop(Waiting)$;
    if $s' \notin Passed$ **then**
        $Passed \leftarrow Passed \cup \{W'\}$;
        $Depend[W'] \leftarrow \{(W, \alpha, W')\}$;
        $Win[W'] \leftarrow (W' \subseteq \gamma(\mathsf{Goal}) \ ? \ 1 : 0)$;
        $Losing[W'] \leftarrow (W' \not\subseteq \gamma(\mathsf{Goal}) \wedge \mathsf{Sink}_\alpha(W') \neq \emptyset \ ? \ 1 : 0)$;
        if $(Losing[W'] \neq 1)$ **then** (* **if losing it is a deadlock state** *)
            $NewTrans \leftarrow \{(W', \alpha, W'') \mid \alpha \in \Sigma, o \in \mathcal{O}, \ W' = \mathsf{Next}_\alpha(W) \cap o \wedge W' \neq \emptyset\}$;
            if $NewTrans = \emptyset \wedge Win[W'] = 0$ **then** $Losing[W'] \leftarrow 1$;
            if $(Win[W'] \vee Losing[W'])$ **then** $Waiting \leftarrow Waiting \cup \{e\}$;
            $Waiting \leftarrow Waiting \cup NewTrans$;
        otherwise (* **reevaluate** *)
            $Win^* \leftarrow \bigvee_{c \in \mathsf{Enabled}(W)} \bigwedge_{W \xrightarrow{c} W''} Win[W'']$;
            if Win^* **then**
                $Waiting \leftarrow Waiting \cup Depend[W]; Win[W] \leftarrow 1$;
            $Losing^* \leftarrow \bigwedge_{c \in \mathsf{Enabled}(W)} \bigvee_{W \xrightarrow{c} W''} Losing[W'']$;
            if $Losing^*$ **then**
                $Waiting \leftarrow Waiting \cup Depend[W]; Losing[W] \leftarrow 1$;
            if $(Win[W'] = 0 \wedge Losing[W'] = 0)$ **then** $Depend[W'] \leftarrow Depend[W'] \cup \{e\}$;
        endif
endwhile

Figure 6.24. *OTFPOR: on-the-fly algorithm for partially observable reachability timed game structures*

sorting the successors in function of their actions. The observation identifier computes and check the observation to see if the states belong to the same observation or not, in particular it is detecting the winning and losing observations. We note that states are split according to the observations and that the state-space is partitioned in function the observations.

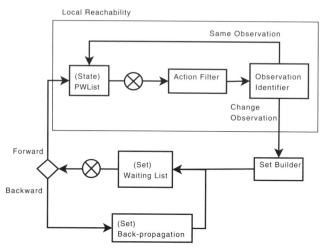

Figure 6.25. *Pipeline architecture for reachability analysis of timed games with partial observability*

6.4.7. *Simulation checking*

UPPAAL-TIGA can be used to check weak alternating simulation relation, i.e., the simulation relation that is defined over the set of pairs of timed *game* automata and that treats *silent* actions separately from other actions.

In this section, we are checking whether there exists a simulation relation between two TGA $A = (L_A, l_{0A}, X_A, \Sigma_c \cup \{\varepsilon_c\}, \Sigma_u \cup \{\varepsilon_u\}, E_A, Inv_A)$ and $B = (L_B, l_{0B}, X_B, \Sigma_c, \Sigma_u, E_B, Inv_B)$ be two TGA. Remark that we have imposed that B has any silent actions, whereas A may have controllable (ε_c) or uncontrollable ε_u silent transitions. It is a natural limitation, because abstract models usually do not have any invisible behavior. Second, A is not allowed to have uncontrollable silent loops, i.e., sequences of states $q_1, \ldots, q_n$ such, that $q_1 \xrightarrow{\varepsilon_u}_u q_2 \xrightarrow{\varepsilon_u}_u \ldots \xrightarrow{\varepsilon_u}_u q_n \xrightarrow{\varepsilon_u}_u q_1$. The presence of such silent loops would complicate the simulation checking algorithm.

Let us define $q \xrightarrow{\varepsilon_u *}_u \xrightarrow{a}_u q'$, iff there exists a sequence of states $q_1, \ldots, q_n$ such, that $q = q_1$, $q_i \xrightarrow{\varepsilon_u}_u q_{i+1}$ (for $i = 1 \ldots n - 1$) and $q_n \xrightarrow{a}_u q'$. We use subscripts c and u to distinguish between controllable and uncontrollable transitions, i.e. $q \xrightarrow{a}_c q'$ is controllable and $q \xrightarrow{a}_u q'$ in uncontrollable.

DEFINITION 6.7(TIMED WEAK ALTERNATING SIMULATION).– A *weak alternating simulation relation* between two TGA A and B is a relation $R \subseteq Q_A \times Q_B$ such that $(q_{0A}, q_{0B}) \in R$ and for every $(q_A, q_B) \in R$ and for every action $a \in \Sigma_c \cup \Sigma_u$:

$$- (q_A \xrightarrow{\varepsilon_c}_c q'_A) \implies ((q'_A, q_B) \in R) \qquad\qquad \text{(silent transitions)}$$

$$- (q_A \xrightarrow{a}_c q'_A) \implies \exists q'_B \ (q_B \xrightarrow{a}_c q'_B \wedge (q'_A, q'_B) \in R) \qquad \text{(controllable)}$$

$$- (q_B \xrightarrow{a}_u q'_B) \implies \exists q'_A \ (q_A \xrightarrow{\varepsilon_u *}_u \xrightarrow{a}_u q'_A \wedge (q'_A, q'_B) \in R) \quad \text{(uncontrollable)}$$

$$- (q_A \xrightarrow{\delta} q'_A) \implies \exists q'_B \ (q_B \xrightarrow{\delta} q'_B \wedge (q'_A, q'_B) \in R) \qquad\qquad \text{(delay)}$$

We write $A \leq B$, if there exists a weak alternating simulation relation between A and B.

The intuition behind this definition is that every controllable transition that can be taken from q_A must be matched by an equally labeled controllable transition from q_B. And on the other hand, every uncontrollable transition in B tends to make B harder to control than A; then we require that it is matched by an equally labeled uncontrollable transition in A. It is also necessary to check that if the controller of A is able to avoid playing any action during a given delay, then the controller of B is able to do the same.

It can be shown that timed weak alternating simulation preserves the satisfiability of formulae of the universal fragment of TCTL (i.e. formulae of the form $A[] \ \phi$, $A <> \ \phi, \phi -- > \psi$). This means that if $A \leq B$ and A satisfies some TCTL formula that does not contain E path quantifier, then B also satisfies this formula. Timed-weak alternating simulation can be checked between *networks* of timed automata as well.

In order to check for timed weak alternating simulation between networks of timed automata in UPPAAL-TIGA, one should use a query of the form $\{A_1, \dots, A_m\} <= \{B_1, \dots B_n\}$. We assume for simplicity that we are checking simulation between single automata. Consider that we are checking $\{A\} \leq \{B\}$. There are several restrictions on the automata A and B in UPPAAL-TIGA. First, B is not allowed to have any silent actions. It is a natural limitation, because abstract models usually do not have any invisible behavior. Second, A is not allowed to have uncontrollable silent loops, i.e., sequences of states $q_1, \dots, q_n$ such that, $q_1 \xrightarrow{\varepsilon}_u q_2 \xrightarrow{\varepsilon}_u \dots \xrightarrow{\varepsilon}_u q_n \xrightarrow{\varepsilon}_u q_1$. The presence of such silent loops would complicate the simulation checking algorithm.

6.4.7.1. *Algorithm*

UPPAAL-TIGA uses a well-known game-theoretic approach to the simulation checking problem that reduces the simulation checking problem to solving a two-players game [ETE 01]. In this game, one player, *Spoiler*, tries to put the models in inconsistent state by taking controllable transitions in A and uncontrollable in B, and the other player, *Duplicator*, tries to prevent *Spoiler* of doing that by repeating *Spoiler*'s transition in the opposite model.

Consider the task of checking weak alternating simulation between TGAs $A = (L_A, l_{0A}, X_A, \Sigma_c \cup \{\varepsilon_c\}, \Sigma_u \cup \{\varepsilon_u\}, E_A, Inv_A)$ and $B = (L_B, l_{0B}, X_B, \Sigma_c, \Sigma_u, E_B,$

Inv_B) $A = (L_A, l_{0A}, X_A, \Sigma_c \cup \{\varepsilon_c\}, \Sigma_u \cup \{\varepsilon_u\}, E_A, Inv_A)$ and $B = (L_B, l_{0B}, X_B,$ $\Sigma_c, \Sigma_u, E_B, Inv_B)$. The game states of a simulation checking game are represented by tuples (l_A, l_B, Z, a), where $l_A \in L_A$, $l_B \in L_B$, $Z \subseteq R_{\geq 0}^{X_A \cup X_B}$ and $a \in \{\perp\} \cup \Sigma$. We will use functions $Z(S)$ and $Type(S)$ that return the third component of a game state S and its owner correspondingly. All the game states (l_A, l_B, Z, a) such that $a = \perp$ are the states of the player $Spoiler$ and we will use the shortcut $(l_A, l_B, Z)_S$ for identifying them. All other states belong to player $Duplicator$ and we will use shortcut $(l_A, l_B, Z, a)_D$ for them. The initial game state is $S_0 = (l_{A0}, l_{B0}, \{\vec{0}\}\nearrow \cap [\![Inv_A(l_{A0})]\!])_S$.

For two game states S_1 and S_2, we will write $S_1 \to S_2$ if there is a game transition from S_1 to S_2. The transition relation of the simulation checking game is constructed as follows:

$- (l_A, l_B, Z)_S \to (l'_A, l_B, Z')_S$, iff $e = (l_A, g, \varepsilon_c, Y, l'_A) \in E_A^c$ and $Z' = Post_e(Z)\nearrow \cap [\![Inv_A(l'_A)]\!]$

$- (l_A, l_B, Z)_S \to (l'_A, l_B, Z', a)_D$, iff $e = (l_A, g, a, Y, l'_A) \in E_A^c$, $a \in \Sigma_c$ and $Z' = Post_e(Z)$

$- (l_A, l_B, Z)_S \to (l_A, l'_B, Z', a)_D$, iff $e = (l_B, g, a, Y, l'_B) \in E_B^u$ and $Z' = Post_e(Z)$

$- (l_A, l_B, Z, a)_D \to (l_A, l'_B, Z')_S$, iff $e = (l_B, g, a, Y, l'_B) \in E_B^c$, $Z' = Post_e(Z)\nearrow \cap [\![Inv_B(l'_B)]\!]$

$- (l_A, l_B, Z, a)_D \to (l'_A, l_B, Z')_S$, iff $e = (l_A, g, a, Y, l'_A) \in E_A^u$, $Z' = Post_e(Z)\nearrow \cap [\![Inv_A(l'_A)]\!]$

$- (l_A, l_B, Z, a)_D \to (l'_A, l_B, Z', a)_D$, iff $e = (l_A, g, \varepsilon_u, Y, l'_A) \in E_A^u$, $Z' = Post_e(Z)$

Each game state S includes a possibly infinite set of clock valuations $Z(S)$, some of them are winning for $Spoiler$. The function $Win(S) \subseteq Z(S)$ will be used to define them.

DEFINITION 6.8.– Let us say that function Win defines the set of winning states of the player $Spoiler$, if the following requirements are fulfilled:

– if $Type(S) = Spoiler$ and $S = (l_A, l_B, Z)_S$, then

$$Win(S) = Z(S) \cap \left(Z(S) \cap (\neg [\![Inv_B(l_B)]\!] \cup \bigcup_{\alpha = S \to S'} Pred_\alpha(Win(S'))) \right)^\searrow,$$

– if $Type(S) = Duplicator$, then
$Win(S) = Z(S) \setminus \bigcup_{\alpha = S \to S'} Pred_\alpha(Z(S') \setminus Win(S'))$,

– Win is the least such function according to the preorder $f \leq g \equiv \forall S(f(S) \subseteq g(S))$.

The first point of this definition stands for the fact that $Spoiler$ wins in some state, if the invariant of A is violated, or if he can delay and move to some other winning state. The second point means that $Duplicator$ loses in some state, if he cannot move to some other game state, which is winning for him.

It can be proved that if Win satisfies Definition 6.8, then $A \leq B$ iff $\vec{0} \notin Win(S_0)$. The winning subsets defined by Win function can be computed incrementally until the fix-point is reached. However, if we see at some point that $\vec{0} \in Win(S_0)$, then we can already build a counterexample showing that simulation is violated and thus avoid building and solving the whole game graph.

Given two models A and B and query $\{A\} <= \{B\}$ UPPAAL-TIGA explores a simulation game graph using on-the fly algorithm which is implemented using the pipeline architecture (see Figure 6.18). Compared to the original algorithm for solving arbitrary timed games we modified the forward and backward filters (where winning conditions are defined) as well as the transition and delay filters (where the game transition relation is defined).

We exploited the fact that simulation checking game is turn-based, i.e., in each game state only one player is permitted to take a move. This allows us to simplify the algorithm to avoid using the expensive function $pred_t$ that is necessary to have in the case when both players can take a move from the same state.

6.5. TAPAAL

6.5.1. *Introduction*

TAPAAL is a platform independent tool for modeling, simulation and verification of timed-arc Petri nets. TAPAAL provides a stand-alone editor and simulator, while the verification module translates timed-arc Petri net models into networks of timed automata and uses the UPPAAL engine for the automatic analysis. The tool is available at www.tapaal.net.

Since the introduction of Petri nets by Petri [PET 62] in 1962, numerous extensions of the basic place/transition model were studied and supported by a number of academic as well as industrial tools [HEI 09]. Many recent studies on Petri net models are concerned with adding timed features that can be associated with places, transitions, arcs, or tokens in the net. A recent overview aiming at a comparison of the different time dependent models (including timed automata) is given in [SRB 08].

The model considered in TAPAAL is a *timed-arc Petri net* [BOL 90, HAN 93]. It associates an age (real number) with each token in the net and time intervals to arcs that restrict the ages of tokens that can be used for firing a transition. The advantages of this model are an intuitive semantics and a number of positive decidability results of problems like coverability and boundedness (for detailed references see [SRB 08]).

On the other hand, the impossibility to describe urgent behaviors limits its modeling power and wider applicability.

TAPAAL extends the TAPN model with new features such as *invariants* for modelling of urgency and *transport arcs* for modeling systems like production lines and work-flow processes. It provides an intuitive modeling environment for editing and simulating of TAPN models. The verification module of TAPAAL allows for automatic checking of bounded TAPN models against safety and liveness requirements via a translation to networks of timed automata. The UPPAAL [UPP 09] engine is then used as a back-end for the actual verification.

The connection between bounded TAPN and timed automata was studied in [SIF 96, SRB 05, BOU 08], and while theoretically satisfactory, the translations described in these papers are not suitable for a tool implementation as they either cause an exponential blow-up in the size or create a new parallel component with a fresh local clock for *each* place in the net. As UPPAAL performance becomes significantly slower with the growing number of parallel processes and clocks, the verification of larger nets with little or no concurrent behavior (few tokens in the net) becomes intractable.

TAPAAL implements a novel translation technique where a new parallel component (with a local clock) is created for every token in the net. One of the main advantages of this approach is the possibility to use *active clock reduction* and *symmetry reduction* techniques recently implemented in UPPAAL. As a result the size of verifiable models increases by orders of magnitude as demonstrated on several examples.

6.5.2. *Definition of timed-arc Petri nets used in TAPAAL*

The set $\mathcal{I}$ of *time intervals* is defined by the following abstract syntax where a and b range over $\mathbb{N}$ and $a < b$

$$I ::= [a, b] \mid [a, a] \mid (a, b] \mid [a, b) \mid (a, b) \mid [a, \infty) \mid (a, \infty) .$$

The set $\mathcal{I}_{Inv}$ of *invariants* is defined as the following subset of time intervals ($\mathcal{I}_{Inv} \subseteq \mathcal{I}$) where b and b' range over $\mathbb{N}$ and $b' > 0$

$$I ::= [0, b] \mid [0, b') \mid [0, \infty) .$$

Let $I \in \mathcal{I}$. Given a time point $d \in \mathbb{R}^{\geq 0}$, the validity of the expression $d \in I$ is defined in the usual way, e.g., $d \in [a, b)$ iff $a \leq d < b$ and $d \in (a, \infty)$ iff $a < d$.

A *timed-arc Petri net with transport arcs and place invariants* (TAPN) is a tuple $N = (P, T, F, c, F_{tarc}, c_{tarc}, \iota)$, where:

- P is a finite set of *places*,
- T is a finite set of *transitions* such that $T \cap P = \emptyset$,
- $F \subseteq (P \times T) \cup (T \times P)$ is a *flow relation*,
- $c : F|_{P \times T} \to \mathcal{I}$ is a function assigning a time interval to every arc from a place to a transition,
- $F_{tarc} \subseteq (P \times T \times P)$ is the set of *transport arcs* which satisfies

$$\forall (p, t, p') \in F_{tarc}, \forall r \in P. \ [(p, t, r) \in F_{tarc} \Rightarrow p' = r \ \wedge$$
$$(r, t, p') \in F_{tarc} \Rightarrow p = r \ \wedge$$
$$(p, t) \notin F \ \wedge \ (t, p') \notin F],$$

- $c_{tarc} : F_{tarc} \to \mathcal{I}$ is a function assigning a time interval to every transport arc, and
- $\iota : P \to \mathcal{I}_{Inv}$ is an *invariant assignment* of invariants to places.

REMARK 6.1.– The conditions imposed on the transport arcs guarantee that for any $p \in P$ and any $t \in T$ there is at most one $p' \in P$ such that $(p, t, p') \in F_{tarc}$ and at most one $p'' \in P$ such that $(p'', t, p) \in F_{tarc}$. In other words, for any given p and t, if there is a transport arc of the form (p, t, p') or (p'', t, p) then the places p' and p'' are uniquely defined. Whenever the places p' and p'' are not relevant for the context, we shall simply denote the transport arcs as $(p, t, \_)$ or $(\_, t, p)$.

The *preset* of a transition t in the net is defined as $^\bullet t = \{p \in P \mid (p, t) \in F \vee (p, t, \_) \in F_{tarc}\}$, and the *postset* of a transition t is defined as $t^\bullet = \{p \in P \mid (t, p) \in F \vee (\_, t, p) \in F_{tarc}\}$.

By $\mathcal{B}(\mathbb{R}^{\geq 0})$ we denote the set of finite multisets on $\mathbb{R}^{\geq 0}$. Let $B \in \mathcal{B}(\mathbb{R}^{\geq 0})$ and $d \in \mathbb{R}^{\geq 0}$. We define $B + d$ in such a way that we add the value d to every element of B, i.e. $B + d \stackrel{def}{=} \{b + d \mid b \in B\}$.

Let $N = (P, T, F, c, F_{tarc}, c_{tarc}, \iota)$ be a TAPN. A *marking* M on the net N is a function $M : P \to \mathcal{B}(\mathbb{R}^{\geq 0})$ such that every $p \in P$ and every $x \in M(p)$ satisfies $x \in \iota(p)$. Each place is thus assigned a certain number of tokens, and each token is annotated with a real number (*age*). We moreover consider only markings such that all their tokens satisfy the place invariants imposed by the invariant assignment ι. By $|M|$, we denote the total number of tokens in the marking M, formally $|M| = \sum_{p \in P} |M(p)|$, where $|M(p)|$ is the cardinality of the multiset $M(p)$. The set of all markings on N is denoted by $\mathcal{M}(N)$.

A *marked TAPN* is a pair (N, M_0), where N is a timed-arc Petri net and M_0 is an initial marking. As *initial markings* we allow only markings with all tokens of age 0.

Let us now outline the dynamics of TAPNs. We introduce two types of transition rules: *firing* of a transition and *time delay*.

For a TAPN N we say that a transition $t \in T$ is *enabled* in a marking M, if:

– in all places $p \in {}^\bullet t$ there is a token x such that its age belongs to the time interval on the arc from p to t, and

– if there is a transport arc of the form (p, t, p') then moreover the age of the token in p satisfies also the invariant imposed by p'.

If a transition t is enabled then it can *fire*. This means that it consumes one token (of an appropriate age) from each place in ${}^\bullet t$, and then produces one new token to every place in $t^\bullet$. The age of the newly produced token is either 0 for the standard arcs, or it preserves the age of the consumed token in case of a transport arc.

Another behavior of the net is a so-called *time delay* step where all tokens in the net grow simultaneously older by a given time factor (a real number in general). A time delay step is allowed only as long as all invariants in places are satisfied.

Formal definitions of transition firing and time delay steps follow.

Transition firing

In a marking M, we can fire a transition t if it is enabled, i.e.

$$\forall p \in {}^\bullet t. \ \exists x \in M(p). \ [x \in c(p, t) \vee (x \in c_{tarc}(p, t, p') \wedge x \in \iota(p'))] \ .$$

Before firing t, we fix the sets $C_t^-(p)$ and $C_t^+(p)$ for all places $p \in P$ so that they satisfy the following equations (note that all operations are on multisets, and there may be several options for fixing these sets):

– for every $p \in P$ such that $(p, t) \in F$
$C_t^-(p) = \{x\}$ where $x \in M(p)$ and $x \in c(p, t)$,

– for every $p \in P$ such that $(t, p) \in F$
$C_t^+(p) = \{0\}$, and

– for every $p, p' \in P$ such that $(p, t, p') \in F_{tarc}$
$C_t^-(p) = \{x\} = C_t^+(p')$ where $x \in M(p)$, $x \in c_{tarc}(p, t, p')$ and $x \in \iota(p')$;

– in all other cases (when the place in the argument is unrelated to the firing of the transition t) we set the above sets to $\emptyset$.

Firing a transition t in the marking M yields a new marking M' defined as

$$\forall p \in P. \ M'(p) = \left(M(p) \setminus C_t^-(p) \right) \cup C_t^+(p).$$

Time delays
In a marking M we can let time pass by $d \in \mathbb{R}^{\geq 0}$ time units, if

$$\forall p \in P. \, \forall x \in M(p). \, (x + d) \in \iota(p)$$

and this time delay step then yields a marking M' defined as

$$\forall p \in P. \, M'(p) = M(p) + d.$$

A TAPN $N = (P, T, F, c, F_{tarc}, c_{tarc}, \iota)$ generates a timed labeled transition system, where states are markings of N, the set of actions is T, and the transition relation is defined by $M \xrightarrow{t} M'$ whenever the firing of a transition t in a marking M yields a marking M', and $M \xrightarrow{d} M'$ whenever a time delay of d time units in a marking M yields a marking M'.

In a marked TAPN (N, M_0), we say that a marking M is reachable iff $M_0 \longrightarrow^* M$. A marked net N is k-*bounded* for a natural number k, if the total number of tokens in any of its reachable markings is less than or equal to k. A marked net is called *bounded*, if it is k-bounded for some k.

6.5.3. *TAPAAL logic*

In order to introduce TAPAAL logic formulae, we have to define the set of atomic proposition $\mathcal{AP}$. Let

$$\mathcal{AP} \stackrel{def}{=} \{p \bowtie n \mid p \in P, n \in \mathbb{N} \text{ and } \bowtie \in \{<, \leq, =, \geq, >\}\}.$$

The interpretation is that a proposition $p \bowtie n$ is true in a marking M, iff the number of tokens in the place p respects the given proposition with respect to n.

We shall now define a subset of computation tree logic used in TAPAAL (essentially mimicking the logic used in UPPAAL, except for the *leads-to* operator). The logical formulae are given by the following abstract syntax:

$$\psi ::= \quad \text{EF} \, \varphi \mid \text{EG} \, \varphi \mid \text{AF} \, \varphi \mid \text{AG} \, \varphi$$
$$\varphi ::= \quad p \bowtie n \mid \neg\varphi \mid \varphi \wedge \varphi,$$

where $p \bowtie n \in \mathcal{AP}$ and EF, EG, AF and AG are the standard CTL temporal operators.

The satisfaction relation $M \models \psi$ for a marking M and a formula ψ is defined inductively as follows:

- $M \models p \bowtie n$, iff $|M(p)| \bowtie n$,
- $M \models \neg\varphi$, iff $M \not\models \varphi$,

- $M \models \varphi_1 \wedge \varphi_2$, iff $M \models \varphi_1$ and $M \models \varphi_2$,
- $M \models \mathsf{EF}\,\varphi$, iff $M \longrightarrow^* M'$ and $M' \models \varphi$
- $M \models \mathsf{EG}\,\varphi$, iff there is a (finite or infinite) alternating run ρ of the form

$$M = M_1 \xrightarrow{d_1} M_1' \xrightarrow{a_1} M_2 \xrightarrow{d_2} M_2' \xrightarrow{a_2} M_3 \xrightarrow{d_3} M_3' \xrightarrow{a_3} M_4 \xrightarrow{d_4} M_4' \xrightarrow{a_4} \dots$$

such that for all i and for all d, $0 \le d \le d_i$ we have $M_i[d] \models \varphi$ (where $M_i[d]$ is the unique marking reachable from M_i by time delay of d time units) and

(i) ρ is infinite, or

(ii) ρ is finite and ends in M_k where for every $d \in \mathbb{R}^{\ge 0}$ we have $M_k \xrightarrow{d}$ and $M_k[d] \models \varphi$, or

(iii) ρ is finite and ends in a state M' (where M' is either of the form M_k or M_k') such that whenever $M' \xrightarrow{d} M'[d]$ is possible for a $d \in \mathbb{R}^{\ge 0}$ then $M'[d] \models \varphi$ and there is no marking M'' such that $M'[d] \xrightarrow{t} M''$ for any $t \in T$,

- $M \models \mathsf{AF}\,\varphi$, iff $M \not\models \mathsf{EG}\,\neg\varphi$, and
- $M \models \mathsf{AG}\,\varphi$, iff $M \not\models \mathsf{EF}\,\neg\varphi$.

REMARK 6.2.– The meaning of the $\mathsf{EG}\,\varphi$ formula is that there should exist a *maximal* run of the system such that at any point the formula φ is satisfied. The conditions (i), (ii) and (iii) list the three possibilities when a run is considered as maximal. It is either if (i) it consists of an infinite alternating sequence of actions and time delays (note that Zeno behaviors are not excluded), or (ii) it ends in a state where the invariants allow time to diverge, or (iii) it ends in a state from which no discrete transitions are possible after any time delay (this includes time-locks).

6.5.4. *Tool details*

TAPAAL offers an editor, simulator and verifier for TAPN. It is written in Java 6.0 using Java Swing for the GUI components and is, therefore, available for the majority of existing platforms.

TAPAAL's graphical *editor* features all necessary elements for the creation of TAPN models, including invariants on places and transport arcs. The user interface supports, among others, a select/move feature for moving a selected sub-net of the model as well as an undo/redo buttons allowing the user to move backward and forward in the history during a creation of larger models. Constructed nets are saved in an interchangeable XML format. An important aspect of the graphical editor is that it disallows to draw syntactically incorrect nets and hence no syntax checks are necessary before calling further TAPAAL modules.

The *simulator* part of TAPAAL allows us to inspect the behavior of a TAPN by graphically simulating the effects of time delays and transition firings. When firing a transition, the user can either manually select the concrete tokens that should be used for the firing or simply allow the simulator to automatically select the tokens based on some predefined strategy (the youngest, the oldest or a random token). The simulator also allows the user to step back and force in the simulated trace, which makes it easier to investigate alternative net behaviors.

TAPAAL's *verification* module allows for checking of safety and liveness queries in the constructed net. Queries are created using a novel graphical query dialog, completely eliminating the possibility of introducing syntactical errors and offering an intuitive and easy to use query formulation mechanism. The TAPAAL query language is a subset of the CTL logic comprising EF, AG, EG, and AF temporal operators,[1] however, several TCTL properties can be verified by encoding them into the net. The actual verification is done by the UPPAAL verification engine via translating TAPN models into networks of timed automata. The verification calls to UPPAAL are seamlessly integrated inside the TAPAAL environment and the returned error traces (if any) are displayed in the TAPAAL's simulator. For the safety questions concrete traces are displayed whenever the command-line UPPAAL engine can output them, otherwise the user is offered an untimed trace and can in the simulation mode experiment with suitable time delays in order to realize the displayed trace in the net. A number of verification/trace options found in UPPAAL are also available in TAPAAL, including a symmetry reduction option which often provides improvements of the verification times in orders of magnitude, though at the expense of disallowing trace options (a current limitation of UPPAAL). Finally, it is possible to check if the constructed net is k-bounded for any given k. If the net is not bounded, the tool provides a suitable under-approximation of the behavior of the net (by asking for a maximum number of tokens that can be used during any transition firing sequence).

6.6. ROMÉO: a tool for the analysis of timed extensions of Petri nets

In this paper, we present the features of ROMÉO, a tool that allows to analyze and simulate timed extensions of Petri nets that are time Petri nets (TPNs). The tool ROMÉO allows state space computation of TPN and on-the-fly model-checking of reachability properties. ROMÉO is a free software available for Linux, MacOSX, and Windows platforms.

It can be downloaded at URL http://romeo.rts-software.org/.

ROMÉO analyzes T-time Petri nets, i.e. nets such that each transition t is associated with a time interval $[a(t), b(t)]$ (in the following, we call such nets time Petri nets). It

---

1. At the moment the EG and AF queries are supported only for nets with transitions that do not contain more than two input and two output places.

does not only allow us to compute the state space of the models but also to perform on-the-fly model-checking of quantitative temporal properties. It is able to translate time Petri nets into timed automata preserving the behavioral semantics (w.r.t. time bisimulation) of the net. The software allows to model and process an extension of time Petri nets that encompass preemption features: time Petri nets with inhibitor arcs (ITPNs). In order to model specifications that are not yet completely defined, parameters can be added to both TPN and ITPN models. ROMÉO is able to deal with such extensions and gives the possibility to check quantitative temporal properties.

The current or past contributors to the software are the following: Olivier (H.) Roux, Didier Lime, Guillaume Gardey, Morgan Magnin, Charlotte Seidner, Louis-Marie Traonouez and Gilles Bénattar.

6.6.1. *Models*

6.6.1.1. *Time Petri nets*

Time Petri nets have been defined by Merlin [MER 74]. Time is integrated to the Petri net model by adding a timing interval associated to each transition. For a given transition, this interval specifies when it can be fired regarding the instant when the transition has been newly enabled the most recently

DEFINITION 6.9(TIME PETRI NET).– A time Petri net is a 7-tuple $\mathcal{N} = \langle P, T, {}^\bullet(.), (.)^\bullet, a, b, M_0 \rangle$ where

– $P = \{P_1, \ldots, P_m\}$ is a finite and non-empty set of *places* ;

– $T = \{t_1, \ldots, t_n\}$ is a finite and non-empty set of *transitions* ;

– ${}^\bullet(.) : T \to \mathbb{N}^P$ is the *backward incidence function* ;

– $(.)^\bullet : T \to \mathbb{N}^P$ is the *forward incidence function* ;

– $a : T \to \mathbb{N}$ and $b : T \to \mathbb{N} \cup \{\infty\}$ are functions giving, for each transition, its *earliest* and *latest* firing times $(a \| eqb)$;

– $M_0 \in \mathbb{N}^P$ is the *initial marking* of the net.

A *marking* M of the net is an element of $\mathbb{N}^P$ such that $\forall p \in P$, $M(p)$ is the number of *tokens* in the place p.

A transition t is said to be *enabled* by the marking M, if the number of tokens in M in each input place of t is greater or equal to the value on the arc between this place and the transition (i.e., $M \geq^\bullet t$). We denote it by $t \in enabled(M)$.

A transition t is said to be *disabled* by the firing of t' from marking M, if it is enabled by M but not by $M - {}^{\bullet}t'$. We then denote it by $t \in disabled(M, t')$.

A transition t is said to be *newly enabled* by the firing of the transition t' from the marking M, if it is enabled by the new marking $M - {}^{\bullet}t' + t'^{\bullet}$ but was not by $M - {}^{\bullet}t'$. We denote it by $t \in \uparrow enabled\,(M, t')$ where $\uparrow enabled\,(\cdot, \cdot)$ is defined as follows:

$$\uparrow enabled\,(M, t') = \{t \in T \,|\, M - {}^{\bullet}t' + t'^{\bullet} \geq^{\bullet} t \wedge (t = t' \vee \neg(M - {}^{\bullet}t' \geq^{\bullet} t))\}.$$

We define the semantics of a dense-time TPN as a time transition system. In this model, two kinds of transitions may occur: *time* transitions when time elapses and *discrete* transitions when a transition of the net is fired.

DEFINITION 6.10(SEMANTICS OF A DENSE-TIME TPN).– The semantics of a *dense-time* TPN $\mathcal{N}$ is defined as a timed transition system $\mathcal{S}_{\mathcal{N}}^{\mathrm{dense}} = (Q, q_0, T, \rightarrow)$ such that

- $Q = \mathbb{N}^P \times (\mathbb{R}^+)^T$;
- $q_0 = (M_0, \overline{0})$;
- $\rightarrow \in Q \times (\mathbb{R}^+ \cup T) \times Q$ is the transition relation including a time transition relation and a discrete transition relation:
  - let $q = (M, \nu) \in Q$ and $q' = (M, \nu') \in Q$ be two states of the net, the continuous time transition relation is defined $\forall d \in \mathbb{R}^+$ by:

$$(M, \nu) \xrightarrow{d} (M, \nu') \text{ if } \forall t_i \in T, \begin{cases} \nu'(t_i) = \nu(t_i) + d \\ M \geq^{\bullet} t_i \Rightarrow \nu'(t_i) \leq b(t_i) \, ; \end{cases}$$

  - let $q = (M, \nu) \in Q$ and $q' = (M', \nu') \in Q$ be two states of the net, the discrete transition relation is defined $\forall t_i \in T$ by

$$(M, \nu) \xrightarrow{t_i} (M', \nu') \text{ ssi } \begin{cases} t_i \in enabled(M) \\ M' = M - {}^{\bullet}t_i + t_i^{\bullet} \\ a(t_i) \leq \nu(t_i) \leq b(t_i) \\ \forall t_k \in T, \nu'(t_k) = \begin{cases} 0, \text{ if } t_k \in \uparrow enabled(M, t_i) \\ \nu(t_k), \text{ otherwise.} \end{cases} \end{cases}$$

In the *dense-time* approach, time is seen as *"jumping" from one integer to the other*, with no care of what may happen between. The behaviors of a discrete-time model are obviously included in the behaviors of the corresponding model with a dense-time semantics. We define the *discrete-time* semantics of a time Petri net $\mathcal{N}$ by a transition system with two kinds of discrete transitions: first, a transition relation modifying the marking of the net and, second, a transition corresponding to a discrete elapsing of time (which is characterized by an increment of one time unit for all the clocks associated to transitions). We choose to write this transition system under the form of a timed transition system $\mathcal{S}_{\mathcal{N}}^{\text{discrete}} = (Q, q_0, T, \rightarrow)$: starting from the definition we previously gave for dense-time semantics, we replace the continuous time transition relation by a discrete-time transition relation

$$(M, \nu) \xrightarrow{1} (M, \nu') \text{ ssi } \forall t_i \in T, \begin{cases} \nu'(t_i) = \nu(t_i) + 1 \\ M \geq^\bullet t_i \Rightarrow \nu'(t_i) \leq b(t_i). \end{cases}$$

6.6.1.2. *Petri Nets with stopwatches*

In order to take into account the global complexity of systems, models now encompass the notion of actions that can be suspended and resumed. This implies extending traditional clock variables by "stopwatches." Several extensions of TPNs that address the modeling of stopwatches have been proposed: scheduling-TPNs [ROU 02], pre-emptive-TPNs [BUC 04] (these two models add resources and priorities attributes to the TPN formalism) and inhibitor hyperarc TPNs (ITPNs) [ROU 04]. ITPNs introduce special inhibitor arcs that control the progress of transitions. These three models belong to the class of PNs extended with stopwatches (SwPNs) [BER 07].

ROMÉO implements ITPNs. Inhibitor hyperarcs make it easier to model systems with priority relations between transitions, but they do not increase the theoretical expressivity of the model compared to inhibitor arcs. That is why we can equivalently work on time Petri nets with inhibitor arcs or inhibitor hyperarcs. For the sake of simplicity, we focus on nets with inhibitor arcs (ITPNs) in this chapter.

DEFINITION 6.11(TIME PETRI NETS WITH INHIBITOR ARCS).– A time Petri net with inhibitor arcs (ITPN) is an n-tuple $\mathcal{N} = (P, T, {}^\bullet(.), (.)^\bullet, {}^\circ(.), a, b, M_0)$, where

   – $P = \{p_1, p_2, \ldots, p_m\}$ is a non-empty finite set of *places*,

   – $T = \{t_1, t_2, \ldots, t_n\}$ is a non-empty finite set of *transitions*,

   – ${}^\bullet(.) \in (\mathbb{N}^P)^T$ is the *backward incidence function*,

   – $(.)^\bullet \in (\mathbb{N}^P)^T$ is the *forward incidence function*,

   – ${}^\circ(.) \in (\mathbb{N}^P)^T$ is the *inhibition function*,

   – $a : T \rightarrow \mathbb{N}$ and $b : T \rightarrow \mathbb{N} \cup \{\infty\}$ are functions giving, for each transition, its *earliest* and *latest* firing times ($a\|eqb$) ;

   – $M_0 \in \mathbb{N}^P$ is the *initial marking* of the net,

A transition t is said to be *inhibited* by the marking M, if the place connected to one of its inhibitor arc is marked with at least as many tokens as the weight of the considered inhibitor arc between this place and t: $0 < {}^\circ t \leq M$. We denote it by $t \in inhibited(M)$. Practically, inhibitor arcs are used to stop the elapsing of time for some transitions: an inhibitor arc between a place p and a transition t means that the stopwatch associated to t is stopped as long as place p is marked with enough tokens.

Transitions that are enabled but inhibited are said to be *suspended*.

A transition t is said to be *active* in the marking M if it is enabled and not inhibited by M.

A transition t is said to be *firable* when it has been enabled and not inhibited for at least $a(t)$ time units.

DEFINITION 6.12(SEMANTICS OF A DENSE-TIME ITPN).– Given a time domain $\mathbb{T}$, the semantics of a dense-time ITPN $\mathcal{N}$ is defined as a timed transition system $\mathcal{S}_{\mathcal{N}}^{\text{dense}} = (Q, q_0, \mathbb{T}, \rightarrow)$ such that:

- $Q = \mathbb{N}^P \times (\mathbb{R}^+)^T$;
- $q_0 = (M_0, \bar{0})$;
- $\rightarrow \in Q \times (T \cup \mathbb{R}) \times Q$ is the transition relation including a continuous time transition relation and a discrete transition relation:
  - the time transition relation is defined $\forall d \in \mathbb{R}^+$ by:

$$(M, \nu) \xrightarrow{d} (M, \nu'), \text{ if } \forall t_i \in T,$$
$$\begin{cases} \nu'(t_i) = \begin{cases} \nu(t_i) + d \text{ if } t_i \in enabled(M) \text{ and } t_i \in active(M) \\ \nu(t_i), \text{ otherwise,} \end{cases} \\ M \geq^\bullet t_i \Rightarrow \nu'(t_i) \leq b(t_i); \end{cases}$$

  - the discrete transition relation is defined $\forall t_i \in T$ by

$$(M, \nu) \xrightarrow{t_i} (M', \nu') \text{ if },$$
$$\begin{cases} t_i \in enabled(M) \text{ and } t_i \in active(M), \\ M' = M -^\bullet t_i + t_i^\bullet, \\ a(t_i) \leq \nu(t_i) \leq b(t_i), \\ \forall t_k \in T, \nu'(t_k) = \begin{cases} 0, \text{ if } t_k \in\uparrow enabled(M, t_i) \\ \nu(t_k), \text{ otherwise.} \end{cases} \end{cases}$$

The discrete-time semantics of ITPNs results from the replacement of the continuous time transition by a discrete-time transition in the definition we previously gave for dense-time semantics

$$(M, \nu) \xrightarrow{1} (M, \nu'), \text{ if } \forall t_i \in T,$$
$$\begin{cases} \nu'(t_i) = \begin{cases} \nu(t_i) + 1, \text{ if } t_i \in enabled(M) \text{ and } t_i \in active(M) \\ \nu(t_i), \text{ otherwise,} \end{cases} \\ M \geq^\bullet t_i \Rightarrow \nu'(t_i) \leq b(t_i). \end{cases}$$

ROMÉO also implements *reset* arcs for both TPNs and ITPNs. Reset arcs allow to remove all the tokens that a place contains, making it easier to model systems with reset functions included.

6.6.1.3. *Parametric Petri nets with stopwatches*

These two classes of Petri nets previously presented can be extended with the use of parameters, for instance to model specifications that are not yet completely defined. In this purpose, parametric time Petri nets and parametric Petri nets with stopwatches [TRA 08] are parametric extensions of respectively time Petri nets and Petri nets with stopwatches, in which the firing intervals of the transitions can be replaced by parametric firing intervals that involve time parameters.

We present below the definition and the semantics of the parametric time Petri net with inhibitor arcs model (PITPN) that extends the ITPN model with parameters.

DEFINITION 6.13(DEFINITION AND SEMANTICS OF PITPN).– A PITPN is an n-tuple $\mathcal{N} = \langle P, T, Par, {}^\bullet(.), (.)^\bullet, {}^\circ(.), a, b, M_0, D_p \rangle$, where

– $Par = \{\lambda_1, \lambda_2, \dots, \lambda_l\}$ is a finite set of *parameters*; let $\Gamma(Par)$ be the set of linear expressions over Par;

– $a : T \to \Gamma(Par)$ is the function that gives the *earliest firing time* of a transition, expressed as a linear expression over the set of parameters;

– $b : T \to \Gamma(Par) \cup \{\infty\}$ is the function that gives the *latest firing time* of a transition, that is either a linear expression over the set of parameters or equal to ∞;

– $D_p \subseteq \mathbb{N}^{Par}$ is the *domain of the parameters*;

and such that for a valuation $\nu \in D_p$, the semantics $[\![\mathcal{N}]\!]_\nu = \langle P, T, {}^\bullet(.), (.)^\bullet, {}^\circ(.), a_\nu, b_\nu, M_0 \rangle$ of $\mathcal{N}$ is a non-parametric ITPN such that a_ν and b_ν define the firing intervals of the transitions by replacing in a and b the parameters by their valuations ν.

6.6.2. *Global architecture*

ROMÉO consists of a graphical user interface (GUI) (written in Tcl/Tk), a dedicated library for networks simulation and a computation module MERCUTION, written in C++. It is dedicated to the design, simulation, state space computation, model-checking, and control of dense-time TPNs and their extension to stopwatches thanks to inhibitor arcs. The tool implements automatic translations of discrete-time TPNs and ITPNs into untimed Petri nets and counter automata. It also allows to symbolically compute the state space of discrete-time ITPNs.

ROMÉO offers a parametric extension for both TPNs and ITPNs. In these latter extensions, ROMÉO supports the use of parametric linear expressions in the time bounds of the transitions, and allows to add linear constraints on the parameters to restrict their domain.

We will give further details on these features in the following sections.

6.6.3. *Systems modeling*

In a system modeling activity, the ROMÉO GUI allows us to model reactive systems or pre-emptive reactive systems by using TPNs or ITPNs. Both benefit from an easy graphical representation and from an easy representation of common real-time features (parallelism, synchronization, resources management, watch-dogs, etc.).

As a design helper, ROMÉO implements on-line simulation and reachability model-checking on TPNs and ITPNs. It allows the early detection of some modeling issues during the conception stage.

6.6.4. *Verification of properties*

Once the systems have been described thanks to a Petri net model (TPNs or ITPNs), a crucial step is to formalize specifications corresponding to safe behaviors. Properties then should be written thanks to observers or a dedicated timed logic.

6.6.4.1. *On-line model checking*

ROMÉO provides an on-line model-checker for reachability. Properties over markings can be expressed and tested. It is then possible to test the reachability of a marking such that it verifies $M(P_1) = 1 \vee M(P_3) \geq 3$, where $M(P_i)$ is the number of tokens in the place P_i of the net. The tool returns a trace leading to such a marking, if reachable.

In [GAR 05a, BOU 06], the authors went further in the model-checking of time Petri nets, by defining a specific TCTL logic for time Petri nets in dense time, called *TPN-TCTL*. The decidability of the model-checking of *TPN-TCTL* on time Petri nets is proved, and they have shown that its complexity is PSPACE.

They have also introduced a restricted subset of *TPN-TCTL* with no recursion in the formulae for which they can propose on-the-fly model-checking. Moreover, this subset appears to be sufficient to verify many interesting properties on time models. Reachability properties can be checked with formulae such as $\exists \lozenge_{[a,b]}(p)$ (where $[a,b]$ is a time interval, with b possibly infinite, and p a property on the markings of the net) and safety properties with $\forall \square_{[a,b]}(p)$. Liveness properties can be checked with $\forall \lozenge_{[a,b]}(p)$ or by using a bounded response property such as $p \rightsquigarrow_{[0,b]} q$. It is equivalent to $\forall \square(p \Rightarrow \forall \lozenge_{[0,b]}(q))$, and thus allows one level of recursion.

The method is extended to the state-class graph in [HAD 06] and leads to efficient model-checking algorithms for TPNs that are implemented in ROMÉO.

6.6.4.1.1. Model-checking of a subset of TCTL on Petri nets with stopwatches

In a dense-time model, it has been shown that state and marking accessibility are not decidable on Petri nets with stopwatches, even if bounded [BER 07]. However, these two problems become decidable once a discrete-time semantics is considered [MAG 06]. Then, an efficient method to compute the symbolic state-space of a Petri net with stopwatches was proposed in [MAG 08].

This method consists of extending the classical symbolic representations of dense time (handled by convex polyhedra) to discrete time. For this purpose, a solution could be to compute the state-space of discrete-time nets as the discretization of the state-space of the associated dense-time model. However, although this solution is correct for time Petri nets, it is not for Petri nets with stopwatches: indeed, in these latter approaches, this method can add wrong discrete behaviors, that is to say behaviors that are not permissible with the discrete-time semantics. A solution has been proposed to overcome this problem: it consists of decomposing the polyhedra that represent the timing information of the net into an union of simpler polyhedra, that assures the validity of the computation of the symbolic successor.

Thus, it is possible to check real-time properties expressed by TCTL formulae on bounded Petri nets with stopwatches in discrete time, through a simple adaptation of the tool Roméo [GAR 05b].

Let us give an intuitive overview of the process. In [GAR 05a, BOU 06], the authors propose a method to check properties expressed in the TCTL logic (or in a subclass of TCTL logic) on time Petri nets by using the zone-based graph. This method is naturally extended to the state-class graph in [HAD 06]. Actually, its principles are in general and can be applied to all time extensions of Petri nets such that the firing domains of the state-classes can be represented by DBM. Besides, Magnin et al. [MAG 08] propose an algorithm to compute the state-space of Petri nets with stopwatches in discrete time by using only DBM. By combining the two previous procedures, an elegant method to check TCTL formulae on Petri nets with stopwatches in discrete time is obtained.

Thanks to the implementation of these algorithms in Roméo, the tool is able to check quantitative temporal properties on Petri nets with stopwatches with a discrete-time semantics.

6.6.4.1.2. Parametric model-checking of Petri nets with stopwatches

Parametric model-checking can be used to synthesize constraints on the parameters of a parametric model to assure that a property is verified. However, the parametric reachability problem is known to be undecidable in general [ALU 93].

For parametric time Petri nets and parametric Petri nets with stopwatches, semi-algorithms are proposed in [TRA 08] to verify parametric TCTL formulae (in which the bounds of the temporal constraints can be replaced by parameters). The goal is to determine the valuations of the parameters, such that for these valuations the model verifies the formula. The method consist of extending the model-checking approach for time Petri nets proposed in [HAD 06], by defining the parametric state-class graph of a parametric model and on-the-fly parametric model-checking semi-algorithms of a subset of parametric TCTL.

These semi-algorithms are implemented in the tool ROMÉO [LIM 09]. As a result, it can synthesize a set of constraints (a disjunction of polyhedra encoded with the *Parma Polyhedra Library* [BAG 02]) that represents the set of solutions.

6.6.4.2. *Off-line model checking*

6.6.4.2.1. Verification based on observers

Observers are a method to model check TPNs and ITPNs. It consists of adding to the Petri net – in a non-intrusive manner – places and transitions to model the property to check. The property is transformed in testing for the reachability of a given marking [TOU 97]. Then, as for the construction of the state-class graph, it is possible to check properties on TPNs/ITPNs with observers.

A main advantage of this approach is the transformation of a property into a reachability or a trace-execution problem. Nevertheless, observers are still a not easy way to model check TPNs and ITPNs. On the one hand, there is no automatic procedure to build observers: it is sometimes quite difficult to turn a property to check into a reachability problem with observers. On the other hand, for each property to be checked, a new state-class graph has to be built and the observer can dramatically increase the size of the state space.

6.6.4.2.2. Verification based on translations into other models

An interesting alternative to check temporal quantitative properties on time Petri nets consists of building a translation of the nets into timed automata. There exists efficient tools working on this model and which are capable to check such properties. There are two main families of translations: on the one hand, *structural translations* (like the translation introduced in [CAS 06] that takes as input a TPN with finite or infinite latest firing times) and, on the other hand, *translations with state space computation* (see, for example, the translation of [LIM 04a, LIM 06] which consists of building the state space of a TPN as a timed automaton).

ROMÉO implements various theoretical methods allowing us to translate the analyzed models into automata, timed automata or stopwatch automata). This method benefits from the existence of efficient *model-checking* tools available on these models (MEC, ALDEBARAN, UPPAAL, KRONOS, HYTECH). These translations extend the class of properties that can be checked by the use of the observers to temporal (LTL, CTL) and quantitative temporal (TCTL) logics.

A first translation consists of the computation of the state-class graphs (SCG) that provide finite representations for the behavior of bounded nets preserving their LTL properties [BER 91a]. For bounded TPNs, the algorithm is based on DBM data structure whereas, for ITPNs, the semi-algorithm is based on polyhedra (using the *Parma Polyhedra Library* [BAG 02]).

Two different methods are implemented for TPNs to generate a TA that preserves its semantics (in the sense of *timed bisimilarity*): the first one is derived from TA framework [GAR 06], the other one from the classical state class graph approach [LIM 03]. In the latter method, we reduce the number of clocks needed during the translation, so that the subsequent verification on the resulting TA is more efficient. In both methods, the automata are generated in UPPAAL or KRONOS input format.

Concerning ITPNs, the approximated and exact methods introduced in [LIM 04b, MAG 05] are implemented. The first one allows a fast translation into a stopwatch automaton using an over-approximating semi-algorithm (DBM-based). Despite the over-approximation, it has already been proved that the SWA is timed-bisimilar to the original ITPN. The SWA is produced in the HYTECH input format and is computed with a low number of stopwatches. Since the number of stopwatches is critical for the complexity of the verification, the method increases the efficiency of the timed analysis of the system; moreover, in some cases, it may just make the analysis possible while it would be a dead end to model the system directly with HYTECH. The second method computes the exact state space of ITPNs. The algorithms may not terminate as the reachability problem is undecidable on dense-time ITPNs, but it may act as a (slower but still efficient) *replacement for the DBM over-approximation* in the cases when the over-approximation introduces an infinite number of markings while the net is actually bounded and prevents this method to yield results.

6.6.5. *Using* ROMÉO *in an example*

The features of ROMÉO that have been previously presented are illustrated in this section in a scheduling problem taken from [BUC 04]. We consider a system of three tasks: $task_1$ and $task_3$ are periodic, $task_2$ is sporadic. The periods are expressed as a function of a time parameter a and are respectively a, $2.a$, and $3.a$ for the tasks 1, 2, and 3. The system has fixed priorities between the tasks: $task_1$ has the greatest priority, then $task_2$, and then $task_3$.

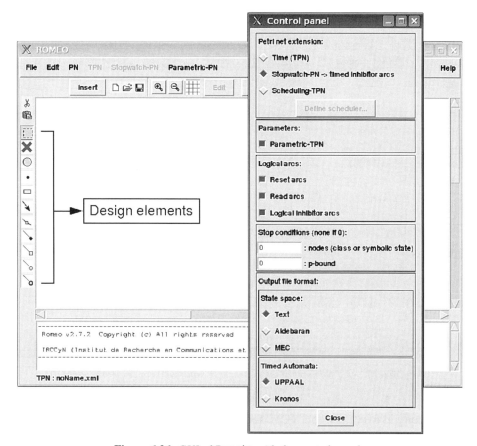

Figure 6.26. *GUI of* ROMÉO *with the control panel*

We design a PITPN model of this system in ROMÉO. The graphical user interface of the tool is presented in Figure 6.26. We choose in the control panel the type of net we want to edit, and we add the elements of the net (places, transitions, arcs).

We obtain the model presented in Figure 6.27, in which the inhibitors arcs, drawn with a circle end, are used to model the priorities between the tasks. Besides, we can restrict the domain of the parameter, so that $D_p = \{30 \le a \le 70\}$.

The simulator of ROMÉO can be used to test scenarios for an early verification of some properties. Then, we can perform model-checking on the model. The interesting problems on this system first concern the schedulability of the three tasks, which is expressed by the property that the PITPN model is safe (i.e. 1-bounded). We can verify

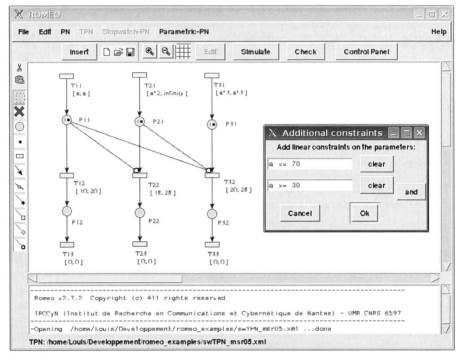

Figure 6.27. *PITPN model of the system with constraints on the parameters*

this property in ROMÉO with a TCTL formula

$$\forall P_i, \ \forall \square_{[0,\infty[}(M(P_i) \leq 1)$$

The result of the parametric model-checking is $a > 48$, as shown in Figure 6.28.

We can add this new constraint in ROMÉO, which assures that the system is now schedulable, and consequently we can verify new properties on the model. For example, we can compute the worst case response time (WCRT) of $task_3$ with the parametric TCTL formulae

$$M(P_{31}) > 0 \rightsquigarrow_{[0,b]} M(P_{32}) > 0.$$

This formula uses a new parameter b that is a maximum bound for the WCRT. The result of the parametric model-checking with ROMÉO is $b \geq 96$ and thus 96 is the WCRT of $task_3$, which is in accordance with [BUC 04] in which $a = 50$.

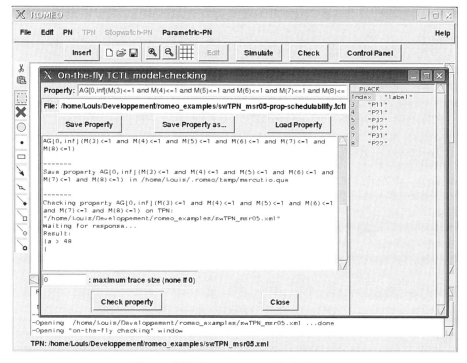

Figure 6.28. *Parametric model-checking*

6.7. Bibliography

[ABA 92] ABADI M., LAMPORT L., "An old-fashioned recipe for real time", *Proceedings of REX Workshop "Real-Time: Theory in Practice"*, vol. 600 of *Lecture Notes in Computer Science*, pp. 1–27, Springer, 1992.

[ABD 01a] ABDULLA P.A., "Using (timed) Petri nets for verification of parameterized (timed) systems", *VEPAS'2001, Verification of Parameterized Systems, ICALP'2001 satellite Workshop*, Crete, Greece, 2001.

[ABD 01b] ABDULLA P.A., NYLÉN A., "Timed Petri Nets and BQQs", *Proceedings of ICATPN'2001, 22nd International Conference on application and theory of Petri nets*, 2001.

[AHU 93] AHUJA R.K., MAGNANTI T.L., ORLIN J.B., *Network Flows – Theory, Algorithms, and Applications*, Prentice Hall, 1993.

[ALU 90a] ALUR R., COURCOUBETIS C., DILL D.L., "Model-checking for real-time systems", *5th Symposium on Logic in Computer Science (LICS'90)*, pp. 414–425, 1990.

[ALU 90b] ALUR R., DILL D.L., "Automata for modeling real-time systems", *Proceedings of International Colloquium on Algorithms, Languages, and Programming*, vol. 443 of *Lecture Notes in Computer Science*, pp. 322–335, 1990.

[ALU 93] ALUR R., HENZINGER T.A., VARDI M.Y., "Parametric real-time reasoning", *ACM Symposium on Theory of Computing*, pp. 592–601, 1993.

[ALU 94] ALUR R., DILL D.L., "A theory of timed automata", *Theoretical Computer Science*, vol. 126, num. 2, 183–235, 1994.

[ALU 01] ALUR R., LA TORRE S., PAPPAS G.J., "Optimal paths in weighted timed automata", *4th International Workshop on Hybrid Systems: Computation and Control*, vol. 2034 of *Lecture Notes in Computer Science*, pp. 49–62, Springer, 2001.

[AMN 01] AMNELL T., BEHRMANN G., BENGTSSON J., D'ARGENIO P.R., DAVID A., FEHNKER A., HUNE T., JEANNET B., LARSEN K.G., MÖLLER M.O., PETTERSSON P., WEISE C., YI W., "UPPAAL – now, next, and future", CASSEZ F., JARD C., ROZOY B., RYAN M. (dir.), *Modelling and Verification of Parallel Processes*, vol. 2067 of *Lecture Notes in Computer Science Tutorial*, pp. 100–125, Springer–Verlag, 2001.

[ARN 03] ARNOLD A., VINCENT A., WALUKIEWICZ I., "Games for synthesis of controllers with partial observation", *Theoretical Computer Science*, vol. 1, num. 303, 7–34, 2003.

[ASA 98] ASARIN E., MALER O., PNUELI A., SIFAKIS J., "Controller synthesis for timed automata", *Proceedings of IFAC Symposium on System Structure & Control*, pp. 469–474, Elsevier Science, 1998.

[BAG 02] BAGNARA R., RICCI E., ZAFFANELLA E., HILL P.M., "Possibly not closed convex polyhedra and the Parma Polyhedra Library", *Proceedings of the 9th International Symposium on Static Analysis*, pp. 213–229, Springer-Verlag, 2002.

[BAI 08] BAIER C., KATOEN J.P., *Principles of Model Checking*, MIT Press, 2008.

[BAL 96] BALARIN F., "Approximate reachability analysis of timed automata", *17th IEEE Real-Time Systems Symposium*, IEEE Computer Society Press, 1996.

[BEH 00] BEHRMANN G., HUNE T., VAANDRAGER F., "Distributed timed model checking – how the search order matters", *Proceedings of 12th International Conference on Computer Aided Verification, Lecture Notes in Computer Science*, Chicago, Springer, July 2000.

[BEH 01a] BEHRMANN G., DAVID A., LARSEN K.G., MÖLLER M.O., PETTERSSON P., YI W., "UPPAAL – Present and Future", *Proceedings of 40th IEEE Conference on Decision and Control*, IEEE Computer Society Press, 2001.

[BEH 01b] BEHRMANN G., FEHNKER A., HUNE T., LARSEN K.G., PETTERSSON P., ROMIJN J., "Efficient guiding towards cost-optimality in UPPAAL", MARGARIA T., YI W. (dir.), *Proceedings of the 7th International Conference on Tools and Algorithms for the Construction and Analysis of Systems*, vol. 2031 of *Lecture Notes in Computer Science*, pp. 174–188, Springer, 2001.

[BEH 01c] BEHRMANN G., FEHNKER A., HUNE T., LARSEN K.G., PETTERSSON P., ROMIJN J., VAANDRAGER F., "Minimum-cost reachability for priced timed automata", BENEDETTO M.D.D., SANGIOVANNI-VINCENTELLI A. (ed.), *Proceedings of the 4th International Workshop on Hybris Systems: Computation and Control*, vol. 2034 of *Lecture Notes in Computer Sciences*, pp. 147–161, Springer, 2001.

[BEH 02] BEHRMANN G., BENGTSSON J., DAVID A., LARSEN K.G., PETTERSSON P., YI
W., "UPPAAL Implementation Secrets", *Proceedings of 7th International Symposium on
Formal Techniques in Real-Time and Fault Tolerant Systems*, 2002.

[BEH 03a] BEHRMANN G., LARSEN K.G., PELANEK R., "To store or not to store", *Proceedings of the 15th International Conference on Computer Aided Verification*, vol. 2725 of
Lecture Notes in Computer Science, pp. 433–445, Springer-Verlag, 2003.

[BEH 03b] BEHRMANN G., DAVID A., LARSEN K.G., YI W., "Unification & sharing in
timed automata verification", *SPIN Workshop 03*, vol. 2648 of *Lecture Notes in Computer
Science*, pp. 225–229, 2003.

[BEH 04a] BEHRMANN G., BOUYER P., LARSEN K., PELNEK R., "Lower and upper bounds
in zone based abstractions of timed automata", *TACAS 2004*, vol. 2988 of *Lecture Notes in
Computer Science*, pp. 312–326, Springer–Verlag, 2004.

[BEH 04b] BEHRMANN G., DAVID A., LARSEN K.G., "A tutorial on UPPAAL", BERNARDO
M., CORRADINI F. (dir.), *Formal Methods for the Design of Real-Time Systems: 4th International School on Formal Methods for the Design of Computer, Communication, and
Software Systems, SFM-RT 2004*, vol. 3185 of *Lecture Notes in Computer Science*, pp. 200–
236, Springer–Verlag, September 2004.

[BEH 05a] BEHRMANN G., BRINKSMA E., HENDRIKS M., MADER A., "Scheduling lacquer
production by reachability analysis – a case study", *Workshop on Parallel and Distributed
Real-Time Systems 2005*, p. 140, IEEE Computer Society, 2005.

[BEH 05b] BEHRMANN G., LARSEN K.G., RASMUSSEN J.I., "Optimal scheduling using
priced timed automata", *ACM SIGMETRICS Performance Evaluation Review*, vol. 32,
num. 4, 34–40, ACM Press, 2005.

[BEH 07] BEHRMANN G., COUGNARD A., DAVID A., FLEURY E., LARSEN K.G., LIME
D., "UPPAAL-TIGA: Time for playing games!", *Proceedings of the 19th International Conference on Computer Aided Verification*, vol. 4590 of *Lecture Notes in Computer Science*,
pp. 121–125, Springer, 2007.

[BEN 98] BENGTSSON J., LARSEN K.G., LARSSON F., PETTERSSON P., WANG Y., WEISE
C., "New generation of UPPAAL", *International Workshop on Software Tools for Technology Transfer*, June 1998.

[BEN 02] BENGTSSON J., Clocks, DBMs and States in Timed Systems, PhD Thesis, Uppsala
University, 2002.

[BER 91a] BERTHOMIEU B., DIAZ M., "Modeling and verification of time dependent systems
using time Petri nets", *IEEE Transactions on Software Engineering*, vol. 17, num. 3, 259–
273, 1991.

[BER 07] BERTHOMIEU B., LIME D., ROUX O.H., VERNADAT F., "Reachability problems and abstract state spaces for time petri nets with stopwatches", *Journal of Discrete Event Dynamic Systems (DEDS)*, vol. 17, num. 2, Springer, 133–158, published in
June 2007.

[BOL 90] BOLOGNESI T., LUCIDI F., TRIGILA S., "From Timed Petri Nets to Timed LO-
TOS", *Proceedings of the IFIP WG 6.1 10th International Symposium on Protocol Specification, Testing and Verification (Ottawa 1990)*, pp. 1–14, North-Holland, Amsterdam,
1990.

[BOU 06] BOUCHENEB H., GARDEY G., ROUX O.H., TCTL model checking of Time Petri
Nets, Report num. number RI2006-14, IRCCyN, 2006.

[BOU 03] BOUYER P., D'SOUZA D., MADHUSUDAN P., PETIT A., "Timed control with
partial observability", *Proceedings of 15th Conference on Computer Aided Verification
(CAV'2003)*, vol. 2725 of *Lecture Notes in Computer Science*, pp. 180-192, Springer, 2003.

[BOU 08] BOUYER P., HADDAD S., REYNIER P.A., "Timed Petri nets and timed automata:
On the discriminating power of zeno sequences", *Information and Computation*, vol. 206,
num. 1, 73–107, 2008.

[BOW 98] BOWMAN H., FACONTI G.P., KATOEN J.P., LATELLA D., MASSINK M., "Auto-
matic verification of a lip synchronisation algorithm using UPPAAL", JAN FRISO GROOTE
B.L., VAN WAMEL J. (dir.), *In Proceedings of the 3rd International Workshop on Formal
Methods for Industrial Critical Systems,* Amsterdam , The Netherlands, 1998.

[BUC 04] BUCCI G., FEDELI A., SASSOLI L., VICARIO E., "Time state space analysis
of real-time preemptive systems", *IEEE Transactions on Software Engineering*, vol. 30,
num. 2, 97–111, February 2004.

[BYG 09] BYG J., JOERGENSEN K., SRBA J., "TAPAAL: editor, simulator and verifier of
timed-arc Petri nets", *ATVA'09, 7th International Symposium on Automated Technology
for Verification and Analysis*, Springer, 2009.

[CAS 00] CASSEZ F., LARSEN K.G., "The impressive power of stopwatches", *CONCUR
2000*, vol. 1877 of *Lecture Notes in Computer Science*, pp. 138–152, Springer-Verlag,
2000.

[CAS 05] CASSEZ F., DAVID A., FLEURY E., LARSEN K.G., LIME D., "Efficient on-the-fly
algorithms for the analysis of timed games", *CONCUR'05*, vol. 3653 of *Lecture Notes in
Computer Science*, pp. 66–80, Springer–Verlag, August 2005.

[CAS 06] CASSEZ F., ROUX O.H., "Structural translation from time petri nets to timed automata – model-checking time petri nets via timed automata", *The Journal of Systems and
Software*, vol. 79, num. 10, 1456–1468, Elsevier, 2006.

[CAS 07] CASSEZ F., DAVID A., LARSEN K.G., LIME D., RASKIN J.F., "Timed control with
observation based and stuttering invariant strategies", *Proceedings of the 5th International
Symposium on Automated Technology for Verification and Analysis*, vol. 4762 of *Lecture
Notes in Computer Science*, pp. 192–206, Springer, 2007.

[CHA 06a] CHATTERJEE K., DOYEN L., HENZINGER T., RASKIN J.F., "Algorithms for
omega-regular games with incomplete information", *Computer Science Logic*, vol. 4207
of *Lecture Notes in Computer Science*, pp. 287–302, Springer, 2006.

[CHA 06b] CHATTERJEE K., HENZINGER T., PITERMAN N., "Algorithms for Buchi Games",
GDV 06, August 2006.

[DAR 97] D'ARGENIO P.R., KATOEN J.P., RUYS T.C., TRETMANS J., "The bounded re-transmission protocol must be on time!", *In Proceedings of the 3rd International Workshop on Tools and Algorithms for the Construction and Analysis of Systems*, vol. 1217 of *Lecture Notes in Computer Science*, pp. 416–431, Springer-Verlag, April 1997.

[DAV 00] DAVID A., YI W., "Modelling and analysis of a commercial field bus protocol", *Proceedings of the 12th Euromicro Conference on Real Time Systems*, pp. 165–172, IEEE Computer Society, 2000.

[DAV 02] DAVID A., BEHRMANN G., LARSEN K.G., YI W., "New UPPAAL architecture", PETTERSSON P., YI W. (ed.), *Workshop on Real-Time Tools*, Uppsala University Technical Report Series, 2002.

[DAV 03] DAVID A., BEHRMANN G., LARSEN K.G., YI W., "A tool architecture for the next generation of UPPAAL", *10th Anniversary Colloquium. Formal Methods at the Cross Roads: From Panacea to Foundational Support, Lecture Notes in Computer Science*, 2003.

[DAV 05] DAVID A., "Merging DBMs Efficiently", *17th Nordic Workshop on Programming Theory*, pp. 54–56, DIKU, University of Copenhagen, October 2005.

[DAV 06] DAVID A., HÅKANSSON J., LARSEN K.G., PETTERSSON P., "Model checking timed automata with priorities using DBM subtraction", *Proceedings of the 4th International Conference on Formal Modelling and Analysis of Timed Systems (FORMATS'06)*, vol. 4202 of *Lecture Notes in Computer Science*, pp. 128–142, 2006.

[DAV 08] DAVID A., LARSEN K.G., LI S., NIELSEN B., "Cooperative testing of uncontrollable timed systems", *4th Workshop on Model-Based Testing MBT'08*, March 2008.

[DAV 09] DAVID A., LARSEN K.G., LI S., NIELSEN B., "Timed testing under partial observability", *Proceedings of the 2nd International Conference on Sofware Testing, Verification, and Validation*, IEEE Computer Society, pp. 61–70, 2009.

[DAW 06] DAWS C., KORDY P., "Symbolic Robustness Analysis of Timed Automata.", *FORMATS*, vol. 4202 of *Lecture Notes in Computer Science*, pp. 143–155, Springer, 2006.

[DEA 01] DE ALFARO L., HENZINGER T.A., MAJUMDAR R., "Symbolic Algorithms for Infinite-State Games", *Proceedings of 12th Conference on Concurrency Theory (CONCUR'01)*, vol. 2154 of *Lecture Notes in Computer Science*, pp. 536–550, Springer, 2001.

[ETE 01] ETESSAMI K., WILKE T., SCHULLER R.A., "Fair simulation relations, parity games, and state space reduction for BÃichi automata", *Automata, Languages and Programming*, vol. 2076 of *Lecture Notes in Computer Science*, pp. 694–707, Springer, 2001.

[FLO 62] FLOYD R.W., "ACM algorithm 97: shortest path", *Communications of the ACM*, vol. 5, num. 6, 345, 1962.

[GAR 05a] GARDEY G., Contribution à la vérification et au contrôle des systèmes temps réel – Application aux réseaux de Petri temporels et aux automates temporisés, PhD Thesis, Nantes University, École Centrale de Nantes, December 2005.

[GAR 05b] GARDEY G., LIME D., MAGNIN M., ROUX O.H., "Roméo: A tool for analyzing time Petri nets", *Proceedings of the 17th International Conference on Computer Aided Verification*, vol. 3576 of *Lecture Notes in Computer Science*, pp. 418–423, Springer, Berlin, 2005.

[GAR 06] GARDEY G., ROUX O.H., ROUX O.F., "State space computation and analysis of time Petri nets", *Theory and Practice of Logic Programming (TPLP). Special Issue on Specification Analysis and Verification of Reactive Systems*, vol. 6, num. 3, pp. 301–320, Cambridge University Press, 2006.

[HAD 06] HADJIDJ R., BOUCHENEB H., "On-the-fly TCTL model checking for time Petri nets using state class graphs", *ACSD*, pp. 111–122, IEEE Computer Society, 2006.

[HAN 93] HANISCH H., "Analysis of place/transition nets with timed-arcs and its application to batch process control", *Proceedings of the 14th International Conference on Application and Theory of Petri Nets (ICATPN'93)*, vol. 691 of *Lecture Notes in Computer Science*, pp. 282–299, 1993.

[HAV 97] HAVELUND K., SKOU A., LARSEN K.G., LUND K., "Formal modelling and analysis of an audio/video protocol: an industrial case study using UPPAAL", *Proceedings of the 18th IEEE Real-Time Systems Symposium*, pp. 2–13, December 1997.

[HEI 09] HEITMANN F., MOLDT D., MORTENSEN K., RÖLKE H., "Petri nets tools database quick overview", *http://www.informatik.uni-hamburg.de/TGI/PetriNets/tools/quick.html*, Accessed: 28.4.2009.

[HEN 92] HENZINGER T.A., NICOLLIN X., SIFAKIS J., YOVINE S., "Symbolic model checking for real-time systems", *Proceedings of IEEE Symposium on Logic in Computer Science*, 1992.

[HEN 94] HENZINGER T.A., "Symbolic model checking for real-time systems", *Information and Computation*, vol. 111, pp. 193–244, 1994.

[HEN 02] HENDRIKS M., LARSEN K.G., "Exact acceleration of real-time model checking", ASARIN E., MALER O., YOVINE S. (ed.), *Electronic Notes in Theoretical Computer Science*, vol. 65, Elsevier Science Publishers, April 2002.

[HEN 03] HENDRIKS M., BEHRMANN G., LARSEN K., NIEBERT P., VAANDRAGER F., "Adding Symmetry Reduction to Uppaal", LARSEN K., NIEBERT P. (dir.), *Proceedings of the First International Workshop on Formal Modeling and Analysis of Timed Systems (FORMATS 2003)*, vol. 2791 of *Lecture Notes in Computer Science*, pp. 46–49, Springer-Verlag, 2003.

[HOL 91] HOLZMANN G.J., *Design and Validation of Computer Protocols*, Prentice-Hall, 1991.

[HOL 98] HOLZMANN G.J., "An analysis of bitstate hashing", *Formal Methods in System Design*, vol. 13, pp. 289–307, 1998.

[HUN 00] HUNE T., LARSEN K.G., PETTERSSON P., "Guided synthesis of control programs using UPPAAL", LAI T.H. (dir.), *Proceedings of the IEEE ICDCS International Workshop on Distributed Systems Verification and Validation*, pp. E15–E22, IEEE Computer Society Press, April 2000.

[IVE 00] IVERSEN T.K., KRISTOFFERSEN K.J., LARSEN K.G., LAURSEN M., MADSEN R.G., MORTENSEN S.K., PETTERSSON P., THOMASEN C.B., "Model-checking real-time control programs – verifying LEGO mindstorms systems using UPPAAL", *Proceedings of 12th Euromicro Conference on Real-Time Systems*, pp. 147–155, IEEE Computer Society Press, June 2000.

[JES 07] JESSEN J.J., RASMUSSEN J.I., LARSEN K.G., DAVID A., "Guided controller synthesis for climate controller using UPPAAL-TIGA", *Proceedings of the 19th International Conference on Formal Modeling and Analysis of Timed Systems*, vol. 4763 of *Lecture Notes in Computer Science*, pp. 227–240, Springer, 2007.

[KRI 02] KRISTENSEN L., MAILUND T., "A generalised sweep-line method for safety properties", *Proc. of FME'02*, vol. 2391 of *Lecture Notes in Computer Science*, pp. 549–567, Springer-Verlag, 2002.

[KRI 96] KRISTOFFERSON K.J., LAROUSSINIE F., LARSEN K.G., PETTERSSON P., YI W., A compositional proof of a real-time mutual exclusion protocol, Report num. RS-96-55, BRICS, December 1996.

[LAM 00] LAMOUCHI H., THISTLE J., "Effective control synthesis for DES under partial observations", *Proceedings of the 39th IEEE Conference on Decision and Control*, pp. 22–28, 2000.

[LAR 95] LARSEN K.G., PETTERSSON P., YI W., "Model-checking for real-time systems", *Proc. of Fundamentals of Computation Theory*, vol. 965 of *Lecture Notes in Computer Science*, pp. 62–88, August 1995.

[LAR 97a] LARSEN K.G., PETTERSSON P., YI W., "UPPAAL in a Nutshell", *International Journal on Software Tools for Technology Transfer*, vol. 1, num. 1–2, 134–152, Springer–Verlag, October 1997.

[LAR 01] LARSEN K.G., BEHRMANN G., BRINKSMA E., FEHNKER A., HUNE T., PETTERSSON P., ROMIJN J., "As cheap as possible: efficient cost-optimal reachability for priced timed automata", BERRY G., COMON H., FINKEL A. (ed.), *Proceedings of CAV 2001*, vol. 2102 of *Lecture Notes in Computer Science*, pp. 493–505, Springer, 2001.

[LAR 97b] LARSSON F., LARSEN K.G., PETTERSSON P., YI W., "Efficient verification of real-time systems: compact data structures and state-space reduction", *Proceedings of the 18th IEEE Real-Time Systems Symposium*, pp. 14–24, IEEE Computer Society Press, December 1997.

[LIM 03] LIME D., ROUX O.H., "State class timed automaton of a time petri net", *The 10th International Workshop on Petri Nets and Performance Models, (PNPM'03)*, IEEE Computer Society, September 2003.

[LIM 04a] LIME D., Vérification d'applications temps réel à l'aide de réseaux de Petri temporels étendus, PhD Thesis, University of Nantes and École Centrale de Nantes, December 2004.

[LIM 04b] LIME D., ROUX O.H., "A translation based method for the timed analysis of scheduling extended time Petri nets", *The 25th IEEE International Real-Time Systems Symposium, (RTSS'04)*, pp. 187–196, Lisbon, Portugal, IEEE Computer Society Press, December 2004.

[LIM 06] LIME D., ROUX O.H., "Model checking of time Petri nets using the state class timed automaton", *Journal of Discrete Events Dynamic Systems - Theory and Applications (DEDS)*, vol. 16, num. 2, 179–205, Kluwer Academic Publishers, 2006.

[LIM 09] LIME D., ROUX O.H., SEIDNER C., TRAONOUEZ L.M., "Romeo: A parametric model-checker for petri nets with stopwatches", KOWALEWSKI S., PHILIPPOU A. (ed.), *15th International Conference on Tools and Algorithms for the Construction and Analysis of Systems (TACAS 2009)*, vol. 5505 of *Lecture Notes in Computer Science*, pp. 54–57, York, UK, Springer, March 2009.

[LIN 01] LINDAHL M., PETTERSSON P., YI W., "Formal design and analysis of a gearbox controller", *Springer International Journal of Software Tools for Technology Transfer (STTT)*, vol. 3, num. 3, 353–368, 2001.

[LIU 98] LIU X., SMOLKA S., "Simple linear-time algorithm for minimal fixed points", *Proceedings 26th Conference on Automata, Languages and Programming (ICALP'98)*, vol. 1443 of *Lecture Notes in Computer Science*, pp. 53–66, Springer, 1998.

[LON 97] LÖNN H., PETTERSSON P., "Formal verification of a TDMA protocol startup mechanism", *Proceedings of the Pacific Rim International Symposium on Fault-Tolerant Systems*, pp. 235–242, December 1997.

[MAG 05] MAGNIN M., LIME D., ROUX O., "An efficient method for computing exact state space of Petri nets with stopwatches", *3rd International Workshop on Software Model-Checking (SoftMC'05)*, Electronic Notes in Theoretical Computer Science, Edinburgh, Scotland, UK, Elsevier, July 2005.

[MAG 06] MAGNIN M., MOLINARO P., ROUX O.H., "Decidability, expressivity and state-space computation of Stopwatch Petri nets with discrete-time semantics.", *8th International Workshop on Discrete Event Systems (WODES'06)*, Ann Arbor, USA, July 2006.

[MAG 08] MAGNIN M., LIME D., ROUX O., "Symbolic state space of Stopwatch Petri nets with discrete-time semantics", CORTADELLA J., REISIG W. (dir.), *The 29th International Conference on Application and Theory of Petri Nets and Other Models of Concurrency (ICATPN 2008)*, Lecture Notes in Computer Science, Xi'an, China, Springer, June 2008.

[MAL 95] MALER O., PNUELI A., SIFAKIS J., "On the synthesis of discrete controllers for timed systems", *Proceedings of the 12th Symposium on Theoretical Aspects of Computer Science (STACS'95)*, vol. 900, pp. 229–242, Springer, 1995.

[MER 74] MERLIN P., A study of the recoverability of computing systems, PhD Thesis, Department of Information and Computer Science, University of California, Irvine, CA, 1974.

[PET 62] PETRI C., Kommunikation mit Automaten, PhD Thesis, Darmstadt, 1962.

[RAS 06] RASMUSSEN J.I., LARSEN K.G., SUBRAMANI K., "On using priced timed automata to achieve optimal scheduling", *Formal Methods in System Design*, vol. 29, num. 1, 97–114, Kluwer Academic Publishers, 2006.

[RAZ 85] RAZOUK R.R., PHELPS C.V., "Performance analysis using timed Petri nets", *Proceedings of Protocol Testing, Specification, and Verification*, pp. 561–576, 1985.

[ROK 93] ROKICKI T.G., Representing and modeling digital circuits, PhD Thesis, Stanford University, 1993.

[ROU 02] ROUX O.H., DÉPLANCHE A.M., "A T-time Petri net extension for real time-task scheduling modeling", *European Journal of Automation (JESA)*, vol. 36, num. 7, 973–987, 2002.

[ROU 04] ROUX O.H., LIME D., "Time Petri nets with inhibitor hyperarcs. Formal semantics and state space computation", CORTADELLA J., REISIG W. (ed.), *The 25th International Conference on Application and Theory of Petri Nets (ICATPN 2004)*, vol. 3099 of *Lecture Notes in Computer Science*, pp. 371–390, Bologna, Italy, Springer-Verlag, June 2004.

[SIF 96] SIFAKIS J., YOVINE S., "Compositional specification of timed systems", *Proceedings of the 13th Annual Symposim on Theoretical Aspects of Computer Science (STACS'96)*, vol. 1046 of *Lecture Notes in Computer Science*, pp. 347–359, Springer-Verlag, 1996.

[SRB 05] SRBA J., "Timed-arc Petri nets vs. networks of timed automata", *Proceedings of the 26th International Conference on Application and Theory of Petri Nets (ICATPN 2005)*, vol. 3536 of *Lecture Notes in Computer Science*, pp. 385–402, Springer-Verlag, 2005.

[SRB 08] SRBA J., "Comparing the expressiveness of timed automata and timed extensions of Petri nets", *Proceedings of the 6th International Conference on Formal Modelling and Analysis of Timed Systems (FORMATS'08)*, vol. 5215 of *Lecture Notes in Computer Science*, pp. 15–32, Springer-Verlag, 2008.

[TOU 97] TOUSSAINT J., SIMONOT-LION F., THOMESSE J.P., "Time constraint verifications methods based time Petri nets", *6th Workshop on Future Trends in Distributed Computing Systems (FTDCS'97)*, pp. 262–267, Tunis, Tunisia, 1997.

[TRA 08] TRAONOUEZ L.M., LIME D., ROUX O.H., "Parametric model-checking of time petri nets with stopwatches using the state-class graph", CASSEZ F., JARD C. (ed.), *6th International Conference on Formal Modelling and Analysis of Timed Systems (FORMATS 2008)*, vol. 5215 of *Lecture Notes in Computer Science*, pp. 280–294, Saint-Malo, France, Springer, September 2008.

[TRI 99] TRIPAKIS S., ALTISEN K., "Controller synthesis for discrete and dense-time systems", *Proceedings of World Congress on Formal Methods in the Development of Computing Systems (FM'99)*, vol. 1708 of *Lecture Notes in Computer Science*, pp. 233–252, Springer, 1999.

[UPP 09] UPPAAL, *www.uppaal.com*, Accessed: 28.4.2009.

[WON 94] WONG-TOI H., Symbolic approximations for verifying real-time systems, PhD Thesis, Stanford University, 1994.

[YI 94] YI W., PETTERSSON P., DANIELS M., "Automatic verification of real-time communicating systems by constraint-solving", HOGREFE D., LEUE S. (ed.), *Proceedings of the 7th International Conference on Formal Description Techniques*, pp. 223–238, North–Holland, 1994.

[ZUB 80] ZUBEREK W.M., "Timed Petri nets and preliminary performance evaluation", *Proceedings of the 7th Anual Symposium on Computer Architecture*, pp. 88–96, ACM Press, 1980.

[ZUB 85] ZUBEREK W.M., "Extended D-timed Petri nets, timeouts, and analysis of communication protocols", *Proceedings of the 1985 ACM Annual Conference on the Range of Computing : mid-80s Perspective*, pp. 10–15, ACM Press, 1985.

Chapter 7

Tools for the Analysis of Hybrid Models

7.1. Introduction

Complex control systems that interact with an external physical environment generally consist of heterogenous components such as software, analog or digital hardware, sensors, and actuators. Mathematical models of such systems and of the external environment are necessary during the design phase: these models make it possible to explore the behavior resulting from the interaction between the controller and the environment, either analytically or by simulation.

Hybrid systems are the result of the composition of the two most commonly used models of dynamical systems: continuous dynamical systems defined by differential equations, and discrete event systems defined by automata, Petri nets, etc. Continuous models are particularly well suited to the "physical" sciences, whereas discrete models are natural abstractions for software or digital hardware. Research on hybrid systems deals with models that combine discrete and continuous dynamics, and, in the last two decades, has attempted to extend analysis methods specific to each type of dynamics in order to study the dynamics of the complete system.

A promising approach, *reachability analysis*, combines ideas borrowed from algorithmic verification of discrete systems (*model-checking*) and from numerical simulation of continuous systems. This approach, which uses graph exploration techniques, numerical analysis and computational geometry, makes it possible to compute (an approximation of) the set of trajectories of the system, for all admissible initial conditions and under all possible disturbances. A successful analysis according to this

Chapter written by Thao DANG, Goran FREHSE, Antoine GIRARD and Colas LE GUERNIC.

method can replace an infinite number of simulations of individual trajectories. It also provides information about the system behavior that can be complementary to the information obtained by analytical methods. Thus, this approach can be viewed as a compromise between purely analytical methods, which give strong results but apply mostly to idealized and isolated subsystems, and validation techniques based on simulation, which apply in practice to much more complex systems but whose results might be erroneous due to numerical errors, etc. As any other analysis technique for complex systems, reachability analysis suffers from the curse of dimensionality and the analysis of systems with more than a few continuous variables is generally considered as very difficult.

In this chapter, we present an overview of different techniques for reachability analysis of hybrid systems. We first introduce the notion of hybrid automaton and the purpose of reachability analysis. Then we present fundamental algorithmic methods that are specific to some classes of hybrid systems: linear hybrid automata (LHA) and piecewise affine hybrid systems. Finally, we present hybridization techniques for the analysis of nonlinear continuous and hybrid systems.

7.2. Hybrid automata and reachability

Hybrid automata are a modeling formalism that combines discrete events with continuous variables that change over time [ALU 95]. Formally, a hybrid automaton $H = (Loc, Var, Lab, Trans, Flow, Inv, Init)$ consists of the following elements:

– a graph whose vertices, called *locations*, are given by a finite set Loc, and whose edges, called *discrete transitions*, are given by a finite set $Trans$;

– a finite set of real-valued variables Var. A *state* of the automaton consists of a location and a value for each variable (formally described as a *valuation* over Var). The set of all states of the automaton is called its *state space*. To simplify the presentation, we assume that the state space is $Loc \times \mathbb{R}^n$, where n is the number of variables. We also simply write x to denote the name of the variable x or its value according to the context;

– for each location, the variables can only take values in a given set called *invariant*. The invariants are given by $Inv \subseteq Loc \times \mathbb{R}^n$;

– for each location, the change of the variables over time is defined by its time-derivative that must be in a given set $Flow \subseteq Loc \times \mathbb{R}^n \times \mathbb{R}^n$. For example, if the system is in a location l, a variable x can take the values of a function $\xi(t)$, if at each time instant t, $(l, \dot{\xi}(t), \xi(t)) \in Flow$, where $\dot{\xi}(t)$ denotes the derivative of $\xi(t)$ with respect to time;

– the *discrete transitions* $Trans \subseteq Loc \times Lab \times 2^{\mathbb{R} \times \mathbb{R}} \times Loc$ specify instantaneous changes of the state of the automaton. A transition (l, α, μ, l') signifies the system can instantaneously jump from any state (l, x) to any state (l', x') if $x' \in Inv(l')$ and $(x, x') \in \mu$. Every transition has a *synchronization label* $\alpha \in Lab$, which is used to model the interaction between several composed automata. Intuitively, if two automata share a common label α, transitions with this label can only be executed in unison, i.e., by simultaneous execution of a transition with this label in both automata. The relation μ is called the *jump relation* of the transition;

  – a set of states $Init \subseteq Loc \times \mathbb{R}^n$ specifies the *initial states* from which all behavior of the automaton begins.

We use a simple model of a bouncing ball as a running example to illustrate the concepts presented in this chapter. Even though this example has only one location, its behaviors consist of alternating time elapse and discrete transitions that show much of the complexity that hybrid systems can exhibit.

EXAMPLE 7.1.– Consider a bouncing ball, whose height above ground and vertical speed are measured by continuous variables x and v. We can model this system with the hybrid automaton shown in Figure 7.1, which has only one location l and one transition. The equations of motion of the ball lead directly to a description of the continuous dynamics in the form of a set of ordinary differential equations

$$Flow = \{(l, \dot{x}, \dot{v}, x, v) \mid \dot{x} = v, \dot{v} = -g\},$$

where g is the gravitational constant. If we suppose the ground to be at height $x = 0$, we can model the fact that the ball does not penetrate the ground as an invariant

$$Inv = \{(l, x, v) | x \geq 0\}.$$

As the ball reaches the ground at $x = 0$, it bounces; we abstract this phenomenon by an instantaneous change of its speed, which changes direction and is reduced by some constant factor $c \leq 1$ that captures the loss of energy due to deformation. This instantaneous change is modeled by a transition (l, α, μ, l), with the jump relation

$$\mu = \{(x, v, x', v') \mid x = 0 \wedge v < 0 \wedge x' = 0 \wedge v' = -cv\}.$$

Note that we include the constraint $v < 0$ since the ball only bounces when it moves toward the ground. If this constraint is omitted, the model erroneously contains the behavior that when the system reaches $x = 0$, it carries out the discrete transition infinitely often in zero time, v converging toward zero. Assuming that initially the ball is at rest at a height x_0, we define the initial states to be

$$Init = \{(l, x, v) | x = x_0, v = 0\},$$

which is indicated in Figure 7.1 by an incoming arrow to the location.

The behavior of a hybrid automaton is defined by its *executions*, which are sequences of time elapse and discrete transitions. Formally, an *execution* σ is a finite or

Figure 7.1. *Hybrid automaton model of a bouncing ball*

infinite sequence of states (l_i, v_i), labels $\alpha_i \in Lab$, delays $\delta_i \in \mathbb{R}^{\geq 0}$ and differentiable functions $\xi_i : \mathbb{R} \to \mathbb{R}^n$

$$\sigma = (l_0, v_0) \xrightarrow{\alpha_0, \delta_0, \xi_0} (l_1, v_1) \xrightarrow{\alpha_1, \delta_1, \xi_1} (l_2, v_2) \xrightarrow{\alpha_2, \delta_2, \xi_2} \cdots , \qquad [7.1]$$

such that for all $i \geq 0$ the following conditions are satisfied:

– $(l_0, v_0) \in Init$, $(l_i, v_i) \in Inv$;
– $\xi_i(0) = v_i$ and for all $t, 0 \leq t \leq \delta_i$, $\xi_i(t) \in Inv(l_i)$, $(l_i, \dot{\xi}_i(t), \xi_i(t)) \in Flow$;
– there is a transition $(l_i, \alpha_i, \mu_i, l_{i+1})$ such that $(\xi_i(\delta_i), v_{i+1}) \in \mu_i$.

A state (l, v) is *reachable*, if there is an execution with $(l, v) = (l_i, \xi_i(t)), 0 \leq t \leq \delta_i$, for some i.

EXAMPLE 7.2.– The continuous component of an execution of the bouncing ball is shown in Figure 7.2(a), for constants $g = 1$, $c = 3/4$ and $x_0 = 1$. The states that are reachable from this initial state are shown in Figure 7.2(b).

The analysis of the reachable states can be used for verifying safety properties of the system, such as whether a set of bad states is reachable or not. The computation of the set of reachable states is generally very costly, especially if the dynamics are complex. For all but the most simple classes of systems, the problem is known to be

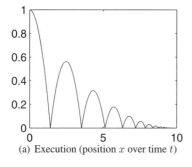

(a) Execution (position x over time t)

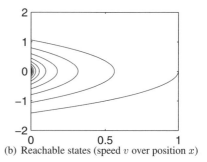

(b) Reachable states (speed v over position x)

Figure 7.2. *Behavior of the bouncing ball model*

undecidable. Therefore, we often resort to computing a simpler over-approximation of the set of reachable states. If the intersection of the over-approximation and the bad states is empty, one is guaranteed that the system is safe. Otherwise, we have to refine the over-approximation or try to find a counter-example, which proves that the system is indeed unsafe.

The basic algorithm for computing the set of reachable states is a simple fixed-point calculation. Starting from the set of initial states $Init$, we add the successor states of time elapse and discrete transitions until no new states are found, and therefore a fixed point is reached. These successors states are computed with the following operators, which are derived directly from the definition of executions: given a set of states Q, the states that are reachable by taking a discrete transition are given by

$$\text{Post}_d(Q) = \{(l', x') \mid \exists (l, \alpha, \mu, l') \in \textit{Trans}, (l, x) \in Q : (x, x') \in \mu\}. \quad [7.2]$$

The states that are reachable from Q by letting time elapse are

$$\text{Post}_c(Q) = \{(l, x) \mid \exists f, t' : (l, f(0)) \in Q \land f(t') = x \land \forall \, 0 \le t \le t' : \\ f(t) \in \textit{Inv}(l) \land (l, \dot{f}(t), f(t)) \in \textit{Flow}\}. \quad [7.3]$$

The set of reachable states $Reach$ can be computed (in general without guarantee of termination), with Algorithm 1.

Algorithm 1

$R := I, R' := \emptyset.$
while $R \ne R'$ **do**
    $R' := R.$
    $R := R \cup \text{Post}_c(R) \cup \text{Post}_d(R).$
end while

The literature on computing the set of reachable states of continuous and hybrid systems can be categorized by the different classes of continuous dynamics that are taken into account. For simple dynamics such as the linear hybrid automata treated in the next section, an exact computation of the operators $Post_d$ and $Post_c$ is possible (noting that the reachability problem remains undecidable) by using standard operations on polyhedra [ALU 95, ASA 95, FRE 05, HEN 97]. For systems with more complex continuous dynamics, we often resort to approximative computation, representing sets of continuous states as polyhedra [ASA 00, CHU 03, GIR 05, GIR 06], ellipsoids [BOT 00, KUR 00], or level sets [TOM 03]. Other approaches are based on constructing a simpler, more abstract discrete or hybrid model, and carrying out the reachability analysis on the simplified model [ALU 02, ASA 03, FRE 05, HEN 98, RAT 05, TIW 03]. All the above techniques construct an explicit representation of the reachable states. There are also implicit techniques such as the construction of barrier certificates [PRA 04]. The central problem of computing the set of reachable states of hybrid systems is how to manipulate and represent complex sets of continuous states. Consequently, the reachability of hybrid systems is strongly connected with reachability of purely continuous systems, and techniques from one domain provide inspiration for the other.

7.3. Linear hybrid automata

Linear hybrid automata are a class of hybrid automata that are syntactically defined as having piecewise constant derivatives and affine maps as jump relations [HEN 96]. More precisely; the continuous dynamics of LHA are given by conjunctions of *linear constraints* on the derivatives of the variables: variables, i.e. constraints of the form

$$a \cdot \dot{x} \bowtie b, \qquad a \in \mathbb{Z}^n, b \in \mathbb{Z}, \bowtie \in \{<, \leq\}. \qquad [7.4]$$

The jump relations are given by conjunctions of linear constraints on the values of the variables before (x) and after (x') the jump

$$a \cdot x + a' \cdot x' \bowtie b, \qquad a, a' \in \mathbb{Z}^n, b \in \mathbb{Z}, \bowtie \in \{<, \leq\}. \qquad [7.5]$$

Finally, invariants and initial states are given by conjunctions of linear constraints on the values of the variables

$$a \cdot x \bowtie b, \qquad a \in \mathbb{Z}^n, b \in \mathbb{Z}, \bowtie \in \{<, \leq\}. \qquad [7.6]$$

Note that discrete time linear dynamics of the form $x_{k+1} = Ax_k + b$ can be modeled by discrete transitions with jump relation $x' = Ax + b$. However, the study of a time-sampled version of a continuous-time hybrid system is generally not conservative and may lead to erroneous conclusions (see Example 7.4).

In the case of LHA, equations [7.2] and [7.3] that define the operators Post$_c$ and Post$_d$ yield first-order logic expressions over linear constraints, which can be computed using standard polyhedral operations, although at a cost that is exponential in the number of variables [ALU 96]. If the fixed-point computation of Algorithm 1 terminates, the result is exactly the set of states that reachable, over an unbounded number of discrete transitions and an infinite time horizon. Termination may occur in practice, but is not guaranteed, and safety properties (no bad states are reachable) of hybrid automata are undecidable [HEN 96].

An enhanced version of Algorithm 1 has been implemented in the tool PHAVer [FRE 05], which uses the *Parma Polyhedra Library* [BAG 02] and exact integer arithmetic to carry out the polyhedral computations. PHAVer also includes techniques to over-approximate polyhedra with other, simpler, polyhedra, which may help in achieving termination and reducing computational costs, and which we briefly introduce in the remainder of this section.

Apart from the most simple systems, the repeated application of the Post operators in Algorithm 1 produces polyhedra of increasing complexity. From a practical point of view, this can manifest itself in three ways: the size of the integer coefficients of the linear constraints may grow rapidly if integer arithmetic is used; the number of constraints of each polyhedron may increase; and, finally, the total number of polyhedra may increase to the point where the computation becomes impractical. In experiments with exact computations of systems with only three to four continuous variables we frequently obtain polyhedra with thousands of constraints where the integer coefficients of each constraint may consist of tens of thousands of bits.

It is therefore important to be able to manage this complexity, i.e. over-approximate a polyhedron conservatively with another polyhedron that has coefficients of a limited size and less constraints. In theory, such an over-approximation immediately guarantees termination since having a bound on the integer coefficients means that there is only a finite number of non-redundant linear constraints, and therefore only a finite number of polyhedra that will eventually be enumerated exhaustively by the algorithm. But in practice, convergence can be extremely slow, and computing polyhedral fixed points efficiently and quickly remains a challenging problem.

EXAMPLE 7.3.– We briefly illustrate the technique used by PHAVer to limit the size of coefficients of the linear constraints of a polyhedron. Consider the triangular polyhedron shown in Figure 7.3(a), which has a constraint with seven-bit coefficients. First, we round the coefficients to three bits. This slightly changes the orientation of the constraint as can be seen in Figure 7.3(b). By solving a linear program, we then find the point at which the constraint is tangential to the original polyhedron (see Figure 7.3(c)). This defines a bound on the inhomogenous coefficient (the right-hand side of the inequality), above which the new constraint contains the old polyhedron. By rounding this coefficient to the next highest integer, we obtain a coefficient that in the example is smaller than the three-bit limit (see Figure 7.3(d)). If the next highest integer were larger than the limit, we would drop the constraint entirely. The same procedure is applied to the other constraints of the polyhedron.

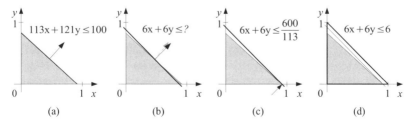

Figure 7.3. *Limiting the integer coefficients of a linear constraint to three bits*

To limit the number of constraints of the polyhedron, we construct a new polyhedron using the most significant of the old constraints. As an approximative measure of significance, we give priority to constraints that are the most opposite to (form the largest spatial angle with) the already chosen constraints. It suffices to compute the scalar product between the coefficient vectors of the constraints, and is therefore relatively fast.

7.4. Piecewise affine hybrid systems

We now turn to hybrid systems whose continuous dynamics is described by a collection of linear or affine differential equations. This is a widely used class for which numerous reachability analysis techniques have been proposed [ASA 00, BOT 00, CHU 03, GIR 05, KUR 00, LAF 01, TIW 03]. While the treatment of the discrete dynamics is identical to the case of LHA, the exact computation of the successor states by time elapse is generally impossible for affine continuous dynamics. In this section, we present methods to over-approximate the continuous successor computation based on discretizing time. A solution based on discretization of the state space is discussed in section 7.5.1. Let us consider continuous dynamics of the form

$$\dot{x} = Ax + Bu, \; u \in U, \qquad\qquad [7.7]$$

where $x \in \mathbb{R}^n$ and $u \in \mathbb{R}^p$ denote the continuous state and input of the system. A and B are real matrices of compatible dimensions. The set of inputs U is generally assumed compact and convex. The input u allows us to model non-determinism, this will be useful for over-approximating nonlinear dynamics in section 7.5.2. Equivalently, the continuous dynamics can be written as $\dot{x} - Ax \in BU$, which corresponds to the form $(l, \dot{x}, x) \in Flow$ given in the definition of hybrid automata. Given a set of initial states $I \subseteq \mathbb{R}^n$ and a time instant $t \geq 0$, we denote $Reach_{[0,t]}(I)$ the set of states reachable by the continuous dynamics during time interval $[0, t]$, from states in I and under all admissible input functions.

7.4.1. Time discretization

Most of the methods for the computation of the set $Reach_{[0,t]}(I)$ use a discretization of the time: given a time step $r = t/N$, we compute a finite sequence of sets $\Omega_0, \ldots, \Omega_{N-1}$ such that Ω_i is an over-approximation of the set of reachable states from I during the time interval $[ir, (i+1)r]$. Then, we have

$$Reach_{[0,t]}(I) \subseteq \Omega_0 \cup \Omega_1 \cup \ldots \cup \Omega_{N-1}.$$

7.4.1.1. Autonomous dynamics

Let us first consider autonomous continuous dynamics ($\dot{x} = Ax$). The computation of the first element of the sequence Ω_0 is illustrated in Figure 7.4. We start by computing the convex hull of the sets I and $e^{rA}I$, where e^{rA} denotes the exponential of

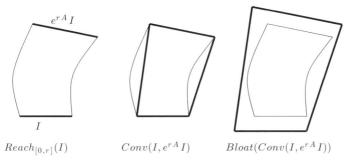

$$Reach_{[0,r]}(I) \qquad\qquad Conv(I, e^{rA}I) \qquad\qquad Bloat(Conv(I, e^{rA}I))$$

Figure 7.4. *Computation of Ω_0, over-approximation of $Reach_{[0,r]}(I)$, for the autonomous dynamics $\dot{x} = Ax$*

the matrix rA. This convex hull is then *bloated*. The bloating factor can be computed explicitly from A, r, and I (see for example [ASA 00]) or by solving a numerical optimization problem [CHU 03]. The elements of the sequence are thus computed by using the recurrence relation

$$\begin{aligned} \Omega_0 &= Bloat(Conv(I, e^{rA}I)), \\ \Omega_{i+1} &= e^{rA}\Omega_i. \end{aligned} \qquad [7.8]$$

The implementation of this algorithm requires to choose a representation for the sets $\Omega_0, \ldots, \Omega_{N-1}$. In order to avoid additional approximations at each iterations of the algorithm, we generally choose a class of sets which is invariant under linear transformations. From this point of view, polytopes [ASA 00, CHU 03] or ellipsoids [BOT 00, KUR 00] are appropriate representations.

EXAMPLE 7.4.– Let us illustrate the need to compute the convex hull in the initialization of the reachability algorithm. For the example of the bouncing ball, the discretized dynamics with a time step r is

$$\begin{aligned} x_{k+1} &= x_k + rv_k, \\ v_{k+1} &= v_k - rg. \end{aligned}$$

The reachable sets for these discretized dynamics and for initial states of $x \in [0.9, 1.1]$ and $v \in [-0.1, 0.1]$ are shown in Figure 7.5. If, initially, we do not compute the convex hull of two consecutive steps, then some discrete transitions may be ignored (see Figure 7.5(a)) (obtained with PHAVer). After the ball bounces four times, the set of current states is empty, which shows clearly that a simple discretization (without guaranteed over-approximation) is not sufficient for hybrid systems analysis. The result of the computation of an over-approximation, using the convex hull operation, is shown in Figure 7.5(b) (obtained with the tool *d/d*t).

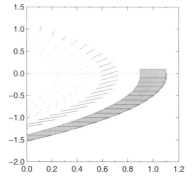 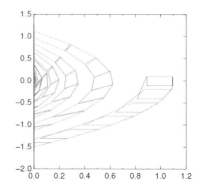

(a) Without using the convex hull, the sequence ends with an empty set ($r = 0.1$)

(b) With convex hull and bloating, we obtain a conservative over-approximation ($r = 0.25$)

Figure 7.5. *The reachable set of the bouncing ball computed using a discretization of the time (speed v against position x)*

7.4.1.2. *Dynamics with inputs*

A similar algorithm is possible for continuous dynamics with inputs as in Equation [7.7]. There are generally two approaches for taking the effect of the inputs into account. The first approach uses tools from continuous optimal control theory and particularly the maximum principle [ASA 00, KUR 00, VAR 98]: at each time step, we determine, at each point of the boundary of Ω_i, the input u that produces the largest successor Ω_{i+1}. The second approach consists of propagating the reachable set by the autonomous dynamics and then to add a set that accounts for the effect of inputs [GIR 05] (see Figure 7.6). In this case, Ω_{i+1} is computed from Ω_i using a recurrence relation of the form

$$\begin{aligned} \Omega_0 &= Bloat(Conv(I, e^{rA}I)) \oplus V, \\ \Omega_{i+1} &= e^{rA}\Omega_i \oplus V, \end{aligned} \qquad [7.9]$$

where the set $V \subseteq \mathbb{R}^n$ can be determined from the matrices A and B, the set of inputs U and the time step r. The operator $\oplus$ denotes the Minkowski sum, which associates with two sets $A \subseteq \mathbb{R}^n$ and $B \subseteq \mathbb{R}^n$ the result $A \oplus B = \{a + b \mid a \in A, \ b \in B\}$.

The two approaches guarantee the computation of an over-approximation $\Omega_0 \cup \ldots \cup \Omega_{N-1}$ of the set of reachable states $Reach_{[0,t]}(I)$. Moreover, the distance between these two sets can be made arbitrarily small by choosing r small enough.

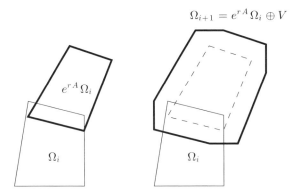

Figure 7.6. *Reachability analysis for linear dynamics with inputs: propagate the reachable set by the autonomous dynamics, add a set that accounts for the effects of inputs*

7.4.2. *Scaling up reachability computations*

In recent years, much effort has been directed at developing scalable methods for reachability analysis [GIR 05, GIR 06, HAN 06, STU 03]. In the following selection, we summarize the contributions of [GIR 05, GIR 06, GIR 08] toward an efficient implementation of the recurrence relation [7.9] and its integration in a reachability analysis tool for hybrid piecewise affine systems.

7.4.2.1. *Reachability using zonotopes*

The choice of the representation of the sets $\Omega_0, \ldots, \Omega_{N-1}$ is crucial for reachability computations and determines the balance between accuracy of the over-approximation and efficiency of the algorithm. For example, the use of polytopes allows us to compute an arbitrarily accurate approximation of the reachable set, but the use of the Minkowski sum in [7.9] will result in increasingly complex polytopes leading to intractable computations even for systems of relatively small dimension. The use of sets of bounded complexity such as ellipsoids or parallelotopes will allow an efficient implementation, but since these classes are not closed under the Minkowski sum, additional approximations will be needed at each step of the computations. The propagation of these approximations through the computations generally has a dramatic impact on the global approximation error of the reachable sets and is known as the *wrapping effect* [KUH 98].

These observations lead us to propose in [GIR 05] the use of zonotopes for the representation of the sets $\Omega_0, \ldots, \Omega_{N-1}$. A zonotope Z is a polytope that can be

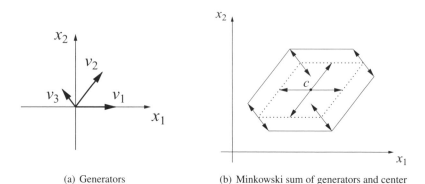

(a) Generators   (b) Minkowski sum of generators and center

Figure 7.7. *Construction of a zonotope from generators v_1, v_2, v_3, and center c*

represented as the Minkowski sum of segments

$$Z = (c, \langle v_1, \ldots, v_m \rangle) = \left\{ c + \sum_{i=1}^{m} \alpha_i v_i \mid \alpha_i \in [-1, 1] \right\}.$$

The vector $c \in \mathbb{R}^n$ is called the *center* and the vectors $v_1, \ldots, v_m \in \mathbb{R}^n$ the *generators* of the zonotope. Figure 7.7 shows an example of a planar zonotope with three generators.

Zonotopes are closed under linear transformation and Minkowski sum. Moreover, the computation of these operations is extremely simple

$$\Phi Z = (\Phi c, \langle \Phi v_1, \ldots, \Phi v_m \rangle),$$
$$Z \oplus Z' = (c + c', \langle v_1, \ldots, v_m, v_1', \ldots, v_{m'}' \rangle),$$

where Φ is a linear transformation (a matrix). Consequently, an implementation of the recurrence [7.9] using zonotopes is very efficient even for high-dimensional systems. However, let us remark that the number of generators of Ω_i increases linearly with the number of iterations. Hence, the linear transformation applied to Ω_i becomes more expensive at each step and the computations may become intractable for a large time horizon N.

A solution to this problem consists of adding a reduction operation at each step: $e^{rA}\Omega_i \oplus V$ is over-approximated by a zonotope with a predetermined number of generators m. This results in faster computations, but the wrapping effect inevitably appears for long-time horizons. The parameter m allows us to adjust the balance between accuracy and efficiency. This method, though presented for time-invariant systems, extends straightforwardly to time-varying systems (meaning that matrices A and B change over time).

7.4.2.2. Efficient implementation for LTI systems

We now specifically consider affine time-invariant systems. For this class of systems an efficient implementation is possible [GIR 06] based on the closed form of Ω_{i+1}:

$$\Omega_{i+1} = e^{(i+1)rA}\Omega_0 \oplus e^{irA}V \oplus \left(e^{(i-1)rA}V \oplus \cdots \oplus V\right).$$

In order to compute efficiently Ω_i, let us define the following auxiliary sequences of sets: $X_0 = \Omega_0$, $V_0 = V$, $S_0 = \{0\}$,

$$\begin{aligned} X_{i+1} &= e^{rA}X_i, \\ V_{i+1} &= e^{rA}V_i, \\ S_{i+1} &= S_i \oplus V_i, \\ \Omega_{i+1} &= X_{i+1} \oplus S_{i+1}. \end{aligned} \qquad [7.10]$$

X_i is an over-approximation of the states reachable by the autonomous dynamics $\dot{x} = Ax$ from the initial states I within $[ir, (i+1)r]$ time. S_i is an over-approximation of the states reachable by system [7.7] from the initial state 0.

The computation of $\Omega_0, \ldots, \Omega_{N-1}$ can be implemented very efficiently using the scheme given by [7.10] and zonotope representations. Indeed, the number of generators of the zonotopes to which the linear transformations are applied, X_i and V_i, does not grow. Thus, the cost of an iteration is constant. This allows fast computations even for large time horizon. The projection of the over-approximation of the reachable set of a five-dimensional linear system, computed with this method, is presented in Figure 7.8. In practice, our algorithm can handle systems with about a hundred variables in a few seconds and using few M-Bytes [GIR 06].

7.4.2.3. Dealing with the discrete transitions

We now go back to hybrid reachability analysis. For the class of piecewise affine hybrid systems, jump relations are usually of the following form:

$$\mu = \{(x, x')|x \in G \wedge x' = R(x)\},$$

where $G = \{x \in \mathbb{R}^n \,|n_G \cdot x = \gamma_G\}$ is a hyperplane and R is an affine transformation. In order to deal with the discrete transitions in a satisfactory (i.e., scalable and accurate) way, we need to approximate the intersection of the continuous reachable sets with the guard G.

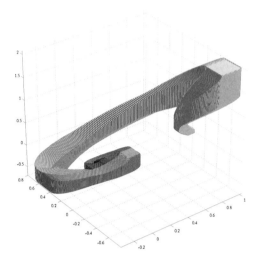

Figure 7.8. *Projection of the over-approximation of the reachable set*
$Reach_{[0,1]}(I)$ *of a five-dimensional linear system*

The previous algorithm returns an over-approximation of the reachable set as a union of zonotopes. Computing the intersection between a zonotope and a hyperplane is a difficult problem, one of the reasons is that it might not be a zonotope. One solution is to express this zonotope as a polytope, then compute the intersection, and finally over-approximate it by a zonotope. Unfortunately, a zonotope with m generators might have more than $(2m)^{n-1}/n^{n-1/2}$ vertices. This approach is intractable. As an example, consider a 10-dimensional system, after only 10 time steps, Ω_{10} may already have hundreds of generators, which leads to more than hundreds of billions of vertices. We present here an alternative method proposed in [GIR 08].

The intersection between our zonotope and the hyperplane is first over-approximated by a polytope of the following form:

$$P = \{x \in \mathbb{R}^n \,|\, n_G \cdot x = \gamma_G \wedge \alpha_j \leq n_j \cdot x \leq \beta_j, j = 1, \ldots, k\},$$

where $n_1, \ldots, n_k \in \mathbb{R}^n$ are vectors selected arbitrarily. In order to do so, for each j, the zonotope is projected on the two-dimensional space generated by the vectors (n_j, n_G). In this plane, the number of vertices of the projected zonotope is proportional to its number of generators. The projection of the hyperplane G is a line. And their intersection, if not empty, is a segment of the form $[\alpha_j, \beta_j] \times \{\gamma_G\}$. This segment can be computed efficiently (see [GIR 08]), and allows the computation of the values $\alpha_1, \ldots \alpha_k, \beta_1, \ldots, \beta_k$ defining the over-approximation P. Moreover, the computed polytope is such that on each of its facets there is a point of the exact intersection between the zonotope and the hyperplane.

In order to continue the reachability computation, P must be over-approximated by a zonotope. If the number of vectors k is equal to $n - 1$, then the polytope P is a zonotope. Its generators can be found by solving a linear system of equations.

7.5. Hybridization techniques for reachability computations

Computing the reachable states for systems with nonlinear differential equations poses significant challenges. Techniques based on time discretization exist, but they often result in excessively large overapproximations [DAN 98]. To obtain more accurate results, one can construct a simplified model by partitioning the state space in small regions and replacing the complex dynamics in each region with a simpler yet conservative approximation. The resulting model is a hybrid automaton, where each partition corresponds to a location, and the transitions from one partition to another are modeled by discrete transitions whose jump relation is the identity relation. The reachability analysis is then carried out on the simplified model [ASA 03, FRE 05, HEN 98]. We call this approach *hybridization*.

7.5.1. *Approximation with linear hybrid automata*

Consider a hybrid automaton H with complex dynamics. We can construct an approximation of H in the form of a linear hybrid automaton $\hat{H}$ by approximating each of the sets *Trans*, *Flow*, *Inv*, *Init* for each location with linear constraints. The approximation is conservative, i.e., every execution of H is also an execution of $\hat{H}$, if the approximated sets $\widehat{Trans}$, $\widehat{Flow}$, $\widehat{Inv}$, $\widehat{Init}$ contain the original ones

$$Trans \subseteq \widehat{Trans}, \quad Flow \subseteq \widehat{Flow}, \quad Inv \subseteq \widehat{Inv}, \quad Init \subseteq \widehat{Init}.$$

If $\hat{H}$ satisfies a safety property, then so does H. If $\hat{H}$ is unsafe, then this might be due to an excessive over-approximation error.

We can increase the accuracy of the over-approximation by partitioning the invariants of H into smaller parts as follows, see [HEN 98] for details. For each location l of H, we introduce a copy l' with copies of incoming and outgoing transitions, and add identity transitions (that do not modify the variables) from l to l' and back. Then, we split the invariants of l and l' into complementary parts, say along the axis of one of the variables, such that each of them is smaller than the original invariant. By repeating this process, we can split the location until all of the resulting invariants are smaller in diameter than a given parameter h. The behavior of the automaton with split invariants is equivalent (up to identity transitions) to that of the original. The accuracy of the above LHA-approximation depends on the diameter of the invariant. By splitting before carrying out the LHA-approximation, we obtain an approximation that is more accurate than approximating the original automaton directly. By choosing a sufficiently small location diameter h, the resulting reachable set of states can be made arbitrarily close to the original, at least for a bounded time horizon and a bounded number of discrete transitions.

For piecewise affine systems, where $Trans$, Inv, $Init$ are given for each location by linear constraints, the over-approximation is a simple problem of existential quantifier elimination. The over-approximation of $Flow$ is

$$\widehat{Flow}(l) = \{(\dot{x}, x) \mid \exists x \in Inv(l) : (\dot{x}, x) \in Flow(l)\}. \qquad [7.11]$$

The splitting of the invariants can be carried out using a set of linear constraints C. For each constraint of the form $\alpha^T x \leq \beta$, we obtain the invariants of l and l' as

$$\begin{aligned}
\widehat{Inv}(l) &= Inv(l) \cap \{x \mid \alpha^T x \leq \beta\}, \\
\widehat{Inv}(l') &= Inv(l) \cap \{x \mid \alpha^T x \geq \beta\}.
\end{aligned} \qquad [7.12]$$

To obtain, e.g. a partition in the form of cubes one could choose $C = \{x_i \leq \beta_i \mid i = 1, \ldots, n\}$. The position of the partition boundary is determined by β_i and can be chosen, e.g. as the middle of the invariant.

EXAMPLE 7.5.– In the case of the bouncing ball, the continuous dynamics is given by the differential equations

$$\begin{aligned}
\dot{x} &= v, \\
\dot{v} &= -g.
\end{aligned}$$

The derivative of the speed v is constant, so in order to obtain LHA dynamics, it suffices to find constant bounds on $\dot{x}$. By splitting the invariant with the set of constraints $C = \{v \leq ih \mid i \in \mathbb{N}\}$, where h is a positive real parameter, we obtain for each location l_i the sets

$$\begin{aligned}
\widehat{Inv}(l_i) &= \{(x, v) \mid x \geq 0 \wedge ih \leq v \leq (i+1)h\}, \\
\widehat{Flow}(l_i) &= \{(\dot{x}, \dot{v}, x, v) \mid ih \leq \dot{x} \leq (i+1)h \wedge \dot{v} = -g\}.
\end{aligned} \qquad [7.13]$$

Note that, the invariant of each location l_i is of diameter h. The reachable states for this approximation for $h = 1/16$ and initial states $Init = \{(l_i, x, v) \mid x \in [0.9, 1.1], v \in [-0.1, 0.1]\}$ are shown in Figure 7.9. Note that Algorithm 1 terminates for the LHA-approximation. The comparison between Figures 7.9 and 7.5(b) shows that the hybridization with LHA is less accurate than time discretization. However, it gives an over-approximation of the reachable states of the original system over an infinite time horizon and an unbounded number of discrete transitions.

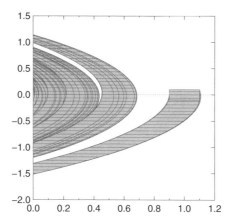

Figure 7.9. *Reachable states of a LHA over-approximation of the bouncing ball (speed v over position x)*

7.5.2. *Hybridization of nonlinear continuous system*

We now focus on the computation of the reachable set of a continuous system described by the following nonlinear differential equations:

$$\dot{x} = f(x), \ x \in X, \hspace{3cm} [7.14]$$

where X is a bounded subset of $\mathbb{R}^n$ et the vector field $f : X \to \mathbb{R}^n$ is L-Lipschitz in X. Recall that f is L-Lipschitz in X if for all $x, x' \in X$, $\|f(x) - f(x')\| \le L\|x - x'\|$.

Given a set of initial states $I \subseteq X$ and a time instant $t \ge 0$, we denote by $Reach_{[0,t]}(\Delta, I)$ the set of all states reachable from I by the system Δ during the time interval $[0, t]$. The exact computation of this reachable set if difficult, and we propose to first over-approximate, by hybridization, the dynamics of Δ. The computation of $Reach_{[0,t]}(\Delta, I)$ can then be performed on this conservative approximation of Δ.

The first step in the construction of an approximate system involves defining a partition of the state space X in disjoint regions of size h. An approximation of the vector field f is then associated with each region. We denote by f_h the resulting approximate vector field, defined in this piecewise manner over the partition of X. The precision of this approximation depends on the parameter h, which will be discussed later. We define a non-deterministic system Δ_h as follows:

$$\dot{x} = f_h(x) + u, \ x \in X, u \in U_h, \hspace{2cm} [7.15]$$

where u is a disturbance input in a set $U_h \subseteq \mathbb{R}^n$ such that

$$\forall x \in X, \ f(x) - f_h(x) \in U_h.$$

The resulting system Δ_h is a hybrid system, and it is easy to see that it is a conservative approximation of Δ, because every trajectory $x(t)$ of Δ is also a trajectory of Δ_h under the input $u(t) = f(x(t)) - f_h(x(t))$. It then follows that the reachable set of Δ is included in that of Δ_h.

7.5.2.1. *Properties of the approximate reachable set*

In order to measure the distance between the exact reachable set $Reach_{[0,t]}(\Delta, I)$ and the approximate set $Reach_{[0,t]}(\Delta_h, I)$, we define the parameter $\varepsilon(h)$ that measures the precision of the vector field approximation as follows: for all $x \in X$, $\|f(x) - f_h(x)\| \leq \varepsilon(h)$ where $\| \cdot \|$ is a norm on $\mathbb{R}^n$. We assume that the finer the partition of X is, the more precise the approximation, that is $\lim_{h \to 0} \varepsilon(h) = 0$. Recall that the Hausdorff distance associated with a norm $\| \cdot \|$ between two sets is defined as

$$d_H(A, B) = \max(\sup_{a \in A} \inf_{b \in B} \|a - b\|, \sup_{b \in B} \inf_{a \in A} \|a - b\|).$$

The following theorem shows the convergence of the reachable set of Δ_h to that of Δ.

THEOREM 7.1([ASA 03]).– *If the vector field f is L-Lipschitz on X, then*

$$d_H\left(Reach_{[0,t]}(\Delta, I), Reach_{[0,t]}(\Delta_h, I)\right) \leq \frac{2\varepsilon(h)}{L}(e^{Lt} - 1).$$

When the parameter h tends to 0, the set $Reach_{[0,t]}(\Delta_h, I)$ converges to the set $Reach_{[0,t]}(\Delta, I)$. The approximation error is proportional to the precision of the approximation of f by f_h. However, it should be noted that the error bound given by the theorem diverge exponentially in t. Hence, when for the reachable sets on a long-time interval, this bound can be large.

We now present a stronger convergence result for the case where the system Δ has a global attractor. A global attractor A is a subset of the state space X that satisfies the following conditions: A is invariant under the dynamics of Δ, and every trajectory of Δ tends asymptotically to A.

THEOREM 7.2([ASA 07]).– *If the system Δ has a global attractor A, then there exists a parameter value h_Δ such that for all $h \leq h_\Delta$ the distance between the sets $Reach_{\mathbb{R}^+}(\Delta, I)$ and $Reach_{\mathbb{R}^+}(\Delta_h, I)$ is bounded. In addition,*

$$\lim_{h \to 0} d_H\left(Reach_{\mathbb{R}^+}(\Delta, I), Reach_{\mathbb{R}^+}(\Delta_h, I)\right) = 0.$$

We notice that when we approximate the dynamics of a continuous system by an LHA, the precision $\varepsilon(h)$ is linear in h and the two theorems hold.

In the following sections, we describe a method for approximating a nonlinear continuous system by a hybrid system with piecewise affine dynamics. This method allows achieving a better precision $\varepsilon(h)$ that is quadratic in h.

7.5.2.2. *Approximation by hybrid systems with piecewise affine dynamics*

This choice is motivated by the availability of tools for analyzing affine continuous systems, as shown in the previous sections.

We first construct a triangulation $\{\mathcal{C}_i\}_{i \in I}$, which is a partition of X where each element $\mathcal{C}_i$ is a simplex (that is, the convex hull of $n + 1$ points linearly independent in $\mathbb{R}^n$). Such a partition can be built from a rectangular partition $\{\mathcal{H}_j\}_{j \in J}$ where each element $\mathcal{H}_j$ is a hypercube of size h. Each hypercube is then partitioned into simplices as follows. We explain this procedure for the hypercube $[0, 1]^n$. Let $\mathcal{P}$ be the set of permutations of $\{1, \ldots, n\}$, for all $p = (i_1, \ldots, i_n) \in \mathcal{P}$, the set

$$\mathcal{S}_p = \{0 \leq x_{i_1} \leq \cdots \leq x_{i_n} \leq 1\}$$

is a simplex, and $\{\mathcal{S}_p\}_{p \in \mathcal{P}}$ defines a triangulation over $[0, 1]^n$. This triangulation construction is simple and memory-efficient because the partition can be generated on-the-fly around the current trajectories, unlike Delaunay triangulations for which dynamical constructions are expensive.

We next define a vector field f_h, which is affine in each simplex $\mathcal{C}_i$. An n-dimensional affine vector field is uniquely defined by its values at $(n + 1)$ points linearly independent. Thus, in each simplex $\mathcal{C}_i$, f_h is uniquely defined by its values at $(n + 1)$ vertices of $\mathcal{C}_i$. In addition, f_h is chosen so that it interpolates f at the vertices of each simplex of the triangulation.

We note that on each faces of a simplex, the values of f_h are determined by the values of f at the vertices of the face. Hence, we can prove that the function f_h is continuous over X, and the resulting system Δ_h is well posed (that is, for an initial condition and an input, there exists a unique trajectory of Δ_h). It remains now to estimate the precision of the approximation of f by f_h.

PROPOSITION 7.1.– *[ASA 03] If f is $C2$ with bounded second derivatives over X, then*

$$\varepsilon(h) = \sup_{x \in X} \|f(x) - f_h(x)\|_\infty \leq \frac{Mn2}{2(n + 1)2} h2$$

where $\|.\|$ is the infinite norm and

$$M = \max_{j=1}^{j=n} \sup_{x \in X} \sum_{p_1=1}^{p_1=n} \sum_{p_2=1}^{p_2=n} \left| \frac{\partial 2 f_j(x)}{\partial x_{p_1} \partial x_{p_2}} \right|.$$

We denote the set $\mathcal{U}_h$ of input values by $\square(\varepsilon(h))$ where $\square(r)$ is the ball of radius

r in the infinite norm. Therefore, f_h converges to f with quadratic rate with regard to h. Consequently, by Theorem 7.1, the rate of the convergence of the approximate reachable set $Reach_{[0,t]}(\Delta_h, I)$ to the set $Reach_{[0,t]}(\Delta_h, I)$ is also quadratic in h.

It should be noted that this hybridization method can be easily extended to nonlinear systems with input of the form $\dot{x} = f(x) + u$ [ASA 03].

EXAMPLE 7.6.– We now show results obtained using this method on a Van der Pol oscillator, which is defined by the dynamics

$$\begin{aligned} \dot{x} &= y, \\ \dot{y} &= y(1 - x^2) - x. \end{aligned}$$

It is well known that this oscillator has a limit cycle that attracts all the trajectories of the system. Thus, it satisfies the condition of the Theorem 7.2. To analyze it, we used a partition with $h = 0.05$. Figure 7.10 depicts the computed reachable set. In this figure, the set drawn in dotted lines is the set of initial states.

7.5.3. *Hybridization and refinement*

Hybridization allows us to obtain a conservative approximation of a continuous or hybrid system by partitioning the state space of the original system into smaller parts. To be sufficiently accurate to show that a given set of bad states is not reachable, the partitions must be sufficiently small, which can very quickly lead to a large number of partitions. By choosing which invariants to split and by how much, we may be able to

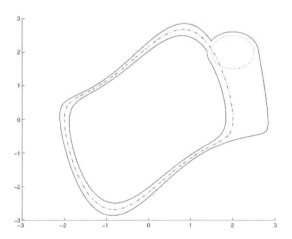

Figure 7.10. *Computed set of reachable states* $Reach_{\mathbb{R}^+}(\Delta)$
of the Van der Pol oscillator and its limit cycle

Algorithm 2

$h := h_{max}$.
while True **do**
    $R_f := Reach(\Delta_h, I)$.
    if $I \cap R_f = \emptyset$ **then**
        Return *'safe'* et terminate.
    else
        Reduce h.
    end if
    $F := F \cap R_f$.
    $R_b = Reach^b(\Delta_h, F)$.
    $I := I \cap R_b$.
    if $I \cap R_b = \emptyset$ **then**
        Return *'safe'* et terminate.
    end if
    if $(h > h_{min})$ **then**
        Reduce h.
    else
        Return *'inconclusive'* and terminate.
    end if
end while

be sufficiently accurate without creating excessively many partitions. This is the goal of *refinement*, i.e. starting out with large partitions and splitting only those that have executions that lead to bad states.

In the following paragraph, we briefly present the simple refinement procedure, called *forward/backward-refinement*, described by Algorithm 2 and illustrated by Figure 7.11. It takes two positive real-valued parameters, h_{min} and h_{max}, that determine an upper and a lower bound on the diameter of the resulting partitions. Initially, we set the partition diameter h to h_{max}. In the first iteration, we partition the system along the axes until the diameter of all partitions is lower than h. Then, we compute the forward reachable states $R_f = Reach^f(\Delta_h, F)$ starting from the set of initial states $Init$ (see Figure 7.11(a)). If this set does not intersect with the set of bad states F, we can conclude that the system is safe and the algorithm terminates. Otherwise, we reduce the partition size and compute the backward reachable states $R_b = Reach^b(\Delta_h, F)$, starting from the intersection of the bad states F and R_f (see Figure 7.11(b)). If R_b does not intersect with the initial states then the system is safe and the algorithm terminates. Otherwise, we reduce the partition size and repeat the computation of the forward reachable states, this time starting from the intersection of $Init$ and R_b. The process is repeated until the system is shown to be safe, or the partition diameter is below h_{min}, in which case the result is inconclusive.

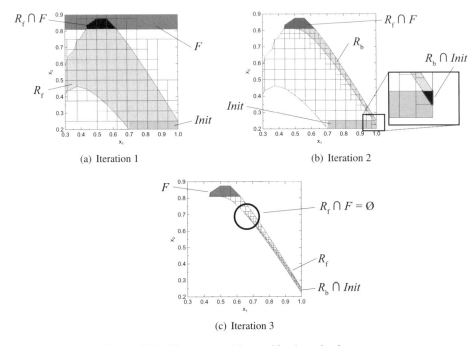

(a) Iteration 1

(b) Iteration 2

(c) Iteration 3

Figure 7.11. *Illustration of forward/backward refinement*

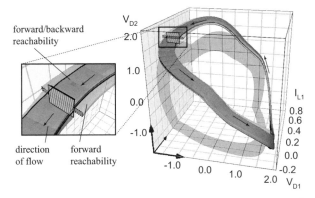

Figure 7.12. *Limit cycle of a voltage-controlled oscillator computed using forward/backward refinement*

This procedure was implemented in the tool PHAVer, and has allowed us to analyze the oscillation of a *voltage controlled oscillator circuit* (VCO) [FRE 06]. The goal was to show the existence of a limit cycle, i.e., to show that from a set of initial states the circuit exhibits stable oscillations. A forward reachability analysis did not terminate due to an accumulating approximation error. Using forward/backward reachability, the accuracy was increased enough to compute a set of states that are guaranteed to remain close to the limit cycle (see Figure 7.12).

7.6. Bibliography

[ALU 95] ALUR R., COURCOUBETIS C., HALBWACHS N., HENZINGER T.A., HO P.H., NICOLLIN X., OLIVERO A., SIFAKIS J., YOVINE S., "The algorithmic analysis of hybrid systems", *Theoretical Computer Science*, vol. 138, num. 1, 3–34, 1995.

[ALU 96] ALUR R., HENZINGER T.A., HO P.H., "Automatic symbolic verification of embedded systems", *IEEE Transactions on Software Engineering*, vol. 22, 181–201, 1996.

[ALU 02] ALUR R., DANG T., IVANCIC F., "Reachability analysis of hybrid systems via predicate abstraction", *HSCC'02*, vol. 2289 of *Lecture Notes in Computer Science*, pp. 35–48, Springer, 2002.

[ASA 95] ASARIN E., MALER O., PNUELI A., "Reachability analysis of dynamical systems having piecewise constant derivatives", *Theoretical Computer Science*, vol. 138, num. 1, 35–65, 1995.

[ASA 00] ASARIN E., DANG T., MALER O., BOURNEZ O., "Approximate reachability analysis of piecewise-linear dynamical systems", *Proceedings of HSCC'00*, vol. 1790 of *Lecture Notes in Computer Science*, pp. 20–31, Springer, 2000.

[ASA 03] ASARIN E., DANG T., GIRARD A., "Reachability analysis of nonlinear systems using conservative approximation", *Proceedings of HSCC'03*, vol. 2623 of *Lecture Notes in Computer Science*, pp. 20–35, Springer, 2003.

[ASA 07] ASARIN E., DANG T., GIRARD A., "Hybridization methods for the analysis of nonlinear systems", *Acta Informatica*, vol. 43, num. 7, 451–476, 2007.

[BAG 02] BAGNARA R., RICCI E., ZAFFANELLA E., HILL P., "Possibly not closed convex polyhedra and the Parma Polyhedra Library", *International Symposium on Static Analysis*, vol. 2477 of *Lecture Notes in Computer Science*, pp. 213–229, Springer, 2002.

[BOT 00] BOTCHKAREV O., TRIPAKIS S., "Verification of hybrid systems with linear differential inclusions using ellipsoidal approximations", *HSCC'00*, vol. 1790 of *Lecture Notes in Compter Science*, pp. 73–88, Springer, 2000.

[CHU 03] CHUTINAN A., KROGH B.H., "Computational techniques for hybrid systems verification", *IEEE Transactions on Automatic Control*, vol. 48, 64–75, 2003.

[DAN 98] DANG T., MALER O., "Reachability analysis via face lifting", *HSCC'98*, vol. 1386 of *Lecture Notes in Computer Science*, pp. 96–109, Springer, 1998.

[FRE 05] FREHSE G., "PHAVer: algorithmic verification of hybrid systems past HyTech", *HSCC'05*, vol. 3414 of *Lecture Notes in Computer Science*, pp. 258–273, Springer, 2005.

[FRE 06] FREHSE G., KROGH B.H., RUTENBAR R.A., "Verifying analog oscillator circuits using forward/backward refinement", *Proceedings of DATE'06*, 2006.

[GIR 05] GIRARD A., "Reachability of uncertain linear systems using zonotopes", *Proceedings of HSCC'05*, vol. 3414 of *Lecture Notes in Computer Science*, pp. 291–305, Springer, 2005.

[GIR 06] GIRARD A., LE GUERNIC C., MALER O., "Efficient computation of reachable sets of linear time-invariant systems with inputs", *Proceedings of HSCC'06*, vol. 3927 of *Lecture Notes in Computer Science*, pp. 257–271, Springer, 2006.

[GIR 08] GIRARD A., LE GUERNIC C., "Zonotope/hyperplane intersection for hybrid systems reachability analysis", *HSCC'08*, vol. 4981 of *Lecture Notes in Compter Science*, Springer, 2008.

[HAN 06] HAN Z., KROGH B., "Reachability analysis of large-scale affine systems using low dimensional polytopes", *HSCC'06*, vol. 3927 of *Lecture Notes in Computer Science*, pp. 287–301, Springer, 2006.

[HEN 96] HENZINGER T.A., "The theory of hybrid automata", *Proceedings of IEEE Symposium on Logic in Computer Science*, pp. 278–292, IEEE Computer Society Press, 1996.

[HEN 97] HENZINGER T.A., HO P.H., WONG TOI H., "HYTECH: a model checker for hybrid systems", *STTT*, vol. 1, num. 1–2, 110–122, 1997.

[HEN 98] HENZINGER T.A., HO P.H., WONG-TOI H., "Algorithmic analysis of nonlinear hybrid systems", *IEEE Transactions on Automatic Control*, vol. 43, 540–554, 1998.

[KUH 98] KÜHN W., "Rigorously computed orbits of dynamical systems without the wrapping effect", *Computing*, vol. 61, 47–68, 1998.

[KUR 00] KURZHANSKI A.B., VARAIYA P., "Ellipsoidal techniques for reachability analysis", *HSCC'00*, vol. 1790 of *Lecture Notes in Computer Science*, pp. 202–214, Springer, 2000.

[LAF 01] LAFFERRIERE G., PAPPAS G.J., YOVINE S., "Symbolic reachability computation for families of linear vector fields", *Journal of Symbolic Computation*, vol. 32, num. 3, 231–253, 2001.

[PRA 04] PRAJNA S., JADBABAIE A., "Safety verification of hybrid systems using barrier certificates", *HSCC'04*, vol. 2993, pp. 477–492, 2004.

[RAT 05] RATSCHAN S., SHE Z., "Safety verification of hybrid systems by constraint propagation based abstraction refinement", *HSCC'05*, vol. 3414 of *Lecture Notes in Computer Science*, pp. 573–589, Springer, 2005.

[STU 03] STURSBERG O., KROGH B.H., "Efficient representation and computation of reachable sets for hybrid systems", *HSCC'03*, vol. 2623 of *Lecture Notes in Computer Science*, pp. 482–497, Springer, 2003.

[TIW 03] TIWARI A., "Approximate reachability for linear systems", *HSCC'03*, vol. 2623 of *Lecture Notes in Computer Science*, pp. 514–525, Springer, 2003.

[TOM 03] TOMLIN C., MITCHELL I., BAYEN A., OISHI M., "Computational techniques for the verification and control of hybrid systems", *Proceedings of the IEEE*, vol. 91, num. 7, 986–1001, 2003.

[VAR 98] VARAIYA P., "Reach set computation using optimal control", *KIT Workshop*, pp. 377–383, 1998.

List of Authors

Béatrice BERARD
LIP6
Pierre and Marie Curie University
Paris
France

Gerd BERHMANN
Computer Science Department
Aalborg University
Aalborg
Denmark

Peter BULYCHEV
Lomonosov Moscow State University
Moscow
Russia

Joakim BYG
Computer Science Department
Aalborg University
Aalborg
Denmark

Franck CASSEZ
CNRS/IRCCyN
Nantes
France

Thomas CHATAIN
LSV
ENS Cachan
Cachan
France

Thao DANG
Verimag
CNRS
Grenoble
France

Alexandre DAVID
Computer Science Department
Aalborg University
Aalborg
Denmark

Susanna DONATELLI
Computer Science Department
Turin University
Turin
Italy

Goran FREHSE
Verimag
University Joseph Fourier Grenoble 1
Grenoble
France

Antoine GIRARD
Laboratoire Jean Kuntzmann
Grenoble
France

Serge HADDAD
LSV
ENS Cachan
Cachan
France

Claude JARD
IRISA
ENS Cachan/Bretagne
Rennes
France

Kenneth Y. JOERGENSEN
Computer Science Department
Aalborg University
Aalborg
Denmark

Kim G. LARSEN
Computer Science Department
Aalborg University
Aalborg
Denmark

Colas LE GERNIC
Verimag
University Joseph Fourier Grenoble 1
Grenoble
France

Didier LIME
IRCCyN
Ecole Centrale de Nantes
Nantes
France

Morgan MAGNIN
IRCCyN
Ecole Centrale de Nantes
Nantes
France

Nicolas MARKEY
LSV/CNRS
ENS Cachan
Cachan
France

Paul PETTERSSON
Mälardalen University
Västerås
Sweden

Jacob Illum RASMUSSEN
Computer Science Department
Aalborg University
Aalborg
Denmark

Olivier H. ROUX
IRCCyN
University of Nantes
Nantes
France

Jiří SRBA
Computer Science Department
Aalborg University
Aalborg
Denmark

Louis-Marie TRAONOUEZ
IRCCyN
Ecole Centrale de Nantes
Nantes
France

Stavros TRIPAKIS
Cadence Research Laboratories
(and CNRS)
Berkeley
USA

Wang YI
Uppsala University
Uppsala
Sweden

Index

A

affine dynamics, 245
algorithms, 67, 68, 71, 76, 82, 87, 92,
    93, 95, 98, 100, 102, 107, 108, 119,
    120, 137

B

bisimulation, 19–22, 33–35
bloating, 235
bouncing ball, 229, 230, 235, 242, 243
Büchi automata, 120

C

clock, 9, 11, 13, 26
clock constraint, 54
configuration, 40, 41, 43, 46, 49, 50,
    57
continuous time Markov chain, 146,
    157
control objective, 70, 76, 85, 86, 91,
    96
controller, 67–73, 76–78, 80, 82, 84,
    86, 87, 89, 92, 95–100

D

decidability, 3, 5, 10, 14, 15, 18, 31,
    34–36

diagnosability, 108, 112–129, 136–138
discrete event system, 108, 115, 137,
    141–143
discrete time Markov chain, 143,
    148
dynamics, 227, 229–232, 234–237, 239,
    241–246

E

expressiveness, 18–21, 23, 24, 31–33,
    35

F

fault diagnosis, 107, 108, 113–116, 122,
    127, 128, 136
flow, 228–231, 234, 241, 242
formal verification, 224

H

hybrid automata, 44, 50, 61, 64, 83, 91,
    103
hybrid automaton, 228–230, 241
hybridization, 228, 241–243, 246, 249

I

implementability, 82, 102

K

Kripke structure, 45–48, 51, 53

L

language, 2, 6, 8, 10, 15, 20–23, 33
linear constraint, 233
linear dynamics, 237
linear hybrid automata, 228, 231, 232, 241
liveness algorithm, 171, 172, 175, 176

M

model checking, 61–65, 165, 166, 205, 206, 210–217, 220, 223, 224, 225

O

optimal control, 71, 87, 88, 99

P

partial observability, 100
PCTL, 148–150, 154
PCTL*, 148, 149, 157
Performance evaluation, 140, 142, 157, 163
PLTL, 149, 154, 155, 157
polyhedron, 233, 234
post operators, 233

R

reachability, 44, 47, 51, 56, 69–71, 76, 78, 80, 81, 83, 85–87, 89–91, 94, 95, 97, 99, 100, 102, 104, 117, 120, 123, 125, 126, 227, 228, 231, 232, 234, 235, 237, 239, 241, 249, 250
reachability algorithm, 171, 173, 174, 181, 183, 187, 190
real-time, 1, 2, 4, 11, 15, 23, 26, 27, 31–36
refinement, 246–250
region, 53–58

region graph, 111, 123, 125–127, 130–132, 134
response time, 40, 49, 50, 53
ROMÉO, 166, 224

S

safety, 70, 71, 79–86, 92, 93, 95–97
scheduling, 4, 23–30, 35, 36
stopwatches, 24, 25, 166, 181, 208, 210, 212–214, 219, 220, 224, 225
strategy, 69–71, 73–77, 80–82, 87, 89, 90, 92, 93, 95–98
synthesis, 67–69, 71, 76, 80, 81, 85, 92, 99, 100, 103–105, 107, 114, 121, 122, 126, 127
system design, 222, 224

T

TCTL, 166, 170, 185, 197, 205, 211–214, 216, 220, 222
temporal logic, 46, 63–65, 140
time discretization, 234, 241, 242
time Petri nets, 4, 10–12, 20, 21, 23–26, 28, 34, 205, 206, 208, 210–213, 220–222, 225
timed automata, 4, 8, 12, 15, 21–24, 32–34, 41, 58, 59, 62–65, 67, 68, 76, 79, 86–88, 99–102, 107, 108, 110, 112, 115, 123–129, 131, 135–138, 165–169, 181, 182, 197, 199, 200, 205, 206, 213, 218–221, 223–225
timed game automata, 165, 166, 185, 186
timed games, 71–74, 76, 78, 83, 89, 90, 92, 93, 95, 97–99, 102, 103
timed language, 44, 51, 56
timed logic, 40, 46, 51
timed transition system, 40
transitions systems, 8

U

UPPAAL, 165, 199, 200, 205

V

verification, 139, 140, 148, 149, 151,
    154, 157, 159–163

W

wrapping effect, 237, 238, 250

Z

Zenoness, 82, 97
zonotope, 237–241, 250